Clayton Walnum

WITHDRAWN

Microsoft®
Direct3D
Programming

KICK START

SAMS

201 West 103rd Street, Indianapolis, Indiana 46290

Microsoft® Direct3D Programming Kick Start

International Standard Book Number: 0-672-32498-9

Library of Congress Catalog Card Number: 2002112961

Printed in the United States of America

First Printing: May 2003

05   04   03   02   4   3   2   1

Trademarks

Warning and Disclaimer

Associate Publisher
Michael Stephens

Acquisitions Editor
Neil Rowe

Development Editor
Mark Renfrow

Managing Editor
Charlotte Clapp

Project Editor
Andy Beaster

Copy Editor
Geneil Breeze

Indexers
Sharon Shock

Proofreader
Tracy Donhardt

Team Coordinator
Cindy Teeters

Designer
Gary Adair

Page Layout
Stacey Richwine-Derome

Contents at a Glance

Table of Contents

Foreword

I have been writing game development books for over a decade, and consistently I see Clayton Walnum's work on the shelves next to mine. His books are concise, consistent, and timely. He is definitely in this for the long haul and his contribution to the game development community is acknowledged. In his new book, "*Microsoft Direct3D Programming Kick Start*," Clayton's practical step-by-step, no nonsense style once again comes through and takes the reader from ground zero to developing working Direct3D 9.0 applications in both MFC and with the standard SDK.

What's interesting about this book is the new approach Clayton has taken by considering both the professional application programmer as well as the game developer. Thus, this single guide will help you both as a game developer interested in migrating to DirectX 9.0 and an application developer that desires to high performance of DirectX 9.0.

In conclusion, if you're interesting in getting a quick start on DirectX 9.0 then this book is highly recommended.

—André Lamothe
CEO Xtreme Games LLC

André LaMothe has been involved in the computing industry and technology for more than a quarter century. He holds degrees in Mathematics, Computer Science, and Electrical Engineering and is one of the rare individuals that actually did work at NASA at the age of 20 doing research. His early teens and 20s were filled with consulting for numerous Silicon Valley companies where he learned the realities of running a business, and worked on his multidisciplinary background in fields such as telecommunications, virtual reality, robotics, compiler design, 3D engines, Artificial Intelligence, and other areas of computing and engineering.

His company Xtreme Games LLC, was one of the first and the last true "indy" publishers with a soul. Later he founded the Xtreme Games Developer Conference (XGDC) to give game developers a low cost alternative to the GDC.

Lately, he has been working on a number of projects including eGamezone Networks, an online distribution system for games that's fair, fun, and has zero ads. Last, but not least he founded a new company Nurve Networks LLC to create hand held video game systems for value minded consumers, and hobbyist's alike. Finally, he is series editor for the world's largest game development series.

On a personal level he likes everything extreme from weightlifting, motorcycles, jet skis, hotrods, to "railing" on his blades. He has even trained extensively with the Shamrock Submission Fighting Team under the tutelage of Crazy Bob Cook, Frank Shamrock, and Javier Mendez. You probably don't want to get in an argument with him over DirectX or OpenGL, right or wrong he will probably make you say uncle!

About the Author

Award-winning author **Clayton Walnum** got his first computer in 1982, when he traded in an IBM Selectric typewriter to buy an Atari 400 computer (16 KB of RAM!). Clay soon learned to combine his interest in writing with his newly acquired computer skills and started selling articles to computer magazines. In 1985, *ANALOG Computing*, a nationally distributed computer magazine, hired him as a technical editor, and before leaving the magazine business in 1989 to become a freelance writer, Clay had worked his way up to executive editor. He has since acquired a degree in computer science and has written nearly 50 books (translated into many languages) covering everything from artificial life to 3D graphics programming. He's also written hundreds of magazine articles and software reviews as well as countless programs. You can reach Clay on his home page at www.claytonwalnum.com or via email at cwalnum@claytonwalnum.com.

Dedications

To Lynn

Acknowledgments

The author would like to thank the many people who made this book possible and who, thanks to their dedicated work, made this book as good as it could be. These folks include, but are not limited to, Neil Rowe, Mark Renfrow, Andy Beaster, Geneil Breeze, and Keith Sink. There are, of course, many people behind the scenes, people I've never had the pleasure of knowing, who also did their bit to get this volume on the shelves. Thanks to all. And, finally, as always, thanks to my family.

We Want to Hear from You!

As the reader of this book, *you* are our most important critic and commentator. We value your opinion and want to know what we're doing right, what we could do better, what areas you'd like to see us publish in, and any other words of wisdom you're willing to pass our way.

As an Associate Publisher for Sams, I welcome your comments. You can email or write me directly to let me know what you did or didn't like about this book—as well as what we can do to make our books better.

Please note that I cannot help you with technical problems related to the *topic* of this book. We do have a User Services group, however, where I will forward specific technical questions related to the book.

When you write, please be sure to include this book's title and author as well as your name, email address, and phone number. I will carefully review your comments and share them with the author and editors who worked on the book.

Email: feedback@samspublishing.com

Mail: Michael Stephens, Associate Publisher
           Sams Publishing
           201 West 103rd Street
           Indianapolis, IN 46290 USA

For more information about this book or another Sams title, visit our Web site at www.samspublishing.com. Type the ISBN (excluding hyphens) or the title of a book in the Search field to find the page you're looking for.

Introduction

Often when graphics programmers take the leap into creating 3D applications, they find themselves confronted with the need for intimate familiarity with mathematics, the science of color, and even to some degree, knowledge of physics. After all, it's no surprise that writing programs that mimic the real world would be challenging, to say the least.

Luckily, thousands of programmers over the years have dedicated themselves to modeling the real world with a series of formulas and algorithms that other programmers can draw on to create 3D applications without needing doctorate degrees in multiple disciplines. Much of this work culminated in the creation of 3D graphics libraries, one of which is Microsoft's Direct3D.

Direct3D places all the knowledge gained by those graphics pioneers at your fingertips, enabling you to create 3D worlds without having to submerse yourself in the mathematical minutia inherent in the code used to create such worlds. In short, Direct3D enables you to *create* 3D worlds rather than reinvent them.

This isn't to say that creating 3D applications requires no graphics programming knowledge at all. To be successful, you need not only to be fluent in the programming language of your choice (in this book, C++) but also must have a basic understanding of what's involved in programming a graphics-based application. In other words, although you don't need to program a lot of mathematical equations or come up with sophisticated and efficient algorithms for manipulating a 3D scene, you should at least have some idea of how such code works.

In this book, then, you get both an introduction to the art of graphics programming in general and graphics programming with Direct3D. Along the way, you'll study everything you need to know to create astonishing 3D worlds with Direct3D.

Who Should Read This Book

This book is aimed at programmers who are fluent with C++ and have some experience with graphics programming. When I say fluent in C++, I mean that you should be able to look at standard C++ code and understand it. Source code in this book is unaccompanied by descriptions of code syntax and usage, except as it applies to Direct3D objects and methods. You need to know the language.

When I say experience with graphics programming, I don't mean that you need to have programmed 3D applications, but just that you know how a computer program creates a simple graphical display, including drawing shapes, displaying text and bitmaps, and how such data gets stored in memory. Some knowledge of display modes and pixel formats will help, but these topics do get coverage as they relate to Direct3D applications.

Other than the technical knowledge described in the previous two paragraphs, you need to bring with you a willingness to spend time carefully reading the book's text and investigating in detail the sample programs presented in each chapter. Taking the time to experiment with the sample programs is also necessary to fully master the Direct3D concepts presented.

Although the individual programming techniques described in these pages are not of themselves overly difficult, putting together a full-featured 3D application requires juggling any number of these techniques, which requires a solid understanding of each. In other words, be willing to spend the time necessary to master each chapter before going on to the next.

System Requirements

The system requirements for this book are the same as those required for developing Direct3D applications with Visual Studio .NET. Specifically, you need the following:

- Visual C++ .NET

- DirectX 9.0 or later

- Windows 2000, Windows XP, or Windows NT 4.0

- 450 MHz Pentium II PC or better

- Windows NT Workstation 4.0: 64 MB; Windows 2000 Professional: 96 MB; Windows 2000 Server: 192 MB; Windows XP Professional: 160 MB

- Super VGA (800×600 or better) monitor

On the Web Site

You don't have to type the code if you don't want to! The full source code for each listing (or example) in this book is available for download from this book's Web site. Go to www.samspublishing.com and type the ISBN (0672324989) in the Search field. You can just copy it from the completed projects!

Exploring Direct3D

Few areas of study in computer science bring you closer to the cutting edge of computer technology than 3D graphics programming. Today's computers—even the desktop variety—can produce stunningly real images in near photographic quality. In fact, using modern 3D graphics programming techniques, computers can produce everything from fabulous games such as The Elder Scrolls III: Morrowind to scenes for blockbuster films such as *Jurassic Park*.

The bad news is that 3D graphics programming techniques require darn near a master's degree in mathematics to understand. Thankfully, many of today's tools hide such gory details, leaving programmers to worry only about creating the images and not about cramming trigonometry, linear algebra, and differential geometry between their ears. One of those tools is Direct3D, a library of graphics routines that makes sophisticated 3D graphics programming accessible to mere mortals.

What Is Direct3D?

Direct3D is a programming interface for producing interactive 3D applications. Using the Direct3D libraries, a programmer can do anything from display simple shapes to compose animated 3D scenes complete with lighting, antialiasing, and texture mapping. Because most of the mathematics is hidden within the library, programmers are relieved of having to decipher lengthy formulas to render images onscreen.

Direct3D was developed by Microsoft to satisfy Windows programmers who wanted to develop games. Before its introduction, most 3D applications had to be written to run under DOS rather than Windows because the Windows graphics routines were too slow and restrictive.

Direct3D is one portion of DirectX, which also includes libraries for programming with sound, input devices, networking, and more.

THE HISTORY OF DIRECTX

Microsoft's first attempt to fix Windows' graphical problems was something called WinG, which was a very small set of functions that enabled programmers to directly access video memory, something Windows never allowed before. Continued development by Microsoft yielded the Game SDK, which was really Microsoft's first attempt at DirectX. Eventually, the Game SDK became DirectX, the name that Microsoft has stuck with ever since.

The Direct3D Library

Direct3D is one part of the DirectX programming library, which provides methods for not only graphics programming but also sound, input, networking, and more. Earlier versions of DirectX included the DirectDraw library for developing 2D applications and Direct3D for developing 3D applications. However, starting with DirectX 8, Microsoft merged DirectDraw into Direct3D, referring to the hybrid as DirectX Graphics.

Direct3D itself comprises a large set of COM interfaces, each of which represents a Direct3D object. For example, you use the IDirect3D9 interface to create device objects, as well as to query for devices, manage graphics adapter modes, inquire about device capabilities, and more. You create an IDirect3D9 object by calling the Direct3DCreate9() function. You can create other types of Direct3D objects from the lower hierarchy interfaces, such as IDirect3DDevice9 and IDirect3DSurface9. (The hierarchy I refer to isn't so much an official organization of the Direct3D interfaces, but rather a perceived one based on the order in which objects are created.) Here's a list of some of the more commonly used Direct3D interfaces:

- IDirect3D9—Represents the main Direct3D object, which is the starting point for every Direct3D application.

- IDirect3DDevice9—Represents a Direct3D device, which is the next highest object in the Direct3D hierarchy. A huge portion of your Direct3D programming is accomplished through this interface.

- IDirect3DSurface9—Represents a Direct3D surface, which, generally, is an area of memory in which graphical data is stored.

- IDirect3DTexture9—Represents a Direct3D texture, which is an image that can be overlaid onto a 3D object to provide extra detail to the object's surface.

- IDirect3DVertexBuffer9—Represents a Direct3D vertex buffer, which is an area of memory that holds the coordinates of points that define 3D shapes.

- IDirect3DIndexBuffer9—Represents a Direct3D index buffer, which holds offsets into vertex buffer data.

You'll learn much more about most of these interfaces as you work your way through the book.

DIRECT3D: AN IMMENSE LIBRARY OF INTERFACES

The main portion of Direct3D features nearly 20 different COM interfaces that represent the objects needed to develop your 3D applications. Direct3D also throws in an extension library that features more than 20 additional COM interfaces. These extra interfaces provide quick and easy ways to accomplish common tasks required by Direct3D. An example of such a task is loading a texture bitmap into memory. This book covers only those interfaces that are most important to getting your full 3D applications up and running. Covering all of the interfaces would require an entire series of books.

What Direct3D Can Do

Direct3D can produce many types of 3D graphical images, including everything from simple 3D objects to interactive, animated scenes. To do all this, Direct3D helps you accomplish many difficult tasks, including these:

- Drawing objects—Direct3D can draw points, lines, and polygons. Using these basic shapes, you can build most any type of 3D image you require. Direct3D polygons are described by a series of vertices that you supply to Direct3D.

- Viewing objects—After you've composed the objects in a scene, you need to tell Direct3D how you want to view those objects. You accomplish this by calling the Direct3D methods that perform several types of transformations, including the world, view, and projection transformations.

- Specifying pixel formats—Direct3D uses a complex set of calculations for determining the color of objects drawn onscreen. However, as the programmer, you can choose between many different pixel formats, which represent different color depths, as well as the types of information included in each color value for a pixel. For example, color information may include RGB values for determining color and alpha information for determining transparency.

- Applying lighting—Shapes drawn with Direct3D functions don't come to life until you've added lighting to the scene. Direct3D not only manipulates many types of light sources—emissive, ambient, diffuse, and specular—but also lets you specify the properties of the surfaces—called *materials*—from which light is reflected.

- Enhancing images—Because of the inherent limitations of computer graphics, Direct3D supplies a number of methods for adding more realism to 3D scenes. These methods implement such image-enhancement techniques as antialiasing, blending, and fog. Antialiasing disguises the stair-step effect so prevalent in lines drawn on a computer display, blending enables the programmer to produce translucent objects, and fog makes images far from the viewpoint seem to fade in the distance.

- Manipulating bitmaps—Direct3D provides various ways of manipulating bitmaps, which are full-color images that can be transferred between the screen and memory.

- Texture mapping—Objects created from color polygons usually lack the detail required to render an effective and realistic scene. For this reason, Direct3D lets the programmer apply texture mapping (which "wraps" a 3D object in a bitmapped pattern) to objects, thus providing all-important graphical details to a scene.

- Performing animation—Because producing smoothly animated scenes requires building frames in memory before transferring those frames to the screen, Direct3D implements *multibuffering*. When you use multibuffering, you first create two or more basic scenes in memory. Then you display one scene onscreen while modifying another scene in memory. When the next scene (or animation frame) is complete, you switch to display the new scene onscreen, leaving you free to modify the next buffer, as required, before switching again.

The Direct3D capabilities described in this section are just some of the most commonly used features. The truth is that Direct3D supplies much more, including bump mapping, environment mapping, tweening, geometry blending, mip-mapping, and so on. Direct3D now has so many features, and is usable under so many development scenarios and languages, that it would be impossible for any reasonably sized, single book to cover everything.

SHOP TALK

THE GOOD OLD DAYS?

I can remember, way back in the day, when we graphics programmers had to write all the code for accomplishing such sophisticated tasks as manipulating bitmaps, texturing surfaces, and applying lighting to a scene.

For example, loading a bitmap into memory wasn't as simple as it is with Direct3D, which requires only a single method call to accomplish the task. Instead, the programmer had to write all of the code needed to examine the bitmap's file for format, size, and color information; allocate the memory to hold the bitmap; and then load the bitmap data into memory. Just to load the bitmap could require 100 lines of code or more. If the image was compressed, writing the code to load the data was even more challenging.

And you don't even want to imagine the mathematics and image manipulation behind such things as texturing and lighting, all of which Direct3D now handles for you. (In the next couple of chapters, you'll get a look at the math needed to manipulate 2D and 3D shapes the "old-fashioned" way.) With Direct3D, you need only supply a little information about the scene you want to render, and the Direct3D methods do most of the work for you.

Direct3D Architecture on Windows

As you probably know, from a programmer's point of view, a computer's operating system comprises many layers of functionality, each of which is represented by a library of functions. Direct3D adds yet another layer to this complex system. Specifically, Direct3D fits between a Windows application and the graphics hardware, much as Windows' standard graphics library, the Graphics Device Interface (GDI), does. Unlike the GDI, which is slow and restrictive, the Direct3D layer gives programmers virtually complete control over the graphics system.

When you write a Windows application using the GDI, you're actually programming through several layers of functionality, starting with the GDI and leading down through the Device Driver Interface (DDI) and finally to the graphics hardware. Figure 1.1 shows the relationship between these layers.

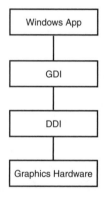

FIGURE 1.1   The hierarchy of layers for a standard Windows application.

The hierarchy of layers for a Direct3D application is a little more complex. This is because a Direct3D application achieves device independence with the Hardware Abstraction Layer (HAL). The manufacturer of the graphics hardware supplies the HAL, which implements the Direct3D-defined functions that the hardware is capable of performing. The HAL reports back to Direct3D the capabilities of the hardware.

So, a Direct3D Windows application interacts with the Direct3D layer, which itself interacts with the HAL or the DDI. The DDI interacts with the graphics hardware. Figure 1.2 shows the relationship between these layers.

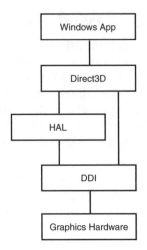

FIGURE 1.2   The hierarchy of layers for a Direct3D Windows application.

Direct3D Example Applications

You may be anxious by now to actually see some of the things that Direct3D can do. You'll be happy to know that the DirectX SDK ships with a lot of Direct3D applications that demonstrate many of the library's features. For example, Figure 1.3 shows the Lighting demo, whereas Figure 1.4 shows the MFCFog example application.

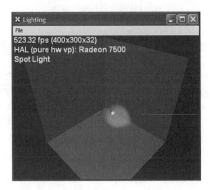

FIGURE 1.3   The Direct3D Lighting demo.

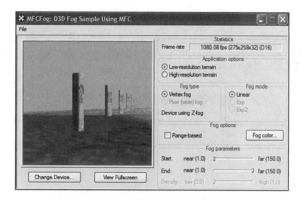

FIGURE 1.4   The Direct3D MFCFog demo.

The DirectX SDK also comes with a number of utility programs to help you with application development. As I mentioned previously, one of the HAL's duties is to report back to Direct3D the capabilities of the graphics hardware. You can view the capabilities of your system by running the DirectX Caps Viewer, shown in Figure 1.5.

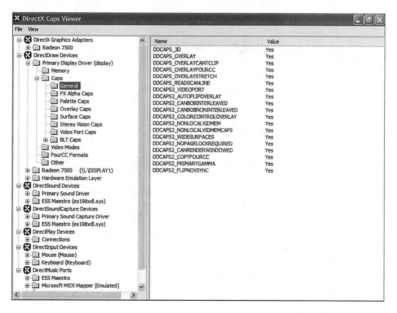

FIGURE 1.5   The DirectX Caps Viewer utility.

The DirectX utilities also include a program for looking up error codes, a mesh viewer, and many more. The Error Lookup utility, shown in Figure 1.6, translates the error values returned by various Direct3D methods into a more descriptive text message.

FIGURE 1.6   The Error Lookup utility.

The mesh viewer, shown in Figure 1.7, enables the user to load and view sophisticated 3D objects from the files that define the objects. The many connected polygons that define 3D objects are referred to as a *mesh*. Meshes are usually stored in a data file on disk from which they are read into a 3D application. The mesh viewer utility is a simple example of such a 3D application.

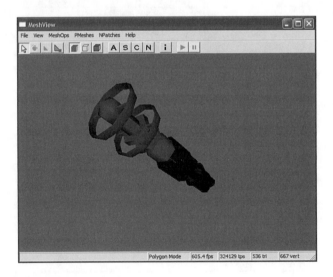

FIGURE 1.7   The mesh viewer utility.

SHOP TALK

LOOKING FOR HELP

Over the years, as I've worked with the different versions of Direct3D, I've always found Microsoft's utility programs and sample code to be more than just a valuable asset but also an essential resource to draw on as I learned to program new features of the DirectX library.

The utility programs such as the DirectX Caps Viewer and DirectX Error Lookup application offer access to exactly the type of information you need when writing Direct3D applications, especially when you're writing those applications for the first time and have little experience to draw on.

Similarly, Microsoft's many example applications cover all of the major programming techniques you need to know to get the most out of Direct3D and other components of DirectX. Studying this source code is essential to understanding intimately the huge library of interfaces that Direct3D places into your hands. In fact, studying Microsoft's example source code should be the next thing you do right after finishing this book.

In Brief

- Direct3D is a library of graphics functions that represents a standard for creating 3D applications.

- Direct3D is one part of the DirectX programming library, which provides methods for not only graphics programming but also sound, input, networking, and more.

- Direct3D itself comprises a large set of COM interfaces, each of which represents a Direct3D object.

- Direct3D helps you accomplish many difficult tasks, including drawing objects, viewing objects, specifying pixel formats, applying lighting, enhancing images, manipulating bitmaps, texture mapping, and performing animation.

- The DirectX SDK ships with a lot of Direct3D applications that demonstrate many of the library's features, including the Lighting demo and the MFCFog example application.

- The DirectX SDK also comes with a number of utility programs to help you with application development.

Writing a Windows Program

2

Because Direct3D programs must be able to run under Windows, before you can actually dig into Direct3D, you need to know how to write a simple Windows program. Luckily, you don't need to know too much about Windows programming. In fact, most of what you need to know, you can learn in this one chapter.

Windows the Old-Fashioned Way

When Windows first become popular, sophisticated programming tools were as scarce as flies in a Raid factory. Programmers wrote Windows applications in straight C (no C++) and compiled them under DOS, strange as that sounds. There were no C compilers that ran under Windows, even though you could program Windows applications with the compilers.

These days, complex libraries such as Microsoft's MFC take much of the drudgery out of writing Windows applications, but such advantages come with a price. MFC itself has a steep learning curve. Moreover, if you don't understand how a conventional Windows program works, learning MFC is even harder.

Anyway, when writing Direct3D programs, you don't want to be stuck with the significant overhead MFC adds to your programs. For this reason, the first step toward learning to write Direct3D programs is to learn to write a basic Windows application the old-fashioned way. You will, however, use C++ rather than C. There's no need to go back to the dark ages!

The Minimum Windows Application

Listing 2.1 is a simple C++ Windows application called BasicWindowsApp. Figure 2.1 shows BasicWindowsApp when you run it.

FIGURE 2.1   The running BasicWindowsApp application.

LISTING 2.1   A Basic Windows Application

```
/////////////////////////////////////////////////////
// BasicWindowsApp.cpp
/////////////////////////////////////////////////////


#include <windows.h>

// Function prototypes.
LRESULT WINAPI WndProc(HWND hWnd, UINT msg,
    WPARAM wParam, LPARAM lParam);
void RegisterWindowClass(HINSTANCE hInstance);
void CreateAppWindow(HINSTANCE hInstance);
WPARAM StartMessageLoop();

// Global variables.
HWND g_hWnd;
```

LISTING 2.1   Continued

```
/////////////////////////////////////////////////
// WinMain()
/////////////////////////////////////////////////
INT WINAPI WinMain(HINSTANCE hInstance, HINSTANCE, LPSTR, INT)
{
    RegisterWindowClass(hInstance);
    CreateAppWindow(hInstance);
    ShowWindow(g_hWnd, SW_SHOWDEFAULT);
    UpdateWindow(g_hWnd);
    INT result = StartMessageLoop();
    return result;
}


/////////////////////////////////////////////////
// WndProc()
/////////////////////////////////////////////////
LRESULT WINAPI WndProc(HWND hWnd, UINT msg, WPARAM wParam, LPARAM lParam)
{
    switch(msg)
    {
    case WM_CREATE:
        return 0;

    case WM_DESTROY:
        PostQuitMessage( 0 );
        return 0;

    case WM_PAINT:
        ValidateRect(g_hWnd, NULL);
        return 0;
    }
    return DefWindowProc(hWnd, msg, wParam, lParam);
}


/////////////////////////////////////////////////
// RegisterWindowClass()
/////////////////////////////////////////////////
void RegisterWindowClass(HINSTANCE hInstance)
{
    WNDCLASSEX wc;
    wc.cbSize = sizeof(WNDCLASSEX);
```

LISTING 2.1   Continued

```
    wc.style = CS_HREDRAW | CS_VREDRAW | CS_OWNDC;
    wc.lpfnWndProc = WndProc;
    wc.cbClsExtra = 0;
    wc.cbWndExtra = 0;
    wc.hInstance = hInstance;
    wc.hIcon = LoadIcon(NULL, IDI_APPLICATION);
    wc.hCursor = (HCURSOR)LoadCursor(NULL, IDC_ARROW);
    wc.hbrBackground = (HBRUSH)GetStockObject(WHITE_BRUSH);
    wc.lpszMenuName = NULL;
    wc.lpszClassName = "WinApp";
    wc.hIconSm = NULL;

    RegisterClassEx(&wc);
}

////////////////////////////////////////////////////
// CreateAppWindow()
////////////////////////////////////////////////////
void CreateAppWindow(HINSTANCE hInstance)
{
    g_hWnd = CreateWindowEx(
        NULL,
        "WinApp",
        "Basic Windows Application",
        WS_OVERLAPPEDWINDOW,
        100,
        100,
        648,
        514,
        GetDesktopWindow(),
        NULL,
        hInstance,
        NULL);
}

////////////////////////////////////////////////////
// StartMessageLoop()
////////////////////////////////////////////////////
WPARAM StartMessageLoop()
{
```

LISTING 2.1   Continued

```
MSG msg;
while(1)
{
    if (PeekMessage(&msg, NULL, 0, 0, PM_REMOVE))
    {
        if (msg.message == WM_QUIT)
            break;
        TranslateMessage(&msg);
        DispatchMessage(&msg);
    }
    else
    {
        // Use idle time here.
    }
}
return msg.wParam;
}
```

As you can see, getting a window up on the screen takes a bit of work. For the most part, though, you can use the code in Listing 2.1 as the beginning of just about any Windows application, so most of your work is already done. In the following sections, you'll learn in general how the program works. However, you need to understand only a few important concepts, such as creating a window, defining a Windows procedure, and handling Windows messages.

Digging into the Program

It's time now to discover exactly how a Windows application works. In the following sections, you'll examine Listing 2.1 a little at a time. By the time you reach the end of this chapter, you'll know how to write and compile a basic Windows application.

The Windows Header File

This line of the program includes some necessary stuff:

```
#include <windows.h>
```

The windows.h file contains many declarations that all Windows programs require. All Windows programs include this header file to access standard Windows function-ality, such as minimize/maximize buttons, resizable windows, and so on.

The Function Prototypes

The next things to notice are the function prototypes and global variables:

```
// Function prototypes.
LRESULT WINAPI WndProc(HWND hWnd, UINT msg,
WPARAM wParam, LPARAM lParam);
void RegisterWindowClass(HINSTANCE hInstance);
void CreateAppWindow(HINSTANCE hInstance);
WPARAM StartMessageLoop();


// Global variables.
HWND g_hWnd;
```

As a C++ programmer, you will recognize these lines as prototypes for the program's functions, as well as a single global variable. You'll dig into all of these functions soon. You'll also see what that single global variable holds.

The WinMain() Function

Now, take a look at the WinMain() function:

```
////////////////////////////////////////////////////
// WinMain()
////////////////////////////////////////////////////
INT WINAPI WinMain(HINSTANCE hInstance, HINSTANCE, LPSTR, INT)
{
    RegisterWindowClass(hInstance);
    CreateAppWindow(hInstance);
    ShowWindow(g_hWnd, SW_SHOWDEFAULT);
    UpdateWindow(g_hWnd);
    INT result = StartMessageLoop();
    return result;
}
```

As you can see, the WinMain() function's signature looks like the following (although in the preceding version of WinMain(), you're not accessing the last three parameters and so have given them no names):

```
INT WINAPI WinMain(HINSTANCE hInstance,
    HINSTANCE hPrevInstance, PSTR lpszCmdLine,
    int nCmdShow)
```

`WinMain()` is the entry point for all Windows programs, in the same way `main()` is the entry point for DOS C/C++ programs. `WinMain()`'s four parameters are

- `hInstance`—The handle of this instance of the program

- `hPrevInstance`—The handle of the previous instance

- `lpszCmdLine`—A pointer to the command line used to run the program

- `nCmdShow`—A set of flags that determine how the application's window should be displayed

GETTING A HANDLE ON HANDLES

Handles are one type of data that you may not be familiar with, if you haven't done much Windows programming. A *handle* is nothing more than a value that identifies a window or some other object. In a traditional Windows program, you almost always refer to a window by its handle, and most Windows API functions that manipulate windows require a handle as their first argument.

An instance of an application is much the same thing as an instance of a class in object-oriented programming. For example, in most cases, the user can run the same Windows application multiple times, having several separate, but identical, windows on the screen. Each window represents an instance of the program.

APPLICATION INSTANCES AND MEMORY

In 16-bit Windows programming, all application instances shared the same memory space. By checking the handle to the previous instance, programmers could prevent multiple instances. If hPrevInstance was NULL, there was no previous instance. If hPrevInstance was not NULL, the application had already been run, and the programmer could display the already existing window, rather than create a new instance of the application.

Under Windows 98 and greater, however, every application gets its own block of virtual memory. For this reason, the hPrevInstance handle in modern Windows programs is always NULL.

Getting back to the program, the `WinMain()` function must perform several important functions to get a window up on the screen:

1. Create and register a class for the window.

2. Create the window.

3. Display the window.

4. Start the application's message loop.

To keep things less confusing, the BasicWindowsApp program performs each of these important steps in a separate function.

Creating the Window Class

The first task in `WinMain()` is to create a class for the application's window, a task that is handled by the `RegisterWindowClass` function. That function looks like this:

```
/////////////////////////////////////////////////////
// RegisterWindowClass()
/////////////////////////////////////////////////////
void RegisterWindowClass(HINSTANCE hInstance)
{
    WNDCLASSEX wc;
    wc.cbSize = sizeof(WNDCLASSEX);
    wc.style = CS_HREDRAW | CS_VREDRAW | CS_OWNDC;
    wc.lpfnWndProc = WndProc;
    wc.cbClsExtra = 0;
    wc.cbWndExtra = 0;
    wc.hInstance = hInstance;
    wc.hIcon = LoadIcon(NULL, IDI_APPLICATION);
    wc.hCursor = (HCURSOR)LoadCursor(NULL, IDC_ARROW);
    wc.hbrBackground = (HBRUSH)GetStockObject(WHITE_BRUSH);
    wc.lpszMenuName = NULL;
    wc.lpszClassName = "WinApp";
    wc.hIconSm = NULL;

    RegisterClassEx(&wc);
}
```

Windows defines a structure for holding the values that make up a window class. `RegisterWindowClass()` declares an instance of this structure like this:

```
WNDCLASS wc;
```

`RegisterWindowClass()` also initializes this structure to the values required for the window class. The WNDCLASS structure defines the window's style, as well as specifies the window's icons, cursor, background color, and menu.

Registering the Window Class

The application-defined function `RegisterWindowClass()` registers the new window class with Windows by calling the Windows API function `RegisterClassEx()`, like this:

```
RegisterClassEx(&wc);
```

`RegisterClassEx()`'s single argument is the address of the initialized WNDCLASS structure.

SHOP TALK

LEARNING MORE ABOUT WINDOWS PROGRAMMING

I won't go into great detail about what all the values of the WNDCLASSEX structure mean, because you can use the program just as it's shown. Nothing in the code really has much to do with Direct3D programming.

If you want to know more, you can consult a Windows programming manual. The important thing to know here is that every Windows application must create an instance of the WNDCLASSEX structure and register it with Windows.

That being said, when you finish with this book, if you plan to go on to program other types of Windows applications—or if you're just curious—I highly recommend that you pick up a general Windows programming book. There's much more to Windows programming than I have room for in this book. In fact, the information here represents maybe one percent of what you need to know to program full-featured Windows applications.

Just a few topics with which Windows programmers must be familiar include using dialog boxes, programming menus, manipulating cursors, drawing text and graphics (not with DirectX), managing bitmaps, and handling a slew of Windows messages that are not mentioned in the following pages.

Creating an Instance of the Window Class

After creating and registering the window class, WinMain() creates an instance of the window class, by calling the function CreateAppWindow(), which looks like this:

```
/////////////////////////////////////////////////////
// CreateAppWindow()
/////////////////////////////////////////////////////
void CreateAppWindow(HINSTANCE hInstance)
{
    g_hWnd = CreateWindowEx(
        NULL,
        "WinApp",                    // Window class's name
        "Basic Windows Application", // Title bar text
        WS_OVERLAPPEDWINDOW,         // The window's style
        100,                         // The window's horizontal position
        100,                         // The window's vertical position
        648,                         // The window's width
        514,                         // The window's height
        GetDesktopWindow(),          // The parent window's handle
        NULL,                        // The window's menu handle
        hInstance,                   // The instance handle
        NULL);
}
```

The comments I've added to the function briefly describe `CreateWindow()`'s arguments. Again, you don't need to know the specifics to create a window for your Direct3D program. I'll explain, when the time comes, anything that needs to be different in upcoming programs.

Showing the Window

At this point, the application has defined a window class and created an instance of that window class. But, so far, nothing is on the screen. To display the new window, `WinMain()` calls the Windows API function `ShowWindow()`:

```
ShowWindow(hWnd, nCmdShow);
```

Finally, to ensure that the window updates its display, the program calls the Windows API function `UpdateWindow()`:

```
UpdateWindow(hWnd);
```

Notice how both of these functions, like most other window-manipulation functions, take a window handle as the first argument.

The Infamous Message Loop

Now that the window is up on the screen, it can start to process the many messages that Windows sends it. The program does this by setting up a message loop, which BasicWindowsApp does in the `StartMessageLoop()` function:

```
/////////////////////////////////////////////////
// StartMessageLoop()
/////////////////////////////////////////////////
WPARAM StartMessageLoop()
{
    MSG msg;
    while(1)
    {
        if (PeekMessage(&msg, NULL, 0, 0, PM_REMOVE))
        {
            if (msg.message == WM_QUIT)
            break;
            TranslateMessage(&msg);
            DispatchMessage(&msg);
        }
        else
        {
```

```
        // Use idle time here.
    }
}
return msg.wParam;
}
```

As you can see, the while loop continues indefinitely, gathering up messages from Windows again and again until the user quits the program. At that point, when the current Windows message is WM_QUIT, a break statement ends the loop.

The PeekMessage() Windows API function retrieves a message from the window's message queue. As long as PeekMessage() returns a nonzero value, the application has messages to handle. If PeekMessage() returns 0, the application has no waiting messages and is considered to be idle. As you'll see in upcoming programs, Direct3D programs use this idle time to process graphics and other program elements.

Inside the loop, the call to TranslateMessage() handles virtual-key messages (messages that represent keystrokes), translating them into character messages that go back into the message queue. The DispatchMessage() function sends the message off to the application's window procedure.

The Window Procedure

When you defined BasicWindowsApp's window class in the WNDCLASSEX structure, you specified the function to which Windows messages should be directed:

```
wc.lpfnWndProc = WndProc;
```

When the program registered the window class, Windows made note of the window procedure passed in the lpfnWndProc structure member. So, calls to DispatchMessage() result in Windows sending the message to WndProc(), where the application either handles the message or sends it back to Windows for default processing.

In BasicWindowsApp, WndProc()'s signature looks like this:

```
LRESULT WINAPI WndProc(HWND hWnd, UINT msg,
    WPARAM wParam, LPARAM lParam)
```

The function's four parameters are

- *hWnd*—The handle of the window to which the message is directed

- *msg*—The message ID (for example, WM_CREATE)

- *wParam*—A 32-bit message parameter

- *lParam*—A 32-bit message parameter

The values of the two 32-bit parameters depend on the type of message. For example, when the user selects a menu item from an application's menu bar, the application gets a WM_COMMAND message, with the menu item's ID in the low word of the wParam parameter.

WndProc()'s job is to determine whether the application needs to handle the message or pass it back to Windows for default processing. (All messages must be dealt with in one of these ways.) In most Windows procedures, the programmer sets up a switch statement with case clauses for the messages the application should handle. BasicWindowsApp handles only three Windows messages: WM_CREATE, WM_DESTROY, and WM_PAINT. Its switch statement looks like the following code snippet:

```
switch(msg)
{
case WM_CREATE:
    return 0;
case WM_DESTROY:
    PostQuitMessage( 0 );
    return 0;
case WM_PAINT:
    ValidateRect(g_hWnd, NULL);
    return 0;
}
```

The following list describes the Windows messages used in the program:

- WM_CREATE—This message means that the program is creating its window. You can do certain kinds of initialization here.

- WM_PAINT—This message means that the window must redraw its display. Because you'll eventually be using Direct3D to draw the application's display, all you need to do here is call the Windows API function ValidateRect(), which tells Windows that the display has been taken care of.

- WM_DESTROY—This message means that the user wants to close the application. All Windows applications must handle WM_DESTROY. The call to the Windows API function PostQuitMessage() ends the program.

Notice that, after handling a message, the function returns a value of zero. Messages not handled in the switch statement must be passed back to Windows. Failure to do this could result in the application being incapable of responding to the user. To pass a message back to Windows, the application calls DefWindowProc():

```
return DefWindowProc(hWnd, msg, wParam, lParam);
```

The function's arguments are the same as the parameters passed to the window procedure. Notice that `WndProc()` returns `DefWindowProc()`'s return value.

Now that you have a general idea of how a "handwritten" Windows application works, you need a little experience building one with Visual C++ .Net.

Building a Basic Windows Application

Now that you know most of the theory behind programming a simple Windows application, it's time to build one for yourself. Load up Visual Studio .NET and perform the following steps:

1. Click the New Project button on Visual Studio .NET's Start page. The New Project dialog box appears, as shown in Figure 2.2.

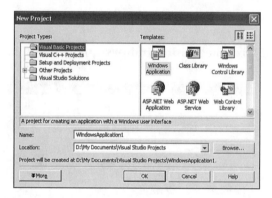

FIGURE 2.2   The New Project dialog box.

2. In the Project Types box, select Visual C++ Projects, as shown in Figure 2.3.

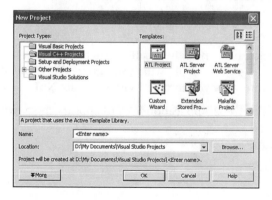

FIGURE 2.3   Selecting the project type.

3. In the Templates box, select Win32 Project, as shown in Figure 2.4.

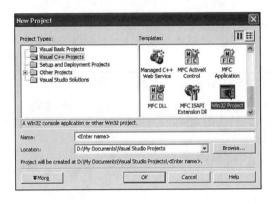

FIGURE 2.4   Selecting the project template.

4. In the Name box, enter **BasicWindowsApp**, as shown in Figure 2.5.

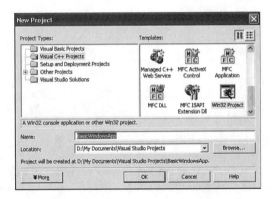

FIGURE 2.5   Entering the project's name.

5. In the Location box, enter the location where the project should be saved, or just leave it set to the default, which should be the Visual Studio Projects folder created for you when you installed Visual Studio .NET.

6. Click OK. The Win32 Application Wizard appears, as shown in Figure 2.6.

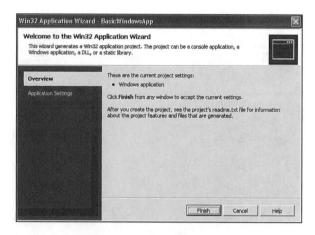

FIGURE 2.6   The Win32 Application Wizard.

7. On the left-hand side of the wizard, click the Application Settings selection. The application settings appear in the wizard, as shown in Figure 2.7.

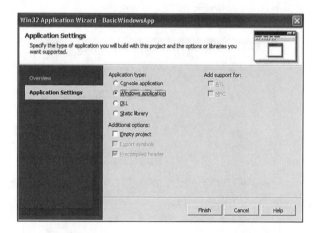

FIGURE 2.7   The application's settings.

8. Select the Empty Project option under the Additional Options heading, as shown in Figure 2.8.

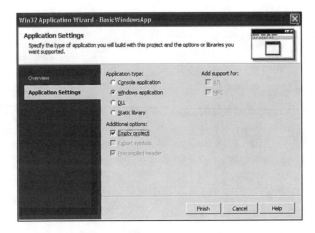

FIGURE 2.8   Choosing the Empty Project option.

9. Click Finish, and Visual Studio .NET creates the project for you.

10. On the Project menu, select the Add New Item command. The Add New Item dialog box appears, as shown in Figure 2.9.

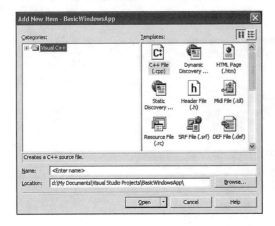

FIGURE 2.9   The Add New Item dialog box.

11. In the Templates box, select the C++ File (.cpp) icon, and in the Name box, enter **BasicWindowsApp.cpp**, as shown in Figure 2.10.

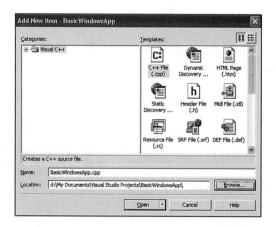

FIGURE 2.10   Entering the file's name.

12. Click Open. The new, blank file appears, as shown in Figure 2.11.

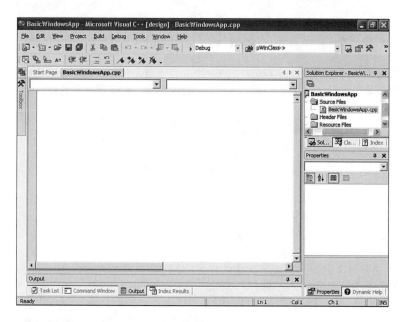

FIGURE 2.11   The newly created file.

13. Type **Listing 2.1** into the new window, or just copy the code from the BasicWindowsApp.cpp file which is available for download at www.samspublishing.com. Type the ISBN (0672324989) in the Search field to find the page you're looking for. Figure 2.12 shows the source code in the code window.

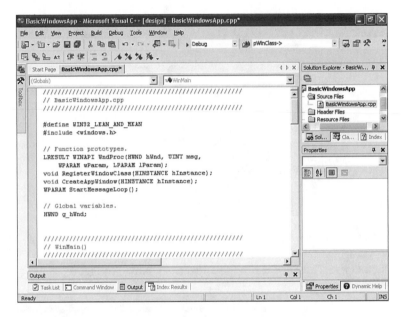

FIGURE 2.12   The source code typed or copied into the window.

14. Press F5 to compile and run the program. Visual Studio asks whether you want to build the out-of-date files, as shown in Figure 2.13. Click Yes.

FIGURE 2.13   Visual Studio asking whether to build out-of-date files.

After completing these steps, you should see the window shown back in Figure 2.1. If the program doesn't work, recheck each of the preceding steps. If you typed the program, make sure that you're typing is correct. It's easy to make mistakes!

This completes your quick course in writing Windows applications. In future chapters, you'll use a similar program as the basis for the DirectX applications you'll be building. However, because you'll be using DirectX rather than Windows to display stuff on the screen, your application's window provides only the basic functionality of a full Windows application. This basic functionality is all you need for the programs in this book. If you want to write an application like a word processor or a spreadsheet, you're reading the wrong programming book!

In Brief

- The windows.h file contains many declarations that all Windows programs require. All Windows programs include this header file.

- `WinMain()` is the entry point for all Windows programs, in the same way that `main()` is the entry point for DOS C/C++ programs.

- A handle is a value that identifies a window or some other object.

- An instance of an application is much the same thing as an instance of a class in object-oriented programming.

- The first task `WinMain()` must complete is to create and register a class for the application's window.

- After creating and registering the window class, `WinMain()` must create an instance of the window class, by calling the Windows API function `CreateWindowEx()`.

- To display the new window, `WinMain()` must call the Windows API function `ShowWindow()`, and to ensure that the window updates its display, the program calls the Windows API function `UpdateWindow()`.

- By setting up a message loop that calls the Windows API functions `PeekMessage()`, `TranslateMessage()`, and `DispatchMessage()`, an application processes the many messages that Windows sends it.

- Calls to `DispatchMessage()` result in Windows sending the current message to the registered window procedure, where the messages are either handled by the application or sent back to Windows for default processing.

Programming 2D Computer Graphics

3

As you've learned, Direct3D provides many powerful functions for creating 3D graphics on your computer. These functions hide many programming details that must be dealt with to produce sophisticated graphics. Still, to understand Direct3D, you need to have a little background in standard 3D programming practices. The first step toward that goal is to understand how your computer programs can manipulate simpler 2D images.

This chapter, then, introduces you to the basics of 2D graphics programming, including the formulas needed to transform (move, rotate, scale, and so on) 2D shapes in various ways. Although transforming 2D shapes requires that you know a set of formulas for manipulating the points that define a shape, you'll discover that these formulas are easy to use, even if you don't really understand exactly how they work.

In this chapter, you learn:

- About screen and Cartesian coordinates
- About using vertices to define 2D shapes
- About translating, scaling, and rotating 2D shapes
- How to use matrices to transform 2D shapes

Understanding Screen and Cartesian Coordinates

Undoubtedly, you have at least some minimal experience with drawing images on a computer screen under Windows. For example, you probably know that to draw a line in a window, you must call the GDI function MoveToEx() to position the starting point of the line and then call the function LineTo() to draw the line. In a program, those two function calls would look something like this:

```
MoveToEx(hDC, x, y, 0);
LineTo(hDC, x, y);
```

The arguments for the MoveToEx() function are a handle to a device context (DC), the X,Y coordinates of the point in the window to which you want to move, and a pointer to a POINT structure in which the function should store the current position before moving to the new position. If this last argument is 0, MoveToEx() doesn't supply the current position. The arguments for the LineTo() function are a handle to a DC and the X,Y coordinates of the end of the line.

Of interest here are the X,Y coordinates used for the end points that define the line. Assuming the default mapping mode of MM_TEXT, both sets of coordinates are based on window coordinates, which, like normal screen coordinates, begin in the upper-left corner of the window, with the X coordinate increasing as you move to the right and the Y coordinate increasing as you move down. Figure 3.1 shows this coordinate system.

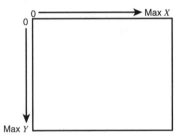

FIGURE 3.1   A window's MM_TEXT coordinate system.

Most computer programmers are familiar with the coordinate system shown in Figure 3.1. Unfortunately, most objects in computer graphics are defined using the *Cartesian* coordinate system, which reverses the Y coordinates so that they increase as you move up from the origin. Also, as shown in Figure 3.2, the Cartesian coordinate system allows negative coordinates. If you remember any of your high school math, you'll recognize Figure 3.2 as the plane on which you graphed equations. In computer graphics, however, you'll use the Cartesian plane as a surface that represents the world in which your graphical objects exist.

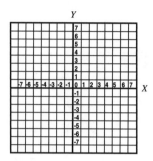

FIGURE 3.2   The Cartesian coordinate system.

You define graphical objects in the Cartesian coordinate system by specifying the coordinates of their *vertices*, which are the points at which the lines that make up the object connect. For example, a triangle can be defined by three points, as shown in Figure 3.3. The defining points in the triangle are (2,5), (5,2), and (2,2).

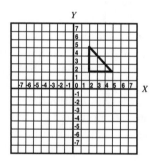

FIGURE 3.3   Defining a triangle in the Cartesian coordinate system.

A problem arises, however, when you try to draw an object defined in the Cartesian coordinate system onscreen. As you can see by Figure 3.4, the figure comes out upside-down due to the reversal of the Y coordinates in the screen's coordinate system as compared with the Cartesian coordinate system. The C++ code that produces the triangle looks like this:

```
MoveToEx(hDC, 2, 5, 0);
LineTo(hDC, 5, 2);
LineTo(hDC, 2, 2);
LineTo(hDC, 2, 5);
```

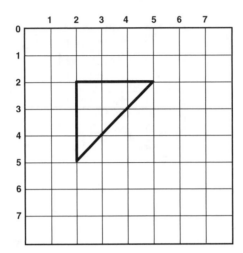

FIGURE 3.4   Drawing a triangle with no mapping between the Cartesian and screen coordinate systems.

Because of the differences between a screen display and the Cartesian coordinate system, you need a way to translate points from one system to the other. In graphics terms, you must *map* points in the Cartesian coordinate system to points in the screen coordinate system so that objects you draw onscreen are positioned correctly. Forgetting about negative coordinates for the time being, mapping point (x1,y1) in the Cartesian coordinate system to point (x2,y2) in the screen coordinate system requires the following simple formulas, shown in C++ program code:

```
x2 = y1;
y2 = maxY - y1;
```

Because the X coordinate is unaffected by the mapping, x2 is simply assigned the value of x1. To reverse the Y coordinate, the original Y coordinate is subtracted from the window's maximum Y coordinate. Of course, for this formula to work, you must know the current size of the window. You can get this value by calling the Windows API function GetClientRect(), which fills a RECT structure with the size of the window's client area. Listing 3.1 draws a triangle in the window, mapping between the Cartesian coordinates and the screen coordinates.

LISTING 3.1   Drawing a Triangle

```
int triangle[6] = {2, 5, 5, 2, 2, 2};
int newX, newY, startX, startY;
RECT clientRect;
GetClientRect(hWnd, &clientRect);
```

LISTING 3.1   Continued

```
int maxY = clientRect.bottom;

for (int x=0; x<3; ++x)
{
    newX = triangle[x*2];
    newY = maxY - triangle[x*2+1];
    if (x == 0)
    {
        MoveToEx(hDC, newX, newY, 0);
        startX = newX;
        startY = newY;
    }
    else
        LineTo(hDC, newX, newY);
}


LineTo(hDC, startX, startY);
```

(Note that the preceding code segment is not complete and will not run on your computer. Later in this chapter, you develop a complete Windows program that demonstrates the topics discussed in this chapter.)

In the preceding code, the first line defines an array that contains the Cartesian coordinates of the triangle. The variables newX and newY will hold the screen coordinates for a point, and the variables startX and startY will hold the screen coordinates for the first point in the triangle. The RECT structure, clientRect, will hold the size of the window's client area.

After declaring the local variables, the code calls GetClientRect() to fill in the clientRect structure, at which point the structure's bottom member will hold the height of the window's client area. The code assigns this value to the local variable maxY.

A for loop then iterates through the triangle's coordinate array. Inside the loop, the currently indexed X,Y coordinates are mapped from Cartesian coordinates to screen coordinates. The first mapped point is used to set the starting point of the triangle. The code uses subsequent points to draw the lines that make up the triangle. The call to LineTo() outside the loop connects the last point of the triangle to the first point.

Defining Vertex and Shape Data Types

As you learned in the previous section, 2D shapes are defined by a set of points, called vertices. Each vertex is connected to the next by a line. When all of the vertices are connected, the shape is finished. To make handling various types of shapes in a program easier, you need to define a couple of new data types. The first data type is for a vertex, and it looks like this:

```
typedef struct vertex
{
    int x, y;
} VERTEX;
```

This structure simply holds the X and Y Cartesian coordinates of a vertex.

The next data type defines a complete shape, like this:

```
typedef struct shape
{
    int numVerts;
    VERTEX* vertices;
} SHAPE;
```

This structure contains an integer to hold the number of vertices in the shape and a pointer to an array of VERTEX structures.

By using these new data types, you can write a more generalized version of the shape-drawing code, placing the loop and the variables on which it depends into its own function. That program code would look something like Listing 3.2.

LISTING 3.2   Drawing Shapes from Generalized Data

```
VERTEX triangleVerts[3] = {2, 5, 5, 2, 2, 2};
SHAPE shape1 = {3, triangleVerts};
DrawShape(shape1);

void DrawShape(SHAPE& shape1)
{
    int newX, newY, startX, startY;
    RECT clientRect;
    GetClientRect(hWnd, &clientRect);
    int maxY = clientRect.bottom;

    for (int x=0; x<shape1.numVerts; ++x)
    {
```

LISTING 3.2   Continued

```
        newX = shape1.vertices[x].x;
        newY = maxY - shape1.vertices[x].y;
        if (x == 0)
        {
            MoveToEx(hDC, newX, newY, 0);
            startX = newX;
            startY = newY;
        }
        else
            LineTo(hDC, newX, newY);
    }

    LineTo(hDC, startX, startY);
}
```

Because the DrawShape() function has been generalized to work with SHAPE structures, the function can draw any type of shape you want to define. For example, to draw a rectangle, you might define shape1 like this:

```
VERTEX rectangleVerts[4] = {10, 10, 100, 10, 100, 50, 10, 50};
SHAPE shape1 = {4, rectangleVerts};
```

In fact, the shapes you define can be as fancy as you want. The shape defined in the following code is shown in Figure 3.5:

```
VERTEX shapeVerts[6] =
    {10, 10, 75, 5, 100, 20, 100, 50, 50, 50, 50, 25};
SHAPE shape1 = {6, shapeVerts};
```

FIGURE 3.5   The SHAPE structure lets you define many types of shapes.

Transforming Shapes

You now know how to create a shape by defining its vertices in Cartesian coordinates, mapping those Cartesian coordinates to screen coordinates, and then drawing lines between the vertices. But drawing a shape onscreen is only the start of the battle. Now, you must write the code needed to manipulate your shapes in various ways so that you can draw the shapes anywhere you want onscreen, as well as in any orientation. Such manipulations are called *transformations*. To transform a shape, you must apply some sort of formula to each vertex. You then use the new vertices to draw the shape.

TRANSFORMING VERTICES, NOT LINES

The fact that only the shape's vertices are transformed is an important point. Although the lines that connect the vertices actually outline a shape, those lines aren't what get transformed. By transforming every vertex in a shape, the lines automatically outline the shape properly when it gets redrawn.

Shape transformations include translation, scaling, and rotation. When you *translate* a shape, you move it to new Cartesian coordinates before drawing it onscreen. For example, you might want to move the shape four units to the right and two units up. When you *scale* a shape, you change its size. You might, for example, want to draw a triangle twice a big as the one you've defined. Finally, when you *rotate* a shape, you turn it to a new angle. Drawing the hands on a clock might involve this type of transformation.

Translating a Shape

Translating a shape to a new position is one of the easiest transformations you can perform. To do this, you simply add or subtract a value from each vertex's X and Y coordinate. Figure 3.6 shows a triangle being translated 3 units on the X axis and 2 units on the Y axis.

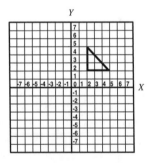
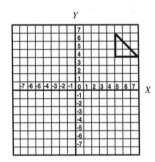

FIGURE 3.6   Translating a triangle.

Suppose that you have the following triangle shape defined:

```
VERTEX triangleVerts[3] = {20, 50, 50, 50, 20, 100};
SHAPE shape1 = {3, triangleVerts};
```

Now, you want to translate that shape 20 units to the right and 30 units up. To do this, you add 20 to each X coordinate and 30 to each Y coordinate, giving the following vertices:

```
VERTEX triangleVerts[3] = {40, 80, 70, 80, 40, 130};
```

So the formula for translating a vertex looks like this:

```
x2 = x1 + xTranslation;
y2 = y1 + yTranslation;
```

In your program, the entire translation would look something like Listing 3.3.

LISTING 3.3   Translating Shapes

```
VERTEX shapeVerts[3] = {20, 50, 50, 50, 20, 100};
SHAPE shape1 = {3, shapeVerts};
Translate(shape1, 20, 30);
DrawShape(shape1);

void Translate(SHAPE& shape, int xTrans, int yTrans)
{
    for (int x=0; x<shape.numVerts; ++x)
    {
        shape.vertices[x].x += xTrans;
        shape.vertices[x].y += yTrans;
    }
}

void DrawShape(SHAPE& shape1)
{
    int newX, newY, startX, startY;
    RECT clientRect;
    GetClientRect(hWnd, &clientRect);
    int maxY = clientRect.bottom;

    for (int x=0; x<shape1.numVerts; ++x)
    {
        newX = shape1.vertices[x].x;
        newY = maxY - shape1.vertices[x].y;
        if (x == 0)
        {
            MoveToEx(hDC, newX, newY, 0);
            startX = newX;
```

LISTING 3.3   Continued

```
            startY = newY;
        }
        else
            LineTo(hDC, newX, newY);
    }

    LineTo(hDC, startX, startY);
}
```

As you can see, the `Translate()` function takes as parameters a reference to a SHAPE structure, the amount of the X translation, and the amount of the Y translation. The function uses a `for` loop to iterate through each of the shape's vertices, adding the translation values to each X and Y coordinate. To translate in the negative direction (moving X left or Y down), you simply make `xTrans` or `yTrans` negative.

Scaling a Shape

Scaling a shape is not unlike translating a shape, except that you multiply each vertex by the scaling factor rather than add or subtract from the vertex. Figure 3.7 shows a triangle being scaled by a factor of 2.

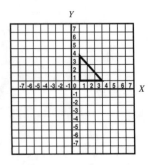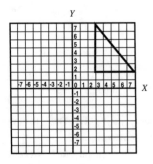

FIGURE 3.7   Scaling a triangle.

Suppose that you have the following triangle shape defined:

```
VERTEX triangleVerts[3] = {20, 50, 50, 50, 20, 100};
SHAPE shape1 = {3, triangleVerts};
```

Now, you want to scale the triangle by a factor of 4. To do this, you multiply each vertex's X and Y coordinates by the scaling factor of 4, giving this set of vertices:

```
VERTEX triangleVerts[3] = {80, 200, 200, 200, 80, 400};
```

So the formula for scaling a vertex looks like this:

```
x2 = x1 * scaleFactor;
y2 = y1 * scaleFactor;
```

In your program, the entire scaling would look something like Listing 3.4.

LISTING 3.4   Scaling Shapes

```
VERTEX triangleVerts[3] = {20, 50, 50, 50, 20, 100};
SHAPE shape1 = {3, triangleVerts};
Scale(shape1, 4);
DrawShape(shape1);

void Scale(SHAPE& shape, float scaleFactor)
{
    for (int x=0; x<shape.numVerts; ++x)
    {
        shape.vertices[x].x =
            (int) (shape.vertices[x].x * scaleFactor);
        shape.vertices[x].y =
            (int) (shape.vertices[x].y * scaleFactor);
    }
}

void DrawShape(SHAPE& shape1)
{
    int newX, newY, startX, startY;
    RECT clientRect;
    GetClientRect(hWnd, &clientRect);
    int maxY = clientRect.bottom;

    for (int x=0; x<shape1.numVerts; ++x)
    {
        newX = shape1.vertices[x].x;
        newY = maxY - shape1.vertices[x].y;
        if (x == 0)
        {
            MoveToEx(hDC, newX, newY, 0);
            startX = newX;
            startY = newY;
        }
        else
```

LISTING 3.4   Continued

```
            LineTo(hDC, newX, newY);
    }

    LineTo(hDC, startX, startY);
}
```

A SIDE EFFECT OF SCALING

Notice that the shape isn't the only thing that gets scaled. The entire coordinate system does, too. That is, a point that was two units from the origin on the X axis would be four units away after scaling by two. To avoid this side effect, you can first translate the shape to the origin (0,0), scale the shape, and then translate it back to its original location.

The Scale() function takes as parameters a reference to a SHAPE structure and the scale factor. Again, the function uses a for loop to iterate through each of the shape's vertices, this time multiplying each X and Y coordinate by the scaling factor. To scale a shape to a smaller size, use a scaling factor less than 1. For example, to reduce the size of a shape by half, use a scaling factor of 0.5. Note that, if you want, you can scale the X coordinates differently from the Y coordinates. To do this, you need both an X scaling factor and a Y scaling factor, giving you a scaling function that looks like Listing 3.5.

LISTING 3.5   A Function that Scales Shapes

```
void Scale(SHAPE& shape, float xScale, float yScale)
{
    for (int x=0; x<shape.numVerts; ++x)
    {
        shape.vertices[x].x =
            (int) (shape.vertices[x].x * xScale);
        shape.vertices[x].y =
            (int) (shape.vertices[x].y * yScale);
    }
}
```

Keep in mind, though, that if you scale the X and Y coordinates differently, you'll distort the shape. Figure 3.8 shows a triangle with an X scaling factor of 1 and a Y scaling factor of 2.

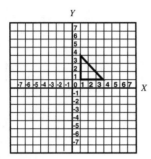 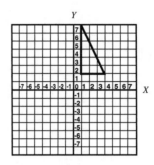

FIGURE 3.8   Scaling a triangle with different X and Y factors.

THE EFFECT OF NEGATIVE SCALING

If you scale a shape with a negative scaling factor, you create a mirror image of the shape.

Rotating a Shape

Rotating a shape is a much more complex operation than translating or scaling, because to calculate the new vertices for the rotated shape, you must resort to more sophisticated mathematics. Specifically, you must calculate sines and cosines. Luckily, as with all the math in this book, you can just plug the rotation formulas into your programs without fully understanding why they do what they do.

Figure 3.9 shows a triangle that's been rotated 45 degrees about the Cartesian origin. Notice that the entire world in which the triangle exists has been rotated, not just the shape itself. It's almost as though the triangle was drawn on a clear piece of plastic the same size as the visible part of the Cartesian plane and then the plastic was rotated 45 degrees to the left, around a pin that secures the plastic where the X and Y axes cross. This is what it means to rotate an object about the origin. If the shape is drawn at the origin, it appears as though only the shape has rotated, rather than the entire world (see Figure 3.10).

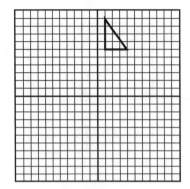
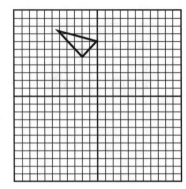

FIGURE 3.9   Rotating a triangle.

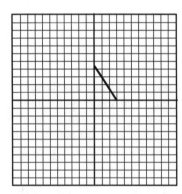
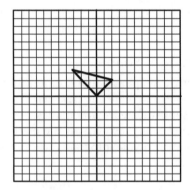

FIGURE 3.10   Rotating a triangle that's drawn at the origin.

Suppose that you have the following triangle shape defined:

```
VERTEX triangleVerts[3] = {20, 50, 50, 50, 20, 100};
SHAPE shape1 = {3, triangleVerts};
```

Now, you want to rotate the triangle 45 degrees. To do this, you apply the following formulas to each vertex in the triangle:

```
rotatedX = x * cos(angle) - y * sine(angle);
rotatedY = y * cos(angle) + x * sine(angle);
```

This gives you the following set of vertices:

```
VERTEX triangleVerts[3] = {-21, 49, 0, 70, -56, 84};
```

Notice that a couple of the coordinates became negative. This is because the rotation caused the triangle to rotate to the left of the Cartesian plane's X axis (see Figure 3.9). Negative values make perfectly acceptable Cartesian coordinates. However, if you were to try and draw this rotated triangle in a window, the shape would be invisible, because windows don't have negative coordinates. To make the rectangle visible, you'd have to translate it to the right, bringing the shape fully to the right of the Cartesian plane's Y axis.

In your program, the entire rotation and translation would look something like Listing 3.6.

LISTING 3.6   Code for a Complete Rotation and Translation

```
VERTEX shapeVerts[3] = {20, 50, 50, 50, 20, 100};
SHAPE shape1 = {3, shapeVerts};
Rotate(shape1, 45);
Translate(shape1, 100, 0);
DrawShape(shape1);

void Rotate(SHAPE& shape, int degrees)
{
    int rotatedX, rotatedY;

    double radians = 6.283185308 / (360.0 / degrees);
    double c = cos(radians);
    double s = sin(radians);

    for (int x=0; x<shape.numVerts; ++x)
    {
        rotatedX =
            (int) (shape.vertices[x].x * c -
            shape.vertices[x].y * s);
        rotatedY =
            (int) (shape.vertices[x].y * c +
            shape.vertices[x].x * s);

        shape.vertices[x].x = rotatedX;
        shape.vertices[x].y = rotatedY;
    }
}


void Translate(SHAPE& shape, int xTrans, int yTrans)
{
```

LISTING 3.6   Continued

```
    for (int x=0; x<shape.numVerts; ++x)
    {
        shape.vertices[x].x += xTrans;
        shape.vertices[x].y += yTrans;
    }
}

void DrawShape(SHAPE& shape1)
{
    int newX, newY, startX, startY;
    RECT clientRect;
    GetClientRect(hWnd, &clientRect);
    int maxY = clientRect.bottom;

    for (int x=0; x<shape1.numVerts; ++x)
    {
        newX = shape1.vertices[x].x;
        newY = maxY - shape1.vertices[x].y;
        if (x == 0)
        {
            MoveToEx(hDC, newX, newY, 0);
            startX = newX;
            startY = newY;
        }
        else
            LineTo(hWnd, newX, newY);
    }

    LineTo(hWnd, startX, startY);
}
```

The `Rotate()` function takes as parameters a reference to a SHAPE structure and the number of degrees to rotate the shape. The function's first task is to convert the degrees to radians. Radians are another way to measure angles and are the type of angle measurement required by Visual C++'s `sin()` and `cos()` functions. A radian is nothing more than the distance around a circle equal to the circle's radius. There are 6.283185308 (two times pi, for you math buffs) radians around a full circle. Therefore, 0 degrees equals 0 radians, 360 degrees equals 6.283185308 radians, with every other angle falling somewhere in between.

After converting the angle to radians, the function calculates the cosine and sine of the angle. Calculating these values in advance saves having to recalculate them many times within the function's for loop. Because the sin() and cos() functions tend to be slow, such recalculations can slow down things considerably (though probably not with such a simple example as this).

As with Translate() and Scale(), the Rotate() function uses a for loop to iterate through each of the shape's vertices, this time recalculating each X and Y using the rotation formula.

DIRECTION OF ROTATION

Positive angles cause the shape to rotate counterclockwise. To rotate a shape clockwise, use negative values for the degrees parameter.

Using Matrix Math in Transformations

In the preceding section, you had to use rotation and transformation calculations to view the triangle shape. Graphics programs often perform all kinds of calculations on the vertices of an object before finally drawing that object onscreen. Translation, scaling, and rotation can all be performed on a single shape just by calling the Translate(), Scale(), and Rotate() functions with the shape's vertices. However, performing so many calculations on many vertices can be time consuming, which is why graphics programmers often use matrix math to transform shapes.

A *matrix* is simply a table of numbers arranged in rows and columns. Similar to arrays in programming, the size of a matrix is defined by the number of rows and columns it has. For example, this is a 4x4 matrix, which has four rows and four columns:

4 3 2 1
5 4 2 8
3 7 0 5
9 3 6 1

On the other hand, the following is a 3x4 matrix, which has three rows and four columns:

4 7 2 4
4 6 7 3
4 5 2 2

Matrices are so similar to arrays, in fact, that arrays are typically used to represent matrices in computer programs. The 3x4 matrix might be represented in a program as follows:

```
int matrix[3][4] =
    {4, 7, 2, 4,
     4, 6, 7, 3,
     4, 5, 2, 2};
```

The advantage of matrices in graphics programming is that you can represent any number of transformations with a single matrix. For example, a single matrix can contain all the values you need to simultaneously translate, scale, and rotate a shape. To do this, you fill the matrix with the appropriate values and then you multiply the matrix times all of the shape's vertices. Of course, the trick is to know what values to place in the matrix. You also need to know how to multiply matrices. You'll learn both tricks in the following sections.

Using Matrix Data Types for 2D Graphics

First, you need data types for the matrices you'll be using in your programs. Programs that deal with 2D graphics typically use two types of matrices: 1×3 and 3×3. The 1×3 matrix is a special type of matrix known as a vector. *Vectors* can represent a vertex in a shape, by holding the vertex's X, Y, and W values. What's W? Although Direct3D sometimes has a special use for this extra value, W is really used most often to simplify the matrix operations. In most cases, W is equal to 1, which means a vector representing a vertex in a shape has this form:

```
X Y 1
```

The data type for a vector, then, looks like this:

```
typedef struct vector
{
    int x, y, w;
} VECTOR;
```

The 3×3 matrix will hold the values needed to transform a vertex, which will be held in the VECTOR data type (which is also a matrix). The data type for the 3×3 matrix looks like this:

```
typedef double MATRIX3X3[3][3];
```

Using Transformation Matrices

The first step in using matrices to transform a shape is to load the matrix with the appropriate values. What values you use and where you place them in the matrix depend on the type of transformations you're doing. A matrix that's set up to translate a shape looks like this:

```
1       0       0
0       1       0
xTrans  yTrans  1
```

Just like when you were using a formula to translate the vertices of a shape, in the preceding matrix the xTrans and yTrans variables are the number of vertical and horizontal units, respectively, that you want to translate the shape. In a program, you'd initialize this matrix like this:

```
MATRIX3X3 m;
m[0][0] = 1.0;      m[0][1] = 0.0;     m[0][2] = 0.0;
m[1][0] = 0.0;      m[1][1] = 1.0;     m[1][2] = 0.0;
m[2][0] = xTrans;   m[2][1] = yTrans;  m[2][2] = 1.0;
```

A matrix for scaling a shape looks like this:

```
xScaleFactor  0             0
0             yScaleFactor  0
0             0             1
```

Here, the variable xScaleFactor is how much you want to scale the shape horizontally, whereas yScaleFactor is how much to scale vertically. In a program, you'd initialize the scaling matrix like this:

```
MATRIX3X3 m;
m[0][0] = xScaleFactor;  m[0][1] = 0.0;           m[0][2] = 0.0;
m[1][0] = 0.0;           m[1][1] = yScaleFactor;  m[1][2] = 0.0;
m[2][0] = 0.0;           m[2][1] = 0.0;           m[2][2] = 1.0;
```

Finally, a matrix for rotating a shape looks as follows:

```
cos(radians)   sin(radians)  0
-sin(radians)  cos(radians)  0
0              0             1
```

Here, the variable `radians` is the angle of rotation in radians. In a program, you'd initialize the rotation matrix like this:

```
MATRIX3X3 m;
m[0][0] = cos(radians);   m[0][1] = sin(radians);  m[0][2] = 0.0;
m[1][0] = -sin(radians);  m[1][1] = cos(radians);  m[1][2] = 0.0;
m[2][0] = 0.0;            m[2][1] = 0.0;           m[2][2] = 1.0;
```

Composing Transformations

Earlier, I said that you can store in a matrix all the values you need to perform translation, scaling, and rotation simultaneously. In the previous section, you saw how each transformation looks when it's stored separately in a matrix. Now, you'll learn about composing transformations, which is the act of combining the translation, scaling, and rotation matrices into one main transformation matrix.

To compose two transformations, you multiply their matrices together, yielding a third master matrix. You can then compose another transformation by multiplying the new matrix by yet another transformation matrix. This composition of matrices can be repeated as often as necessary. Figure 3.11 illustrates an example of matrix composition. Figure 3.12 shows another way of looking at this matrix composition. In Figure 3.12, the results of each composition aren't shown.

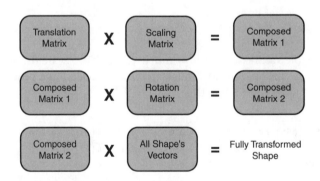

FIGURE 3.11   Matrix composition.

FIGURE 3.12   Another view of matrix composition.

Now, if you only knew how to multiply matrices! A matrix can be multiplied by any other matrix as long as the first matrix has the same number of columns as the second matrix has rows. So a 1×3 matrix can be multiplied by a 3×3 matrix, which is fortunate because that's exactly what you need to do to multiply a matrix times a vector in 2D graphics programs. Also, a 3×3 matrix can be multiplied by a 3×3 matrix, something else you need to do in a 2D graphics program to compose transformations. You'll look at multiplying vectors a little later in this chapter, but Listing 3.7 is a function that multiplies two 3×3 matrices.

LISTING 3.7   Multiplying 3×3 Matrices

```
void MultMatrix(MATRIX3X3& product,
    MATRIX3X3& matrix1, MATRIX3X3& matrix2)
{
    for (int x=0; x<3; ++x)
        for (int y=0; y<3; ++y)
        {
            double sum = 0;
            for (int z=0; z<3; ++z)
                sum += matrix1[x][z] * matrix2[z][y];
            product[x][y] = sum;
        }
}
```

The function's three parameters are a reference to a 3×3 matrix in which to hold the product of the multiplication and references to the two matrices that should be multiplied. Listing 3.8 is an example of how to use the function.

LISTING 3.8   Using the `MultMatrix()` Function

```
MATRIX3X3 m1, m2, m3;

m1[0][0] = 1.0; m1[0][1] = 0.0; m1[0][2] = 0.0;
m1[1][0] = 0.0; m1[1][1] = 1.0; m1[1][2] = 0.0;
m1[2][0] = 0.0; m1[2][1] = 0.0; m1[2][2] = 1.0;

m2[0][0] = 9.0; m2[0][1] = 8.0; m2[0][2] = 7.0;
m2[1][0] = 6.0; m2[1][1] = 5.0; m2[1][2] = 4.0;
m2[2][0] = 3.0; m2[2][1] = 2.0; m2[2][2] = 3.0;

MultMatrix(m3, m1, m2);
```

Here, the code first declares three 3×3 matrices, m1, m2, and m3. Next, m1 and m2 are initialized, after which the call to `MultMatrix3X3()` multiplies m1 times m2 and stores the result in m3. Can you tell what m3 will hold after the multiplication? The answer is that m3 will contain exactly the same values as m2. Why? Because the values stored in m1 are what is known as an *identity matrix*, which, for a 3×3 matrix, looks like this:

1 0 0
0 1 0
0 0 1

THE IDENTITY MATRIX

An identity matrix is sort of the matrix equivalent of the number 1. Just as any number times 1 equals the original number (for example, $5 \times 1 = 5$), so also any matrix times an identity matrix equals the original matrix (for example, m1 × I = m1). An identity matrix contains all zeroes except for the line of 1s that runs diagonally from the upper-left corner to the lower-right corner.

An identity matrix is often used in graphics programming to initialize the main matrix that'll be used to compose transformations. By initializing this main matrix to the identity matrix, you know that there aren't any strange values left over in the matrix that'll foul up your matrix multiplications.

Performing the Transformation

After you compose your transformations, you have a main matrix that contains the exact values you need to simultaneously translate, scale, and rotate a shape. To perform this transformation, you only need to multiply the main transformation matrix by each of the shape's vectors. This operation requires a matrix multiplication function that can handle not only 1×3 vectors and 3×3 matrices, but also can apply the multiplication to a whole list of vectors. Listing 3.9 is a function that does just that.

LISTING 3.9   Transformations with Matrices

```
void Transform(SHAPE& shape, MATRIX3X3& m)
{
    int transformedX, transformedY;

    for (int x=0; x<shape.numVerts; ++x)
    {
        transformedX = (int) (shape.vertices[x].x * m[0][0] +
            shape.vertices[x].y * m[1][0] + m[2][0]);
        transformedY = (int) (shape.vertices[x].x * m[0][1] +
            shape.vertices[x].y * m[1][1] + m[2][1]);
        shape.vertices[x].x = transformedX;
        shape.vertices[x].y = transformedY;
    }
}
```

This function takes as parameters a reference to a SHAPE structure and a reference to a MATRIX3X3 array. When this function has finished, the vertices in the SHAPE structure, shape, will have been transformed by the values in the transformation matrix, m.

Using Some Matrix Utility Functions

Now that you have some idea of how the matrix operations work, you can start using them in your programs. To do that, however, you need a couple of utility functions that make handling matrices a little easier. First, you need a function that can initialize a matrix to an identity matrix. Such a function looks like Listing 3.10.

LISTING 3.10   Initializing an Identity Matrix

```
void InitMatrix(MATRIX3X3& m)
{
    m[0][0]=1; m[0][1]=0; m[0][2]=0;
    m[1][0]=0; m[1][1]=1; m[1][2]=0;
    m[2][0]=0; m[2][1]=0; m[2][2]=1;
}
```

The InitMatrix() function takes as a parameter a reference to a MATRIX3X3 array into which the function loads the values that comprise a 3×3 identity matrix.

Another thing you'll need to do is copy a matrix. The CopyMatrix() function looks like Listing 3.11.

LISTING 3.11   Copying a Matrix

```
void CopyMatrix(MATRIX3X3& dst, MATRIX3X3& src)
{
   for (int i=0; i<3; ++i)
      for (int j=0; j<3; ++j)
         dst[i][j] = src[i][j];
}
```

This function takes as parameters references to the destination and source matrices, both of which are the type MATRIX3X3. The function copies the src matrix into the dst matrix.

Using Functions for Composing Transformations

The last task in writing functions for a 2D graphics program using matrices is to rewrite the Translate(), Scale(), and Rotate() functions so that they use the new matrix data types. The Translate() function ends up looking like Listing 3.12.

LISTING 3.12   Translating with Matrices

```
void Translate(MATRIX3X3& m, int xTrans, int yTrans)
{
    MATRIX3X3 m1, m2;

    m1[0][0]=1;        m1[0][1]=0;        m1[0][2]=0;
    m1[1][0]=0;        m1[1][1]=1;        m1[1][2]=0;
    m1[2][0]=xTrans;   m1[2][1]=yTrans;   m1[2][2]=1;

    MultMatrix(m2, m1, m);
    CopyMatrix(m, m2);
}
```

This function takes as parameters a reference to the matrix that holds the current state of the transformation and the X and Y translation values. First, the function loads a local matrix with the values that create a translation matrix, after which it multiplies the translation matrix times the main transformation matrix. The result of the multiplication, stored in the local matrix m2, is then copied into the transformation matrix.

Rewriting the Scale() function for use with matrices results in Listing 3.13.

LISTING 3.13   Scaling with Matrices

```
void Scale(MATRIX3X3& m, double xScale, double yScale)
{
    MATRIX3X3 m1, m2;

    m1[0][0]=xScale; m1[0][1]=0;        m1[0][2]=0;
    m1[1][0]=0;      m1[1][1]=yScale;   m1[1][2]=0;
    m1[2][0]=0;      m1[2][1]=0;        m1[2][2]=1;

    MultMatrix(m2, m1, m);
    CopyMatrix(m, m2);
}
```

The Scale() function takes as parameters a reference to the current transformation matrix and the X and Y scaling factors. The function first initializes the local matrix m1 to the scaling matrix. It then multiplies the scaling matrix times the current transformation matrix, storing the results in the local matrix m2. The program finally copies m2 into the transformation matrix.

The last function you need is the matrix version of Rotate(). That function looks like
Listing 3.14.

LISTING 3.14   Rotating with Matrices

```
void Rotate(MATRIX3X3& m, int degrees)
{
    MATRIX3X3 m1, m2;

    if (degrees == 0) return;

    double radians = 6.283185308 / (360.0 / degrees);
    double c = cos(radians);
    double s = sin(radians);

    m1[0][0]=c;  m1[0][1]=s; m1[0][2]=0;
    m1[1][0]=-s; m1[1][1]=c; m1[1][2]=0;
    m1[2][0]=0;  m1[2][1]=0; m1[2][2]=1;

    MultMatrix(m2, m1, m);
    CopyMatrix(m, m2);
}
```

The Rotate() function takes as parameters a reference to the current transformation
matrix and the number of degrees to rotate the shape. The function first checks
whether degrees is zero. If it is, the function returns immediately to avoid a division-
by-zero error. Then, the function converts the degrees to radians and calculates the
cosine and sine of the angle. Next, Rotate() initializes the rotation matrix and multiplies that matrix times the current transformation matrix, storing the results in the
local matrix m2. Finally, m2 gets copied into the transformation matrix.

Now that you have a set of matrix functions, you might want to see exactly how you
would use those functions in a program to translate, scale, and rotate a shape.
Listing 3.15 shows you how.

LISTING 3.15   Performing Transformations with the Matrix Functions

```
MATRIX3X3 m;
InitMatrix(m);
Translate(m, 10, 15);
Scale(m, 0.5, 0.5);
Rotate(m, 45);
Transform(shape1, m);
DrawShape(shape1);
```

The code segment first declares a 3×3 transformation matrix called m. It then calls InitMatrix() to initialize m to an identity matrix. At this point, m looks like this:

```
1.0000000000000    0.0000000000000    0.0000000000000
0.0000000000000    1.0000000000000    0.0000000000000
0.0000000000000    0.0000000000000    1.0000000000000
```

The call to Translate() composes m with a translation matrix containing the values 10 and 15, which leaves m containing the translation. The transformation matrix, m, now looks like this:

```
1.0000000000000    0.0000000000000    0.0000000000000
0.0000000000000    1.0000000000000    0.0000000000000
10.000000000000    15.000000000000    1.0000000000000
```

After the call to Scale(), m contains the translation and scaling values:

```
0.5000000000000    0.0000000000000    0.0000000000000
0.0000000000000    0.5000000000000    0.0000000000000
10.000000000000    15.000000000000    1.0000000000000
```

Finally, the call to Rotate() leaves m containing the full transformation—translation, scaling, and rotation—for the shape:

```
0.35355339055702     0.35355339062953     0.0000000000000
-0.35355339062953    0.35355339055702     0.0000000000000
10.000000000000      15.000000000000      1.0000000000000
```

The call to Transform() applies the translation matrix m to all of the vertices in shape1, after which DrawShape() draws the newly transformed shape onscreen.

Building a 2D Graphics Application

You now have all the information you need to write a 2D graphics program that can draw various shapes as well as translate, scale, and rotate those shapes. In Chapter 2, "Writing a Windows Program," you learned how to write C++ Windows programs that don't rely on the Microsoft Foundation Classes, and for the Direct3D programs you'll develop later in this book, you will use those programming techniques. However, you develop the programs in this chapter and in Chapter 4, "Programming 3D Computer Graphics," using Visual Studio's application wizards and MFC. Perform the steps in the following sections to create a program called Graphics2D that demonstrates the principles you learned in this chapter.

Creating the Basic Project

In the first set of steps that follow, you create the basic project and modify the application's user interface. (The following steps assume that you have experience with using Visual C++ to write Windows applications. If you don't know how to perform any of the following steps, consult your Visual C++ documentation.)

1. Create a new MFC application named Graphics2D, as shown in Figure 3.13.

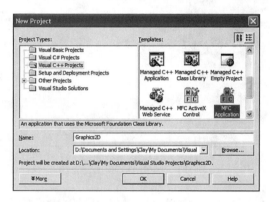

FIGURE 3.13   Creating the Graphics2D project.

2. In the MFC Application Wizard dialog box, click the Application Type selection. Then set the Application Type option to Single Document and the Use of MFC option to Use MFC in a Static Library, as shown in Figure 3.14.

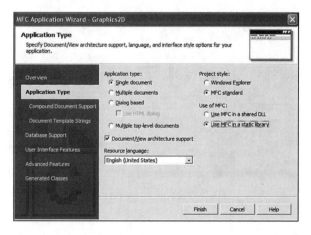

FIGURE 3.14   The Application Type options.

3. Click the User Interface Features selection. Then turn off the Initial Status Bar option, as shown in Figure 3.15.

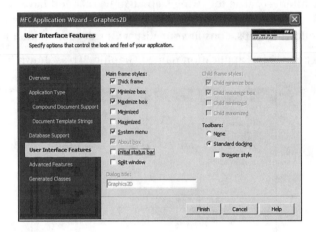

FIGURE 3.15   The User Interface Features options.

4. Again in the MFC Application Wizard dialog box, click the Advanced Features selection. Then turn off the Printing and Print Preview and ActiveX Controls options, as shown in Figure 3.16.

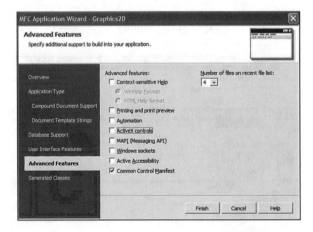

FIGURE 3.16   The Advanced Features options.

5. Click Finish to generate the project's source code files.

Editing the Project's Resources

Next, you modify the application's resources, including menus and dialog boxes. Perform the following steps to get your program's resources ready to go:

1. Double-click the Graphics2D.rc file in the Solution Explorer to bring up the Resource View pane.

2. Double-click the Menu folder, and then double-click IDR_MAINFRAME to bring up the menu editor (see Figure 3.17).

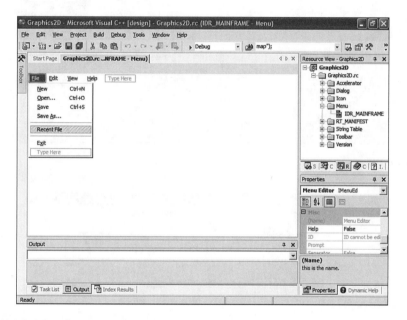

FIGURE 3.17   The menu editor.

3. Delete all entries from the File menu except Exit (see Figure 3.18).

4. Delete the Edit and View menus, leaving the File and Help menus, as shown in Figure 3.19.

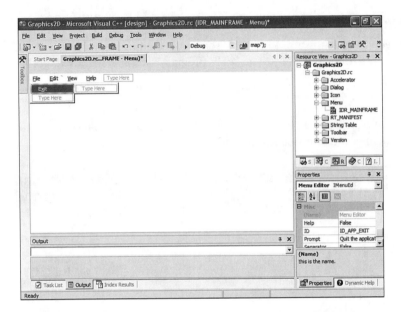

FIGURE 3.18   The new File menu.

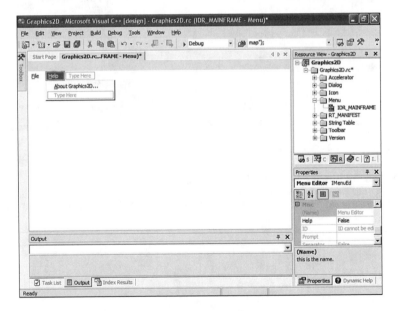

FIGURE 3.19   The menu bar after deleting the Edit menu.

5. Add a Transform menu, giving it the commands Translate, Scale, and Rotate (see Figure 3.20).

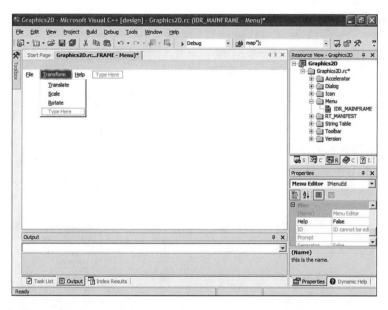

FIGURE 3.20   The new Transform menu.

6. Close the menu editor and bring up the dialog box editor (see Figure 3.21) by double-clicking the Dialog folder in the Resource View pane and then double-clicking IDD_ABOUTBOX.

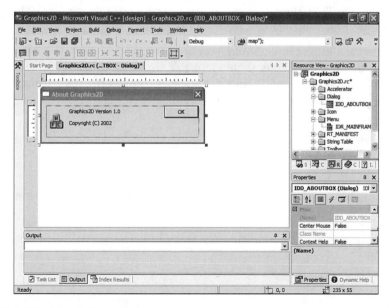

FIGURE 3.21   The dialog editor.

7. Modify the About dialog box so that it looks like Figure 3.22.

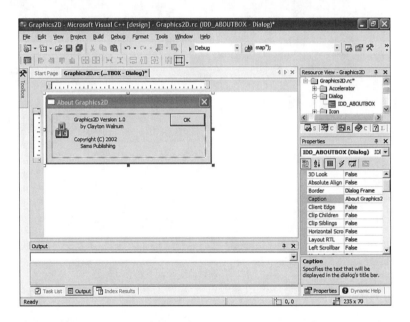

FIGURE 3.22   The new About dialog box.

8. Close the dialog box editor and double-click Accelerator in the Resource View pane. You'll see the IDR_MAINFRAME accelerator ID (see Figure 3.23). Delete the IDR_MAINFRAME accelerator table from the browser window.

9. Select the Project menu's Add Resource command, and create a new dialog box. The finished dialog box should look like Figure 3.24. (Be sure to give the dialog box the IDD_TRANSFORM ID, and give the edit controls the IDs IDC_XAXIS and IDC_YAXIS.)

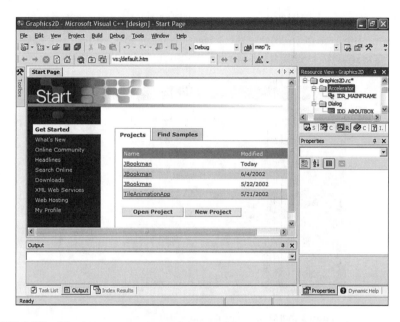

FIGURE 3.23   The lDR_MAINFRAME accelerator table.

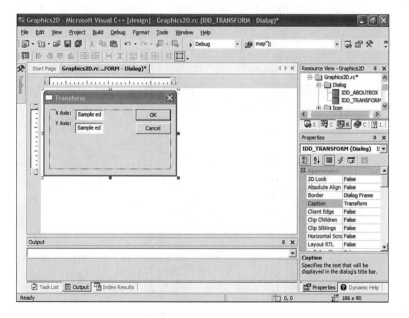

FIGURE 3.24   The Transform dialog box.

10. Double-click the dialog box to bring up the MFC Class Wizard dialog box. Name the Transform dialog box's class CTransformDlg and set the Base Class type to CDialog (see Figure 3.25). Click Finish to create the class.

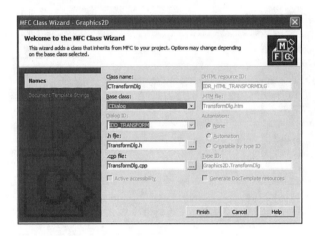

FIGURE 3.25   Creating the CTransformDlg class.

11. Switch to the Class View pane and then right-click the CTransformDlg class. Select the Add/Add Variable command from the menu that appears. Use this command to add public variables called m_xAxis and m_yAxis of type double. Associate these variables with the edit controls, as shown in Figure 3.26.

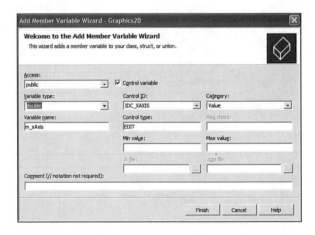

FIGURE 3.26   Creating a variable for one of the edit controls.

12. Press Ctrl+Shift+S to save all your changes.

Creating Message-Response Functions

In the next set of steps, you add message-response functions for the commands in the Transform menu and for the WM_RBUTTONDOWN Windows message.

1. In the Class View pane, click on the CGraphics2DView class. In the class's Properties window, click the Events button (the one that looks like a lightning bolt) to display the many events to which the class can respond.

2. Add COMMAND functions for the ID_TRANSFORM_ROTATE, ID_TRANSFORM_SCALE, and ID_TRANSFORM_TRANSLATE commands. Stick with the default names of OnTransformRotate(), OnTransformScale(), and OnTransformTranslate(), as shown in Figure 3.27.

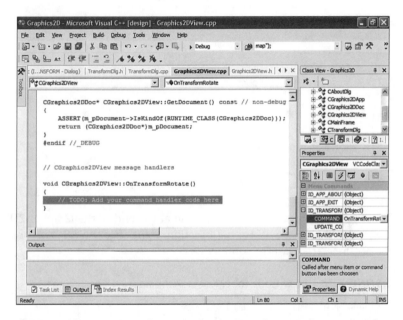

FIGURE 3.27   Adding response functions for the Transform menu commands.

3. Find the OnTransformRotate() function at the end of the Graphics2DView.cpp file, and add Listing 3.16 to that function, right after the // TODO: Add your command handler code here comment.

LISTING 3.16   New Code for OnTransformRotate()

```
CTransformDlg dlg;
dlg.m_xAxis = 0;
dlg.m_yAxis = 0;
```

LISTING 3.16   Continued

```
INT_PTR response = dlg.DoModal();

if (response == IDOK)
    m_rotate = (int) dlg.m_xAxis;
```

4. Find the `OnTransformScale()` function at the end of the Graphics2DView.cpp file, and add Listing 3.17 to that function, right after the `// TODO: Add your command handler code here` comment.

LISTING 3.17   New Code for `OnTransformScale()`

```
CTransformDlg dlg;
dlg.m_xAxis = 1;
dlg.m_yAxis = 1;

INT_PTR response = dlg.DoModal();

if (response == IDOK)
{
    m_xScale = dlg.m_xAxis;
    m_yScale = dlg.m_yAxis;
}
```

5. Find the `OnTransformTranslate()` function at the end of the Graphics2DView.cpp file, and add Listing 3.18 to that function, right after the `// TODO: Add your command handler code here` comment.

LISTING 3.18   New Code for `OnTransformTranslate()`

```
CTransformDlg dlg;
dlg.m_xAxis = 0;
dlg.m_yAxis = 0;

INT_PTR response = dlg.DoModal();

if (response == IDOK)
{
    m_xTranslate = dlg.m_xAxis;
    m_yTranslate = dlg.m_yAxis;
}
```

6. In the class's Properties window, click the Messages button (the one to the right of the lightning bolt) to display the many Windows messages to which the class can respond.

7. Create a response function named OnRButtonDown() for the WM_RBUTTONDOWN message, as shown in Figure 3.28.

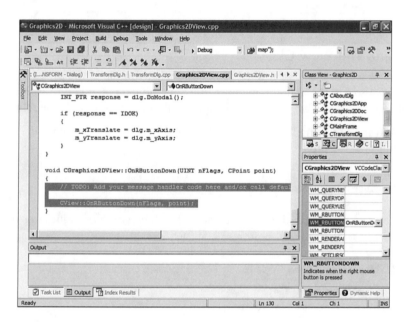

FIGURE 3.28 Adding the OnRButtonDown() function.

8. Add Listing 3.19 to the OnRButtonDown() function, right after the // TODO: Add your message handler code here and/or call default comment.

LISTING 3.19 New Code for OnRButtonDown()

```
MATRIX3X3 m;
InitMatrix(m);

Translate(m, (int) m_xTranslate, (int) m_yTranslate);
Scale(m, m_xScale, m_yScale);
Rotate(m, m_rotate);
Transform(m_polygon, m);

m_rotate = 0;
m_xScale = 1;
```

LISTING 3.19   Continued

```
m_yScale = 1;
m_xTranslate = 0;
m_yTranslate = 0;

Invalidate(TRUE);
```

Finishing the View Class

In the next set of steps, you add the source code that completes the CGraphics2DView class. You also add the required member function and data member declarations to the CGraphics2DView class's header file. Perform the following steps to complete these tasks:

1. Add the following lines near the top of the Graphics2DView.cpp file, right after the #endif compiler directive:

   ```
   #include <math.h>
   #include "TransformDlg.h"
   ```

2. Add Listing 3.20 to the CGraphics2DView class's constructor, right after the // TODO: add construction code here comment.

LISTING 3.20   New Code for CGraphics2DView Constructor

```
m_polygon.numVerts = 4;
m_polygon.vertices = m_vectors;
m_vectors[0].x = 0;
m_vectors[0].y = 0;
m_vectors[0].w = 1;
m_vectors[1].x = 100;
m_vectors[1].y = 0;
m_vectors[1].w = 1;
m_vectors[2].x = 100;
m_vectors[2].y = 50;
m_vectors[2].w = 1;
m_vectors[3].x = 0;
m_vectors[3].y = 75;
m_vectors[3].w = 1;

m_rotate = 0;
m_xScale = 1;
m_yScale = 1;
m_xTranslate = 0;
m_yTranslate = 0;
```

3. Add the following line to the `CGraphics2DView` class's `OnDraw()` function, right after the `// TODO: add draw code for native data here` comment:

    `DrawShape(pDC, m_polygon);`

4. Again in `OnDraw()`, uncomment the `pDC` parameter.

5. Also in Graphics2DView.cpp, add the functions in Listing 3.21 to the end of the file. Note that because this is an MFC program, Windows API functions such as `MoveToEx()` and `LineTo()` have been replaced with their MFC counterparts, but their functionality is the same.

LISTING 3.21   New Functions for the `CGraphics2DView` Class

```
void CGraphics2DView::InitMatrix(MATRIX3X3& m)
{
    m[0][0]=1; m[0][1]=0; m[0][2]=0;
    m[1][0]=0; m[1][1]=1; m[1][2]=0;
    m[2][0]=0; m[2][1]=0; m[2][2]=1;
}

void CGraphics2DView::CopyMatrix(MATRIX3X3& dst, MATRIX3X3& src)
{
    for (int i=0; i<3; ++i)
        for (int j=0; j<3; ++j)
            dst[i][j] = src[i][j];
}

void CGraphics2DView::MultMatrix(MATRIX3X3& product,
        MATRIX3X3& matrix1, MATRIX3X3& matrix2)
{
    for (int x=0; x<3; ++x)
        for (int y=0; y<3; ++y)
        {
            double sum = 0;
            for (int z=0; z<3; ++z)
                sum += matrix1[x][z] * matrix2[z][y];
            product[x][y] = sum;
        }
}

void CGraphics2DView::Translate(MATRIX3X3& m, int xTrans, int yTrans)
{
    MATRIX3X3 m1, m2;
```

LISTING 3.21   Continued

```
    m1[0][0]=1;         m1[0][1]=0;         m1[0][2]=0;
    m1[1][0]=0;         m1[1][1]=1;         m1[1][2]=0;
    m1[2][0]=xTrans;    m1[2][1]=yTrans;    m1[2][2]=1;

    MultMatrix(m2, m1, m);
    CopyMatrix(m, m2);
}


void CGraphics2DView::Scale(MATRIX3X3& m, double xScale, double yScale)
{
    MATRIX3X3 m1, m2;

    m1[0][0]=xScale; m1[0][1]=0;       m1[0][2]=0;
    m1[1][0]=0;      m1[1][1]=yScale;  m1[1][2]=0;
    m1[2][0]=0;      m1[2][1]=0;       m1[2][2]=1;

    MultMatrix(m2, m1, m);
    CopyMatrix(m, m2);
}


void CGraphics2DView::Rotate(MATRIX3X3& m, int degrees)
{
    MATRIX3X3 m1, m2;

    if (degrees == 0) return;

    double radians = 6.283185308 / (360.0 / degrees);
    double c = cos(radians);
    double s = sin(radians);

    m1[0][0]=c;  m1[0][1]=s; m1[0][2]=0;
    m1[1][0]=-s; m1[1][1]=c; m1[1][2]=0;
    m1[2][0]=0;  m1[2][1]=0; m1[2][2]=1;

    MultMatrix(m2, m1, m);
    CopyMatrix(m, m2);
}
```

LISTING 3.21   Continued

```cpp
void CGraphics2DView::Transform(SHAPE& shape, MATRIX3X3& m)
{
    int transformedX, transformedY;

    for (int x=0; x<shape.numVerts; ++x)
    {
        transformedX = (int) (shape.vertices[x].x * m[0][0] +
            shape.vertices[x].y * m[1][0] + m[2][0]);
        transformedY = (int) (shape.vertices[x].x * m[0][1] +
            shape.vertices[x].y * m[1][1] + m[2][1]);
        shape.vertices[x].x = transformedX;
        shape.vertices[x].y = transformedY;
    }
}


void CGraphics2DView::DrawShape(CDC* pDC, SHAPE& shape1)
{
    int newX, newY, startX, startY;
    RECT clientRect;

    GetClientRect(&clientRect);
    int maxY = clientRect.bottom;

    for (int x=0; x<shape1.numVerts; ++x)
    {
        newX = shape1.vertices[x].x;
        newY = maxY - shape1.vertices[x].y;
        if (x == 0)
        {
            pDC->MoveTo(newX, newY);
            startX = newX;
            startY = newY;
        }
        else
            pDC->LineTo(newX, newY);
    }

    pDC->LineTo(startX, startY);
}
```

6. Load Graphics2DView.h and add Listing 3.22 to the top of the file, right before the `CGraphics2DView` class declaration.

LISTING 3.22   New Code for the `CGraphics2DView` Class's Header File

```
typedef double MATRIX3X3[3][3];

typedef struct vector
{
    int x, y, w;
} VECTOR;

typedef struct shape
{
    int numVerts;
    VECTOR* vertices;
} SHAPE;
```

7. Also in Graphics2DView.h, add Listing 3.23 to the `CGraphics2DView` class's Attributes section, right after the `CGraphics2DDoc* GetDocument()` const line.

LISTING 3.23   New Code for the `CGraphics2DView` Class's Attributes Section

```
protected:
    SHAPE m_polygon;
    VECTOR m_vectors[4];
    int m_rotate;
    double m_xScale, m_yScale;
    double m_xTranslate, m_yTranslate;
```

8. Again in Graphics2DView.h, add Listing 3.24 to the `CGraphics2DView` class's Implementation section, right after the `protected` keyword.

LISTING 3.24   New Code for the `CGraphics2DView` Class's Implementation Section

```
void DrawShape(CDC* pDC, SHAPE& shape1);
void Translate(MATRIX3X3& m, int xTrans, int yTrans);
void Scale(MATRIX3X3& m, double xScale, double yScale);
void Rotate(MATRIX3X3& m, int degrees);
void Transform(SHAPE& shape, MATRIX3X3& m);
void MultMatrix(MATRIX3X3& product,
    MATRIX3X3& matrix1, MATRIX3X3& matrix2);
void InitMatrix(MATRIX3X3& m);
void CopyMatrix(MATRIX3X3& dst, MATRIX3X3& src);
```

Your Graphics2D program is now complete. To create the application, press Ctrl+Shift+B. To run the application, press F5 on your keyboard.

Running the Graphics2D Application

When you run the Graphics2D application, you see the window shown in Figure 3.29. Notice the polygon drawn in the window's lower-left corner. This is the shape that you'll transform using the commands in the Transform menu. To perform a transformation, you first choose the type of transformation from the Transform menu. After entering the appropriate values into the dialog box that appears, right-click the program's window to apply the transformation you created to the shape.

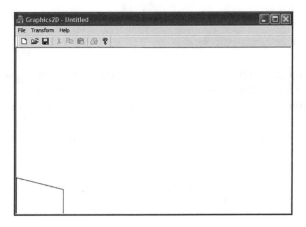

FIGURE 3.29   The Graphics2D application at startup.

For example, choose the Translate command from the Transform menu. You see the dialog box shown in Figure 3.30. Enter the values 100 and 50 into the dialog box's edit controls and then click OK. You've just set up a transformation that will translate the polygon in the window 100 units on the X axis and 50 units on the Y axis. To apply the transformation to the shape, right-click inside the window. You then see a window like that shown in Figure 3.31, with the polygon moved up and to the right.

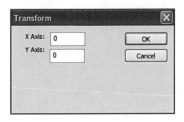

FIGURE 3.30   The Transform dialog box.

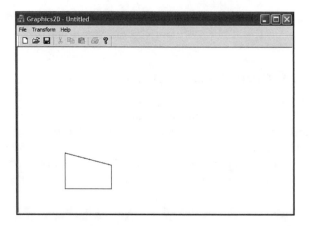

FIGURE 3.31   The translated polygon.

If you want, you can compose several transformations and apply them to the shape all at once. As an example, now select the Rotate command from the Transform menu, and enter 20 into the Transform dialog box's first edit field (the second edit field isn't used for rotations, nor are you really rotating around the X axis). After clicking OK, select the Transform menu's Scale command. Enter the values 0.5 and 1 in the dialog box's edit fields. When you click OK, the program composes both transformations—the rotation and the scaling—into the single transformation matrix. Right-click in the window to apply the transformations to the shape. You see the window shown in Figure 3.32.

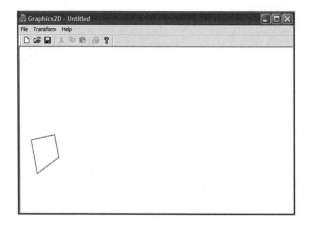

FIGURE 3.32   The rotated and scaled polygon.

SHOP TALK

A SMALL MATTER OF INFINITY

As you mess around with the various transformations you can perform with the Graphics2D application, soon you'll run into trouble. Although the application's window on the screen has a finite size, the Cartesian coordinate system in which your 3D object appears is infinite in all directions.

In the case of Graphics2D, the application's window shows only a small portion of the upper-right quadrant of the Cartesian plane. As I discovered as I tested the program, it's not only possible, but downright easy, accidentally to rotate the shape out of this quadrant so that the shape no longer appears in the window. Similarly, you can translate the shape to a set of coordinates that don't appear in the window.

If the shape disappears, try performing a translation on the object to bring it back into view. Of course, unless you have some idea of where the object is located in the Cartesian plane, you may end up translating the shape even farther away from your viewing area. Bringing the shape back into the window is an exercise in frustration, so watch what you're doing.

Take some time now to experiment with the various types of transformations until you're sure you understand how they work. Keep in mind that each new transformation you enter acts on the shape's current vertices—that is, if you should rotate the shape 20 degrees twice in a row, the shape will end up rotated 40 degrees. To start from scratch with the polygon back in the lower-left corner of the window, restart the program.

Understanding How the Graphics2D Program Works

Now that you've had a chance to experiment with the Graphics2D application, you may want a quick rundown of how it does its thing. First, look at the Graphics2DView.h file. The CGraphics2DView class declares a number of data members, including m_polygon, which is a SHAPE structure that holds information about the current shape. The data member m_vectors is an array of VECTOR structures that hold the vertices of the m_polygon object. Finally, the data members m_rotate, m_xScale, m_yScale, m_xTranslate, and m_yTranslate hold the values for the currently selected transformations.

Look now at the Graphics2DView.cpp file. When the program runs, the CGraphics2DView class's constructor first initializes the m_polygon structure and the shape's vertices, which are stored in the m_vectors[] array. The constructor also initializes the transformation variables m_rotate, m_xScale, m_yScale, m_xTranslate, and m_yTranslate to their default values. These default values won't affect the shape's vertices if you happen to right-click in the window before setting the transformation variables with the commands in the Transform menu.

When the application's window appears onscreen, the CGraphics2DView class's OnDraw() function displays the shape by calling the DrawShape() function. This DrawShape() function is similar to the previous version, except that it now requires two arguments: a pointer to a device context and a reference to a SHAPE structure.

When you select a command from the Transform menu, the appropriate command-response function takes over, initializing and displaying the Transform dialog box, and then saving your response in the appropriate transformation variables. When you select the Scale command, for example, the OnTransformScale() function gets called. In that function, the program first sets the dialog box's m_xAxis and m_yAxis data members to 1, so that the default scaling values of 1 for both axes are in the edit controls when the dialog box appears. The call to the dialog box's DoModal() function then displays the dialog box so that you can enter new values into the edit controls. When you click OK, the program stores your responses in the m_xScale and m_yScale variables.

Finally, when you right-click in the application's window, the program calls the OnRButtonDown() function, which applies the selected transformations to the shape's vertices. First, the function declares a matrix called m to hold the transformations and calls InitMatrix() to initialize m to an identity matrix. Calling the Translate(), Scale(), and Rotate() functions (with the appropriate transformation variables as arguments) then composes the transformations in the matrix, after which a call to Transform() applies the transformations to the shape's vertices. The function then resets the transformation variables to their default values and calls Invalidate() to force the application's window to redraw.

You can add a couple of enhancements to the Graphics2D program to make it easier to use. First, try adding a response function for the WM_LBUTTONDOWN message that resets the shape to its starting point in the window. To do this, you'd reinitialize the shape's vertices to their starting values (as is done in the CGraphics2DView class's constructor) and then call Invalidate(TRUE) to force the window to repaint.

You may also want to add a dialog box that displays the values of the shape's current vertices. That way, if you should transform the shape such that it no longer appears in the window, you can see the type of translation you need to bring the shape back into view. To do this, you need to create a new dialog box with App Studio, and then create a new menu command that displays the dialog box. The response functions for the current Transform menu commands show you how to respond to a menu command and how to initialize and display a dialog box.

Exploring the Program Listings

Listings 3.25 and 3.26 show the complete code for the CGraphics2DView class, including the Graphics2DView.h header file and the Graphics2DView.cpp implementation file. Many other files were created by AppWizard when you started the Graphics2D application project. Because you didn't modify those files, they aren't shown here. However, you can easily view any of the project's files by loading them with Visual C++'s editor (or any other text editor).

LISTING 3.25   The `CGraphics2DView` Class's Header File

```
// Graphics2DView.h : interface of the CGraphics2DView class
//


#pragma once

typedef double MATRIX3X3[3][3];

typedef struct vector
{
    int x, y, w;
} VECTOR;

typedef struct shape
{
    int numVerts;
    VECTOR* vertices;
} SHAPE;

class CGraphics2DView : public CView
{
protected: // create from serialization only
    CGraphics2DView();
    DECLARE_DYNCREATE(CGraphics2DView)

// Attributes
public:
    CGraphics2DDoc* GetDocument() const;
protected:
    SHAPE m_polygon;
    VECTOR m_vectors[4];
    int m_rotate;
    double m_xScale, m_yScale;
    double m_xTranslate, m_yTranslate;

// Operations
public:

// Overrides
    public:
```

LISTING 3.25   Continued

```
    virtual void OnDraw(CDC* pDC);   // overridden to draw this view
virtual BOOL PreCreateWindow(CREATESTRUCT& cs);
protected:

// Implementation
public:
    virtual ~CGraphics2DView();
#ifdef _DEBUG
    virtual void AssertValid() const;
    virtual void Dump(CDumpContext& dc) const;
#endif

protected:
    void DrawShape(CDC* pDC, SHAPE& shape1);
    void Translate(MATRIX3X3& m, int xTrans, int yTrans);
    void Scale(MATRIX3X3& m, double xScale, double yScale);
    void Rotate(MATRIX3X3& m, int degrees);
    void Transform(SHAPE& shape, MATRIX3X3& m);
    void MultMatrix(MATRIX3X3& product,
        MATRIX3X3& matrix1, MATRIX3X3& matrix2);
    void InitMatrix(MATRIX3X3& m);
    void CopyMatrix(MATRIX3X3& dst, MATRIX3X3& src);

// Generated message map functions
protected:
    DECLARE_MESSAGE_MAP()
public:
    afx_msg void OnTransformRotate();
    afx_msg void OnTransformScale();
    afx_msg void OnTransformTranslate();
    afx_msg void OnRButtonDown(UINT nFlags, CPoint point);
};

#ifndef _DEBUG  // debug version in Graphics2DView.cpp
inline CGraphics2DDoc* CGraphics2DView::GetDocument() const
   { return reinterpret_cast<CGraphics2DDoc*>(m_pDocument); }
#endif
```

LISTING 3.26   The `CGraphics2DView` Class's Implementation File

```cpp
// Graphics2DView.cpp : implementation of the CGraphics2DView class
//

#include "stdafx.h"
#include "Graphics2D.h"

#include "Graphics2DDoc.h"
#include "Graphics2DView.h"

#ifdef _DEBUG
#define new DEBUG_NEW
#endif

#include <math.h>
#include "TransformDlg.h"

// CGraphics2DView

IMPLEMENT_DYNCREATE(CGraphics2DView, CView)

BEGIN_MESSAGE_MAP(CGraphics2DView, CView)
    ON_COMMAND(ID_TRANSFORM_ROTATE, OnTransformRotate)
    ON_COMMAND(ID_TRANSFORM_SCALE, OnTransformScale)
    ON_COMMAND(ID_TRANSFORM_TRANSLATE, OnTransformTranslate)
    ON_WM_RBUTTONDOWN()
END_MESSAGE_MAP()

// CGraphics2DView construction/destruction

CGraphics2DView::CGraphics2DView()
{
    // TODO: add construction code here
    m_polygon.numVerts = 4;
    m_polygon.vertices = m_vectors;
    m_vectors[0].x = 0;
    m_vectors[0].y = 0;
    m_vectors[0].w = 1;
    m_vectors[1].x = 100;
    m_vectors[1].y = 0;
    m_vectors[1].w = 1;
    m_vectors[2].x = 100;
```

LISTING 3.26   Continued

```
    m_vectors[2].y = 50;
    m_vectors[2].w = 1;
    m_vectors[3].x = 0;
    m_vectors[3].y = 75;
    m_vectors[3].w = 1;

    m_rotate = 0;
    m_xScale = 1;
    m_yScale = 1;
    m_xTranslate = 0;
    m_yTranslate = 0;
}


CGraphics2DView::~CGraphics2DView()
{
}


BOOL CGraphics2DView::PreCreateWindow(CREATESTRUCT& cs)
{
    // TODO: Modify the Window class or styles here by modifying
    //   the CREATESTRUCT cs

    return CView::PreCreateWindow(cs);
}


// CGraphics2DView drawing

void CGraphics2DView::OnDraw(CDC* pDC)
{
    CGraphics2DDoc* pDoc = GetDocument();
    ASSERT_VALID(pDoc);

    // TODO: add draw code for native data here
    DrawShape(pDC, m_polygon);
}



// CGraphics2DView diagnostics

#ifdef _DEBUG
void CGraphics2DView::AssertValid() const
```

LISTING 3.26   Continued

```
{
    CView::AssertValid();
}


void CGraphics2DView::Dump(CDumpContext& dc) const
{
    CView::Dump(dc);
}


CGraphics2DDoc* CGraphics2DView::GetDocument() const
{
    ASSERT(m_pDocument->IsKindOf(RUNTIME_CLASS(CGraphics2DDoc)));
    return (CGraphics2DDoc*)m_pDocument;
}
#endif //_DEBUG


// CGraphics2DView message handlers

void CGraphics2DView::OnTransformRotate()
{
    // TODO: Add your command handler code here
    CTransformDlg dlg;
    dlg.m_xAxis = 0;
    dlg.m_yAxis = 0;

    INT_PTR response = dlg.DoModal();

    if (response == IDOK)
        m_rotate = (int) dlg.m_xAxis;
}

void CGraphics2DView::OnTransformScale()
{
    // TODO: Add your command handler code here
    CTransformDlg dlg;
    dlg.m_xAxis = 1;
    dlg.m_yAxis = 1;

    INT_PTR response = dlg.DoModal();
```

LISTING 3.26   Continued

```
    if (response == IDOK)
    {
        m_xScale = dlg.m_xAxis;
        m_yScale = dlg.m_yAxis;
    }
}

void CGraphics2DView::OnTransformTranslate()
{
    // TODO: Add your command handler code here
    CTransformDlg dlg;
    dlg.m_xAxis = 0;
    dlg.m_yAxis = 0;

    INT_PTR response = dlg.DoModal();

    if (response == IDOK)
    {
        m_xTranslate = dlg.m_xAxis;
        m_yTranslate = dlg.m_yAxis;
    }
}

void CGraphics2DView::OnRButtonDown(UINT nFlags, CPoint point)
{
    // TODO: Add your message handler code here and/or call default
    MATRIX3X3 m;
    InitMatrix(m);

    Translate(m, (int) m_xTranslate, (int) m_yTranslate);
    Scale(m, m_xScale, m_yScale);
    Rotate(m, m_rotate);
    Transform(m_polygon, m);

    m_rotate = 0;
    m_xScale = 1;
    m_yScale = 1;
    m_xTranslate = 0;
    m_yTranslate = 0;

    Invalidate(TRUE);
```

LISTING 3.26   Continued

```
        CView::OnRButtonDown(nFlags, point);
}


void CGraphics2DView::InitMatrix(MATRIX3X3& m)
{
    m[0][0]=1; m[0][1]=0; m[0][2]=0;
    m[1][0]=0; m[1][1]=1; m[1][2]=0;
    m[2][0]=0; m[2][1]=0; m[2][2]=1;
}


void CGraphics2DView::CopyMatrix(MATRIX3X3& dst, MATRIX3X3& src)
{
    for (int i=0; i<3; ++i)
        for (int j=0; j<3; ++j)
            dst[i][j] = src[i][j];
}


void CGraphics2DView::MultMatrix(MATRIX3X3& product,
        MATRIX3X3& matrix1, MATRIX3X3& matrix2)
{
    for (int x=0; x<3; ++x)
        for (int y=0; y<3; ++y)
        {
            double sum = 0;
            for (int z=0; z<3; ++z)
                sum += matrix1[x][z] * matrix2[z][y];
            product[x][y] = sum;
        }
}


void CGraphics2DView::Translate(MATRIX3X3& m, int xTrans, int yTrans)
{
    MATRIX3X3 m1, m2;

    m1[0][0]=1;       m1[0][1]=0;       m1[0][2]=0;
    m1[1][0]=0;       m1[1][1]=1;       m1[1][2]=0;
    m1[2][0]=xTrans;  m1[2][1]=yTrans;  m1[2][2]=1;

    MultMatrix(m2, m1, m);
    CopyMatrix(m, m2);
}
```

LISTING 3.26   Continued

```
void CGraphics2DView::Scale(MATRIX3X3& m, double xScale, double yScale)
{
    MATRIX3X3 m1, m2;

    m1[0][0]=xScale; m1[0][1]=0;      m1[0][2]=0;
    m1[1][0]=0;      m1[1][1]=yScale; m1[1][2]=0;
    m1[2][0]=0;      m1[2][1]=0;      m1[2][2]=1;

    MultMatrix(m2, m1, m);
    CopyMatrix(m, m2);
}

void CGraphics2DView::Rotate(MATRIX3X3& m, int degrees)
{
    MATRIX3X3 m1, m2;

    if (degrees == 0) return;

    double radians = 6.283185308 / (360.0 / degrees);
    double c = cos(radians);
    double s = sin(radians);

    m1[0][0]=c;  m1[0][1]=s; m1[0][2]=0;
    m1[1][0]=-s; m1[1][1]=c; m1[1][2]=0;
    m1[2][0]=0;  m1[2][1]=0; m1[2][2]=1;

    MultMatrix(m2, m1, m);
    CopyMatrix(m, m2);
}

void CGraphics2DView::Transform(SHAPE& shape, MATRIX3X3& m)
{
    int transformedX, transformedY;

    for (int x=0; x<shape.numVerts; ++x)
    {
        transformedX = (int) (shape.vertices[x].x * m[0][0] +
            shape.vertices[x].y * m[1][0] + m[2][0]);
        transformedY = (int) (shape.vertices[x].x * m[0][1] +
            shape.vertices[x].y * m[1][1] + m[2][1]);
        shape.vertices[x].x = transformedX;
```

LISTING 3.26   Continued

```
        shape.vertices[x].y = transformedY;
    }
}


void CGraphics2DView::DrawShape(CDC* pDC, SHAPE& shape1)
{
    int newX, newY, startX, startY;
    RECT clientRect;

    GetClientRect(&clientRect);
    int maxY = clientRect.bottom;

    for (int x=0; x<shape1.numVerts; ++x)
    {
        newX = shape1.vertices[x].x;
        newY = maxY - shape1.vertices[x].y;
        if (x == 0)
        {
            pDC->MoveTo(newX, newY);
            startX = newX;
            startY = newY;
        }
        else
            pDC->LineTo(newX, newY);
    }

    pDC->LineTo(startX, startY);
}
```

In Brief

- To draw a line in a window, you must call the GDI function MoveToEx() to position the starting point of the line and then call the function LineTo() to draw the line.

- Most objects in computer graphics are defined using the Cartesian coordinate system.

- You define graphical objects in the Cartesian coordinate system by specifying the coordinates of their vertices.

- Shape transformations include translation, scaling, and rotation.

- Translation, scaling, and rotation can all be performed on a single shape just by using matrix math.

- Using matrices in graphics programming enables you to represent any number of transformations with a single matrix.

Programming 3D Computer Graphics

4

You probably noticed that this book is about Direct3D, which you use to create 3D applications. That means that, although you now know how to manipulate 2D shapes, you've still got to convert what you know about 2D shapes to 3D. Of course, when I talk about 3D graphics in this book, I'm really only talking about 2D graphics that simulate 3D. After all, a computer screen has no depth.

In this chapter, then, you learn to convert the 2D formulas you experimented with in Chapter 3, "Programming 2D Computer Graphics," to formulas that can be used to manipulate 3D shapes onscreen. Specifically, in this chapter, you learn:

- About the 3D Cartesian coordinate system
- How to define vertices for 3D objects
- About parallel and perspective projection
- How to use matrices to transform 3D objects
- How to animate 3D objects

Understanding the 3D Coordinate System

You already learned about the Cartesian coordinate system (see the section "Understanding Screen and Cartesian Coordinates in Chapter 3), which is a way of specifying points in a 2D grid. If you recall, the Cartesian plane has X and Y axes, allowing you to specify a point by defining its X and Y coordinate. Unfortunately, you can't describe 3D objects with only two axes. That's because 3D objects have depth, as well as width and height. Therefore, you need a new coordinate system in which to define your 3D objects. To create that new coordinate system, you simply add a Z axis to the Cartesian plane, changing the plane into a cube, as shown in Figure 4.1.

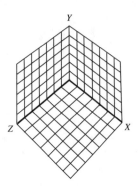

FIGURE 4.1 The 3D coordinate system.

Although the X, Y, and Z axes of the 3D coordinate system can be interpreted to be pointing in any direction, this book treats the X axis as running left and right, the Y axis running up and down, and the Z axis running away from the viewer and into the screen. This is a logical axis orientation for many computer programs because it leaves the coordinate system's X and Y axes running in the same direction as their screen-coordinate counterparts.

Defining a 3D Object

Creating a 2D shape was a simple matter of defining a set of vertices and then drawing lines between those vertices. (For a review, see the section "Defining Vertex and Shape Data Types" in Chapter 3.) Defining a 3D object, on the other hand, is a bit more difficult, thanks to the addition of the Z axis, which adds many vertices to a simple shape. For example, a 2D square requires only four vertices, whereas a cube, which is the 3D equivalent of a square, requires eight (see Figure 4.2).

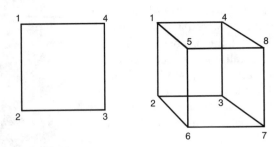

FIGURE 4.2 Comparing 2D vertices to 3D vertices.

With so many extra vertices floating around in your 3D world, there often may be some confusion about how to connect the vertices to form the required object correctly. For that reason, 3D objects require that not only their vertices be defined but also their *edges*, which are the lines that connect the vertices to form the 3D object. A 3D object that's constructed of vertices and edges is called a *wireframe model*.

To define a wireframe model, you must have a list of vertices and a list of edges. Obviously, you're going to need some new data types to define wireframe models in your programs. First, you need a data type that describes a vertex for a 3D object. Such a vertex requires that three coordinates—X, Y, and Z—be defined. Because you'll be using matrices to transform your 3D objects, the structure also requires the W member (see the section "Using Matrix Data Types for 2D Graphics" in Chapter 3) and so looks like this:

```
typedef struct vertex
{
    int x, y, z, w;
} VERTEX;
```

Next, you need a data type for the object's edges. To draw one of an object's edges, you need to know the starting vertex and the ending vertex. To draw the edge, you simply draw a line between the two vertices. So, the data type for an edge looks like this:

```
typedef struct edge
{
    UINT vertex1, vertex2;
} EDGE;
```

Here, the structure member vertex1 is the starting point of the edge, and vertex2 is the ending point.

Finally, now that you have data types for 3D vertices and edges, you can define the data type for a wireframe model like this:

```
typedef struct model
{
    UINT numVerts;
    VERTEX* vertices;
    UINT numEdges;
    EDGE* edges;
} MODEL;
```

As you can see, the MODEL structure contains two unsigned integers that hold the number of vertices and edges in the object. In addition, a pointer to the VERTEX data type holds the address of the object's vertex list, and a pointer to the EDGE data type holds the address of the object's edge list.

To further clarify how to create a wireframe model, you'll now use the preceding data types to define the wireframe cube shown in Figure 4.3. First, you must number the vertices so that you have a consistent way of referring to them. This number scheme is also shown in Figure 4.3. Then, you must define each of the cube's vertices, which have these X, Y, Z coordinates: (0, 4, 0), (4, 4, 0), (4, 4, -4), (0, 4, -4), (0, 0, 0), (4, 0, 0), (4, 0, -4), and (0, 0, -4). So, the cube's vertex list looks like this:

```
VERTEX cubeVerts[8] =
    {0, 4, 0,
     4, 4, 0,
     4, 4, -4,
     0, 4, -4,
     0, 0, 0,
     4, 0, 0,
     4, 0, -4,
     0, 0, -4};
```

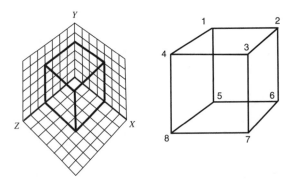

FIGURE 4.3   A wireframe cube.

Notice that the Z coordinates are either 0 or less than 0. Why? Look again at the grid in Figure 4.3. Imagine that the surface formed by the X and Y axes is your computer's screen. Now, imagine that the values on the Z axis get smaller the further "into" the screen they go. In that case, points that are on the computer's screen have a Z coordinate of 0, whereas points that are "beyond" the screen have negative Z values.

LOCAL AND WORLD COORDINATES

The coordinates that define a 3D wireframe model, such as those in the cubeVerts structure, are referred to as *local coordinates*. The local coordinates are changed into *world coordinates* when a program transforms the model's vertices using translation, scaling, or rotation. Finally, a graphics program converts the world coordinates to screen coordinates, so that the model can be drawn onscreen.

Now, you need to create an edge list that specifies how the vertices are connected. If you look carefully at the cube, you'll see that it has 12 edges. The edge list for the cube, then, is defined like this:

```
EDGE cubeEdges[12] =
    {1, 2,
     2, 3,
     3, 4,
     4, 1,

     5, 6,
     6, 7,
     7, 8,
     8, 5,

     5, 1,
     6, 2,
     7, 3,
     8, 4};
```

The first four pairs of vertices in the edge list form the top of the cube. The second four form the bottom, with the last four connecting the bottom to the top. Compare this edge list to the numbered vertices in Figure 4.3.

Now, that the cube's vertices and edges are defined, you can define the cube itself, like this:

```
MODEL cube = {8, cubeVerts, 12, cubeEdges};
```

Moving from Local Coordinates to Screen Coordinates

At this point, you probably want to draw your 3D cube onscreen. However, you're confronted with a major problem: The cube's vertices are described using X, Y, and Z coordinates, whereas the screen is described using only X and Y coordinates. How the heck can you take care of the Z coordinate? There are actually two methods: *parallel projection* and *perspective projection*.

Implementing Parallel Projection

Using parallel projection, you can draw a 3D wireframe model onscreen simply by ignoring all the Z coordinates. This has the effect of squashing the model down into a simple 2D shape. In the case of your cube model, the picture onscreen would be nothing more than a square. Listing 4.1 shows a function to draw the cube using parallel projection.

LISTING 4.1   Drawing with Parallel Projection

```
void DrawModel(CDC* pDC, MODEL& model)
{
    int newX, newY;
    RECT clientRect;

    GetClientRect(&clientRect);
    int maxY = clientRect.bottom;

    for (UINT i=0; i<model.numEdges; ++i)
    {
        UINT vertNum = model.edges[i].vertex1;
        newX = model.vertices[vertNum-1].x;
        newY = maxY - model.vertices[vertNum-1].y - 1;
        pDC->MoveTo(newX, newY);

        vertNum = model.edges[i].vertex2;
        newX = model.vertices[vertNum-1].x;
        newY = maxY - model.vertices[vertNum-1].y - 1;
        pDC->LineTo(newX, newY);
    }
}
```

This function first calls `GetClientRect()` to determine the window's maximum Y coordinate. The function then uses a `for` loop to draw each of the object's edges. Inside the loop, the function gets the vertex number for the starting point of the edge and uses that number to index the array of vertices to obtain the vertex's X and Y coordinates. `DrawParallel()` uses these coordinates in a call to `MoveTo()` to position the line's starting point. The X and Y coordinates for the edge's second vertex are then obtained in the same way, except that this time the coordinates are used in a call to `LineTo()` to draw the edge.

SIMILARITIES BETWEEN 2D AND 3D SHAPES

Although the addition of a Z coordinate in 3D graphics complicates the programming, 2D and 3D shapes have more in common than they have differences. For example, the X and Y coordinates for each vertex in a shape are mapped to the screen exactly as they are in the `DrawShape()` function presented in Chapter 3.

Perspective Projection

Although parallel projection is easy to implement in a program, it doesn't produce particularly satisfactory results (unless you're writing a drafting program). What's the point of drawing 3D objects so that they look like 2D shapes? A key element of 3D images is that they appear to have depth; this illusion is created in 3D programs by the use of perspective projection, which makes distant objects look smaller than close-up objects. (This technique is called *perspective foreshortening*.) For example, using perspective projection to view your 3D cube would make the back of the cube, which is farther away, look smaller than the front of the cube, as shown in Figure 4.4.

FIGURE 4.4   A wireframe cube drawn using perspective projection.

You may think that the cube in Figure 4.4 looks a little peculiar. That's because the cube was drawn as if your eye were positioned exactly on the cube's front, lower-left corner. If you don't believe that the view is accurate, find a small box, close one eye, and then position your open eye on the box's lower-left corner. You'll see an image very similar to Figure 4.4.

The formulas you need for perspective projection look like this in C++ code:

```
double t = 1.0 / (1.0 - zCoord / eye);
perspX = (int) (xCoord * t);
perspY = (int) (yCoord * t);
```

The variable t is a value used to scale the X and Y coordinates based on the Z coordinate. The smaller the Z coordinate (the farther it is from the origin), the greater the effect of the scaling. The variables xCoord, yCoord, and zCoord are the coordinates of one of the model's vertices. The variables perspX and perspY are the screen coordinates of the vertex after applying perspective projection. The variable eye is used to determine how great an effect the perspective projection has on the model. When the eye is close to the model (eye is a small number), you get more of a perspective effect (as shown in the first drawing in Figure 4.5) than when the eye is far away from the model (as shown in the second drawing in Figure 4.5).

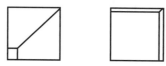

FIGURE 4.5   The effects of the eye variable on projection.

Now that you have a formula for applying perspective projection, you need a function that will apply the projection to each vertex of a wireframe model. Listing 4.2 shows such a function.

LISTING 4.2 Drawing with Perspective Projection

```
void PerspProject(MODEL& model, double eye)
{
    for (UINT i=0; i<model.numVerts; ++i)
    {
        int xCoord = model.vertices[i].x;
        int yCoord = model.vertices[i].y;
        int zCoord = model.vertices[i].z;
        double t = 1.0 / (1.0 - zCoord / eye);
        model.vertices[i].x = (int) (xCoord * t);
        model.vertices[i].y = (int) (yCoord * t);
    }
}
```

The preceding function takes as parameters a reference to a MODEL structure and the eye value needed to calculate the viewpoint. PerspProject() uses a for loop to iterate through all the vertices in the model, applying the perspective projection to each. Listing 4.3 shows how to define the model, apply perspective, and then draw the resultant object.

LISTING 4.3 The Perspective Projection Process

```
VERTEX cubeVerts[8] =
    {0,   100, 0,    1,
     100, 100, 0,    1,
     100, 100, -100, 1,
     0,   100, -100, 1,
     0,   0,   0,    1,
     100, 0,   0,    1,
     100, 0,   -100, 1,
     0,   0,   -100, 1};

EDGE cubeEdges[12] =
    {1, 2,
     2, 3,
     3, 4,
     4, 1,
     5, 6,
     6, 7,
     7, 8,
     8, 5,
     5, 1,
     6, 2,
     7, 3,
```

LISTING 4.3   Continued

```
    8, 4};

MODEL cube;
cube.numVerts = 8;
cube.vertices = cubeVerts;
cube.numEdges = 12;
cube.edges = cubeEdges;

PerspProject(cube, 200);
DrawModel(pDC, cube);
```

Transforming 3D Objects

As you can see, drawing a 3D object is not particularly difficult. Unfortunately, the objects you've managed to draw so far have not exactly been awe-inspiring. This is because your viewing angle has been locked onto the object's front, lower-left corner. To view 3D objects from different angles, you must learn how to transform them. Luckily, transforming 3D objects is not much different from transforming 2D objects, which you already know how to do. (See the section "Transforming Shapes" in Chapter 3.) You simply have to take the new Z coordinate into consideration.

In the following sections, you see how to use matrix math to apply translation, scaling, and rotation to 3D objects. Because you now have to deal with the Z axis, as well as the X and Y axes, you need a new 4×4 matrix data type. That data type looks like this:

```
typedef double MATRIX4X4[4][4];
```

You also need new functions for dealing with 4×4 matrices. The InitMatrix(), CopyMatrix(), and MultMatrix() functions now look like Listing 4.4.

LISTING 4.4   New Matrix-Handling Functions

```
void InitMatrix(MATRIX4X4& m)
{
    m[0][0]=1; m[0][1]=0; m[0][2]=0; m[0][3]=0;
    m[1][0]=0; m[1][1]=1; m[1][2]=0; m[1][3]=0;
    m[2][0]=0; m[2][1]=0; m[2][2]=1; m[2][3]=0;
    m[3][0]=0; m[3][1]=0; m[3][2]=0; m[3][3]=1;
}


void CopyMatrix(MATRIX4X4& dst, MATRIX4X4& src)
{
    for (int i=0; i<4; ++i)
```

LISTING 4.4   Continued

```
      for (int j=0; j<4; ++j)
         dst[i][j] = src[i][j];
}


void MultMatrix(MATRIX4X4& product,
      MATRIX4X4& matrix1, MATRIX4X4& matrix2)
{
   for (int x=0; x<4; ++x)
      for (int y=0; y<4; ++y)
      {
         double sum = 0;
         for (int z=0; z<4; ++z)
            sum += matrix1[x][z] * matrix2[z][y];
         product[x][y] = sum;
      }
}
```

Programming 3D Translation

When you translate an object, you move it to a new location in the 3D coordinate system. When you did this with 2D shapes, you were able to translate the shape on its X and Y axes. (See the section "Translating a Shape" in Chapter 3.) Now, with 3D objects, you also can translate on the Z axis. The addition of the Z axis means that you must modify the matrix you use to apply the translation. So, a translation matrix for a 3D object looks like this:

```
1       0       0       0
0       1       0       0
0       0       1       0
xTrans  yTrans  zTrans  1
```

As you can see, the main difference between this translation matrix and the 2D version is that you're now using a 4×4 matrix, and you've added the zTrans variable, which is the amount to translate on the Z axis. The function to compose this translation with the main transformation matrix looks like Listing 4.5.

LISTING 4.5   3D Translations with Matrices

```
void Translate(MATRIX4X4& m,
      int xTrans, int yTrans, int zTrans)
{
   MATRIX4X4 m1, m2;
```

LISTING 4.5   Continued

```
    m1[0][0]=1;      m1[0][1]=0;      m1[0][2]=0;      m1[0][3]=0;
    m1[1][0]=0;      m1[1][1]=1;      m1[1][2]=0;      m1[1][3]=0;
    m1[2][0]=0;      m1[2][1]=0;      m1[2][2]=1;      m1[2][3]=0;
    m1[3][0]=xTrans; m1[3][1]=yTrans; m1[3][2]=zTrans; m1[3][3]=1;

    MultMatrix(m2, m1, m);
    CopyMatrix(m, m2);
}
```

This `Translate()` function looks and acts much like the 2D version you wrote in Chapter 3. However, the 3D `Translation()` function enables you to translate an object on the Z axis, as well as on the X and Y axes.

Programming 3D Scaling

When you scale a 3D object, you multiply its vertices by some scaling factor, which effectively enlarges or reduces the object. When you did this with 2D shapes, you were able to scale only the X and Y coordinates. (See the section "Scaling a Shape" in Chapter 3.) Now, with 3D objects, you also can scale the Z coordinate. Just as with the 3D translation, the addition of the Z axis means that you must modify the matrix that you use to apply the scaling, like this:

```
xFactor  0         0         0
0        yFactor   0         0
0        0         zFactor   0
0        0         0         1
```

Again, the main difference between this scaling matrix and the 2D version is that you're now using a 4×4 matrix. In addition, you've added the `zFactor` variable, which is the amount to scale on the Z axis. The function to compose the scaling with the main transformation matrix looks like Listing 4.6.

LISTING 4.6   3D Scaling with Matrices

```
void Scale(MATRIX4X4& m,
    double xScale, double yScale, double zScale)
{
    MATRIX4X4 m1, m2;

    m1[0][0]=xScale; m1[0][1]=0;      m1[0][2]=0;      m1[0][3]=0;
    m1[1][0]=0;      m1[1][1]=yScale; m1[1][2]=0;      m1[1][3]=0;
    m1[2][0]=0;      m1[2][1]=0;      m1[2][2]=zScale; m1[2][3]=0;
    m1[3][0]=0;      m1[3][1]=0;      m1[3][2]=0;      m1[3][3]=1;
```

LISTING 4.6   Continued

```
    MultMatrix(m2, m1, m);
    CopyMatrix(m, m2);
}
```

Programming 3D Rotation

When you rotate a 3D object, you turn it to a new orientation on the display. When you did this with 2D shapes, you were able to rotate only around one axis. (See the section "Rotating a Shape" in Chapter 3.) You didn't know it at the time, but you were actually rotating the shape around the Z axis. Now, with 3D objects, you also can rotate around the X and Y axes. (Figure 4.6 shows these rotations in relation to the X, Y, and Z axes.) There is, however, no simple matrix that can perform all three types of rotations simultaneously. Instead, you must treat each rotation as a separate transformation.

FIGURE 4.6   3D rotations.

The matrix for rotation around the Z axis now looks like this:

```
cos(radians)    sin(radians    0  0
-sin(radians)   cos(radians)   0  0
0               0              0  0
0               0              0  1
```

As you can see, the rotation around the Z axis is now done with a 4×4 matrix.

The function to compose the Z rotation with the main transformation matrix looks like Listing 4.7.

LISTING 4.7   3D Rotation Around the Z Axis with Matrices

```
void RotateZ(MATRIX4X4& m, int zAngle)
{
    MATRIX4X4 m1, m2;

    if (zAngle == 0) return;

    double radians = 6.283185308 / (360.0 / zAngle);
    double c = cos(radians);
    double s = sin(radians);

    m1[0][0]=c;   m1[0][1]=s;  m1[0][2]=0;  m1[0][3]=0;
    m1[1][0]=-s;  m1[1][1]=c;  m1[1][2]=0;  m1[1][3]=0;
    m1[2][0]=0;   m1[2][1]=0;  m1[2][2]=1;  m1[2][3]=0;
    m1[3][0]=0;   m1[3][1]=0;  m1[3][2]=0;  m1[3][3]=1;

    MultMatrix(m2, m1, m);
    CopyMatrix(m, m2);
}
```

The rotation matrix for rotating around the X axis looks a little bit different:

```
1            0               0              0
0            cos(radians)    sin(radians)   0
0            -sin(radians)   cos(radians)   0
0            0               0              1
```

Notice that the matrix still requires the program to calculate the sine and cosine of the rotation angle, but now those values appear in a different part of the matrix. The function to compose the X rotation with the main transformation matrix looks like Listing 4.8.

LISTING 4.8   3D Rotation Around the X Axis with Matrices

```
void RotateX(MATRIX4X4& m, int xAngle)
{
    MATRIX4X4 m1, m2;

    if (xAngle == 0) return;

    double radians = 6.283185308 / (360.0 / xAngle);
    double c = cos(radians);
    double s = sin(radians);
```

LISTING 4.8   Continued

```
m1[0][0]=1;  m1[0][1]=0;  m1[0][2]=0; m1[0][3]=0;
m1[1][0]=0;  m1[1][1]=c;  m1[1][2]=s; m1[1][3]=0;
m1[2][0]=0;  m1[2][1]=-s; m1[2][2]=c; m1[2][3]=0;
m1[3][0]=0;  m1[3][1]=0;  m1[3][2]=0; m1[3][3]=1;

MultMatrix(m2, m1, m);
CopyMatrix(m, m2);
}
```

Finally, the matrix for rotation around the Y axis also requires sines and cosines, but, again, they're located in a different part of the matrix:

```
cos(radians)   0      sin(radians)        0
-sin(radians)  0      cos(radians)        0
0              0      0                   0
0              0      0                   1
```

The function to compose the Y rotation with the main transformation matrix looks like Listing 4.9.

LISTING 4.9   3D Rotation Around the X Axis with Matrices

```
void RotateY(MATRIX4X4& m, int yAngle)
{
    MATRIX4X4 m1, m2;

    if (yAngle == 0) return;

    double radians = 6.283185308 / (360.0 / yAngle);
    double c = cos(radians);
    double s = sin(radians);

    m1[0][0]=c;  m1[0][1]=0;  m1[0][2]=-s; m1[0][3]=0;
    m1[1][0]=0;  m1[1][1]=1;  m1[1][2]=0;  m1[1][3]=0;
    m1[2][0]=s;  m1[2][1]=0;  m1[2][2]=c;  m1[2][3]=0;
    m1[3][0]=0;  m1[3][1]=0;  m1[3][2]=0;  m1[3][3]=1;

    MultMatrix(m2, m1, m);
    CopyMatrix(m, m2);
}
```

Building a 3D Graphics Application

You now have all the information you need to write a 3D graphics program that can draw wireframe models, as well as translate, scale, and rotate those models. Perform the following steps to create a program called Graphics3D that demonstrates the principles you learned in this chapter. If you need help placing the following code segments in the program, refer to the listings near the end of this chapter.

In the first set of steps that follow, you create the basic application and modify the application's user interface. (If you don't know how to perform any of the following steps, consult your Visual C++ documentation.) To complete these tasks, perform the following steps:

1. Create a new MFC Application named Graphics3D, as shown in Figure 4.7.

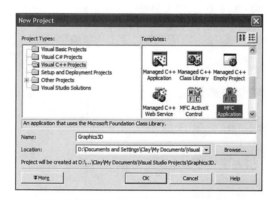

FIGURE 4.7   Creating the Graphics3D project.

2. In the MFC Application Wizard dialog box, click the Application Type selection. Then set the Application Type option to Single Document and the Use of MFC option to Use MFC in a Static Library, as shown in Figure 4.8.

3. Click the User Interface Features selection. Then turn off the Initial Status Bar option, as shown in Figure 4.9.

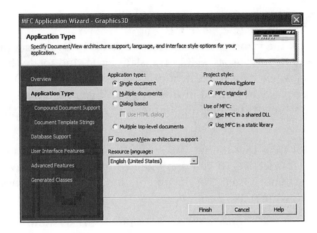

FIGURE 4.8   The Application Type options.

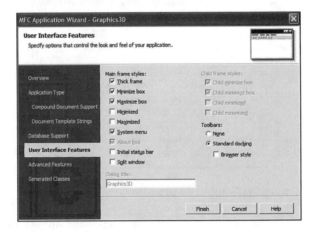

FIGURE 4.9   The User Interface Features options.

4. Again in the MFC Application Wizard dialog box, click the Advanced Features selection. Then turn off the Printing and Print Preview and ActiveX Controls options, as shown in Figure 4.10.

5. Click Finish to generate the project's source code files.

6. Double-click the Graphics3D.rc file in the Solution Explorer to bring up the Resource View pane.

7. Double-click the Menu folder, and then double-click IDR_MAINFRAME to bring up the menu editor (see Figure 4.11).

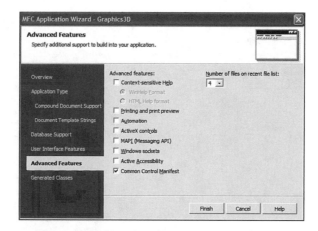

FIGURE 4.10   The Advanced Features options.

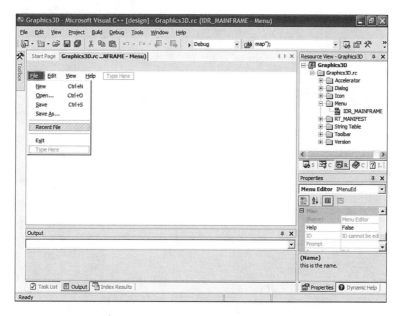

FIGURE 4.11   The menu editor.

8. Delete all entries from the File menu except Exit (see Figure 4.12).

9. Delete the Edit and View menus, leaving the File and Help menus, as shown in Figure 4.13.

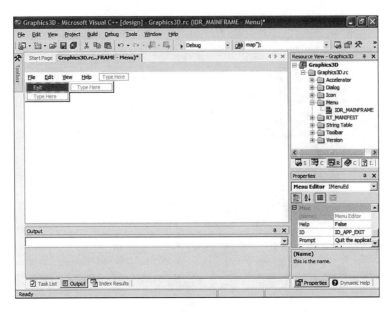

FIGURE 4.12   The new File menu.

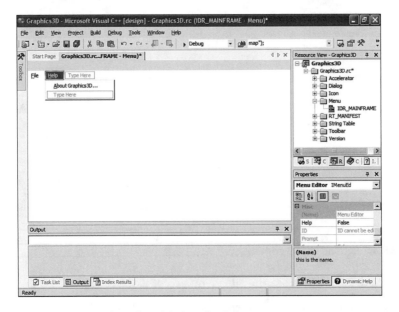

FIGURE 4.13   The menu bar after deleting the Edit menu.

10. Add a Transform menu, giving it the commands Translate, Scale, Rotate, and Animate (see Figure 4.14).

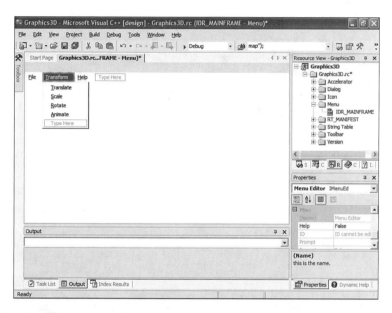

FIGURE 4.14   The new Transform menu.

11. Close the menu editor and bring up the dialog box editor (see Figure 4.15) by double-clicking the Dialog folder in the Resource View pane and then double-clicking IDD_ABOUTBOX.

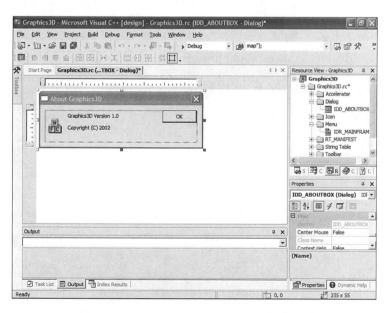

FIGURE 4.15   The dialog box editor.

12. Modify the About dialog box so that it looks like Figure 4.16.

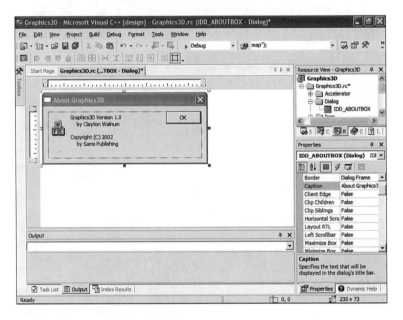

FIGURE 4.16   The new About dialog box.

13. Close the dialog box editor and double-click Accelerator in the Resource View pane. You'll see the IDR_MAINFRAME accelerator ID (see Figure 4.17). Delete the IDR_MAINFRAME accelerator table from the browser window.

14. Select the Project menu's Add Resource command and create a new dialog box. The finished dialog box should look like Figure 4.18. (Be sure to give the dialog box the IDD_TRANSFORM ID, and give the edit controls the IDs IDC_XAXIS, IDC_YAXIS, and IDC_ZAXIS.)

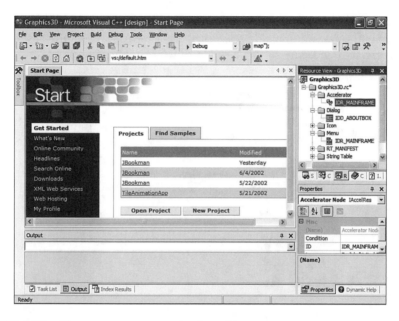

FIGURE 4.17   The IDR_MAINFRAME accelerator table.

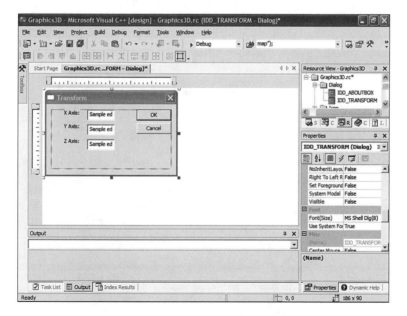

FIGURE 4.18   The Transform dialog box.

15. Double-click the dialog box to bring up the MFC Class Wizard dialog box. Name the Transform dialog box's class `CTransformDlg` and set the Base Class type to `CDialog` (see Figure 4.19). Click Finish to create the class.

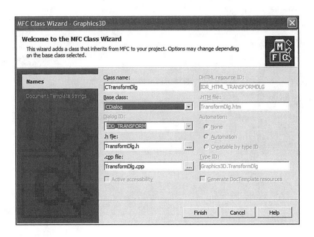

FIGURE 4.19   Creating the `CTransformDlg` class.

16. Switch to the Class View pane and then right-click the `CTransformDlg` class. Select the Add/Add Variable command from the menu that appears. Use this command to add public variables called `m_xAxis`, `m_yAxis`, and `m_zAxis` of type `double`. Associate these variables with the edit controls, as shown in Figure 4.20.

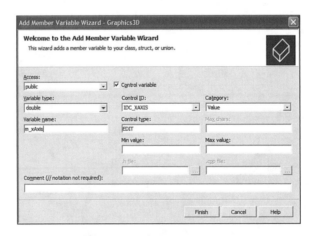

FIGURE 4.20   Creating a variable for one of the edit controls.

17. Press Ctrl+Shift+S to save all your changes.

Now you can add message-response functions for the commands in the Transform menu and for the WM_RBUTTONDOWN, WM_TIMER, and WM_DESTROY Windows message. To complete these tasks, perform the following steps:

1. In the Class View pane, click on the CGraphics3DView class. In the class's Properties window, click the Events button (the one that looks like a lightning bolt) to display the many events to which the class can respond.

2. Add COMMAND functions for the ID_TRANSFORM_ROTATE, ID_TRANSFORM_SCALE, ID_TRANS-FORM_TRANSLATE, and ID_TRANSFORM_ANIMATE commands. Stick with the default names of OnTransformRotate(), OnTransformScale(), OnTransformTranslate(), and OnTransformAnimate() as shown in Figure 4.21.

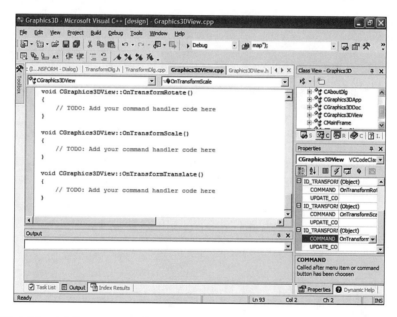

FIGURE 4.21   Adding response functions for the Transform menu commands.

3. Add an UPDATE_COMMAND_UI function for the ID_TRANSFORM_ANIMATE command. Name the function OnUpdateTransformAnimate(), as shown in Figure 4.22.

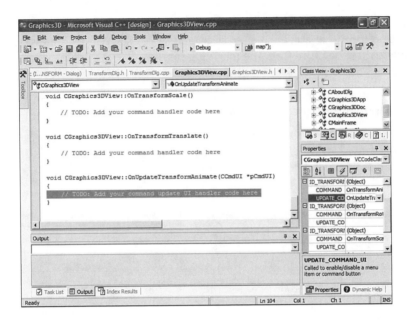

FIGURE 4.22   Adding an update command function for the Transform menu.

4. Find the OnTransformRotate() function at the end of the Graphics3DView.cpp file, and add Listing 4.10 to that function, right after the // TODO: Add your command handler code here comment.

LISTING 4.10   Code for the OnTransformRotate() Function

```
CTransformDlg dlg;
dlg.m_xAxis = 0;
dlg.m_yAxis = 0;
dlg.m_zAxis = 0;

int response = dlg.DoModal();

if (response == IDOK)
{
    m_xRotate += (int) dlg.m_xAxis;
    m_yRotate += (int) dlg.m_yAxis;
    m_zRotate += (int) dlg.m_zAxis;
}
```

5. Find the `OnTransformScale()` function at the end of the Graphics3DView.cpp file, and add Listing 4.11 to that function, right after the `// TODO: Add your command handler code here` comment.

LISTING 4.11   Code for the `OnTransformScale()` Function

```
CTransformDlg dlg;
dlg.m_xAxis = 1;
dlg.m_yAxis = 1;
dlg.m_zAxis = 1;

int response = dlg.DoModal();

if (response == IDOK)
{
    m_xScale *= dlg.m_xAxis;
    m_yScale *= dlg.m_yAxis;
    m_zScale *= dlg.m_zAxis;
}
```

6. Find the `OnTransformTranslate()` function at the end of the Graphics3DView.cpp file, and add Listing 4.12 to that function, right after the `// TODO: Add your command handler code here` comment.

LISTING 4.12   Code for the `OnTransformTranslate()` Function

```
CTransformDlg dlg;
dlg.m_xAxis = 0;
dlg.m_yAxis = 0;
dlg.m_zAxis = 0;

int response = dlg.DoModal();

if (response == IDOK)
{
    m_xTranslate += dlg.m_xAxis;
    m_yTranslate += dlg.m_yAxis;
    m_zTranslate += dlg.m_zAxis;
}
```

7. Find the `OnTransformAnimate()` function at the end of the Graphics3DView.cpp file, and add Listing 4.13 to that function, right after the `// TODO: Add your command handler code here` comment.

LISTING 4.13   Code for the `OnTransformAnimate()` Function

```
if (m_animate)
{
    KillTimer(1);
    m_animate = FALSE;
}
else
{
    SetTimer(1, 50, NULL);
    m_animate = TRUE;
}
```

8. Find the `OnUpdateTransformAnimate()` function at the end of the Graphics3DView.cpp file, and add the following lines to that function, right after the `// TODO: Add your command update UI handler code here` comment:

```
if (m_animate)
    pCmdUI->SetCheck(TRUE);
else
    pCmdUI->SetCheck(FALSE);
```

9. In the class's Properties window, click the Messages button (the one to the right of the lightning bolt) to display the many Windows messages to which the class can respond.

10. Create a response function named `OnRButtonDown()` for the `WM_RBUTTONDOWN` message, as shown in Figure 4.23.

11. Add the following lines to the `OnRButtonDown()` function, right after the `// TODO: Add your message handler code here and/or call default` comment:

```
InitModel();
TransformModel();
Invalidate(TRUE);
```

12. Create a response function named `OnTimer()` for the `WM_TIMER` message, as shown in Figure 4.24.

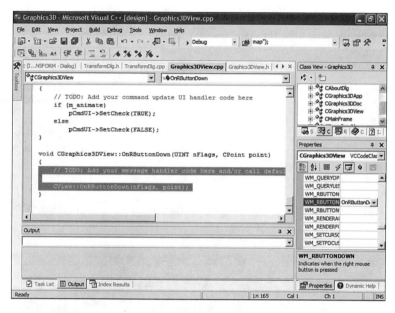

FIGURE 4.23   Adding the `OnRButtonDown()` function.

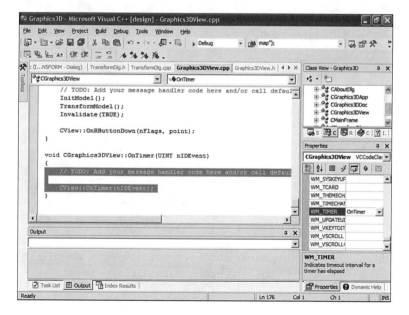

FIGURE 4.24   Adding the `OnTimer()` function.

13. Add Listing 4.14 to the OnTimer() function, right after the // TODO: Add your message handler code here and/or call default comment.

LISTING 4.14   Code for the OnTimer() Function

```
m_xRotate += 5;
m_yRotate += 5;
m_zRotate += 5;
InitModel();
TransformModel();
Invalidate(TRUE);
```

14. Create a response function named OnDestroy() for the WM_DESTROY message, as shown in Figure 4.25.

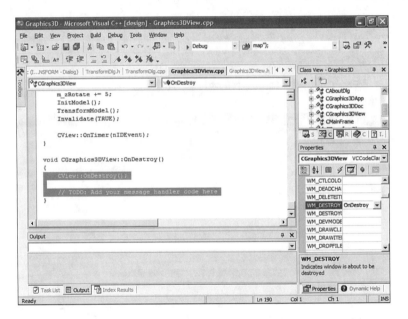

FIGURE 4.25   Adding the OnDestroy() function.

15. Add the following line to the OnDestroy() function, right after the // TODO: Add your message handler code here and/or call default comment:

```
KillTimer(1);
```

In the following set of steps, you add the source code that completes the CGraphics3DView class. You also add the required member function and data member declarations to the CGraphics3DView class's header file.

1. Add the following lines near the top of the Graphics3DView.cpp file, right after the #endif compiler directive:

```
#include <math.h>
#include "TransformDlg.h"
```

2. Add Listing 4.15 to the CGraphics3DView class's constructor, right after the // TODO: add construction code here comment.

LISTING 4.15   Code for the Class's Constructor

```
InitModel();

m_xRotate = 0;
m_yRotate = 0;
m_zRotate = 0;
m_xScale = 1;
m_yScale = 1;
m_zScale = 1;
m_xTranslate = 0;
m_yTranslate = 0;
m_zTranslate = 0;

TransformModel();

m_animate = FALSE;
```

3. Add the following line to the CGraphics3DView class's OnDraw() function, right after the // TODO: add draw code for native data here comment:

```
DrawModel(pDC, m_cube);
```

4. Also in Graphics3DView.cpp, add Listing 4.16 to the end of the file.

LISTING 4.16   New Functions for the Class's Implementation File

```
void CGraphics3DView::InitModel()
{
    VERTEX cubeVerts[8] =
        {0,    100, 0,    1,
         100, 100, 0,    1,
```

LISTING 4.16   Continued

```
                    100, 100, -100, 1,
                    0,   100, -100, 1,
                    0,   0,   0,    1,
                    100, 0,   0,    1,
                    100, 0,   -100, 1,
                    0,   0,   -100, 1};

          EDGE cubeEdges[14] =
              {1, 2,
               2, 3,
               3, 4,
               4, 1,
               5, 6,
               6, 7,
               7, 8,
               8, 5,
               5, 1,
               6, 2,
               7, 3,
               8, 4,
               3, 8,
               4, 7};

          memcpy(m_cubeVerts, cubeVerts, sizeof(m_cubeVerts));
          memcpy(m_cubeEdges, cubeEdges, sizeof(m_cubeEdges));
          m_cube.numVerts = 8;
          m_cube.vertices = m_cubeVerts;
          m_cube.numEdges = 14;
          m_cube.edges = m_cubeEdges;
     }

     void CGraphics3DView::TransformModel()
     {
          MATRIX4X4 m;
          InitMatrix(m);

          Translate(m, (int) m_xTranslate,
               (int) m_yTranslate, (int) m_zTranslate);
          Scale(m, m_xScale, m_yScale, m_zScale);
          RotateX(m, m_xRotate);
          RotateY(m, m_yRotate);
```

LISTING 4.16   Continued

```
    RotateZ(m, m_zRotate);
    Transform(m_cube, m);
    PerspProject(m_cube, 300);
}


void CGraphics3DView::DrawModel(CDC* pDC, MODEL& model)
{
    int newX, newY;
    RECT clientRect;

    GetClientRect(&clientRect);
    int maxY = clientRect.bottom;

    for (UINT i=0; i<model.numEdges; ++i)
    {
        UINT vertNum = model.edges[i].vertex1;
        newX = model.vertices[vertNum-1].x;
        newY = maxY - model.vertices[vertNum-1].y - 1;
        pDC->MoveTo(newX, newY);

        vertNum = model.edges[i].vertex2;
        newX = model.vertices[vertNum-1].x;
        newY = maxY - model.vertices[vertNum-1].y - 1;
        pDC->LineTo(newX, newY);
    }
}


void CGraphics3DView::PerspProject(MODEL& model, double eye)
{
    for (UINT i=0; i<model.numVerts; ++i)
    {
        int xCoord = model.vertices[i].x;
        int yCoord = model.vertices[i].y;
        int zCoord = model.vertices[i].z;
        double t = 1.0 / (1.0 - zCoord / eye);
        model.vertices[i].x = (int) (xCoord * t);
        model.vertices[i].y = (int) (yCoord * t);
    }
}


void CGraphics3DView::InitMatrix(MATRIX4X4& m)
```

LISTING 4.16   Continued

```
{
    m[0][0]=1; m[0][1]=0; m[0][2]=0; m[0][3]=0;
    m[1][0]=0; m[1][1]=1; m[1][2]=0; m[1][3]=0;
    m[2][0]=0; m[2][1]=0; m[2][2]=1; m[2][3]=0;
    m[3][0]=0; m[3][1]=0; m[3][2]=0; m[3][3]=1;
}

void CGraphics3DView::CopyMatrix(MATRIX4X4& dst, MATRIX4X4& src)
{
    for (int i=0; i<4; ++i)
        for (int j=0; j<4; ++j)
            dst[i][j] = src[i][j];
}

void CGraphics3DView::MultMatrix(MATRIX4X4& product,
        MATRIX4X4& matrix1, MATRIX4X4& matrix2)
{
    for (int x=0; x<4; ++x)
        for (int y=0; y<4; ++y)
        {
            double sum = 0;
            for (int z=0; z<4; ++z)
                sum += matrix1[x][z] * matrix2[z][y];
            product[x][y] = sum;
        }
}

void CGraphics3DView::Translate(MATRIX4X4& m,
        int xTrans, int yTrans, int zTrans)
{
    MATRIX4X4 m1, m2;

    m1[0][0]=1;       m1[0][1]=0;       m1[0][2]=0;       m1[0][3]=0;
    m1[1][0]=0;       m1[1][1]=1;       m1[1][2]=0;       m1[1][3]=0;
    m1[2][0]=0;       m1[2][1]=0;       m1[2][2]=1;       m1[2][3]=0;
    m1[3][0]=xTrans; m1[3][1]=yTrans; m1[3][2]=zTrans; m1[3][3]=1;

    MultMatrix(m2, m1, m);
    CopyMatrix(m, m2);
}
```

LISTING 4.16   Continued

```
void CGraphics3DView::Scale(MATRIX4X4& m,
    double xScale, double yScale, double zScale)
{
    MATRIX4X4 m1, m2;

    m1[0][0]=xScale; m1[0][1]=0;      m1[0][2]=0;      m1[0][3]=0;
    m1[1][0]=0;      m1[1][1]=yScale; m1[1][2]=0;      m1[1][3]=0;
    m1[2][0]=0;      m1[2][1]=0;      m1[2][2]=zScale; m1[2][3]=0;
    m1[3][0]=0;      m1[3][1]=0;      m1[3][2]=0;      m1[3][3]=1;

    MultMatrix(m2, m1, m);
    CopyMatrix(m, m2);
}


void CGraphics3DView::RotateX(MATRIX4X4& m, int xAngle)
{
    MATRIX4X4 m1, m2;

    if (xAngle == 0) return;

    double radians = 6.283185308 / (360.0 / xAngle);
    double c = cos(radians);
    double s = sin(radians);

    m1[0][0]=1;  m1[0][1]=0;   m1[0][2]=0;  m1[0][3]=0;
    m1[1][0]=0;  m1[1][1]=c;   m1[1][2]=s;  m1[1][3]=0;
    m1[2][0]=0;  m1[2][1]=-s;  m1[2][2]=c;  m1[2][3]=0;
    m1[3][0]=0;  m1[3][1]=0;   m1[3][2]=0;  m1[3][3]=1;

    MultMatrix(m2, m1, m);
    CopyMatrix(m, m2);
}


void CGraphics3DView::RotateY(MATRIX4X4& m, int yAngle)
{
    MATRIX4X4 m1, m2;

    if (yAngle == 0) return;
```

LISTING 4.16   Continued

```
    double radians = 6.283185308 / (360.0 / yAngle);
    double c = cos(radians);
    double s = sin(radians);

    m1[0][0]=c;   m1[0][1]=0;   m1[0][2]=-s;  m1[0][3]=0;
    m1[1][0]=0;   m1[1][1]=1;   m1[1][2]=0;   m1[1][3]=0;
    m1[2][0]=s;   m1[2][1]=0;   m1[2][2]=c;   m1[2][3]=0;
    m1[3][0]=0;   m1[3][1]=0;   m1[3][2]=0;   m1[3][3]=1;

    MultMatrix(m2, m1, m);
    CopyMatrix(m, m2);
}

void CGraphics3DView::RotateZ(MATRIX4X4& m, int zAngle)
{
    MATRIX4X4 m1, m2;

    if (zAngle == 0) return;

    double radians = 6.283185308 / (360.0 / zAngle);
    double c = cos(radians);
    double s = sin(radians);

    m1[0][0]=c;   m1[0][1]=s;   m1[0][2]=0;   m1[0][3]=0;
    m1[1][0]=-s;  m1[1][1]=c;   m1[1][2]=0;   m1[1][3]=0;
    m1[2][0]=0;   m1[2][1]=0;   m1[2][2]=1;   m1[2][3]=0;
    m1[3][0]=0;   m1[3][1]=0;   m1[3][2]=0;   m1[3][3]=1;

    MultMatrix(m2, m1, m);
    CopyMatrix(m, m2);
}

void CGraphics3DView::Transform(MODEL& shape, MATRIX4X4& m)
{
    int transformedX, transformedY, transformedZ;

    for (UINT i=0; i<shape.numVerts; ++i)
    {
        transformedX = (int) (shape.vertices[i].x * m[0][0] +
```

LISTING 4.16   Continued

```
            shape.vertices[i].y * m[1][0] +
            shape.vertices[i].z * m[2][0] + m[3][0]);
        transformedY = (int) (shape.vertices[i].x * m[0][1] +
            shape.vertices[i].y * m[1][1] +
            shape.vertices[i].z * m[2][1] + m[3][1]);
        transformedZ = (int) (shape.vertices[i].x * m[0][2] +
            shape.vertices[i].y * m[1][2] +
            shape.vertices[i].z * m[2][2] + m[3][2]);
        shape.vertices[i].x = transformedX;
        shape.vertices[i].y = transformedY;
        shape.vertices[i].z = transformedZ;
    }
}
```

5. Load Graphics3DView.H, and add Listing 4.17 to the top of the file, right before the CGraphics3DView class declaration.

LISTING 4.17   Code for the Class's Header File

```
typedef double MATRIX4X4[4][4];

typedef struct vertex
{
    int x, y, z, w;
} VERTEX;

typedef struct edge
{
    UINT vertex1, vertex2;
} EDGE;

typedef struct model
{
    UINT numVerts;
    VERTEX* vertices;
    UINT numEdges;
    EDGE* edges;
} MODEL;
```

6. Also in Graphics3DView.H, add Listing 4.18 to the CGraphics3DView class's Attributes section, right after the CGraphics3DDoc* GetDocument() const line.

LISTING 4.18   Code for the Class's Attributes Section

```
protected:
    VERTEX m_cubeVerts[8];
    EDGE m_cubeEdges[14];
    MODEL m_cube;
    int m_xRotate, m_yRotate, m_zRotate;
    double m_xScale, m_yScale, m_zScale;
    double m_xTranslate, m_yTranslate, m_zTranslate;
    BOOL m_animate;
```

7. Again in Graphics3DView.H, add Listing 4.19 to the CGraphics3DView class's Implementation section, right after the protected keyword.

LISTING 4.19   Code for the Class's Implementation Section

```
void InitModel();
void TransformModel();
void DrawModel(CDC* pDC, MODEL& model);
void PerspProject(MODEL& model, double eye);
void Translate(MATRIX4X4& m,
    int xTrans, int yTrans, int zTrans);
void Scale(MATRIX4X4& m,
    double xScale, double yScale, double zScale);
void RotateX(MATRIX4X4& m, int xAngle);
void RotateY(MATRIX4X4& m, int yAngle);
void RotateZ(MATRIX4X4& m, int zAngle);
void Transform(MODEL& model, MATRIX4X4& m);
void MultMatrix(MATRIX4X4& product,
    MATRIX4X4& matrix1, MATRIX4X4& matrix2);
void InitMatrix(MATRIX4X4& m);
void CopyMatrix(MATRIX4X4& dst, MATRIX4X4& src);
```

Your Graphics3D program is now complete. To create the application, press Ctrl+Shift+B. To run the application, press F5.

Running the Graphics3D Application

When you run Graphics3D, you see the window shown in Figure 4.26, which displays a cube wireframe model in the lower-left corner. (Note that the model has an X on the back part of the cube, which helps you keep track of which side is which as you manipulate the object.) This program works similarly to Graphics2D, which you developed in Chapter 3. To transform the object onscreen, select the Translate, Scale, or Rotate commands from the Transform menu. You can apply as many transformations as you want to the object because they are not applied to the object until you right-click in the application's window. Figure 4.27 shows the cube translated 100 units on the X and Y axis and rotated 20 degrees around the Y axis.

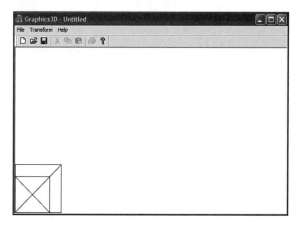

FIGURE 4.26   The Graphics3D application.

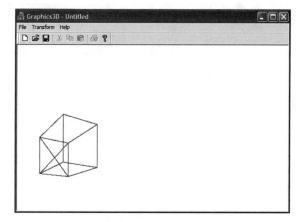

FIGURE 4.27   The cube translated and rotated.

Unlike the Graphics2D application, Graphics3D has an Animate command in the Transform menu. When you select this command, the program continually rotates the object around all three axes. The speed of the animation depends on the speed of your computer and the size of the window. If things are running too slowly, try making the window smaller so that the program has less area to redraw for each frame of the animation.

How the Graphics3D Program Works

First, look at the Graphics3DView.h file. The CGraphics3DView class declares a number of data members, including m_cube, which is a MODEL structure that holds information about the current wireframe model. The data member m_cubeVerts[] is an array of VERTEX structures that hold the vertices of the m_cube object, whereas m_cubeEdges[] is an array of EDGE structures that hold the object's edge list. The data members m_xRotate, m_yRotate, m_zRotate, m_xScale, m_yScale, m_zScale, m_xTranslate, m_yTranslate, and m_zTranslate hold the values for the current state of the transformations. Finally, m_animate is a flag that indicates whether the program should animate the model.

Look now at the Graphics3DView.cpp file. When the program runs, the CGraphics3DView class's constructor calls the local function InitModel() to initialize the m_cube structure and the model's vertices and edges. The constructor also initializes the transformation variables m_xRotate, m_yRotate, m_zRotate, m_xScale, m_yScale, m_zScale, m_xTranslate, m_yTranslate, and m_zTranslate to their default values. These default values are used in the constructor's call to TransformModel(), which applies the default transformation to the cube model before the model is displayed for the first time. Finally, the constructor initializes the m_animate flag to FALSE.

SHOP TALK

ACCUMULATING TRANSFORMATIONS

If you're anything like me when I started learning about 3D graphics programming, keeping track of all the transformations is driving you right up the wall. Because of the way transformations can accumulate in a matrix, you have to be sure of the order in which your program performs transformations, as well as making sure that you properly initialize matrices as appropriate for each frame of animation.

For example, unlike the Graphics2D application, which reset its transformation variables to their default values after each transformation, Graphics3D keeps the current state of the transformation in the m_xRotate, m_yRotate, m_zRotate, m_xScale, m_yScale, m_zScale, m_xTranslate, m_yTranslate, and m_zTranslate data members.

Instead of resetting the transformation variables to their default values, Graphics3D resets the model's vertices to their starting values before applying a transformation. This ensures that all transformations start off fresh and that the program applies the current perspective projection only once to the model's vertices.

Applying the perspective again and again without resetting the model's vertices to their starting values would cause the model to look more and more stretched along the Z axis. Similarly, in the case of this chapter's Graphics3D application, forgetting to reset the vertices to their starting locations would cause strange displays as the 3D object is transformed incorrectly.

When the application's window appears onscreen, the CGraphics3DView class's OnDraw() function displays the model by calling the local DrawModel() function.

When you select a command from the Transform menu, the appropriate command-response function takes over, initializing and displaying the Transform dialog box and then saving your response in the appropriate transformation variables. For example, when you select the Scale command, the OnTransformScale() function is called. In that function, the program first sets the dialog box's m_xAxis, m_yAxis, and m_zAxis data members to 1, so that the default scaling values of 1 for the three axes are in the edit controls when the dialog box appears. The call to the dialog box's DoModal() function then displays the dialog box, so that you can enter new values into the edit controls. When you click OK, the program updates the m_xScale, m_yScale, and m_zScale variables based on your response.

When you right-click in the application's window, the program calls the OnRButtonDown() function, which applies the selected transformations to the shape's vertices. First, the function calls InitModel() to ensure that the model's vertices are set to their starting values. Then, OnRButtonDown() calls TransformModel() to apply the current transformation and calls Invalidate() to force the application's window to redraw its display.

Finally, when you select the Transform menu's Animate command, the message-response function OnTransformAnimate() is called. The first time this function is called, the m_animate flag is FALSE, so OnTransformAnimate() calls SetTimer() to start a windows timer and changes m_animate to TRUE. If OnTransformAnimate() is called when m_animate is TRUE, the program calls KillTimer() to turn off the windows timer and toggles m_animate back to FALSE.

After SetTimer() is called, the program starts to receive WM_TIMER messages. The application handles these messages with the OnTimer() function, which increments the angle of rotation for each of the object's axes, and then calls InitModel(), TransformModel(), and Invalidate() to apply the new rotation and to force the window to display the new animation frame.

Although selecting the Transform menu's Animate command a second time turns off the window's timer, you might exit the program with the animation feature still active. Because you should kill timers that your application starts, Graphics3D uses the OnDestroy() function, which the program calls whenever the application receives a WM_DESTROY message, to call KillTimer(). Because Windows sends the WM_DESTROY message whenever you exit the application, this extra call to KillTimer() ensures that the timer is never left running.

The last function of interest is OnUpdateTransformAnimate(), which is called whenever you display the Transform menu and is responsible for checking and unchecking the Animate command in the menu. This function simply checks the value of m_animate and calls the SetCheck() function with a value of TRUE or FALSE.

SHOP TALK

MANIPULATING ANIMATION

Animated 3D displays, like the one shown by this chapter's Graphics3D application, offer a great opportunity for exploring and learning. You can modify the program in many ways to see how your modifications affect the display.

For example, another way to speed up the Graphics3D program if it runs too slowly on your system is to change the number of degrees by which the OnTimer() function increments the m_xRotate, m_yRotate, and m_zRotate variables. The bigger the increment, the faster the model rotates onscreen. Of course, larger increments also mean less fluid animation.

If your display looks like it's rotating in a room with a strobe light, your rotation angles are too large. If the angles get even larger, the animation will lose the logic of its motion, making the shape look as if it's randomly appearing in various positions instead of rotating in a logical way around its three axes. Of course, if that's the effect you want, go for it!

If nothing else, increasing the rotation angle and watching the results are instructional. You might even want to add to the application some keystroke or menu commands that enable you to change certain parameters "on-the-fly." For example, you could program the "A" key to increase the rotation angle each time it's pressed.

How about adding a response function for the WM_LBUTTONDOWN message that resets the shape to its starting point in the window. To do this, you'd reinitialize the shape's vertices to their starting values and then call Invalidate(TRUE) to force the window to repaint.

You also may want to add a dialog box that displays the values of the shape's current vertices. That way, if you should transform the shape such that it no longer appears in the window, you can see the type of translation you need to bring the shape back into view. To do this, you need to create a new dialog box and then create a new menu command that displays the dialog box. The response functions for the current Transform menu commands show you how to respond to a menu command and how to initialize and display a dialog box.

Finally, you may want to animate other transformations besides just rotations. You could go so far as to provide an animation feature for each of the possible transformations, one for each axis. For example, you might want to add commands to animate the translations along the X, Y, and Z axes. If you do this, you'll want to check for the size of the window so that you don't translate the object out of view.

Presenting the Program Listings

Listings 4.20 and 4.21 show the complete code for the CGraphics3DView class, including the Graphics3DView.h header file and the Graphics3DView.cpp implementation file. Many other files were created by AppWizard when you started the Graphics3D application project. Because you did not modify those files, they are not shown here. However, you easily can view any of the project's files by loading them with Visual C++'s editor (or any other text editor).

LISTING 4.20   The CGraphics3DView Class's Header File

```
// Graphics3DView.h : interface of the CGraphics3DView class
//


#pragma once

typedef double MATRIX4X4[4][4];

typedef struct vertex
{
    int x, y, z, w;
} VERTEX;

typedef struct edge
{
    UINT vertex1, vertex2;
} EDGE;

typedef struct model
{
    UINT numVerts;
    VERTEX* vertices;
    UINT numEdges;
    EDGE* edges;
} MODEL;

class CGraphics3DView : public CView
{
protected: // create from serialization only
    CGraphics3DView();
    DECLARE_DYNCREATE(CGraphics3DView)

// Attributes
public:
    CGraphics3DDoc* GetDocument() const;

protected:
    VERTEX m_cubeVerts[8];
    EDGE m_cubeEdges[14];
    MODEL m_cube;
    int m_xRotate, m_yRotate, m_zRotate;
```

LISTING 4.20   Continued

```
    double m_xScale, m_yScale, m_zScale;
    double m_xTranslate, m_yTranslate, m_zTranslate;
    BOOL m_animate;

// Operations
public:

// Overrides
    public:
    virtual void OnDraw(CDC* pDC);  // overridden to draw this view
virtual BOOL PreCreateWindow(CREATESTRUCT& cs);
protected:

// Implementation
public:
    virtual ~CGraphics3DView();
#ifdef _DEBUG
    virtual void AssertValid() const;
    virtual void Dump(CDumpContext& dc) const;
#endif

protected:
    void InitModel();
    void TransformModel();
    void DrawModel(CDC* pDC, MODEL& model);
    void PerspProject(MODEL& model, double eye);
    void Translate(MATRIX4X4& m,
        int xTrans, int yTrans, int zTrans);
    void Scale(MATRIX4X4& m,
        double xScale, double yScale, double zScale);
    void RotateX(MATRIX4X4& m, int xAngle);
    void RotateY(MATRIX4X4& m, int yAngle);
    void RotateZ(MATRIX4X4& m, int zAngle);
    void Transform(MODEL& model, MATRIX4X4& m);
    void MultMatrix(MATRIX4X4& product,
        MATRIX4X4& matrix1, MATRIX4X4& matrix2);
    void InitMatrix(MATRIX4X4& m);
    void CopyMatrix(MATRIX4X4& dst, MATRIX4X4& src);

// Generated message map functions
protected:
```

LISTING 4.20   Continued

```
    DECLARE_MESSAGE_MAP()
public:
    afx_msg void OnTransformAnimate();
    afx_msg void OnTransformRotate();
    afx_msg void OnTransformScale();
    afx_msg void OnTransformTranslate();
    afx_msg void OnUpdateTransformAnimate(CCmdUI *pCmdUI);
    afx_msg void OnRButtonDown(UINT nFlags, CPoint point);
    afx_msg void OnTimer(UINT nIDEvent);
    afx_msg void OnDestroy();
};


#ifndef _DEBUG  // debug version in Graphics3DView.cpp
inline CGraphics3DDoc* CGraphics3DView::GetDocument() const
   { return reinterpret_cast<CGraphics3DDoc*>(m_pDocument); }
#endif
```

LISTING 4.21   The CGraphics3DView Class's Implementation File

```
// Graphics3DView.cpp : implementation of the CGraphics3DView class
//

#include "stdafx.h"
#include "Graphics3D.h"

#include "Graphics3DDoc.h"
#include "Graphics3DView.h"

#ifdef _DEBUG
#define new DEBUG_NEW
#endif

#include <math.h>
#include "TransformDlg.h"

// CGraphics3DView

IMPLEMENT_DYNCREATE(CGraphics3DView, CView)

BEGIN_MESSAGE_MAP(CGraphics3DView, CView)
    ON_COMMAND(ID_TRANSFORM_ANIMATE, OnTransformAnimate)
```

LISTING 4.21   Continued

```
    ON_COMMAND(ID_TRANSFORM_ROTATE, OnTransformRotate)
    ON_COMMAND(ID_TRANSFORM_SCALE, OnTransformScale)
    ON_COMMAND(ID_TRANSFORM_TRANSLATE, OnTransformTranslate)
    ON_UPDATE_COMMAND_UI(ID_TRANSFORM_ANIMATE, OnUpdateTransformAnimate)
    ON_WM_RBUTTONDOWN()
    ON_WM_TIMER()
    ON_WM_DESTROY()
END_MESSAGE_MAP()

// CGraphics3DView construction/destruction

CGraphics3DView::CGraphics3DView()
{
    // TODO: add construction code here
    InitModel();

    m_xRotate = 0;
    m_yRotate = 0;
    m_zRotate = 0;
    m_xScale = 1;
    m_yScale = 1;
    m_zScale = 1;
    m_xTranslate = 0;
    m_yTranslate = 0;
    m_zTranslate = 0;

    TransformModel();

    m_animate = FALSE;
}

CGraphics3DView::~CGraphics3DView()
{
}

BOOL CGraphics3DView::PreCreateWindow(CREATESTRUCT& cs)
{
    // TODO: Modify the Window class or styles here by modifying
    //   the CREATESTRUCT cs
```

LISTING 4.21   Continued

```
    return CView::PreCreateWindow(cs);
}

// CGraphics3DView drawing

void CGraphics3DView::OnDraw(CDC* pDC)
{
    CGraphics3DDoc* pDoc = GetDocument();
    ASSERT_VALID(pDoc);

    // TODO: add draw code for native data here
    DrawModel(pDC, m_cube);
}



// CGraphics3DView diagnostics

#ifdef _DEBUG
void CGraphics3DView::AssertValid() const
{
    CView::AssertValid();
}

void CGraphics3DView::Dump(CDumpContext& dc) const
{
    CView::Dump(dc);
}

CGraphics3DDoc* CGraphics3DView::GetDocument() const
{
    ASSERT(m_pDocument->IsKindOf(RUNTIME_CLASS(CGraphics3DDoc)));
    return (CGraphics3DDoc*)m_pDocument;
}
#endif //_DEBUG



// CGraphics3DView message handlers

void CGraphics3DView::OnTransformAnimate()
{
```

LISTING 4.21 Continued

```
    // TODO: Add your command handler code here
    if (m_animate)
    {
        KillTimer(1);
        m_animate = FALSE;
    }
    else
    {
        SetTimer(1, 50, NULL);
        m_animate = TRUE;
    }
}

void CGraphics3DView::OnTransformRotate()
{
    // TODO: Add your command handler code here
    CTransformDlg dlg;
    dlg.m_xAxis = 0;
    dlg.m_yAxis = 0;
    dlg.m_zAxis = 0;

    int response = dlg.DoModal();

    if (response == IDOK)
    {
        m_xRotate += (int) dlg.m_xAxis;
        m_yRotate += (int) dlg.m_yAxis;
        m_zRotate += (int) dlg.m_zAxis;
    }
}

void CGraphics3DView::OnTransformScale()
{
    // TODO: Add your command handler code here
    CTransformDlg dlg;
    dlg.m_xAxis = 1;
    dlg.m_yAxis = 1;
    dlg.m_zAxis = 1;

    int response = dlg.DoModal();
```

LISTING 4.21   Continued

```
    if (response == IDOK)
    {
        m_xScale *= dlg.m_xAxis;
        m_yScale *= dlg.m_yAxis;
        m_zScale *= dlg.m_zAxis;
    }
}

void CGraphics3DView::OnTransformTranslate()
{
    // TODO: Add your command handler code here
    CTransformDlg dlg;
    dlg.m_xAxis = 0;
    dlg.m_yAxis = 0;
    dlg.m_zAxis = 0;

    int response = dlg.DoModal();

    if (response == IDOK)
    {
        m_xTranslate += dlg.m_xAxis;
        m_yTranslate += dlg.m_yAxis;
        m_zTranslate += dlg.m_zAxis;
    }
}

void CGraphics3DView::OnUpdateTransformAnimate(CCmdUI *pCmdUI)
{
    // TODO: Add your command update UI handler code here
    if (m_animate)
        pCmdUI->SetCheck(TRUE);
    else
        pCmdUI->SetCheck(FALSE);
}

void CGraphics3DView::OnRButtonDown(UINT nFlags, CPoint point)
{
    // TODO: Add your message handler code here and/or call default
    InitModel();
    TransformModel();
    Invalidate(TRUE);
```

LISTING 4.21   Continued

```
        CView::OnRButtonDown(nFlags, point);
}

void CGraphics3DView::OnTimer(UINT nIDEvent)
{
    // TODO: Add your message handler code here and/or call default
    m_xRotate += 5;
    m_yRotate += 5;
    m_zRotate += 5;
    InitModel();
    TransformModel();
    Invalidate(TRUE);

    CView::OnTimer(nIDEvent);
}

void CGraphics3DView::OnDestroy()
{
    CView::OnDestroy();

    // TODO: Add your message handler code here
    KillTimer(1);
}

void CGraphics3DView::InitModel()
{
    VERTEX cubeVerts[8] =
        {0,   100, 0,    1,
         100, 100, 0,    1,
         100, 100, -100, 1,
         0,   100, -100, 1,
         0,   0,   0,    1,
         100, 0,   0,    1,
         100, 0,   -100, 1,
         0,   0,   -100, 1};

    EDGE cubeEdges[14] =
        {1, 2,
         2, 3,
         3, 4,
         4, 1,
```

LISTING 4.21   Continued

```
        5, 6,
        6, 7,
        7, 8,
        8, 5,
        5, 1,
        6, 2,
        7, 3,
        8, 4,
        3, 8,
        4, 7};

    memcpy(m_cubeVerts, cubeVerts, sizeof(m_cubeVerts));
    memcpy(m_cubeEdges, cubeEdges, sizeof(m_cubeEdges));
    m_cube.numVerts = 8;
    m_cube.vertices = m_cubeVerts;
    m_cube.numEdges = 14;
    m_cube.edges = m_cubeEdges;
}


void CGraphics3DView::TransformModel()
{
    MATRIX4X4 m;
    InitMatrix(m);

    Translate(m, (int) m_xTranslate,
        (int) m_yTranslate, (int) m_zTranslate);
    Scale(m, m_xScale, m_yScale, m_zScale);
    RotateX(m, m_xRotate);
    RotateY(m, m_yRotate);
    RotateZ(m, m_zRotate);
    Transform(m_cube, m);
    PerspProject(m_cube, 300);
}


void CGraphics3DView::DrawModel(CDC* pDC, MODEL& model)
{
    int newX, newY;
    RECT clientRect;

    GetClientRect(&clientRect);
    int maxY = clientRect.bottom;
```

LISTING 4.21   Continued

```
    for (UINT i=0; i<model.numEdges; ++i)
    {
        UINT vertNum = model.edges[i].vertex1;
        newX = model.vertices[vertNum-1].x;
        newY = maxY - model.vertices[vertNum-1].y - 1;
        pDC->MoveTo(newX, newY);

        vertNum = model.edges[i].vertex2;
        newX = model.vertices[vertNum-1].x;
        newY = maxY - model.vertices[vertNum-1].y - 1;
        pDC->LineTo(newX, newY);
    }
}

void CGraphics3DView::PerspProject(MODEL& model, double eye)
{
    for (UINT i=0; i<model.numVerts; ++i)
    {
        int xCoord = model.vertices[i].x;
        int yCoord = model.vertices[i].y;
        int zCoord = model.vertices[i].z;
        double t = 1.0 / (1.0 - zCoord / eye);
        model.vertices[i].x = (int) (xCoord * t);
        model.vertices[i].y = (int) (yCoord * t);
    }
}

void CGraphics3DView::InitMatrix(MATRIX4X4& m)
{
    m[0][0]=1; m[0][1]=0; m[0][2]=0; m[0][3]=0;
    m[1][0]=0; m[1][1]=1; m[1][2]=0; m[1][3]=0;
    m[2][0]=0; m[2][1]=0; m[2][2]=1; m[2][3]=0;
    m[3][0]=0; m[3][1]=0; m[3][2]=0; m[3][3]=1;
}

void CGraphics3DView::CopyMatrix(MATRIX4X4& dst, MATRIX4X4& src)
{
    for (int i=0; i<4; ++i)
        for (int j=0; j<4; ++j)
            dst[i][j] = src[i][j];
}
```

LISTING 4.21   Continued

```cpp
void CGraphics3DView::MultMatrix(MATRIX4X4& product,
    MATRIX4X4& matrix1, MATRIX4X4& matrix2)
{
    for (int x=0; x<4; ++x)
        for (int y=0; y<4; ++y)
        {
            double sum = 0;
            for (int z=0; z<4; ++z)
                sum += matrix1[x][z] * matrix2[z][y];
            product[x][y] = sum;
        }
}

void CGraphics3DView::Translate(MATRIX4X4& m,
    int xTrans, int yTrans, int zTrans)
{
    MATRIX4X4 m1, m2;

    m1[0][0]=1;       m1[0][1]=0;       m1[0][2]=0;       m1[0][3]=0;
    m1[1][0]=0;       m1[1][1]=1;       m1[1][2]=0;       m1[1][3]=0;
    m1[2][0]=0;       m1[2][1]=0;       m1[2][2]=1;       m1[2][3]=0;
    m1[3][0]=xTrans; m1[3][1]=yTrans; m1[3][2]=zTrans; m1[3][3]=1;

    MultMatrix(m2, m1, m);
    CopyMatrix(m, m2);
}

void CGraphics3DView::Scale(MATRIX4X4& m,
    double xScale, double yScale, double zScale)
{
    MATRIX4X4 m1, m2;

    m1[0][0]=xScale; m1[0][1]=0;       m1[0][2]=0;       m1[0][3]=0;
    m1[1][0]=0;       m1[1][1]=yScale; m1[1][2]=0;       m1[1][3]=0;
    m1[2][0]=0;       m1[2][1]=0;       m1[2][2]=zScale; m1[2][3]=0;
    m1[3][0]=0;       m1[3][1]=0;       m1[3][2]=0;       m1[3][3]=1;

    MultMatrix(m2, m1, m);
    CopyMatrix(m, m2);
}
```

LISTING 4.21   Continued

```
void CGraphics3DView::RotateX(MATRIX4X4& m, int xAngle)
{
    MATRIX4X4 m1, m2;

    if (xAngle == 0) return;

    double radians = 6.283185308 / (360.0 / xAngle);
    double c = cos(radians);
    double s = sin(radians);

    m1[0][0]=1;  m1[0][1]=0;   m1[0][2]=0;  m1[0][3]=0;
    m1[1][0]=0;  m1[1][1]=c;   m1[1][2]=s;  m1[1][3]=0;
    m1[2][0]=0;  m1[2][1]=-s;  m1[2][2]=c;  m1[2][3]=0;
    m1[3][0]=0;  m1[3][1]=0;   m1[3][2]=0;  m1[3][3]=1;

    MultMatrix(m2, m1, m);
    CopyMatrix(m, m2);
}

void CGraphics3DView::RotateY(MATRIX4X4& m, int yAngle)
{
    MATRIX4X4 m1, m2;

    if (yAngle == 0) return;

    double radians = 6.283185308 / (360.0 / yAngle);
    double c = cos(radians);
    double s = sin(radians);

    m1[0][0]=c;  m1[0][1]=0;   m1[0][2]=-s;  m1[0][3]=0;
    m1[1][0]=0;  m1[1][1]=1;   m1[1][2]=0;   m1[1][3]=0;
    m1[2][0]=s;  m1[2][1]=0;   m1[2][2]=c;   m1[2][3]=0;
    m1[3][0]=0;  m1[3][1]=0;   m1[3][2]=0;   m1[3][3]=1;

    MultMatrix(m2, m1, m);
    CopyMatrix(m, m2);
}
```

LISTING 4.21 Continued

```
void CGraphics3DView::RotateZ(MATRIX4X4& m, int zAngle)
{
    MATRIX4X4 m1, m2;

    if (zAngle == 0) return;

    double radians = 6.283185308 / (360.0 / zAngle);
    double c = cos(radians);
    double s = sin(radians);

    m1[0][0]=c;   m1[0][1]=s; m1[0][2]=0; m1[0][3]=0;
    m1[1][0]=-s;  m1[1][1]=c; m1[1][2]=0; m1[1][3]=0;
    m1[2][0]=0;   m1[2][1]=0; m1[2][2]=1; m1[2][3]=0;
    m1[3][0]=0;   m1[3][1]=0; m1[3][2]=0; m1[3][3]=1;

    MultMatrix(m2, m1, m);
    CopyMatrix(m, m2);
}


void CGraphics3DView::Transform(MODEL& shape, MATRIX4X4& m)
{
    int transformedX, transformedY, transformedZ;

    for (UINT i=0; i<shape.numVerts; ++i)
    {
        transformedX = (int) (shape.vertices[i].x * m[0][0] +
            shape.vertices[i].y * m[1][0] +
            shape.vertices[i].z * m[2][0] + m[3][0]);
        transformedY = (int) (shape.vertices[i].x * m[0][1] +
            shape.vertices[i].y * m[1][1] +
            shape.vertices[i].z * m[2][1] + m[3][1]);
        transformedZ = (int) (shape.vertices[i].x * m[0][2] +
            shape.vertices[i].y * m[1][2] +
            shape.vertices[i].z * m[2][2] + m[3][2]);
        shape.vertices[i].x = transformedX;
        shape.vertices[i].y = transformedY;
        shape.vertices[i].z = transformedZ;
    }
}
```

In Brief

- To create a 3D coordinate system from a 2D one, you simply add a Z axis to the Cartesian plane, changing the plane into a cube.

- Defining a 3D object requires defining not only vertices but also edges, which are the lines that connect the vertices to form the 3D object.

- The coordinates that define a 3D wireframe model are referred to as local coordinates.

- Local coordinates are changed into world coordinates when a program transforms the model's vertices using translation, scaling, or rotation.

- A graphics program converts world coordinates to screen coordinates so that the model can be drawn onscreen.

- Using parallel projection, you can draw a 3D wireframe model onscreen simply by ignoring all of the Z coordinates, but the result will lack the appearance of depth.

- 3D programs create the illusion of depth using perspective projection, which makes distant objects look smaller than close-up objects.

- The main difference between 2D transformations and 3D transformations is that 3D transformations are performed using a 4×4 matrix rather than a 3×3 matrix.

Getting Direct3D Up and Running

5

Every Direct3D program has to initialize Direct3D before the program can render to the screen. As a programmer, you'll face this overhead with every Direct3D program you write, so you might as well get it out of the way now. Not only that, until you learn to do these things, you can't do anything else with Direct3D. So, in this chapter, you study Direct3D objects and Direct3D devices. Specifically, today you will learn:

- How to create a Direct3D object

- How to create a Direct3D device object

- About display modes and pixel formats

- How to check for device availability

- How to clear a Direct3D display

Creating a Direct3D Object

The first step in writing a Direct3D program is to create a Direct3D object, which provides you access to the `IDirect3D8` interface. This interface provides the methods you need to get your Direct3D application up and running, including methods to check for display modes, create Direct3D devices, and more. Later in this chapter, you'll learn to call some of these methods, but for now, here's how you create your Direct3D object:

```
IDirect3D9* g_pDirect3D = NULL;
g_pDirect3D = Direct3DCreate9(D3D_SDK_VERSION);
if (g_pDirect3D == NULL)
    return E_FAIL;
```

Here, the code first declares a pointer to the IDirect3D9 interface. The pointer is named g_pDirect3D and is a global variable in your program. To obtain the pointer to the Direct3D object, you call the Direct3DCreate9() method, which is declared in the DirectX API like this:

```
IDirect3D9* Direct3DCreate9(
  UINT SDKVersion
);
```

As you can see, Direct3DCreate9() returns a pointer to the IDirect3D9 interface and requires a single argument. Supplying the value for this argument is easy; you currently have only one choice: D3D_SDK_VERSION.

After calling Direct3DCreate9(), you should check the value returned by the method. If the value is NULL, the call to Direct3DCreate9() failed; otherwise, the return value is the pointer to your Direct3D object.

You might have noticed the constant E_FAIL in the previous example of creating a Direct3D object. The DirectX SDK defines this constant for you. Obviously, it represents an error value that you can use to indicate the failure of the call to Direct3DCreate9(). The DirectX SDK defines hundreds of such error constants, many of which you'll learn about as you proceed through this book.

WATCHING OUT FOR NULLS

Always check for a NULL value in the returned pointer and handle the error if it occurs. Because your Direct3D program will be completely crippled if it's unable to get this pointer, you'd probably handle the error by giving the user a quick message and then terminating the application.

Creating a Direct3D Device

After you create your Direct3D object, it's time to create a Direct3D device, which is an object of the IDirect3DDevice9 interface. This object provides your program with access to a slew of methods for handling graphical resources, drawing shapes, manipulating images and textures, and much more. In fact, a great deal of the graphical work your Direct3D application performs will be done through the IDirect3DDevice9 object.

Here's how you use your Direct3D object's pointer to create a device object for your application:

```
IDirect3DDevice9* g_pDirect3DDevice = NULL;
HRESULT hResult = g_pDirect3D->CreateDevice(D3DADAPTER_DEFAULT,
```

```
        D3DDEVTYPE_HAL, g_hWnd, D3DCREATE_SOFTWARE_VERTEXPROCESSING,
        &D3DPresentParams, &g_pDirect3DDevice);
if (FAILED(hResult))
    return E_FAIL;
```

As you can see, you first need to declare a pointer to the IDirect3DDevice9 interface. In this example, the pointer is named g_pDirect3DDevice and is initialized to NULL, something you should do with all your pointers. To create the Direct3D device object and obtain a pointer to it, your program must call the Direct3D object's CreateDevice() method. The DirectX API declares that method like this:

```
HRESULT CreateDevice(
  UINT Adapter,
  D3DDEVTYPE DeviceType,
  HWND  hFocusWindow,
  DWORD BehaviorFlags,
  D3DPRESENT_PARAMETERS* pPresentationParameters,
  IDirect3DDevice8** ppReturnedDeviceInterface
);
```

This method requires six arguments, which are used as follows:

- *Adapter*—A number that specifies the adapter for which Direct3D should create the device

- *DeviceType*—Specifies the type of device object to create

- *hFocusWindow*—A handle to the window with which the device will be associated

- *BehaviorFlags*—A set of flags that specify the required behaviors for the device

- *pPresentationParameters*—A pointer to an instance of the D3DPRESENT_PARAMETERS structure

- *ppReturnedDeviceInterface*—The address of a pointer to the IDirect3DDevice9 interface

Obviously, there's a lot more going on with the CreateDevice() call than there was with the Direct3DCreate9() call.

First, let's talk about the adapter, which is the first argument in the call. The adapter referred to here is the graphics hardware that the user has installed in his machine. This hardware is usually a graphics card installed in the computer. Most systems have only one adapter, but it's possible to have more than one, which is why the CreateDevice() method insists that you specify the adapter to use.

Although a system can have more than one adapter, only one can be the default adapter. Because you're not going to be doing anything too wild and crazy in this book, the default adapter will work fine for everything you need to do. As luck would have it, the DirectX SDK defines a constant, D3DADAPTER_DEFAULT, that you can use to specify the default adapter.

That takes care of the first argument. Now take a gander at the second. This second argument specifies the type of device to create. Direct3D defines three types of devices, each of which has its own constant, defined in the D3DDEVTYPE structure, which looks like this:

```
typedef enum _D3DDEVTYPE {
    D3DDEVTYPE_HAL        = 1,
    D3DDEVTYPE_REF        = 2,
    D3DDEVTYPE_SW         = 3,

    D3DDEVTYPE_FORCE_DWORD = 0xffffffff
} D3DDEVTYPE;
```

You can forget that fourth constant in the structure; it's currently unused. Here's what the other three mean:

- D3DDEVTYPE_HAL—A device that takes advantage of any 3D hardware installed on the machine. (*HAL* stands for *hardware abstraction layer*.)

- D3DDEVTYPE_REF—A device in which all Direct3D features are performed by software. This is called the reference device. (*REF* stands for *reference*.)

- D3DDEVTYPE_SW—Currently unsupported. (*SW* stands for *software*.)

For the best results, you'll want to use D3DDEVTYPE_HAL. If you do that, though, you'll need to query the device to discover what Direct3D features the user's system supports. The advantage of the D3DDEVTYPE_REF type of device is that all features of Direct3D can be tested on any machine, because Direct3D performs all of these features in software. No 3D hardware is required. However, because all the complex processing happens with software, this type of device is much slower than the hardware device. Typically, D3DDEVTYPE_REF is used only for testing.

Moving on, the third argument is simply your application's window handle. If you recall from Chapter 2, "Writing a Windows Program," you acquire the handle when you call the Windows API function CreateWindowEx(). Nothing more to say about this argument.

The fourth argument is a value containing the flags that specify how the device should behave. There are actually seven of these flags, but in this book, you only need to know two: D3DCREATE_HARDWARE_VERTEXPROCESSING and D3DCREATE_SOFTWARE_VERTEX-PROCESSING. The former specifies that Direct3D should process vertices (a fancy word for points in a shape) using hardware, and the latter specifies using software for the same purpose. In this book, you'll use D3DCREATE_SOFTWARE_VERTEXPROCESSING, which ensures compatibility with all systems at the cost of slightly less efficiency.

Now we get to the fifth argument, which is a monster—even its name is intimidating. Don't panic, though. You'll soon master this beast. The fifth argument is the address of a D3DPRESENT_PARAMETERS structure. The DirectX SDK defines the structure like this:

```
typedef struct _D3DPRESENT_PARAMETERS_ {
    UINT                    BackBufferWidth;
    UINT                    BackBufferHeight;
    D3DFORMAT               BackBufferFormat;
    UINT                    BackBufferCount;

    D3DMULTISAMPLE_TYPE     MultiSampleType;

    D3DSWAPEFFECT           SwapEffect;
    HWND                    hDeviceWindow;
    BOOL                    Windowed;
    BOOL                    EnableAutoDepthStencil;
    D3DFORMAT               AutoDepthStencilFormat;
    DWORD                   Flags;

    UINT                    FullScreen_RefreshRateInHz;
    UINT                    FullScreen_PresentationInterval;
} D3DPRESENT_PARAMETERS;
```

Even I'm getting nervous. Okay, not really. This isn't as bad as it looks, especially considering that you can use standard settings and forget about it. In fact, you really need to know only a couple of these settings to get started. You'll run into several others throughout this book. For now, just know this:

- hDeviceWindow—Your window's handle.

- Windowed—TRUE for a windowed application and FALSE for a full-screen application.

The other members of this structure, you can take on faith for now, filling them in with the values shown in Listing 5.1 (and ignoring the rest).

LISTING 5.1   Initializing the D3DPRESENT_PARAMETERS Structure

```
D3DPRESENT_PARAMETERS D3DPresentParams;
ZeroMemory(&D3DPresentParams, sizeof(D3DPRESENT_PARAMETERS));
D3DPresentParams.Windowed = FALSE;
D3DPresentParams.BackBufferCount = 1;
D3DPresentParams.BackBufferWidth = 800;
D3DPresentParams.BackBufferHeight = 600;
D3DPresentParams.BackBufferFormat = D3DFMT_X8R8G8B8;
D3DPresentParams.SwapEffect = D3DSWAPEFFECT_DISCARD;
D3DPresentParams.hDeviceWindow = g_hWnd;
```

Notice, in this example, how a call to the ZeroMemory() function initializes the entire structure to zeroes. Notice also that the example sets Windowed to FALSE and hDeviceWindow to g_hWnd, which is a global variable that holds the application's window handle.

A WINDOW OR NOT?

It might seem strange to tell Direct3D that you don't want a window and then have to pass along a window handle. Remember, though, that even a full-screen display is actually a window, albeit one without any of the visible elements of a window. In the case of a full-screen application, you can think of hDeviceWindow as holding a handle to the full screen.

Finally, you've made it all the way to the last argument in the call to CreateDevice(). This argument is named ppReturnedDeviceInterface and is nothing more than the address where CreateDevice() should store the pointer to your Direct3D device. After the call to CreateDevice(), if ppReturnedDeviceInterface remains NULL, the call to CreateDevice() failed.

Releasing Direct3D Objects

You know that when you allocate memory in a program, you need to release it before the application terminates. This is just the way programmers in polite society do things. The same is true of Direct3D objects: When you're finished with them, you have to remove them from memory. To do this, you must call each object's Release() method. For example, here's how you would release the Direct3D objects you just created:

```
if (g_pDirect3DDevice)
    g_pDirect3DDevice->Release();
if (g_pDirect3D)
    g_pDirect3D->Release();
```

You need to look at a couple of things here. First, notice how the code checks whether the object pointers are NULL before trying to release them. This is why it's so important to set these pointers to NULL when you first declare them so that the only time they can contain a value other than NULL is when the program successfully creates the Direct3D objects. You don't want to call Release() through a bad or NULL pointer! If you do, you'll almost certainly crash the program.

The other thing to notice here is that the program releases the objects in the reverse order they were created. Because of this, every Direct3D program always releases the Direct3D object last because it's always the first to be created. To tell you the truth, nothing bad seems to happen if you don't follow this rule, but the key word here is "seems." You have to figure that they make these rules for a reason.

Your First Direct3D Program

That's enough theory for now. Before your head starts spinning, you should spend a little time making sure that you understand what you've just read. To help you toward this goal, you'll now build your first Direct3D program. This program won't seem to do much of anything. But if it works okay, you should successfully create and release a Direct3D object and a Direct3D device object.

Creating the Basic Project

Perform the following steps to get the main Windows application up and running:

1. Start a new empty Win32 project named BasicDirect3DApp, as shown in Figures 5.1 and 5.2.

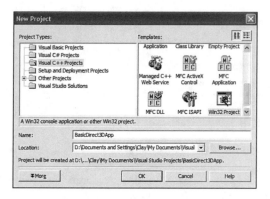

FIGURE 5.1   Creating the BasicDirect3DApp project.

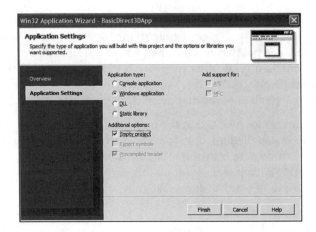

FIGURE 5.2   Be sure to choose the Empty Project setting.

2. On the Project menu, select the Add New Item command. The Add New Item dialog box appears.

3. Add a new C++ File (.cpp) named BasicDirect3DApp.cpp, as shown in Figure 5.3.

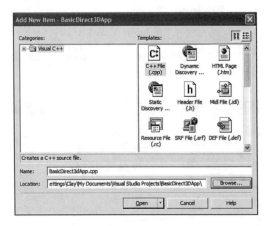

FIGURE 5.3   Creating the main source-code file.

4. Copy the contents of the BasicWindowsApp.cpp file (from Chapter 2) into the new BasicDirect3DApp code window.

5. Change the name in the comment at the top of the file to BasicDirect3DApp.cpp.

6. In the `RegisterWindowClass()` function change `wc.lpszClassName = "WinApp"` to `wc.lpszClassName = "Direct3DApp"`.

7. In the `CreateAppWindow()` function, change `"WinApp"` to `"Direct3DApp"`, and then change `"Basic Windows Application"` to `"Basic Direct3D Application"`.

8. Compile and run the application to make sure that it works okay. You should see the window shown in Figure 5.4.

FIGURE 5.4   Creating the main source-code file.

Adding the Direct3D Stuff

You're now ready to start programming your Direct3D application. Perform the following steps:

1. Add the following lines to the program's function prototypes:

```
HRESULT InitDirect3D();
void Render();
void CleanUpDirect3D();
```

2. Add the following lines to the program's global variables:

```
IDirect3D8* g_pDirect3D = NULL;
IDirect3DDevice8* g_pDirect3DDevice = NULL;
```

3. In the `WinMain()` function, replace the line `StartMessageLoop()` with the following:

```
HRESULT hResult = InitDirect3D();
if (SUCCEEDED(hResult))
    WPARAM result = StartMessageLoop();
CleanUpDirect3D();
```

4. Add the functions in Listing 5.2 to the program.

   LISTING 5.2   New Functions for BasicDirec3DApp

```
/////////////////////////////////////////////////////
// InitDirect3D()
/////////////////////////////////////////////////////
HRESULT InitDirect3D()
{
    g_pDirect3D = Direct3DCreate8(D3D_SDK_VERSION);
    if (g_pDirect3D == NULL)
        return E_FAIL;
    D3DPRESENT_PARAMETERS D3DPresentParams;
    ZeroMemory(&D3DPresentParams, sizeof(D3DPRESENT_PARAMETERS));
    D3DPresentParams.Windowed = FALSE;
    D3DPresentParams.BackBufferCount = 1;
    D3DPresentParams.BackBufferWidth = 800;
    D3DPresentParams.BackBufferHeight = 600;
    D3DPresentParams.BackBufferFormat = D3DFMT_X8R8G8B8;
    D3DPresentParams.SwapEffect = D3DSWAPEFFECT_DISCARD;
    D3DPresentParams.hDeviceWindow = g_hWnd;
    HRESULT hResult = g_pDirect3D->CreateDevice(D3DADAPTER_DEFAULT,
        D3DDEVTYPE_HAL, g_hWnd, D3DCREATE_SOFTWARE_VERTEXPROCESSING,
        &D3DPresentParams, &g_pDirect3DDevice);
    if (FAILED(hResult))
        return E_FAIL;
    return D3D_OK;
}


/////////////////////////////////////////////////////
// CleanUpDirect3D()
/////////////////////////////////////////////////////
void CleanUpDirect3D()
{
    if (g_pDirect3DDevice)
        g_pDirect3DDevice->Release();
```

LISTING 5.2 Continued

```
    if (g_pDirect3D)
        g_pDirect3D->Release();
}
```

Adding the Required References

If you try to compile the program at this point, you'll end up with a bunch of errors. This is because your project doesn't yet know where to find the Direct3D header and library files it needs to build the application. Go ahead and try to compile. When you get your list of errors, look at the top three. They should look like this:

```
error C2143: syntax error : missing ';' before '*'
error C2501: 'IDirect3D9' : missing storage-class or type specifiers
error C2501: 'g_pDirect3D' : missing storage-class or type specifiers
```

You're getting these errors because the program doesn't recognize the IDirect3D9* data type, which, as you now know, is a pointer to the IDirect3D9 interface. You should also see similar errors for the IDirect3DDevice9* data type, like this:

```
error C2143: syntax error : missing ';' before '*'
error C2501: 'IDirect3DDevice9' : missing storage-class or type specifiers
error C2501: 'g_pDirect3DDevice' : missing storage-class or type specifiers
```

There's a slew of other similar errors, where the program doesn't recognize the Direct3D symbols you're using. To resolve these errors, you need to tell the program where these symbols are defined. To do that, first add the line #include <d3d9.h> near the top of the program, right after the line #include <windows.h> that's already there.

Now, you need to tell your project where to find that header file. Perform the following steps to accomplish this task:

1. Right-click the project's name in the Solution Explorer and select Properties from the menu that appears. The BasicDirect3DApp Property Pages dialog box appears, as shown in Figure 5.5.

2. Click the C/C++ selection in the left pane, and select General from the displayed choices, as shown in Figure 5.6.

3. In the Additional Include Directories box, enter the path to the DirectX 9 SDK's include folder. If you installed the SDK using the default settings, this path should be c:\DXSDK\include, as shown in Figure 5.6.

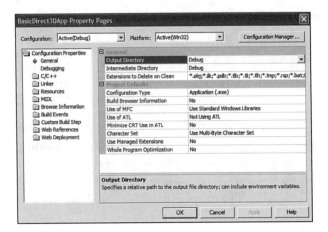

FIGURE 5.5 The project's property pages.

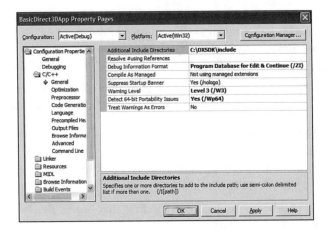

FIGURE 5.6 The general C/C++ settings.

4. Dismiss the dialog box by clicking OK.

Now you should be able to compile the program successfully. However, when the linker gets busy, you get the following errors:

```
error LNK2019: unresolved external symbol _Direct3DCreate9@4 referenced in
    function "long __cdecl InitFullScreenDirect3D(void)"
    (?InitFullScreenDirect3D@@YAJXZ)
BasicDirect3DApp fatal error LNK1120: 1 unresolved externals
```

You're getting these errors because, even though the project now knows how all those Direct3D symbols are declared, it doesn't know where the actual code for the objects is defined. In other words, you now need to tell the project where the Direct3D library files are located. Here's how:

1. Right-click the project's name in the Solution Explorer, and bring up the BasicDirect3DApp Property Pages dialog box again.

2. Click the Linker selection in the left pane, and select General from the displayed choices.

3. In the Additional Library Directories box, enter the path to the DirectX 9 SDK's library folder. If you installed the SDK using the default settings, this path should be C:\DXSDK\lib, as shown in Figure 5.7.

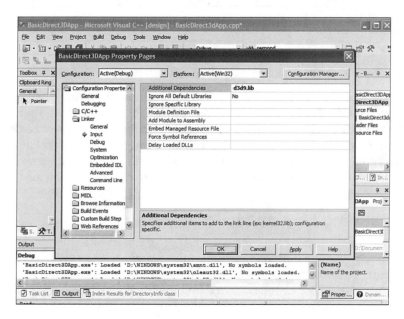

FIGURE 5.7 The general linker settings.

4. Click the Linker's Input selection in the left pane.

5. In the Additional Dependencies box in the right pane, enter **d3d9.lib**—which is the Direct3D 9 library file—as shown in Figure 5.8.

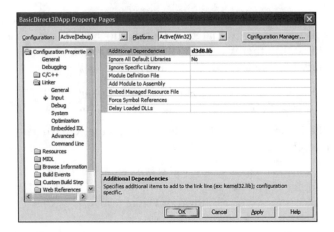

FIGURE 5.8   The linker input settings.

6. Dismiss the dialog box by clicking OK.

Now you should be able to compile, link, and run the application. When you do, your screen will probably flicker a couple of times and then you'll see your full-screen Direct3D window. Unfortunately, because you haven't yet drawn anything in the window, all you see is a plain white screen. To get out of the program Alt+Tab back to Visual Studio and then exit the program by clicking the toolbar's Stop Debugging button or by selecting Stop Debugging from the Debug menu.

Understanding Display Modes

To continue programming your first Direct3D program, you need to know about display modes. For the most part, a display mode comprises screen resolution and color depth. For example, most computer displays these days are set to 800×600 resolution with 32-bit color or 1024×768 resolution with 32-bit color. You can access dozens of other display modes as long as the graphics hardware in the computer supports them.

Most supported display modes, however, are archaic and are of no use to you as a Direct3D programmer. For example, we could get into a whole bag of worms here and talk about things like palletized display modes and monochrome display modes and other not-so-cool stuff, but you want to get started with game programming as soon as you can. So, for the purposes of this book, you'll need to know only about the nine most commonly used display modes on today's computers, as shown in Table 5.1.

TABLE 5.1   Some Common Display Modes

Resolution	Color Setting
640×480	16-bit color
640×480	24-bit color
640×480	32-bit color
800×600	16-bit color
800×600	24-bit color
800×600	32-bit color
1024×768	16-bit color
1024×768	24-bit color
1024×768	32-bit color

When I said these were the only settings you need to know, I meant that you should understand what these display modes represent on the screen and in memory. This is because your Direct3D applications will most likely have to deal with them at one time or another.

Now, I think you understand that an 800×600 display is 800 dots horizontally and 600 dots vertically. If not, you do now. The tricky part of a display mode is the color depth. To really understand how your computer displays a dot of a particular color, you need to know about pixel formats. A *pixel*, of course, is one of those tiny dots on your screen. The pixel format determines how the information that represents that dot is stored in the computer's memory.

The first thing to know is that the number of bits in a color determines how much video card memory each pixel on the screen consumes. For example, 16 bits is 2 bytes, so each pixel of a 16-bit color display requires two bytes. So, if your computer display is set to 800×600 resolution with 16-bit color, your video card requires 800×600×2 bytes of memory, or a total of 960,000 bytes of memory. If the same display uses 32-bit color, the video card memory is 1,920,000 bytes or twice that required by the 16-bit scenario.

For your purposes in this book, colors on the screen are created by combining red, green, and blue. These are called *RGB color modes*. One of the simplest display modes to understand is the 24-bit mode, which uses three bytes for each pixel. One byte represents red intensity, one represents green, and the last represents blue. Because a byte of memory can hold a value from 0 to 255, each of these three color elements can be set to one of 256 intensities, from 0 (none of the color) to 255 (full intensity of the color).

So, if you have a 24-bit pixel with the RGB values 255,0,0, you have a red dot on the screen. The RGB values 0,255,0 give you a green dot, and, as you've undoubtedly already guessed, 0,0,255 is a blue dot. The rest of the colors range from 0,0,0, which is black, to 255,255,255, which is white. If you've ever heard that black is the absence of all color and white is the presence of all color, you now know what that means.

Now that you know about 24-bit color, forget about it. That's right; forget it. As most programmers know, computers hate to work with odd numbers of bytes, and that's exactly what you have with 24-bit color. Direct3D programs, too, are not too fond of 24-bit color displays and work much better with either 16- or 32-bit displays. In this book, you'll work almost exclusively with 32-bit displays.

The most common 32-bit display mode still uses three bytes for the red, green, and blue color elements, but it adds a fourth byte for something called an alpha value. You don't need to know too much about alpha values yet. Just know that an alpha value specifies a color's transparency. Table 5.2 shows some of the 16-, 24-, and 32-bit pixel formats and the constants that the DirectX SDK defines for them.

TABLE 5.2 Pixel Formats

Format	Description
D3DFMT_R5G6B5	16-bit RGB pixel format with 5 bits for red, 6 bits for green, and 5 bits for blue
D3DFMT_X1R5G5B5	16-bit pixel format with 5 bits for each color
D3DFMT_A1R5G5B5	16-bit pixel format with 5 bits for each color and 1 bit for alpha
D3DFMT_A4R4G4B4	16-bit ARGB pixel format with 4 bits for each color and alpha value
D3DFMT_X4R4G4B4	16-bit RGB pixel format with 4 bits for each color
D3DFMT_R8G8B8	24-bit RGB pixel format with 8 bits per channel
D3DFMT_A8R8G8B8	32-bit ARGB pixel format with 8 bits for each color and alpha
D3DFMT_X8R8G8B8	32-bit RGB pixel format with 8 bits for each color (fourth byte unused)
D3DFMT_A2B10G10R10	32-bit pixel format using 10 bits for each color and 2 bits for alpha
D3DFMT_G16R16	32-bit pixel format using 16 bits each for green and red

Checking for Display-Mode Availability

When your Direct3D application first runs, it really should check for the availability of the display mode your application needs. You never know what kind of computer your program will be running on, and although most computers these days can handle any of the display modes you'll need, your program may be unlucky enough to have to run on a computer from the Stone Age. In such a case, the program has to know that it can't run properly and must inform the user of this sad fact.

The DirectX API supplies a method to take care of this problem. To discover whether a particular display mode is available, just call the Direct3D object's CheckDeviceType() method, which the SDK declares like this:

```
HRESULT CheckDeviceType(
  UINT Adapter,
  D3DDEVTYPE CheckType,
  D3DFORMAT DisplayFormat,
```

```
    D3DFORMAT BackBufferFormat,
    BOOL Windowed
);
```

This method requires five arguments, which are described as follows:

- *Adapter*—A number that specifies the adapter for which Direct3D should create the device

- *CheckType*—The type of device object for which you're checking

- *DisplayFormat*—The display format for which to check

- *BackBufferFormat*—The back buffer display format for which to check

- *Windowed*—A Boolean value that specifies whether the required device will be used in a windowed (TRUE) or full-screen (FALSE) application

In this book, the first argument will always be D3DADAPTER_DEFAULT, for the default adapter. The second argument can be either D3DDEVTYPE_HAL for a hardware-assisted device or D3DDEVTYPE_REF for a software device. The third and fourth arguments are, for your purposes, one of the values from Table 5.2, usually D3DFMT_X8R8G8B8. Finally, the fifth argument should be TRUE if your application will run in a window or FALSE if it's full-screen.

If the call succeeds (that is, the pixel format you want is available), CheckDeviceType() returns the value D3D_OK. So, a typical call to CheckDeviceType() in your programs might look like this:

```
HRESULT hResult = g_pDirect3D->CheckDeviceType(D3DADAPTER_DEFAULT,
    D3DDEVTYPE_REF, D3DFMT_X8R8G8B8, D3DFMT_X8R8G8B8, FALSE);
if (hResult != D3D_OK)
    return E_FAIL;
```

Windowed Versus Full-Screen Applications

Checking for a specific pixel format is usually something you do when starting up a full-screen Direct3D application. This is because, with a full-screen application, you can use whatever display mode you want, as long as the hardware supports it. However, if you're running your Direct3D application in a window, you have to share the display with any other applications that might also be running. This means that you're stuck with whatever mode the user has her machine set to. Your program must either adapt to the current display mode or ask the user to change it. This is why most Direct3D games run in full-screen mode.

But the windowed mode is cool for quickie types of games that the user may want to switch to from another application or for the types of demo programs you'll see in this book. Moreover, windowed games don't seem as isolated to the user as a full-screen game, even though a full-screen game is still a Windows application, and the user can switch back and forth with ease (assuming that the Direct3D application has been properly programmed).

When writing a windowed Direct3D application, it makes more sense to check the current display mode than it does to check for the availability of a specific one. After all, only one mode will be available, although you'll probably still want to check for hardware support if your application relies on hardware acceleration.

SHOP TALK

LIVING WITH DISPLAY MODES

Whether you're writing full-screen or windowed applications, you need to pay special attention to display modes. Full-screen applications have a lesser problem with display modes because they can reset the display mode to any one supported by the user's hardware. However, in both full-screen and windowed Direct3D applications, a close relationship exists between the display mode and the other graphics the program uses to create its display.

For example, when I first started with Direct3D, I can remember a few hard-to-track-down bugs that occurred because of Direct3D methods that "invisibly" returned errors (I didn't handle the errors in the program). These errors were due to problems between the current display mode and various rendering commands and resulted in mysterious display anomalies. Without tracking down the errors, I had no idea why the display was incorrect.

An example might be a bitmap that's larger than the Direct3D surface that represents the screen or window area to which the bitmap must be drawn. Trying to transfer such a bitmap to the display will cause the Direct3D method to fail and return an error. To the program's user, it will appear as if the bitmap just mysteriously didn't appear. Direct3D errors don't crash your programs, so, unless you capture and analyze every returned error code (which really is unreasonable), many errors can result in strange behavior.

Windowed Direct3D applications, especially, must be aware of the current display mode and adjust themselves appropriately to ensure that the program runs successfully. This might require just initializing a few coordinate variables to values appropriate for the current display mode. Or, at the other extreme, it could mean providing a different set of artwork for each display mode under which the program should run.

To check the current display mode, you can call the Direct3D object's `GetAdapterDisplayMode()` method, which the DirectX SDK declares like this:

```
HRESULT GetAdapterDisplayMode(
  UINT Adapter,
  D3DDISPLAYMODE* pMode
);
```

This method's two arguments are the adapter to check and a pointer to a D3DDISPLAY-MODE structure into which the call will place the information you need about the current display mode. The DirectX SDK declares this structure like this:

```
typedef struct _D3DDISPLAYMODE {
    UINT            Width;
    UINT            Height;
    UINT            RefreshRate;
    D3DFORMAT       Format;
} D3DDISPLAYMODE;
```

The Width and the Height members of this structure represent the current screen resolution, and the Format member represents the current pixel format. You don't need to worry about the RefreshRate member. So, if the user's system is set to a resolution of 800×600 with the 32-bit RGB pixel format when your program calls GetAdapterDisplayMode(), you'll end up with Width equal to 800, Height equal to 600, and Format equal to D3DFMT_X8R8G8B8. The actual call would look something like this:

```
D3DDISPLAYMODE d3ddisplaymode;
HRESULT hResult = g_pDirect3D->
    GetAdapterDisplayMode(D3DADAPTER_DEFAULT, &d3ddisplaymode);
if (hResult != D3D_OK)
    return E_FAIL;
```

After you have the display mode information, you can use it to create the device for your application, as shown in Listing 5.3.

LISTING 5.3   Creating the Device Object

```
D3DPRESENT_PARAMETERS D3DPresentParams;
ZeroMemory(&D3DPresentParams, sizeof(D3DPRESENT_PARAMETERS));
D3DPresentParams.Windowed = TRUE;
D3DPresentParams.BackBufferFormat = d3ddisplaymode.Format;
D3DPresentParams.SwapEffect = D3DSWAPEFFECT_DISCARD;
D3DPresentParams.hDeviceWindow = g_hWnd;
HRESULT hResult = g_pDirect3D->CreateDevice(D3DADAPTER_DEFAULT,
    D3DDEVTYPE_HAL, g_hWnd, D3DCREATE_SOFTWARE_VERTEXPROCESSING,
    &D3DPresentParams, &g_pDirect3DDevice);
if (FAILED(hResult))
    return E_FAIL;
```

That's it. Later in this chapter, in the section "Programming a Windowed Application," you'll see how to write a windowed Direct3D application.

Drawing to the Display

Because you don't want to look at that plain white screen that you get with your program as it stands now (blinding, isn't it?), you need to learn a couple of new Direct3D methods. The first of these is Clear(), which is a method of the Direct3D device object. The DirectX SDK declares Clear() like this:

```
HRESULT Clear(
  DWORD Count,
  CONST D3DRECT* pRects,
  DWORD Flags,
  D3DCOLOR Color,
  float Z,
  DWORD Stencil
);
```

As you can see, this method has quite a few arguments. Here's what they mean:

- *Count*—The number of rectangles in the pRects array or 0 if pRects is NULL.

- *pRects*—A pointer to an array of D3DRECT structures that describe the rectangles to clear or NULL to clear the entire viewport rectangle.

- *Flags*—The flags that specify the surfaces to be cleared. Can be a combination of D3DCLEAR_STENCIL, D3DCLEAR_TARGET, and D3DCLEAR_ZBUFFER.

- *Color*—A 32-bit value that specifies the color to which to clear the rectangles.

- *Z*—A new z value for the depth buffer.

- *Stencil*—The integer value to store in the stencil buffer.

A typical call to Clear() looks like this:

```
g_pDirect3DDevice->Clear(0, 0, D3DCLEAR_TARGET,
    D3DCOLOR_XRGB(0,0,255), 0, 0);
```

The third argument, D3DCLEAR_TARGET, tells Direct3D to clear the surface to the color specified in the fourth argument. The fourth argument is a D3DCOLOR value, which you can create using the XRGB macro. This macro takes the red, green, and blue color intensities as arguments. The remaining four arguments can be all zeroes.

After you have cleared the surface, you need to display it. All this task requires is a call to the Direct3D device object's Present() method, which the DirectX SDK declares like this:

```
HRESULT Present(
  CONST RECT* pSourceRect,
```

```
  CONST RECT* pDestRect,
  HWND hDestWindowOverride,
  CONST RGNDATA* pDirtyRegion
);
```

I'm not even going to tell you what these arguments mean because you're not going to use any of them in this book. Feel free to look them up in the documentation. For the purposes of the programs you'll be developing in these pages, here's what a call to Present() looks like:

```
g_pDirect3DDevice->Present(NULL, NULL, NULL, NULL);
```

That's right, all NULLs. Makes it all so much easier, eh? Seriously, though, this call to Present() displays the entire surface, overwriting all that nonsense that used to be on the screen.

You're now ready to add to your Direct3D application. When you're finished, your full-screen application will present you with a cool blue screen rather than the mess you had before. Just load up the project and follow these steps:

1. Find the InitFullScreenDirect3D() function, and add Listing 5.4 right after the first return E_FAIL line.

   LISTING 5.4   Code for the InitFullScreenDirect3D() Function

   ```
   HRESULT hResult = g_pDirect3D->CheckDeviceType(D3DADAPTER_DEFAULT,
       D3DDEVTYPE_REF, D3DFMT_X8R8G8B8, D3DFMT_X8R8G8B8, FALSE);
   if (hResult != D3D_OK)
   {
       MessageBox(g_hWnd,
           "Sorry. This program won't\nrun on your system.",
           "DirectX Error", MB_OK);
       return E_FAIL;
   }
   ```

2. Remove the HRESULT from in front of the call to CreateDevice().

3. Add the function shown in Listing 5.5 to the program.

   LISTING 5.5   The Render() Function

   ```
   /////////////////////////////////////////////////////////
   // Render()
   /////////////////////////////////////////////////////////
   void Render()
   ```

LISTING 5.5   Continued

```
{
    static red = 0;
    red = red + 2;
    if (red > 255)
        red = 0;
    g_pDirect3DDevice->Clear(0, 0, D3DCLEAR_TARGET,
        D3DCOLOR_XRGB(red,0,0), 0, 0);
    g_pDirect3DDevice->Present(NULL, NULL, NULL, NULL);
}
```

4. Find the `StartMessageLoop()` function and place the following line after the `// Use idle time` comment that's already there:

```
Render();
```

5. Find the `WndProc()` function and add the following lines right before the `switch` statement's ending brace:

```
case WM_KEYDOWN:
    switch(wParam)
    {
    case VK_ESCAPE:
        PostQuitMessage(WM_QUIT);
        break;
    }
```

Now you're ready to compile and run the application. When you do, you see a black screen that smoothly changes to red. To exit the application, press your keyboard's Escape key.

Programming a Windowed Application

Now let's see how to convert the full-screen program to a windowed Direct3D application. This task is actually pretty easy for a simple program like BasicDirect3DApp. The process can, however, be much more complicated for a full-featured application. This is because, as you already learned, a windowed application cannot change the display mode. That is, a windowed Direct3D application must work with whatever the current display mode is.

The first step in converting the program is to remove the call to `CheckDeviceType()`, as well as the related error code. Listing 5.6 is the source code you need to remove from the `InitDirect3D()` function.

LISTING 5.6   Code to Remove from `InitDirect3D()`

```
HRESULT hResult = g_pDirect3D->CheckDeviceType(D3DADAPTER_DEFAULT,
    D3DDEVTYPE_REF, D3DFMT_X8R8G8B8, D3DFMT_X8R8G8B8, FALSE);
if (hResult != D3D_OK)
{
    MessageBox(g_hWnd,
        "Sorry. This program won't\nrun on your system.",
        "DirectX Error", MB_OK);
    return E_FAIL;
}
```

Because you have to use whatever the current display mode is, there's no point in calling `CheckDeviceType()` to see whether a specific mode is available.

Although you can't change the display mode, you do have to know what the display mode is currently set to. You do this by calling `GetAdapterDisplayMode()`. So, to continue modifying the program, place the following source code where the call to `CheckDeviceType()` used to be:

```
D3DDISPLAYMODE d3ddisplaymode;
HRESULT hResult = g_pDirect3D->
    GetAdapterDisplayMode(D3DADAPTER_DEFAULT, &d3ddisplaymode);
if (hResult != D3D_OK)
    return E_FAIL;
```

Now you need to use the settings returned into the `D3DDISPLAYMODE` structure to create your Direct3D device. To do this, remove the source code shown in Listing 5.7.

LISTING 5.7   Initialization Code to Remove

```
D3DPRESENT_PARAMETERS D3DPresentParams;
ZeroMemory(&D3DPresentParams, sizeof(D3DPRESENT_PARAMETERS));
D3DPresentParams.Windowed = FALSE;
D3DPresentParams.BackBufferCount = 1;
D3DPresentParams.BackBufferWidth = 800;
D3DPresentParams.BackBufferHeight = 600;
D3DPresentParams.BackBufferFormat = D3DFMT_X8R8G8B8;
D3DPresentParams.SwapEffect = D3DSWAPEFFECT_DISCARD;
D3DPresentParams.hDeviceWindow = g_hWnd;
```

Then replace the code you removed with the following version, which sets up the parameters to create a Direct3D device for a windowed application:

```
D3DPRESENT_PARAMETERS D3DPresentParams;
ZeroMemory(&D3DPresentParams, sizeof(D3DPRESENT_PARAMETERS));
D3DPresentParams.Windowed = TRUE;
D3DPresentParams.BackBufferFormat = d3ddisplaymode.Format;
D3DPresentParams.SwapEffect = D3DSWAPEFFECT_DISCARD;
D3DPresentParams.hDeviceWindow = g_hWnd;
```

And that's all there is to the conversion. When you run the program now, the Direct3D display is constrained to the application's window.

In Brief

- The first step in writing a Direct3D program is to create a Direct3D object, which provides you access to the `IDirect3D8` interface.

- After you create your Direct3D object, you create a Direct3D device, which is an object of the `IDirect3DDevice9` interface.

- When you're finished with Direct3D objects, you have to remove them from memory. To do this, you must call each object's `Release()` method.

- You need to tell the program where Direct3D symbols are defined. To do that, first add the line `#include <d3d9.h>` near the top of the program.

- You must also tell the compiler where the header and library files are located.

- A display mode comprises screen resolution and color depth.

- To understand how your computer displays a dot of a particular color, you need to know about pixel formats.

- For your purposes in this book, colors on the screen are created by combining red, green, and blue.

- When a full-screen Direct3D application first runs, it should check for the availability of the required display modes.

- A windowed Direct3D application must share the display with any other applications that might also be running. This means that you're stuck with whatever mode the user has his machine set to.

- After a Direct3D application has rendered its display, it must call the Direct3D device object's `Present()` method.

Understanding Direct3D Surfaces

6

Surfaces are an important topic to Direct3D programmers because surfaces enable applications to store and manipulate graphics in a number of ways. In fact, without surfaces, you wouldn't even be able to see what's supposed to be on the screen. In this chapter, you'll see why. Specifically, today you will learn:

- What surfaces do for your program

- The different types of surfaces

- Creating and accessing surfaces

- Creating animation with Direct3D surfaces

- Restoring lost devices and surfaces

Exploring Direct3D Surfaces

Throughout this book and with all your future Direct3D programs, you'll be working a lot with something called *surfaces*. A surface is really nothing more than an area of memory in which you can store graphical information. For example, the stuff you see on the screen or in a window is stored in a surface, as are the images you may need to build that display. In this book, you'll learn about four different kinds of surfaces:

- The primary surface

- Back-buffer surfaces

- Image surfaces

- Texture surfaces

The Primary Surface

The *primary surface*, sometimes called the *front buffer*, is what you're looking at on the screen when you run a Direct3D program. This surface may contain the graphical data for the entire screen, or, in the case of a windowed application, the display you see in the application's window. The primary surface is the only type of surface that every Direct3D application must create and maintain, although the other types of surfaces are important.

PRIMARY SURFACE CREATION

You don't have to worry about explicitly creating a primary surface. Because it must always exist, just creating your Direct3D device object automatically creates the primary surface.

The Back-Buffer Surface

A *back buffer* is an area of memory where you can draw a display out of view of the user. After you draw onto the back buffer, you call the Present() method to make the back buffer the new primary surface. Rendering your display this way prevents nasty stuff like flicker and tearing, problems that plagued graphics programmers until they came up with the idea of back buffers.

The back buffer is so important to rendering smooth animation on a display that you can automatically create a back buffer at the same time that you create the application's Direct3D device. Remember that D3DPRESENT_PARAMETERS structure you learned about in Chapter 5, "Getting Direct3D Up and Running"? As a reminder, here's what it looks like:

```
typedef struct _D3DPRESENT_PARAMETERS_ {
    UINT                    BackBufferWidth;
    UINT                    BackBufferHeight;
    D3DFORMAT               BackBufferFormat;
    UINT                    BackBufferCount;

    D3DMULTISAMPLE_TYPE     MultiSampleType;

    D3DSWAPEFFECT           SwapEffect;
    HWND                    hDeviceWindow;
    BOOL                    Windowed;
    BOOL                    EnableAutoDepthStencil;
    D3DFORMAT               AutoDepthStencilFormat;
    DWORD                   Flags;

    UINT                    FullScreen_RefreshRateInHz;
    UINT                    FullScreen_PresentationInterval;
} D3DPRESENT_PARAMETERS;
```

You may remember that you had to fill in values for this structure and then had to pass the structure to the `CreateDevice()` method when you created your Direct3D device object. You can see that the first four members of the structure have to do with back buffers. I kind of skipped over these members when you first learned about the `D3DPRESENT_PARAMETERS` structure. So, here's what you use these first four structure members for:

- `BackBufferWidth`—The width of the back buffer, which is usually the same as the width of the primary surface.

- `BackBufferHeight`—The height of the back buffer, which is usually the same as the height of the primary surface.

- `BackBufferFormat`—The pixel format of the back buffer, which is usually the same as the pixel format of the primary surface.

- `BackBufferCount`—The number of back buffers to create. In this book, this value will always be 1.

Image Surfaces

Most Direct3D applications need a place to store images required by the program. For example, you might have a bitmap that shows a background scene. Before you can use such an image, it needs to be loaded into memory. Specifically, it needs to be placed into an *image surface*. An image surface is something you must create explicitly in your program. To do this, you call the Direct3D device object's `CreateOffscreenPlainSurface()` method, which the DirectX SDK declares like this:

```
HRESULT CreateOffscreenPlainSurface(
    UINT Width,
    UINT Height,
    D3DFORMAT Format,
    DWORD Pool,
    IDirect3DSurface9** ppSurface,
    HANDLE* pHandle
);
```

Here's what the method's six arguments mean:

- *Width*—The desired width of the surface.

- *Height*—The desired height of the surface.

- *Format*—The surface's pixel format, which is usually the same as the primary surface's pixel format.

- *Pool*—The surface's pool type, which, for the purposes of this book, will always be `D3DPOOL_DEFAULT`.

- *ppSurface*—The address where the method should store the pointer to the new surface object.

- *pHandle*—Currently, this argument should always be set to NULL.

So, suppose that you have a 640×480, 32-bit color bitmap that you want to load into memory. You might create a surface for the bitmap with the code shown in Listing 6.1.

LISTING 6.1   Creating an Off-Screen Surface

```
IDirect3DSurface9* g_pBitmapSurface = NULL;
hResult = g_pDirect3DDevice->CreateOffscreenPlainSurface(640, 480,
    D3DFMT_X8R8G8B8, D3DPOOL_DEFAULT, &g_pBitmapSurface, NULL);
if (FAILED(hResult))
{
    // Handle error here.
}
```

The first line here declares a pointer to the IDirect3DSurface9 interface, an object of which is created by CreateOffscreenPlainSurface(). If the call to CreateOffscreenPlainSurface() fails, it returns an error value. You can easily check whether the method call failed by using the FAILED() macro, as shown in the example.

GROUPING BITMAPS

You can create as many surfaces as your program requires, memory permitting. However, if you have a lot of small bitmaps, it's usually more efficient to group them together into a single bitmap and then transfer the rectangles you need from the bitmap.

After the surface is created, you need to load the bitmap into it. The DirectX SDK provides the D3DXLoadSurfaceFromFile() function for exactly this purpose. The SDK declares that function like this:

```
HRESULT D3DXLoadSurfaceFromFile(
  LPDIRECT3DSURFACE9 pDestSurface,
  CONST PALETTEENTRY* pDestPalette,
  CONST RECT* pDestRect,
  LPCTSTR pSrcFile,
  CONST RECT* pSrcRect,
  DWORD Filter,
  D3DCOLOR ColorKey,
  D3DXIMAGE_INFO* pSrcInfo
);
```

Here's what the arguments mean:

- *pDestSurface*—A pointer to the surface to which to load the image.

- *pDestPalette*—A pointer to the palette to which to load the image's colors. You'll use only NULL for this argument because you won't be dealing with palletized graphics.

- *pDestRect*—The rectangular area of the surface to which to load the image or NULL for the entire surface.

- *pSrcFile*—A string holding the path to the file to load.

- *pSrcRect*—The rectangular area of the image to copy or NULL for the entire image.

- *Filter*—The type of filtering to use, usually D3DX_DEFAULT. You don't have to worry about filtering because you won't be using it in this book.

- *ColorKey*—The color value that should be changed to transparent black or 0 to disable color keying.

- *pSrcInfo*—A pointer to a D3DXIMAGE_INFO structure containing information about the image. Usually, you'll use NULL here.

You don't need to deal with most of these arguments. You only need the surface pointer, the file path, and the default filter. So, to load that 640×480, 32-bit color bitmap, you'd write something like Listing 6.2.

LISTING 6.2 Loading a Surface

```
HRESULT hResult = D3DXLoadSurfaceFromFile(g_pBitmapSurface, NULL, NULL,
    "image.bmp", NULL, D3DX_DEFAULT, 0, NULL);
if (FAILED(hResult))
{
    DXTRACE_ERR("Couldn't load bitmap.", hResult);
}
```

ERROR TRACING

The DXTRACE_ERR() macro enables you to easily display all the information you need about an error. For example, if this call to D3DXLoadSurfaceFromFile() fails, the DXTRACE_ERR() macro displays the message box shown in Figure 6.1.

Unfortunately, displaying message boxes in a Direct3D program can be a little tricky. You'll probably need to Alt+Tab away from the application to see the dialog box. This is because your Direct3D application continually draws its display, erasing anything that was there before, including message boxes. As you'll soon discover, though, there's a way around this problem.

FIGURE 6.1   Displaying a Direct3D error.

Transferring Image Data Between Surfaces

You're cooking now. You've managed to create a surface for an image and then load the image from disk into the surface. All you have to do now is show the image. To accomplish this task, you must transfer the image to the back buffer and then call the Present() method.

Transferring the image to the back buffer is as easy as a call to the Direct3D device object's CopyRects() method. First, though, you need to find a way to access the back buffer. You can get the needed pointer by calling the Direct3D device object's GetBackBuffer() method, which the DirectX SDK declares like this:

```
HRESULT GetBackBuffer(
  UINT iSwapChain,
  UINT BackBuffer,
  D3DBACKBUFFER_TYPE Type,
  IDirect3DSurface9** ppBackBuffer
);
```

In this method call, the four arguments are as follows:

- *iSwapChain*—The ID of the swap chain. In this book, you'll always use 0 for this argument.

- *BackBuffer*—The index of the back buffer to get. Unless you're using multiple back buffers, this will be 0.

- *Type*—Must be D3DBACKBUFFER_TYPE_MONO.

- *ppBackBuffer*—The address where the method should store the returned pointer.

A typical call to GetBackBuffer() might look like Listing 6.3.

LISTING 6.3   Getting a Pointer to the Back-Buffer Surface

```
IDirect3DSurface9* pBackBuffer = NULL;
HRESULT hResult = g_pDirect3DDevice->GetBackBuffer(0, 0,
    D3DBACKBUFFER_TYPE_MONO, &pBackBuffer);
```

LISTING 6.3   Continued

```
if (FAILED(hResult))
{
    // Handle error here.
}
```

Now, you're ready for the StretchRect() method, which the DirectX SDK declares like this:

```
HRESULT StretchRect(
    IDirect3DSurface9 *pSourceSurface,
    CONST RECT *pSourceRect,
    IDirect3DSurface9 *pDestSurface,
    CONST RECT *pDestRect,
    D3DTEXTUREFILTERTYPE Filter
);
```

Here's what all the arguments mean:

- *pSourceSurface*—A pointer to the surface from which to copy.

- *pSourceRect*—A pointer to a RECT structure containing the coordinates of the rectangle to copy. Use NULL to copy the entire surface.

- *pDestSurface*—A pointer to the surface to which to copy the data.

- *pDestRect*—A pointer to a RECT structure containing the coordinates of the destination rectangle. Use NULL to specify the entire surface.

- *Filter*—The filter type, which can be D3DTEXF_NONE, D3DTEXF_POINT, or D3DTEXF_LINEAR.

For the time being, you won't worry about all the rectangle stuff because you'll be copying only the full image surface to the back buffer. Later in this chapter, you'll refine your use of this method. Listing 6.4 shows what the code looks like.

LISTING 6.4   Copying a Bitmap Between Surfaces

```
g_hResult = g_pDirect3DDevice->StretchRect(g_pBitmapSurface,
    NULL, pBackBuffer, NULL, D3DTEXF_NONE);
if (FAILED(hResult))
{
    // Handle error here.
}
```

At this point, all you need to do is call the Direct3D device object's Present() method to view the bitmap you loaded. Want to try it? Build the program presented in the following section to see all these things working.

Using Surfaces for Real

So far, you've learned how to create and load Direct3D surfaces, as well as how to transfer images between surfaces. These Direct3D techniques are among the most important you'll learn, because virtually every Direct3D program must perform them. In this section, you put together all these techniques by building a working Direct3D program that loads and displays a bitmap.

Creating the Basic Project

Perform the following steps to get the main Windows application up and running:

1. Start a new empty Win32 project named SurfaceApp, as shown in Figures 6.2 and 6.3.

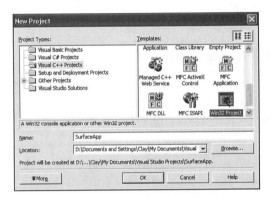

FIGURE 6.2 Creating the SurfaceApp project.

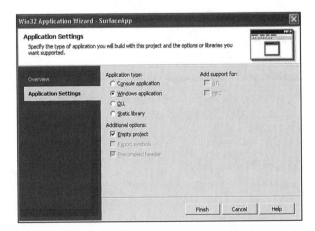

FIGURE 6.3 Choose the Empty Project setting.

2. On the Project menu, select the Add New Item command. The Add New Item dialog box appears.

3. Add a new C++ file (.cpp) named SurfaceApp.cpp, as shown in Figure 6.4.

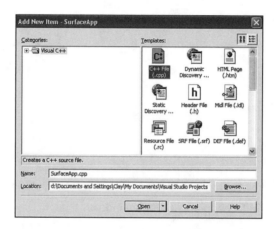

FIGURE 6.4   Creating the SurfaceApp.cpp source-code file.

4. Copy the contents of the BasicWindowsApp.cpp file (from Chapter 2) into the new SurfaceApp code window.

5. Change the name in the comment at the top of the file to SurfaceApp.cpp.

6. In the `RegisterWindowClass()` function, change `wc.lpszClassName = "WinApp"` to `wc.lpszClassName = "SurfaceApp"`.

7. In the `CreateAppWindow()` function, change `"WinApp"` to `"SurfaceApp"`, and then change `"Basic Windows Application"` to `"Direct3D Surface Application"`.

8. Compile and run the application to make sure that it works okay. You should see the window shown in Figure 6.5.

FIGURE 6.5   The SurfaceApp application's window.

Adding the DirectX References

Next, you need to tell the program where the required DirectX header files and libraries are located. To do that, follow these steps:

1. Near the top of the program, right after the line `#include <windows.h>`, add the following include directives:

```
#include <d3d9.h>
#include <d3dx9tex.h>
#include <dxerr9.h>
```

2. Right-click the project's name in the Solution Explorer, and select Properties from the menu that appears. The SurfaceApp Property Pages dialog box appears, as shown in Figure 6.6.

3. Click the C/C++ selection in the left pane, and select General from the displayed choices.

4. In the Additional Include Directories box, enter the path to the DirectX 9 SDK's include folder. If you installed the SDK using the default settings, this path should be `c:\DXSDK\include`, as shown in Figure 6.7.

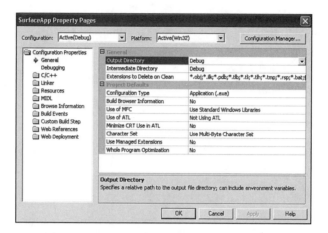

FIGURE 6.6   The project's property pages.

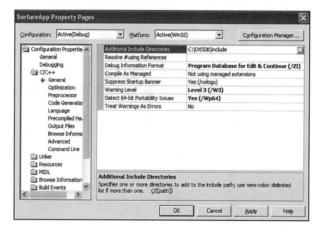

FIGURE 6.7   The general C/C++ settings.

5. Click the Linker selection in the left pane, and select General from the displayed choices.

6. In the Additional Library Directories box, enter the path to the DirectX 9 SDK's library folder. If you installed the SDK using the default settings, this path should be C:\DXSDK\lib, as shown in Figure 6.8

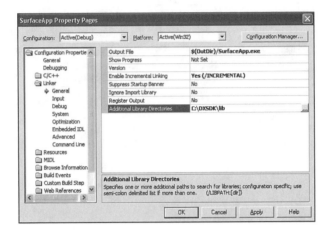

FIGURE 6.8   The general linker settings.

7. Click the Linker's Input selection in the left pane.

8. In the Additional Dependencies box in the right pane, enter **d3d9.lib**, **d3dx9.lib**, and **dxerr9.lib**, as shown in Figure 6.9, and then dismiss the dialog box.

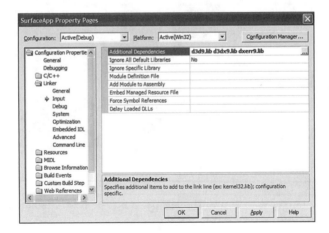

FIGURE 6.9   The linker input settings.

Adding Source Code

Now all you have to do is add the Direct3D code that'll get this project going. Follow these steps to accomplish this task:

1. Add the following lines to the program's function prototypes:

    ```
    HRESULT InitDirect3D();
    void Render();
    void CleanUpDirect3D();
    ```

2. Add the following lines to the program's global variables:

    ```
    IDirect3D9* g_pDirect3D = NULL;
    IDirect3DDevice9* g_pDirect3DDevice = NULL;
    IDirect3DSurface9* g_pBitmapSurface = NULL;
    HRESULT g_hResult = D3D_OK;
    char g_szErrorMsg[256];
    ```

3. In the `WinMain()` function, replace the line `StartMessageLoop()` with Listing 6.5.

    LISTING 6.5   New Code for `WinMain()`

    ```
    HRESULT hResult = InitDirect3D();
    if (SUCCEEDED(hResult))
        WPARAM result = StartMessageLoop();
    CleanUpDirect3D();
    CloseWindow(g_hWnd);
    if (g_hResult != D3D_OK)
        DXTRACE_ERR(g_szErrorMsg, g_hResult);
    ```

4. Add the line `Render();` after the idle time comment in the `StartMessageLoop()` function.

5. Find the `WndProc()` function and add Listing 6.6 right before the `switch` statement's ending brace.

    LISTING 6.6   New Code for `WndProc()`

    ```
    case WM_KEYDOWN:
        switch(wParam)
        {
        case VK_ESCAPE:
            PostQuitMessage(WM_QUIT);
            break;
        }
    ```

6. Add the functions shown in Listing 6.7 to the program.

LISTING 6.7   New Functions for the Application

```
/////////////////////////////////////////////////
// InitDirect3D()
/////////////////////////////////////////////////
HRESULT InitDirect3D()
{
    g_pDirect3D = Direct3DCreate9(D3D_SDK_VERSION);
    if (g_pDirect3D == NULL)
    {
        MessageBox(g_hWnd,
            "Couldn't create DirectX object.",
            "DirectX Error", MB_OK);
        return E_FAIL;
    }

    HRESULT hResult = g_pDirect3D->CheckDeviceType(D3DADAPTER_DEFAULT,
        D3DDEVTYPE_HAL, D3DFMT_X8R8G8B8, D3DFMT_X8R8G8B8, FALSE);
    if (hResult != D3D_OK)
    {
        MessageBox(g_hWnd,
            "Sorry. This program won't\nrun on your system.",
            "DirectX Error", MB_OK);
        return E_FAIL;
    }

    D3DPRESENT_PARAMETERS D3DPresentParams;
    ZeroMemory(&D3DPresentParams, sizeof(D3DPRESENT_PARAMETERS));
    D3DPresentParams.Windowed = FALSE;
    D3DPresentParams.BackBufferCount = 1;
    D3DPresentParams.BackBufferWidth = 640;
    D3DPresentParams.BackBufferHeight = 480;
    D3DPresentParams.BackBufferFormat = D3DFMT_X8R8G8B8;
    D3DPresentParams.SwapEffect = D3DSWAPEFFECT_DISCARD;
    D3DPresentParams.hDeviceWindow = g_hWnd;
    hResult = g_pDirect3D->CreateDevice(D3DADAPTER_DEFAULT,
        D3DDEVTYPE_HAL, g_hWnd, D3DCREATE_SOFTWARE_VERTEXPROCESSING,
        &D3DPresentParams, &g_pDirect3DDevice);
```

LISTING 6.7   Continued

```
    if (FAILED(hResult))
    {
        MessageBox(g_hWnd,
            "Failed to create Direct3D device.",
            "DirectX Error", MB_OK);
        return E_FAIL;
    }

    g_hResult = g_pDirect3DDevice->CreateOffscreenPlainSurface(640, 480,
        D3DFMT_X8R8G8B8, D3DPOOL_DEFAULT, &g_pBitmapSurface, NULL);
    if (FAILED(g_hResult))
    {
        strcpy(g_szErrorMsg, "Error creating bitmap surface.");
        PostQuitMessage(WM_QUIT);
    }
    g_hResult = D3DXLoadSurfaceFromFile(g_pBitmapSurface, NULL, NULL,
        "image.bmp", NULL, D3DX_DEFAULT, 0, NULL);
    if (FAILED(g_hResult))
    {
        strcpy(g_szErrorMsg, "Couldn't load bitmap file.");
        PostQuitMessage(WM_QUIT);
    }

    return D3D_OK;
}


/////////////////////////////////////////////////////
// CleanUpDirect3D()
/////////////////////////////////////////////////////
void CleanUpDirect3D()
{
    if (g_pBitmapSurface)
        g_pBitmapSurface->Release();
    if (g_pDirect3DDevice)
        g_pDirect3DDevice->Release();
    if (g_pDirect3D)
        g_pDirect3D->Release();
}
```

LISTING 6.7   Continued

```
/////////////////////////////////////////////////////
// Render()
/////////////////////////////////////////////////////
void Render()
{
    IDirect3DSurface9* pBackBuffer = NULL;
    g_hResult = g_pDirect3DDevice->GetBackBuffer(0, 0,
        D3DBACKBUFFER_TYPE_MONO, &pBackBuffer);
    if (FAILED(g_hResult))
    {
        strcpy(g_szErrorMsg, "Error getting back buffer.");
        PostQuitMessage(WM_QUIT);
    }
    g_hResult = g_pDirect3DDevice->StretchRect(g_pBitmapSurface,
        NULL, pBackBuffer, NULL, D3DTEXF_NONE);
    if (FAILED(g_hResult))
    {
        strcpy(g_szErrorMsg, "Error copying image buffer.");
        PostQuitMessage(WM_QUIT);
    }
    g_pDirect3DDevice->Present(NULL, NULL, NULL, NULL);
    if (pBackBuffer)
        pBackBuffer->Release();
}
```

7. Copy the image.bmp file from the sample code's Chapter06\SurfaceApp directory to your SurfaceApp project's working directory, or supply a 640×480, 32-bit color bitmap of your own and name it image.bmp. (See this book's introduction for instructions on obtaining the sample source code.)

You can now compile and run the application. When you do, you should see the screen shown in Figure 6.10 (unless you used your own bitmap, in which case the image will be different). Press Esc to exit the program.

FIGURE 6.10   The running SurfaceApp application.

The Program Details

This program uses two techniques for error handling: one to handle errors before the program creates the Direct3D device and one for after. In the first case, the program doesn't really need to do anything special because Direct3D initialization hasn't gotten far enough to affect the display. In that case, the type of error handling shown in Listing 6.8 works just fine.

LISTING 6.8   Error Handling

```
if (hResult != D3D_OK)
{
    MessageBox(g_hWnd,
        "Sorry. This program won't\nrun on your system.",
        "DirectX Error", MB_OK);
    return E_FAIL;
}
```

The message box appears on the screen without difficulty and by returning E_FAIL to WinMain(), the program never even enters its message loop.

Things get a lot trickier, though, after the application has created its Direct3D device object because the display mode will have been changed to that required by your program, and, if the program's main loop has started, the Render() function will be constantly redrawing the screen.

The solution I came up with is to have two global variables, one for results returned from Direct3D methods and one to hold an error string. The program defines these variables like this:

```
HRESULT g_hResult = D3D_OK;
char g_szErrorMsg[256];
```

The Direct3D code in the program sets these values if an error occurs. It also calls the Windows API function PostQuitMessage(), which terminates the message loop and sends program execution back to WinMain(), as shown in Listing 6.9.

LISTING 6.9   Setting Error Values

```
g_hResult = g_pDirect3DDevice->CreateOffscreenPlainSurface(640, 480,
    D3DFMT_X8R8G8B8, D3DPOOL_DEFAULT, &g_pBitmapSurface, NULL);
if (FAILED(g_hResult))
{
    strcpy(g_szErrorMsg, "Error creating bitmap surface.");
    PostQuitMessage(WM_QUIT);
}
```

All WinMain() has to do is check for the error value and display an error message if an error occurred. A call to the Windows API CloseWindow() ensures that the application's window stays out of the way:

```
CloseWindow(g_hWnd);
if (g_hResult != D3D_OK)
    DXTRACE_ERR(g_szErrorMsg, g_hResult);
```

One other important thing to notice about this program is the way it releases surfaces when it's finished with them. In the Render() function, the program must release the back-buffer surface:

```
pBackBuffer->Release();
```

And in the `CleanUpDirect3D()` function, the program must release the bitmap surface:

```
if (g_pBitmapSurface)
    g_pBitmapSurface->Release();
```

Digging Deeper into the `StretchRect()` Method

Many times, you'll need the `StretchRect()` method to copy only a small part of a source surface to a specific location in the destination surface. This is an easy process, requiring only that you provide the function with `RECT` structures that specify the source and destination rectangles.

For example, suppose that you have a 640×480 bitmap and you want to copy a 128×64 rectangle from the location 256,64 in the bitmap. Suppose further that you want to copy this rectangle to the location 100,200 in the source surface. Listing 6.10 shows what the code might look like.

LISTING 6.10   Copying a Portion of a Bitmap

```
RECT SrcRect;
RECT DstRect;
SrcRect.left = 256;
SrcRect.right = SrcRect.left + 128;
SrcRect.top = 64;
SrcRect.bottom = SrcRect.top + 64;
DstRect.left = 100;
DstRect.top = 200;
DstRect.right = DstRect.left + 128;
DstRect.bottom = DstRect.top + 64;

HRESULT hResult = g_pDirect3DDevice->StretchRect(g_pBitmapSurface,
    &SrcRect, pBackBuffer, &DstRect, D3DTEXF_NONE);
```

Building the CopyRectsApp Application

Now that you've seen a new way to use the `StretchRect()` method, you'll put your knowledge to the test with a new example application. The following steps, divided into several sections, guide you through this process.

Creating the Basic CopyRectsApp Project

Perform the following steps to get the main Direct3D application project started:

1. Start a new empty Win32 project named CopyRectsApp. (Don't forget to set the Additional Options to Empty Project.)

2. Add to the project a new C++ File (.cpp) named CopyRectsApp.cpp.

3. Copy the contents of the SurfaceApp.cpp file into the new CopyRectsApp.cpp code window.

4. Change the name in the comment at the top of the file to CopyRectsApp.cpp.

5. In the `RegisterWindowClass()` function, change `wc.lpszClassName = "SurfaceApp"` to `wc.lpszClassName = "CopyRectsApp"`.

6. In the `CreateAppWindow()` function, change `"SurfaceApp"` to `"CopyRectsApp"`, and then change `"Direct3D Surface Application"` to `"Copy Rectangles Application"`.

Adding the DirectX References

Next, you need to tell the program where the required DirectX header files and libraries are located. To do that, follow these steps:

1. Right-click the project's name in the Solution Explorer, and select Properties from the menu that appears. The CopyRectsApp Property Pages dialog box appears.

2. Click the C/C++ selection in the left-hand pane, and select General from the displayed choices.

3. In the Additional Include Directories box, enter the path to the DirectX 9 SDK's include folder. If you installed the SDK using the default settings, this path should be `C:\DXSDK\include`.

4. Click the Linker selection in the left-hand pane, and select General from the displayed choices.

5. In the Additional Library Directories box, enter the path to the DirectX 9 SDK's library folder. If you installed the SDK using the default settings, this path should be `C:\DXSDK\lib`.

6. Click the Linker's Input selection in the left-hand pane.

7. In the Additional Dependencies box in the right-hand pane, enter **d3d9.lib**, **d3dx9.lib**, and **dxerr9.lib**.

8. Build the application (Ctrl+Shift+B) to make sure that everything is okay. Don't try to run it yet, though, because you'll just get an error.

Adding Source Code

The final step is to add the source code that'll get everything up and running. Follow these steps to get that task done:

1. Near the top of the program, add Listing 6.11 to the function prototypes.

   LISTING 6.11   New Function Prototypes

   ```
   void PaintBackground();
   int ColumnRow2RectNum(int iCol, int iRow, int iNumCols);
   HRESULT PlaceRectangle(IDirect3DSurface9* pBackBuffer,
       IDirect3DSurface9* pSrcSurface, int iRectNumber,
       int iDstCol, int iDstRow, int iNumRectCols, int iNumDstCols,
       int iRectSize, int iXOffset, int iYOffset);
   int RectNumber2SourceX(int iRectNumber, int iNumCols, int iRectSize);
   int RectNumber2SourceY(int iRectNumber, int iNumCols, int iRectSize);
   int Column2X(int iCol, int iRectSize, int iNumCols);
   int Row2Y(int iRow, int iRectSize);
   ```

   These lines declare the new functions you'll be adding to the program.

2. Again, near the top of the program, add the following line to the global variables:

   ```
   IDirect3DSurface9* g_pBackBuffer = NULL;
   ```

3. Add Listing 6.12 right after the program's includes.

   LISTING 6.12   New Constant Definitions

   ```
   // Constants.
   const COLUMNSINRECTFILE = 3;
   const RECTSIZE = 128;
   const DSTCOLUMNCOUNT = 3;
   const DSTROWCOUNT = 2;
   const XOFFSET = 128;
   const YOFFSET = 112;
   ```

   You'll see what these constants do a little later in the chapter, when you explore the source code in detail.

4. Go to the InitDirect3D() function, and in the call to CreateOffscreenPlainSurface(), change the 640 and 480 to 384 and 256.

   The rectangle bitmap is smaller than the image the original application loaded.

5. In the call to `D3DXLoadSurfaceFromFile()`, change the image filename from Image.bmp to Image02.bmp.

6. Add Listing 6.13 to the `InitDirect3D()`, right before the final return statement.

LISTING 6.13   New Code for `InitDirect3D()`

```
g_hResult = g_pDirect3DDevice->GetBackBuffer(0, 0,
    D3DBACKBUFFER_TYPE_MONO, &g_pBackBuffer);
if (FAILED(g_hResult))
{
    strcpy(g_szErrorMsg, "Couldn't get back buffer.");
    PostQuitMessage(WM_QUIT);
}
```

These lines get a pointer to the application's back buffer, which the program needs to draw images on the back buffer.

7. Add the following lines to the beginning of the `CleanUpDirect3D()` function:

```
if (g_pBackBuffer)
    g_pBackBuffer->Release();
```

These lines release the back buffer when the program is finished with it.

8. Replace the current `Render()` function with the one shown in Listing 6.14.

LISTING 6.14   New `Render()` Function

```
/////////////////////////////////////////////////////
// Render()
/////////////////////////////////////////////////////
void Render()
{
    PaintBackground();
    g_pDirect3DDevice->Present(NULL, NULL, NULL, NULL);
}
```

This function calls the helper function that draws the map on the back buffer. The call to `Present()` makes the back buffer visible to the user.

9. Add the `PaintBackground()` function shown in Listing 6.15 to the program.

LISTING 6.15   New `PaintBackground()` Function

```
////////////////////////////////////////////////////
// PaintBackground()
////////////////////////////////////////////////////
void PaintBackground()
{
    g_pDirect3DDevice->Clear(0, NULL, D3DCLEAR_TARGET,
        D3DCOLOR_XRGB(0,0,96), 1.0f, 0);
    g_hResult = PlaceRectangle(g_pBackBuffer, g_pBitmapSurface, 0, 2, 1,
        COLUMNSINRECTFILE, DSTCOLUMNCOUNT, RECTSIZE, XOFFSET, YOFFSET);
    g_hResult = PlaceRectangle(g_pBackBuffer, g_pBitmapSurface, 1, 1, 1,
        COLUMNSINRECTFILE, DSTCOLUMNCOUNT, RECTSIZE, XOFFSET, YOFFSET);
    g_hResult = PlaceRectangle(g_pBackBuffer, g_pBitmapSurface, 2, 0, 1,
        COLUMNSINRECTFILE, DSTCOLUMNCOUNT, RECTSIZE, XOFFSET, YOFFSET);
    g_hResult = PlaceRectangle(g_pBackBuffer, g_pBitmapSurface, 3, 2, 0,
        COLUMNSINRECTFILE, DSTCOLUMNCOUNT, RECTSIZE, XOFFSET, YOFFSET);
    g_hResult = PlaceRectangle(g_pBackBuffer, g_pBitmapSurface, 4, 1, 0,
        COLUMNSINRECTFILE, DSTCOLUMNCOUNT, RECTSIZE, XOFFSET, YOFFSET);
    g_hResult = PlaceRectangle(g_pBackBuffer, g_pBitmapSurface, 5, 0, 0,
        COLUMNSINRECTFILE, DSTCOLUMNCOUNT, RECTSIZE, XOFFSET, YOFFSET);
}
```

This function draws the source rectangles onto the destination surface.

10. Add the `PlaceRectangle()` function shown in Listing 6.16 to the program.

LISTING 6.16   New `PlaceRectangle()` Function

```
////////////////////////////////////////////////////
// PlaceRectangle()
////////////////////////////////////////////////////
HRESULT PlaceRectangle(IDirect3DSurface9* pBackBuffer,
    IDirect3DSurface9* pSrcSurface, int iRectNumber,
    int iDstCol, int iDstRow, int iNumRectCols, int iNumDstCols,
    int iRectSize, int iXOffset, int iYOffset)
{
    RECT SrcRect;
    RECT DstRect;
    SrcRect.left = RectNumber2SourceX(iRectNumber,
        iNumRectCols, iRectSize);
```

LISTING 6.16   Continued

```
    SrcRect.right = SrcRect.left + iRectSize;
    SrcRect.top = RectNumber2SourceY(iRectNumber,
        iNumRectCols, iRectSize);
    SrcRect.bottom = SrcRect.top + iRectSize;
    DstRect.left = Column2X(iDstCol, iRectSize, iNumDstCols) + iXOffset;
    DstRect.top = Row2Y(iDstRow, iRectSize) + iYOffset;
    DstRect.right = DstRect.left + (SrcRect.right - SrcRect.left);
    DstRect.bottom = DstRect.top + (SrcRect.bottom - SrcRect.top);

    HRESULT hResult = g_pDirect3DDevice->StretchRect(g_pBitmapSurface,
        &SrcRect, pBackBuffer, &DstRect, D3DTEXF_NONE);
    return hResult;
}
```

This function draws a single rectangle on the back buffer.

11. Add the functions shown in Listing 6.17 to the program.

LISTING 6.17   New Functions for the Application

```
//////////////////////////////////////////////////
// ColumnRow2RectNum()
//////////////////////////////////////////////////
int ColumnRow2RectNum(int iCol, int iRow, int iNumCols)
{
    return iRow * iNumCols + iCol;
}


//////////////////////////////////////////////////
// RectNumber2SourceX()
//////////////////////////////////////////////////
int RectNumber2SourceX(int iRectNumber, int iNumCols, int iRectSize)
{
    return (iRectNumber - ((int)(iRectNumber / iNumCols))
        * iNumCols) * iRectSize;
}


//////////////////////////////////////////////////
// RectNumber2SourceY()
//////////////////////////////////////////////////
```

LISTING 6.17   Continued

```
int RectNumber2SourceY(int iRectNumber, int iNumCols, int iRectSize)
{
    return ((int)(iRectNumber / iNumCols)) * iRectSize;
}


////////////////////////////////////////////////////////
// Column2X()
////////////////////////////////////////////////////////
int Column2X(int iCol, int iRectSize, int iNumCols)
{
    return (iCol - ((int)((iCol / iNumCols)) *
        iNumCols)) * iRectSize;
}


////////////////////////////////////////////////////////
// Row2Y()
////////////////////////////////////////////////////////
int Row2Y(int iRow, int iRectSize)
{
    return iRow * iRectSize;
}
```

These functions contain the math needed to locate and display a source rectangle. After you finish building the program, you'll explore these functions in greater detail.

12. Copy the Image02.bmp file from the sample code's Chapter06\CopyRectsApp directory and place the file in your application's main directory.

   This is the bitmap file that contains the source rectangles.

Now compile and run the program. When you do, you should see the window in Figure 6.11. Notice how the program copies the lettered rectangles in reverse order, proving that the rectangles are being displayed one at a time, rather than the entire source bitmap being copied all at once.

FIGURE 6.11   The running CopyRectsApp application.

Exploring the CopyRectsApp Program

Now that you've built the program and seen it run, it's time to see how the source code works. You don't need to look at the Windows code, because you should already know how it works. So, the following sections explain how CopyRectsApp creates its display.

Loading the Images and Getting the Back Buffer

The first source code of interest is where the program loads its image file, as shown in Listing 6.18.

LISTING 6.18   Loading the Image File

```
g_hResult = g_pDirect3DDevice->CreateOffscreenPlainSurface(384, 256,
    D3DFMT_X8R8G8B8, D3DPOOL_DEFAULT, &g_pBitmapSurface, NULL);
if (FAILED(g_hResult))
{
    strcpy(g_szErrorMsg, "Error creating bitmap surface.");
    PostQuitMessage(WM_QUIT);
}
```

LISTING 6.18   Continued

```
g_hResult = D3DXLoadSurfaceFromFile(g_pBitmapSurface, NULL, NULL,
    "Image02.bmp", NULL, D3DX_DEFAULT, 0, NULL);
if (FAILED(g_hResult))
{
    strcpy(g_szErrorMsg, "Couldn't load bitmap file.");
    PostQuitMessage(WM_QUIT);
}
```

This part of the program creates a 384×256 surface and loads the Image02.bmp file, which holds the source rectangles, into it.

After getting the image loaded into memory, the program gets a pointer to the back buffer (see Listing 6.19), which it needs to draw the display.

LISTING 6.19   Getting the Back Buffer

```
g_hResult = g_pDirect3DDevice->GetBackBuffer(0, 0,
    D3DBACKBUFFER_TYPE_MONO, &g_pBackBuffer);
if (FAILED(g_hResult))
{
    strcpy(g_szErrorMsg, "Couldn't get back buffer.");
    PostQuitMessage(WM_QUIT);
}
```

Rendering During Idle Time

With all the initialization complete, the program enters its message loop. Whenever there are no messages to process (which is most of the time), the program calls the Render() function:

```
void Render()
{
    PaintBackground();
    g_pDirect3DDevice->Present(NULL, NULL, NULL, NULL);
}
```

Here, a call to the PaintBackground() function draws the display, and the call to Present() makes the back buffer visible.

Drawing the Screen

The `PaintBackground()` function is where the program draws each rectangle in its proper location. First the method call clears the back buffer:

```
g_pDirect3DDevice->Clear(0, NULL, D3DCLEAR_TARGET,
    D3DCOLOR_XRGB(0,0,96), 1.0f, 0);
```

The `PaintBackground()` function then processes each rectangle, one at a time, by calling the application-defined `PlaceRectangle()` function for each, as shown in Listing 6.20.

LISTING 6.20   Getting the Back Buffer

```
g_hResult = PlaceRectangle(g_pBackBuffer, g_pBitmapSurface, 0, 2, 1,
    COLUMNSINRECTFILE, DSTCOLUMNCOUNT, RECTSIZE, XOFFSET, YOFFSET);
g_hResult = PlaceRectangle(g_pBackBuffer, g_pBitmapSurface, 1, 1, 1,
    COLUMNSINRECTFILE, DSTCOLUMNCOUNT, RECTSIZE, XOFFSET, YOFFSET);
g_hResult = PlaceRectangle(g_pBackBuffer, g_pBitmapSurface, 2, 0, 1,
    COLUMNSINRECTFILE, DSTCOLUMNCOUNT, RECTSIZE, XOFFSET, YOFFSET);
g_hResult = PlaceRectangle(g_pBackBuffer, g_pBitmapSurface, 3, 2, 0,
    COLUMNSINRECTFILE, DSTCOLUMNCOUNT, RECTSIZE, XOFFSET, YOFFSET);
g_hResult = PlaceRectangle(g_pBackBuffer, g_pBitmapSurface, 4, 1, 0,
    COLUMNSINRECTFILE, DSTCOLUMNCOUNT, RECTSIZE, XOFFSET, YOFFSET);
g_hResult = PlaceRectangle(g_pBackBuffer, g_pBitmapSurface, 5, 0, 0,
    COLUMNSINRECTFILE, DSTCOLUMNCOUNT, RECTSIZE, XOFFSET, YOFFSET);
```

Drawing a Single Rectangle

The `PlaceRectangle()` function is where the program calls on Direct3D to draw the bitmaps. You may recall that the whole point of this program is to show that you don't need to copy an entire surface. Instead, you can copy any part of one surface and copy it to any part of another surface. To do this, you first need to declare the RECT structures that will hold the source and destination rectangles. The `PlaceRectangle()` function takes care of that detail like this:

```
RECT SrcRect;
RECT DstRect;
```

The next task is to fill the first RECT structure with the coordinates of the rectangle the program needs to copy to the back buffer. Because the rectangles are all in one bitmap, the program needs to use a little math to get the job done. To get the left edge of the required rectangle, the program calls the application-defined `RectNumber2SourceX()` function:

```
SrcRect.left = RectNumber2SourceX(iRectNumber,
    iNumRectCols, iRectSize);
```

The `RectNumber2SourceX()` function takes a rectangle number and returns the pixel location of the rectangle's left edge within the bitmap. The function requires the following arguments:

- The rectangle number

- The number of columns in the rectangle bitmap (that is, how many rectangles across in the bitmap)

- The size of a rectangle (the width, which, in this example, should be the same as the height)

You can use this function (and the others you'll soon see) with any size rectangle bitmap as long as you provide the correct values for the arguments. For example, if you had a rectangle bitmap that was 10 rectangles across with each rectangle being 64 pixels square, you'd use 10 and 64, respectively, for the function's second and third arguments.

The location of the rectangle's right edge is just the location of the left edge plus the rectangle's width:

```
SrcRect.right = SrcRect.left + iRectSize;
```

The program gets the location of the rectangle's top edge by calling the application-defined `RectNumber2SourceY()` function, which works similarly to its counterpart, `RectNumber2SourceX()`:

```
SrcRect.top = RectNumber2SourceY(iRectNumber,
    iNumRectCols, iRectSize);
```

The location of the rectangle's bottom edge is simply the location of the top edge plus the rectangle's height:

```
SrcRect.bottom = SrcRect.top + iRectSize;
```

Now that the source `RECT` structure is filled in, it's time to tackle the destination `RECT` structure. To get the pixel X coordinate for the rectangle's destination upper-left corner, the program calls the application-defined function `Column2X()`:

```
DstRect.left = Column2X(iDstCol, iRectSize, iNumDstCols) + iXOffset;
```

The `Column2X()` function takes the destination column in which the rectangle needs to be drawn and returns the pixel X coordinate for that column. It requires the following arguments:

- The destination column

- The rectangle's size (that is, the rectangle's width, which, in this example, should be the same as its height)
- The number of columns in the destination surface, by which I mean the number of rectangles across in the final image that will be displayed on the screen

Notice that the program sums the value returned by Column2X() with iXOffset. The iXOffset value determines how far to the right the image's left edge gets drawn. If you left off iXOffset, the map would be drawn on the screen's left edge.

To get the Y coordinate for the rectangle's destination upper-left corner, the program calls the application-defined function Column2Y():

```
DstRect.top = Row2Y(iDstRow, iRectSize) + iYOffset;
```

The Row2Y() function takes the destination row in which the rectangle needs to be drawn and returns the pixel Y coordinate for the row. It requires the following arguments:

- The destination row
- The rectangle's size

The destination RECT structure's remaining members are easily calculated using existing values:

```
DstRect.right = DstRect.left + (SrcRect.right - SrcRect.left);
DstRect.bottom = DstRect.top + (SrcRect.bottom - SrcRect.top);
```

Finally, a call to the Direct3D device object's StretchRect() method draws the rectangle on the back buffer:

```
HRESULT hResult = g_pDirect3DDevice->StretchRect(g_pBitmapSurface,
    &SrcRect, pBackBuffer, &DstRect, D3DTEXF_NONE);
```

Performing Computer Animation with Surfaces

The world is filled with all kinds of animation, including everything from a child's simple flip book to cartoons and feature films. Every form of animation has one thing in common: The appearance of movement comes from rapidly projecting a series of images one after the other.

The simplest form of animation is that flip book I mentioned, which is a small pad of paper with an image on each page. To create the animation effect, you look at the pad while you flip the pages. Because each image is slightly different from the one before, your eyes and brain interpret the changing images as smooth motion.

Feature films work exactly the same way, except that each image in the animation sequence is projected on a screen rather than drawn in a book. Still, if you examine a reel of movie film, you'll see a series of images, each slightly different from the one before.

Computer animation is different only in the details. When you see some sort of movielike effect on your computer's screen, it's nothing more than a series of images being drawn one after the other on your computer's screen. How the computer draws those images are the details you learn about in this section.

As an example, look at Figure 6.12, which shows four images that make up part of an animation sequence. In this sequence, an arrow rotates from an upward position to a downward position. If you were rapidly to display these images one after another, the arrow would appear to rotate.

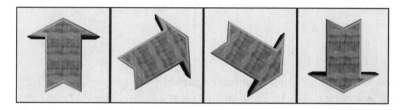

FIGURE 6.12   Four images of an animation sequence.

Understanding Computer Animation

You already know just about everything you need to know to use Direct3D to display an animation sequence. In short, here are the steps you need to complete:

1. Load the animation images into memory.

2. Draw an animation image onto the back buffer.

3. Display the back buffer.

4. Go back to step 2.

Loading the Animation Frames

Up to this point, I've been calling the pictures that make up an animation sequence "animation images." But the real name for such an image is a *frame*. An animation sequence is made up of a series of frames, each of which is displayed one after the other.

The animation sequence with the arrow, then, has four frames. Each frame needs to be loaded into memory. The simplest way to do this is to create a surface for each frame and then load each image into its respective surface. Listing 6.21 shows how you might create the surfaces.

LISTING 6.21   Creating Surfaces for an Animation Sequence

```
IDirect3DSurface9* g_pBitmapSurfaces[4];
for (int x=0; x<4; ++x)
{
    g_pBitmapSurfaces[x] = NULL;
    g_hResult = g_pDirect3DDevice->CreateOffscreenPlainSurface(400, 400,
        D3DFMT_X8R8G8B8, D3DPOOL_DEFAULT, &g_pBitmapSurfaces[x], NULL);
    if (FAILED(g_hResult))
    {
        strcpy(g_szErrorMsg, "Error creating bitmap surface.");
        PostQuitMessage(WM_QUIT);
        break;
    }
}
```

Here, you've created an array of pointers, named g_pBitmapSurfaces[4]. This array holds the pointers to each of the frame surfaces, four in all. In the for loop, the program creates each surface and stores its pointer in the array.

Now you can load the surfaces with their images (see Listing 6.22), which are the four animation frames, the filenames of which are Frame01.bmp through Frame04.bmp.

LISTING 6.22   Loading Surfaces for an Animation Sequence

```
for (int x=0; x<4; ++x)
{
    char filename[15];
    wsprintf(filename, "%s%d%s", "Frame0", x+1, ".bmp");
    g_hResult = D3DXLoadSurfaceFromFile(g_pBitmapSurfaces[x], NULL, NULL,
        filename, NULL, D3DX_DEFAULT, 0, NULL);
    if (FAILED(g_hResult))
    {
        strcpy(g_szErrorMsg, "Couldn't load bitmap file.");
        PostQuitMessage(WM_QUIT);
        break;
    }
}
```

STORING ANIMATION IMAGES

In most professional applications, the animation frames wouldn't be in separate files and loaded into separate surfaces. Instead, the entire animation sequence would be stored in a single bitmap, which itself would be loaded into a single surface. The application would then use a little math to determine which parts of the bitmap to display for each frame of the animation.

Drawing Frames on the Back Buffer

At this point, you've got your animation frames loaded into memory and ready to go. Now you need to display each frame, one after the other, on the screen. All this happens in your application's rendering function, where you must perform the following tasks:

1. Check whether it's time to display the next frame.

2. Update the frame counter.

3. Get access to the back buffer.

4. Copy the appropriate animation frame to the back buffer.

Checking the Timer

The speed at which the animation runs depends on how fast you display the frames. The faster the *frame rate*, the faster the action looks on the screen. To control the speed, then, your program needs some sort of timer.

There are several ways to implement a timer, some more crude than others. To keep things simple for this example, we'll use nothing more than a `for` loop as a timer. For example, Listing 6.23 shows what such a timer function might look like.

LISTING 6.23   A Timer Function

```
BOOL IsTimeForNextFrame()
{
    static DWORD count = 0;
    count = count + 1;
    if (count > 100000)
    {
        count = 0;
        return TRUE;
    }
    else
        return FALSE;
}
```

This function returns TRUE if it's time to display the next frame, and FALSE otherwise. In this case, the timer variable count must reach 100,000 between each frame of the animation.

Frankly, this is a horrible way to time animation sequences, because the speed of the animation depends on the speed of the computer on which it's running. But for right now, we're keeping things as simple as possible.

Updating the Frame Counter

Your application must display the animation frames in order and then loop back to the start of the sequence after displaying the last frame. To know which frame is next to display, you need to keep track of a frame counter. Here's how to do that:

```
static frameNum = 0;
frameNum = frameNum + 1;
if (frameNum == 4)
    frameNum = 0;
```

Here, the variable frameNum counts from 0 to 3 and then starts over again. The variable gets incremented once for each frame of the animation, so you can use this counter to determine which frame to display.

Getting Access to the Back Buffer

When it's time to display the next frame of the animation, you need to draw the correct image on the back buffer. Obviously, then, you need to have access to the back buffer. You already know how to get this access, by calling the GetBackBuffer() method, as shown in Listing 6.24.

LISTING 6.24   Getting a Pointer to the Back Buffer

```
IDirect3DSurface9* pBackBuffer = NULL;
g_hResult = g_pDirect3DDevice->GetBackBuffer(0, 0,
    D3DBACKBUFFER_TYPE_MONO, &pBackBuffer);
if (FAILED(g_hResult))
{
    strcpy(g_szErrorMsg, "Error getting back buffer.");
    PostQuitMessage(WM_QUIT);
    return;
}
```

Copying a Frame to the Back Buffer

Copying an animation frame to the back buffer is no different from copying any other image from one surface to another. You already know how to do this by using the StretchRect() method of the Direct3D device object. The call to StretchRect() looks something like Listing 6.25.

LISTING 6.25   Copying a Frame of the Animation Sequence

```
RECT SrcRect;
RECT DstRect;
SrcRect.left = 0;
SrcRect.right = 399;
SrcRect.top = 0;
SrcRect.bottom = 399;
DstRect.left = 200;
DstRect.top = 100;
DstRect.right = 599;
DstRect.bottom = 499;

HRESULT hResult = g_pDirect3DDevice->StretchRect(g_pBitmapSurfaces[frameNum],
    &SrcRect, pBackBuffer, &DstRect, D3DTEXF_NONE);
```

Here, the code first defines a RECT structure to hold the size and position of the source rectangle, which is the area of the image you want to copy to the back buffer. In this program, you want to copy the entire 400×400 image, so the left, right, top, and bottom members of the RECT structure are set as shown.

Next, the code defines a RECT structure to hold the destination coordinates to which the source rectangle should be copied. With the source and destination structures initialized, a quick call to StretchRect(), giving the structures as the appropriate arguments, copies the animation frame to the back buffer.

Displaying the Back Buffer

At this point, you've managed to get the image data for the next animation frame copied to the back buffer. However, as you no doubt recall, the back buffer is hidden away in memory, out of sight of the user. You may also recall that you bring the back buffer into view by calling the Direct3D device object's Present() method:

```
g_pDirect3DDevice->Present(NULL, NULL, NULL, NULL);
```

Building the AnimationApp Application

You're now ready to build a complete program that demonstrates the concepts presented in this chapter. Perform the steps outlined in the following sections to build the AnimationApp program.

Creating the Basic AnimationApp Project

Perform the following steps to start the main Direct3D application project:

1. Start a new empty Win32 project named AnimationApp. (Don't forget to set the Application Settings to Empty Project.)

2. On the Project menu, select the Add New Item command. The Add New Item dialog box appears.

3. Add a new C++ File (.cpp) named AnimationApp.cpp.

4. Copy the contents of the SurfaceApp.cpp file into the new AnimationApp code window.

5. Change the name in the comment at the top of the file to AnimationApp.cpp.

6. In the `RegisterWindowClass()` function, change `wc.lpszClassName = "SurfaceApp"` to `wc.lpszClassName = "AnimationApp"`.

7. In the `CreateAppWindow()` function, change `"SurfaceApp"` to `"AnimationApp"`, and then change `"Direct3D Surface Application"` to `"Direct3D Animation Application"`.

Adding the DirectX References

Next, you need to tell the program where the required DirectX header files and libraries are located. To do that, follow these steps:

1. In the project's C/C++ property settings, enter the path to the DirectX 9 SDK's include folder. If you installed the SDK using the default settings, this path should be `C:\DXSDK\include`.

2. In the project's Linker property settings, enter the path to the DirectX 9 SDK's library folder. If you installed the SDK using the default settings, this path should be `C:\DXSDK\lib`.

3. Also in the project's Linker property settings, in the Additional Dependencies box, enter **d3d9.lib**, **d3dx9.lib**, and **dxerr9.lib**.

4. Copy the Image.bmp file into your AnimationApp main directory. You can find this file in the sample source code's Chapter06\SurfaceApp directory.

5. Compile and run the application to make sure that it works. When the main screen appears, press Escape to exit the application.

6. You can now delete the Image.bmp file you copied to the AnimationApp directory. You will no longer need it.

Adding Source Code

Now it's time to add the source code. Follow these steps to complete this task:

1. Near the top of the program, add the following line to the function prototypes:

```
BOOL IsTimeForNextFrame();
```

   This declares a new function that controls the speed of the animation.

2. Again near the top of the program, in the global variables, replace the line

```
IDirect3DSurface9* g_pBitmapSurface = NULL;
```

   with

```
IDirect3DSurface9* g_pBitmapSurfaces[8];
```

   This array holds pointers to the bitmaps that make up the animation sequence.

3. Right at the beginning of the WinMain() function, add the following lines:

```
for (int x=0; x<8; ++x)
    g_pBitmapSurfaces[x] = NULL;
```

   These lines ensure that the members of the pointer array start off all NULL.

4. In the InitDirect3D() function, change the lines

```
D3DPresentParams.BackBufferWidth = 640;
D3DPresentParams.BackBufferHeight = 480;
```

   to

```
D3DPresentParams.BackBufferWidth = 800;
D3DPresentParams.BackBufferHeight = 600;
```

   These lines set up the screen to the 800×600 resolution.

5. In the same function, replace the lines

```
g_hResult = g_pDirect3DDevice->CreateOffscreenPlainSurface(640, 480,
    D3DFMT_X8R8G8B8, D3DPOOL_DEFAULT, &g_pBitmapSurface, NULL);
if (FAILED(g_hResult))
{
    strcpy(g_szErrorMsg, "Error creating bitmap surface.");
    PostQuitMessage(WM_QUIT);
}
```

```
g_hResult = D3DXLoadSurfaceFromFile(g_pBitmapSurface, NULL, NULL,
    "image.bmp", NULL, D3DX_DEFAULT, 0, NULL);
if (FAILED(g_hResult))
{
    strcpy(g_szErrorMsg, "Couldn't load bitmap file.");
    PostQuitMessage(WM_QUIT);
}
```

with Listing 6.26.

LISTING 6.26   New Lines for `InitDirect3D()`

```
for (int x=0; x<8; ++x)
{
    g_hResult = g_pDirect3DDevice->CreateOffscreenPlainSurface(400, 400,
        D3DFMT_X8R8G8B8, D3DPOOL_DEFAULT, &g_pBitmapSurfaces[x], NULL);
    if (FAILED(g_hResult))
    {
        strcpy(g_szErrorMsg, "Error creating bitmap surface.");
        PostQuitMessage(WM_QUIT);
        break;
    }
    char filename[15];
    wsprintf(filename, "%s%d%s", "Frame0", x+1, ".bmp");
    g_hResult = D3DXLoadSurfaceFromFile(g_pBitmapSurfaces[x], NULL, NULL,
        filename, NULL, D3DX_DEFAULT, 0, NULL);
    if (FAILED(g_hResult))
    {
        strcpy(g_szErrorMsg, "Couldn't load bitmap file.");
        PostQuitMessage(WM_QUIT);
        break;
    }
}
```

These lines load eight bitmaps into the image surfaces, storing pointers to the surfaces in the pointer array.

6. In the `CleanUpDirect3D()` function, replace the lines

```
if (g_pBitmapSurface)
    g_pBitmapSurface->Release();
```

with the lines

```
for (int x=0; x<8; ++x)
{
    if (g_pBitmapSurfaces[x])
        g_pBitmapSurfaces[x]->Release();
}
```

These lines release all the surfaces whose pointers are stored in the pointer array.

7. Replace the current Render() function with the one shown in Listing 6.27.

LISTING 6.27 The New Render() Function

```
////////////////////////////////////////////////////////
// Render()
////////////////////////////////////////////////////////
void Render()
{
    if (IsTimeForNextFrame())
    {
        static frameNum = 0;
        frameNum = frameNum + 1;
        if (frameNum == 8)
            frameNum = 0;

        IDirect3DSurface9* pBackBuffer = NULL;
        g_hResult = g_pDirect3DDevice->GetBackBuffer(0, 0,
            D3DBACKBUFFER_TYPE_MONO, &pBackBuffer);
        if (FAILED(g_hResult))
        {
            strcpy(g_szErrorMsg, "Error getting back buffer.");
            PostQuitMessage(WM_QUIT);
            return;
        }

        g_pDirect3DDevice->Clear(0, NULL, D3DCLEAR_TARGET,
            D3DCOLOR_XRGB(0,0,0), 1.0f, 0);

        RECT SrcRect;
        RECT DstRect;
        SrcRect.left = 0;
```

LISTING 6.27   Continued

```
        SrcRect.right = 399;
        SrcRect.top = 0;
        SrcRect.bottom = 399;
        DstRect.left = 200;
        DstRect.top = 100;
        DstRect.right = 599;
        DstRect.bottom = 499;

        HRESULT hResult = g_pDirect3DDevice->
            StretchRect(g_pBitmapSurfaces[frameNum],
                &SrcRect, pBackBuffer, &DstRect, D3DTEXF_NONE);

        g_pDirect3DDevice->Present(NULL, NULL, NULL, NULL);
        if (pBackBuffer)
            pBackBuffer->Release();
    }
}
```

This performs the animation by displaying the different bitmaps one after the other.

8. Add the `IsTimeForNextFrame()` function shown in Listing 6.28 to the program.

LISTING 6.28   The New `IsTimeForNextFrame()` Function

```
////////////////////////////////////////////////////
// IsTimeForNextFrame()
////////////////////////////////////////////////////
BOOL IsTimeForNextFrame()
{
    static DWORD count = 0;
    count = count + 1;
    if (count > 100000)
    {
        count = 0;
        return TRUE;
    }
    else
        return FALSE;
}
```

This function acts as a timer for the animation sequence.

9. Copy the image files Frame01.bmp through Frame08.bmp from the sample source code's Chapter06\AnimationApp directory to your own AnimationApp directory.

You can now compile and run the program. When you do, you see the screen shown in Figure 6.13, except on your screen, the star shape should be spinning. Exactly how fast it's spinning will depend on the speed of your computer.

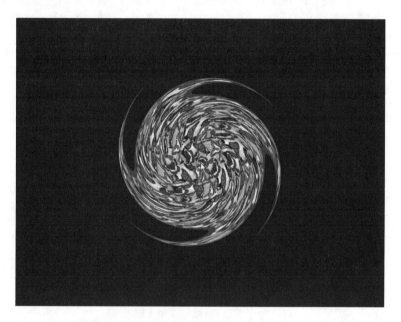

FIGURE 6.13   The AnimationApp program.

SHOP TALK

HANDLING LOST DEVICES AND SURFACES

I'm willing to bet that one thing about the Direct3D programs you've developed so far has been driving you crazy. Have you noticed how, if you Alt+Tab back to the desktop from one of these Direct3D applications, you can never get the program up and running again—at least, not without shutting it down and restarting?

The truth is that, in this situation, the program really is still running. You can even see its window. The problem is that, after returning to the desktop, the program's window has lost all its graphics and now looks just like any other empty Windows window. This happens because, when you Alt+Tab away from a Direct3D application and back to the desktop, the Windows desktop takes over the video card, throwing away the device object and all the surfaces you worked so hard to get up and running.

This may seem like a huge problem, but it is actually an easy one to fix. First, when your Direct3D program loses its surfaces, even though the program can no longer draw to the screen, all drawing functions continue to work in the sense that they won't crash your program. They simply return the error code `D3DERR_DEVICELOST`. Second, a Direct3D device object provides a method named `TestCooperativeLevel()` that can tell your program at any time whether it still has access to its device and surfaces.

But how do you know when the player wants to return to the program? When the Direct3D application's window regains the focus, `TestCooperativeLevel()` stops returning `D3DERR_DEVICELOST` and returns `D3DERR_DEVICENOTRESET` instead. This return code tells the program that it can take the device back and start drawing graphics again. To get everything going again, you pretty much have to reinitialize Direct3D just as you did when the program first ran, re-creating the device and the surfaces.

So that you can see all this lost-device stuff in action, you'll now add this functionality to the AnimationApp project. Just perform the following steps to get the job done:

1. Load the AnimationApp project into Visual Studio.

2. Add the following line to the function prototypes near the top of the program:

   ```
   BOOL CheckDevice();
   ```

3. Add the function shown in Listing 6.29 to the program.

LISTING 6.29   The New `CheckDevice()` Function

```
/////////////////////////////////////////////////////
// CheckDevice()
/////////////////////////////////////////////////////
BOOL CheckDevice()
{
    HRESULT hResult = g_pDirect3DDevice->TestCooperativeLevel();
    if (hResult == D3DERR_DEVICELOST)
        return FALSE;
    else if (hResult == D3DERR_DEVICENOTRESET)
    {
        CleanUpDirect3D();
        InitDirect3D();
        return TRUE;
    }
    else
        return TRUE;
}
```

4. Find the Render() function and add the following lines right after the first if statement's opening brace:

```
BOOL bDeviceOK = CheckDevice();
if (!bDeviceOK) return;
```

Now you can compile and run the project. When the program's display comes up on the screen, Alt+Tab back to the desktop. Then, select the AnimationApp's window, and everything springs back to life.

In the CheckDevice() function, you can see that the program has three possible paths of execution. The first is if TestCooperativeLevel() returns D3DERR_DEVICELOST, in which case CheckDevice() return FALSE, which causes the program to skip its rendering.

The second path of execution occurs when TestCooperativeLevel() returns D3DERR_DEVICENOTRESET. In this case, ProcessGame() calls CleanUpDirect3D() to delete all existing Direct3D objects and then calls InitDirect3D() to get Direct3D up and running again.

Finally, the third possibility is when TestCooperativeLevel() doesn't return D3DERR_DEVICELOST or D3DERR_DEVICENOTRESET, returning D3D_OK instead. In this case, the program simply goes about its normal business with no interruption, redrawing the screen.

In Brief

- A surface is an area of memory in which you can store graphical information.

- The primary surface, sometimes called the front buffer, is what you're looking at on the screen when you run a Direct3D program.

- A back-buffer surface is an area of memory where you can draw a display out of view of the user.

- To create a surface in which to store images, you call the Direct3D device object's CreateOffscreenPlainSurface() method.

- To load a bitmap into a surface, the DirectX SDK provides the D3DXLoadSurfaceFromFile() function.

- To display an image, you must transfer it to the back buffer with the StretchRect() method and then call the Present() method.

- The Direct3D device object's GetBackBuffer() method returns a pointer to the back-buffer surface.

- The TestCooperativeLevel() method tells your program at any time whether the program still has access to its device and surfaces.

Drawing Graphics Primitives

As all graphics programmers know, one of the first things to learn when tackling a new graphics library is how to draw graphics primitives, such as lines and rectangles. To perform these elementary drawing tasks with Direct3D, you need to know how Direct3D manages *points* and *vertices*. In this chapter, you see how Direct3D uses points and vertices to draw graphics primitives. Specifically, you learn:

- How to express points as coordinates
- How to define shapes with vertices
- How to create and use a vertex buffer
- How to use Direct3D to draw primary shapes

Defining a Point

Everything starts with a point. This is true whether you're talking about a single dot on the screen or about a fully rendered 3D town in the latest edition of Might & Magic. A point is the basic building block for every shape and is the form of data that determines where that shape is located in a 3D world. (Refer to Chapters 3 and 4 for a non-Direct3D discussion of points.)

To see how points work, imagine those graphs that you used to deal with in high school math. Such a graph might have looked like Figure 7.1.

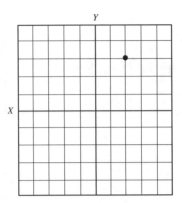

FIGURE 7.1   A simple graph.

In this graph, the single point shown has a coordinate of 2,3, which means the point is located two units on the X axis and three units on the Y axis. You start counting from the center of the graph where the two axes cross. This location has a coordinate of 0,0 and is called the *origin*.

To refresh your memory, points to the right of the origin on the X axis are positive and points to the left of the origin on the X axis are negative. Similarly, points above the origin on the Y axis are positive, and points below the origin on the Y axis are negative. With this in mind, you can see that the point in Figure 7.2 is located at -3,-2.

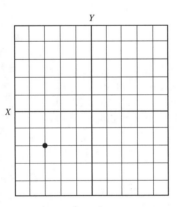

FIGURE 7.2   A point with negative coordinates.

No doubt this is the way you remember graphing points. With 3D graphics, though, things are a little different. First, you'll generally be interested only in positive coordinates, which limits you to the upper-right quadrant of the graph. Also, a 3D coordinate system requires three values, not just two. This third value is called Z, and represents depth, by which I mean how far "behind" the screen a point appears to be. You could say that the point in Figure 7.1 is located at 2,3,0.

Defining a Shape with Vertices

A point defines a single location somewhere in 3D space. You'd have a real job on your hand, however, if you had to use nothing but points to draw your displays. This is why 3D programmers use something called a *vertex*. A vertex is a point that defines where two edges of a shape come together. For example, a triangle has three vertices, as shown in Figure 7.3. (Refer to Chapters 3 and 4 for a non-Direct3D discussion of vertices.)

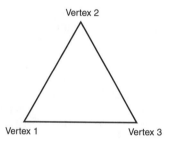

Vertex 2

Vertex 1   Vertex 3

FIGURE 7.3   The vertices of a triangle.

Because a vertex is a special type of point, it's defined just like any other point, with X,Y,Z coordinates. So, if you wanted to draw a triangle on the screen, you might use coordinates such as (1,1,0), (3,4,0), and (4,1,0), which would give you the triangle shown in Figure 7.4.

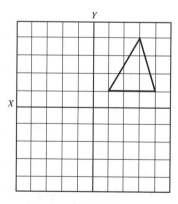

FIGURE 7.4   A triangle with vertices at (1,1,0), (3,4,0), and (4,1,0).

Using Vertex Buffers

All this talk of points and vertices brings us to this chapter's first Direct3D topic: vertex buffers. A *vertex buffer* is a block of memory that contains the vertices needed to draw a shape. For example, if you wanted to draw that triangle we've been talking about, you'd need to create a vertex buffer that holds the triangle's three vertices. Before creating the buffer, though, you need to tell Direct3D what your vertices are like.

Defining a Custom Vertex Type

Originally, I said that a vertex was a kind of point, a set of which defines a shape. Up until now, you've been thinking of a vertex as having the same types of values as a point, by which I mean X,Y,Z coordinates. With Direct3D, however, a vertex can be much more, can include all kinds of information about a point, including its color, texture coordinates, blending information, and more.

FLEXIBLE VERTICES

The various values you can use with a vertex are managed in Direct3D using what's called *flexible vertex format* (FVF) flags. FVF flags are constants defined by Direct3D that specify the types of information contained in a vertex. When your program provides one or more of these flags, Direct3D can correctly interpret your vertex data and display it on the screen.

As an example, consider the simplest possible vertex, which is the 3D coordinates of a point. Direct3D defines the D3DFVF_XYZ flag to describe this type of vertex. You can represent such a vertex with this simple structure:

```
struct CUSTOMVERTEX
{
    FLOAT x, y, z;
};
```

This structure defines a data type for your vertices. To actually create a set of vertices that describe a shape, you might write something like this:

```
CUSTOMVERTEX triangleVertices[] =
{
    {320.0f,  120.0f, 0.0f,},
    {420.0f, 320.0f, 0.0f,},
    {220.0f, 320.0f, 0.0f,},
};
```

Here, you create an array of CUSTOMVERTEX structures. The three vertices defined here represent a triangle. However, the triangle's coordinates are such that the shape will appear in the center of a 640×480 screen. In other words, the vertices here represent screen coordinates rather than the type of coordinates you used with the graph examples. In the case of the screen, the origin is the upper-left corner, with positive X values going to the right, and positive Y values going down, as shown in Figure 7.5.

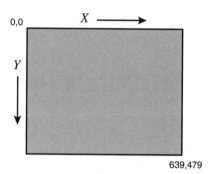

FIGURE 7.5   Transformed screen coordinates.

These types of screen values are called *transformed coordinates*, which are simply values that tell Direct3D the exact screen coordinates at which you want a shape drawn. Unfortunately, the simplest vertex type of D3DFVF_XYZ describes untransformed coordinates, so we need to specify a different type. In this case, a suitable vertex type would be D3DFVF_XYZRHW, which tells Direct3D that every vertex is represented by X,Y,Z values, as well as an RHW value, a type of value that you don't need to deal with yet. Just think of this value as being 1.0 for now. (By the way, RHW stands for "reciprocal of homogeneous W.")

```
struct CUSTOMVERTEX
{
    FLOAT x, y, z, rhw;
};
```

And here's how you'd describe the vertices for the triangle:

```
CUSTOMVERTEX triangleVertices[] =
{
    {320.0f,  120.0f, 0.0f, 1.0f},
    {420.0f, 320.0f, 0.0f, 1.0f},
    {220.0f, 320.0f, 0.0f, 1.0f},
};
```

You're getting close to defining the complete vertex type you need. You're missing only one thing: color. If Direct3D were to draw the shape you've defined here, you'd get a plain, white triangle. To use color, you need to add a color value to your vertex data type, like this:

```
struct CUSTOMVERTEX
{
    FLOAT x, y, z, rhw;
    DWORD color;
};
```

Now, you need to add a color value to your array of vertices. An easy way to do this is to use Direct3D's D3DCOLOR_XRGB() macro, which enables you to specify a color using its RGB values. Here's the end result:

```
CUSTOMVERTEX triangleVertices[] =
{
    {320.0f,  120.0f, 0.0f, 1.0f, D3DCOLOR_XRGB(255,0,0),},
    {420.0f, 320.0f, 0.0f, 1.0f, D3DCOLOR_XRGB(0,255,0),},
    {220.0f, 320.0f, 0.0f, 1.0f, D3DCOLOR_XRGB(0,0,255),},
};
```

Each vertex of this triangle has been assigned a color, either red, green, or blue. To describe this type of vertex to Direct3D, you need two FVF flags ORed together, like this:

```
D3DFVF_XYZRHW | D3DFVF_DIFFUSE
```

The D3DFVF_DIFFUSE flag tells Direct3D that you're using color values along with the X, Y, Z, and RHW values.

Creating the Vertex Buffer

You now have your custom vertex data type defined, and you have created an array of vertices that represent a triangle with red, green, and blue points. The next step is to create a vertex buffer into which to store the values of the vertices. Your Direct3D device object defines the CreateVertexBuffer() method for exactly this task. Here's how Direct3D declares this method:

```
HRESULT CreateVertexBuffer(
    UINT Length,
    DWORD Usage,
    DWORD FVF,
    D3DPOOL Pool,
    IDirect3DVertexBuffer9** ppVertexBuffer
    HANDLE* pHandle
);
```

Here's what the method's six arguments mean:

- *Length*—The desired size of the buffer.

- *Usage*—Flags that specify how the buffer is to be used. In this book, you'll always use 0.

- *FVF*—The vertex format. This is where you use the values such as D3DFVF_XYZRHW and D3DFVF_DIFFUSE.

- *Pool*—A value that specifies memory usage for the buffer. In this book, you'll always use D3DPOOL_DEFAULT.

- *ppVertexBuffer*—The address where the method should store the pointer to the new vertex-buffer object.

- *pHandle*—Currently, this argument should always be NULL.

In your programs, an actual call to CreateVertexBuffer() will look something like Listing 7.1.

LISTING 7.1   Creating a Vertex Buffer

```
IDirect3DVertexBuffer9* pVertexBuf = NULL;
HRESULT hResult = g_pDirect3DDevice->CreateVertexBuffer(
    3*sizeof(CUSTOMVERTEX), 0, D3DFVF_XYZRHW | D3DFVF_DIFFUSE,
    D3DPOOL_DEFAULT, &pVertexBuf, NULL);
if(FAILED(hResult))
{
    DXTRACE_ERR("Error creating vertex buffer", hResult);
    return;
}
```

As you can see, the type of pointer returned by CreateVertexBuffer() is IDirect3DVertexBuffer9. This is the interface that represents vertex-buffer objects.

Loading the Vertex Buffer

The last step in creating your vertex buffer is loading the vertex data into the buffer. Before you can do that, though, you must lock the buffer so that Direct3D knows to leave it alone while you're working with it. You lock the buffer by calling the vertex-buffer object's Lock() method, which Direct3D declares like this:

```
HRESULT Lock(
  UINT OffsetToLock,
  UINT SizeToLock,
```

```
    BYTE** ppbData,
    DWORD Flags
);
```

Here's what the method's four arguments mean:

- *OffsetToLock*—Index of the first byte to lock. In this book, you'll always use 0.

- *SizeToLock*—The number of bytes to lock. In this book, you'll always use 0, which tells Direct3D to lock the entire buffer, no matter its size.

- *ppbData*—The address where the method should store the pointer to the vertex buffer's data.

- *Flags*—A set of flags that specify how to lock the buffer. In this book, you'll always use 0.

Putting this all together, your own call to Lock() might look like Listing 7.2.

LISTING 7.2   Locking a Vertex Buffer

```
VOID* pVertices;
hResult = pVertexBuf->Lock(0, 0, (BYTE**)&pVertices, 0);
if(FAILED(hResult))
{
    DXTRACE_ERR("Error locking vertex buffer", hResult);
    return;
}
```

With the vertex buffer locked, a quick call to memcpy() is all you need to transfer the data from your program into the buffer:

```
memcpy(pVertices, triangleVertices, sizeof(triangleVertices));
```

Last but not least, don't forget to unlock the vertex buffer by calling the buffer object's Unlock() method:

```
pVertexBuf->Unlock();
```

Rendering Graphics Primitives

To draw your rectangle, you need to know about Direct3D's *graphics primitives*. Direct3D can draw six types of graphics primitives in sets called lists or strips:

- Point lists—A list of individual points

- Line lists—A list of individual lines

- Line strips—A list of connected lines

- Triangle lists—A list of individual triangles

- Triangle strips—A list of connected triangles

- Triangle fans—A list of triangles connected into a fan shape

ELEMENTARY SHAPES, DEAR WATSON

In case you've never run into them before, graphics primitives are elementary shapes, such as points, lines, or triangles. 3D displays comprise many thousands of graphics primitives that combine to create the illusion of one or more 3D objects.

Using just these six graphics primitives, a Direct3D application can render any type of display it needs, from a simple cube to a detailed underground dungeon filled with horrific creatures.

Rendering a Basic Triangle

Direct3D can't just throw a shape onto the screen because it has a lot of work to do as it calculates how a 3D object will look. To perform these calculations, Direct3D needs some information from your application. In the case of drawing a graphics primitive, Direct3D must know at least the following:

- Where the vertices are stored

- How to shade the shape

- What type of shape to draw

To tell Direct3D where the vertices are stored, your program calls the Direct3D device object's SetStreamSource() method, which Direct3D declares like this:

```
HRESULT SetStreamSource(
  UINT StreamNumber,
  IDirect3DVertexBuffer9* pStreamData,
  UINT OffsetInBytes,
  UINT Stride
);
```

Here's what the method's four arguments mean:

- *StreamNumber*—The datastream to use. You'll usually provide 0 for this argument.

- *pStreamData*—A pointer to the vertex-buffer object that contains the vertices to render.

- *OffsetInBytes*—The number of bytes from the start of the buffer to the vertex data.

- *Stride*—The size of each set of vertex data.

So, in your program, the call to SetStreamSource() might look like this:

```
g_pDirect3DDevice->SetStreamSource(0, pVertexBuf, 0,
    sizeof(CUSTOMVERTEX));
```

Next, you need to tell Direct3D how to apply shading to the graphics primitive. In this simple case, you can call the Direct3D device object's SetFVF() method, which Direct3D declares like this:

```
HRESULT SetFVF(
    DWORD FVF
);
```

The FVF argument is the value that holds the vertex-format flags. If you include color values in the vertex data, Direct3D can use those colors to provide a simple type of lighting. The actual call in your program, then, looks something like this:

```
g_pDirect3DDevice->SetFVF(D3DFVF_XYZRHW | D3DFVF_DIFFUSE);
```

Finally, you're ready to draw the shape. To do this, call the Direct3D device object's DrawPrimitive() method, which Direct3D declares as follows:

```
HRESULT DrawPrimitive(
    D3DPRIMITIVETYPE PrimitiveType,
    UINT StartVertex,
    UINT PrimitiveCount
);
```

Here's what the method's three arguments mean:

- *PrimitiveType*—One of the constants that specify primitive types. For a triangle list, use D3DPT_TRIANGLELIST.

- *StartVertex*—The vertex at which to start drawing. In this book, you'll always use 0 for this argument.

- *PrimtiveCount*—The number of shapes to draw. In a triangle list, each shape is represented by three vertices, so if you had to draw two rectangles, your vertex buffer would have six vertices, and you'd set this argument to 2.

To draw a single triangle, the call to `DrawPrimitive()` might look like this:

```
g_pDirect3DDevice->DrawPrimitive(D3DPT_TRIANGLELIST, 0, 1);
```

There's only one last detail to consider. Before you start drawing a Direct3D display, you must call the Direct3D device object's `BeginScene()` method, and when you're finished drawing, you must call the `EndScene()` method, after which you call `Present()`. The whole process looks like Listing 7.3.

LISTING 7.3   Rendering a Scene

```
g_pDirect3DDevice->SetStreamSource(0, pVertexBuf, 0,
    sizeof(CUSTOMVERTEX));
g_pDirect3DDevice->SetFVF(D3DFVF_XYZRHW | D3DFVF_DIFFUSE);
g_pDirect3DDevice->BeginScene();
g_pDirect3DDevice->DrawPrimitive(D3DPT_TRIANGLELIST, 0, 1);
g_pDirect3DDevice->EndScene();
g_pDirect3DDevice->Present( NULL, NULL, NULL, NULL );
```

SWAPPING BUFFERS

Experienced graphics programmers, especially those who have programmed animated displays, know about a programming technique called *page flipping*, where one frame of a scene is rendered offscreen in memory while another is displayed to the user. Such a program had a command or function called something like Swap that switched the visible screen with the hidden scene. In the case of Direct3D, the `Present()` method performs much the same task.

Building the TriangleApp Application

The TriangleApp application presented in this section summarizes and demonstrates the Direct3D programming techniques covered so far in this chapter. Perform the steps outlined in the following sections to build this sample application.

Creating the Basic Project

Perform the following steps to get the main Direct3D application project started:

1. Start a new empty Win32 project named TriangleApp.

2. On the Project menu, select the Add New Item command. The Add New Item dialog box appears.

3. Add a new C++ File (.cpp) named TriangleApp.cpp.

4. Copy the contents of the BasicDirect3D.cpp file (the non-windowed version from Chapter 5, "Getting Direct3D Up and Running") into the new TriangleApp code window.

5. Change the name in the comment at the top of the file to TriangleApp.cpp.

6. In the `RegisterWindowClass()` function, change `wc.lpszClassName = "WinApp"` to `wc.lpszClassName = "TriangleApp"`.

7. In the `CreateAppWindow()` function, change `"WinApp"` to `"TriangleApp"`, and then change `"Basic Windows Application"` to `"Triangle Application"`.

Adding the DirectX References

Next, you need to tell the program where the required DirectX header files and libraries are located. To do that, follow these steps:

1. Near the top of the program, right after the line `#include <d3d9.h>`, add the following include directives:

```
#include <d3dx9tex.h>
#include <dxerr9.h>
```

2. Right-click the project's name in the Solution Explorer, and select Properties from the menu that appears. The TriangleApp Property Pages dialog box appears.

3. Click the C/C++ selection in the left-hand pane, and select General from the displayed choices.

4. In the Additional Include Directories box, enter the path to the DirectX 9 SDK's include folder. If you installed the SDK using the default settings, this path should be `c:\DXSDK\include`.

5. Click the Linker selection in the left-hand pane, and select General from the displayed choices.

6. In the Additional Library Directories box, enter the path to the DirectX 9 SDK's library folder. If you installed the SDK using the default settings, this path should be `c:\DXSDK\lib`.

7. Click the Linker's Input selection in the left-hand pane.

8. In the Additional Dependencies box in the right-hand pane, enter **d3d9.lib**, **d3dx9.lib**, and **dxerr9.lib**.

9. Compile and run the application to make sure that it works. Press Escape to exit the application.

Adding Source Code

Now all you have to do is add the Direct3D code that'll get your triangle onto the
screen. Most of the changes you need to make are in the Render() function, so just
replace the current Render() with Listing 7.4.

LISTING 7.4   A Render() Function that Draws a Single Triangle

```
/////////////////////////////////////////////////
// Render()
/////////////////////////////////////////////////
void Render()
{
    CUSTOMVERTEX triangleVertices[] =
    {
        {400.0f,  180.0f, 0.0f, 1.0f, D3DCOLOR_XRGB(255,0,0),},
        {500.0f, 380.0f, 0.0f, 1.0f, D3DCOLOR_XRGB(0,255,0),},
        {300.0f, 380.0f, 0.0f, 1.0f, D3DCOLOR_XRGB(0,0,255),},
    };

    IDirect3DVertexBuffer9* pVertexBuf = NULL;
    HRESULT hResult = g_pDirect3DDevice->CreateVertexBuffer(
        3*sizeof(CUSTOMVERTEX), 0, D3DFVF_XYZRHW | D3DFVF_DIFFUSE,
        D3DPOOL_DEFAULT, &pVertexBuf);

    if(FAILED(hResult))
    {
        DXTRACE_ERR("Error creating vertex buffer", hResult);
        return;
    }

    VOID* pVertices;
    hResult = pVertexBuf->Lock(0, 0, (void**)&pVertices, 0);
    if(FAILED(hResult))
    {
        DXTRACE_ERR("Error locking vertex buffer", hResult);
        return;
    }
    memcpy(pVertices, triangleVertices, sizeof(triangleVertices));
    pVertexBuf->Unlock();

    g_pDirect3DDevice->Clear(0, NULL, D3DCLEAR_TARGET,
        D3DCOLOR_XRGB(0,0,0), 1.0f, 0 );
    g_pDirect3DDevice->SetStreamSource(0, pVertexBuf, 0,
```

LISTING 7.4   Continued

```
        sizeof(CUSTOMVERTEX));
    g_pDirect3DDevice->SetFVF(D3DFVF_XYZRHW | D3DFVF_DIFFUSE);

    g_pDirect3DDevice->BeginScene();
    g_pDirect3DDevice->DrawPrimitive(D3DPT_TRIANGLELIST, 0, 1);
    g_pDirect3DDevice->EndScene();

    g_pDirect3DDevice->Present( NULL, NULL, NULL, NULL );

    if (pVertexBuf)
        pVertexBuf->Release();
}
```

Finally, add the declaration for the CUSTOMVERTEX structure near the top of the program, right after the global variables:

```
struct CUSTOMVERTEX
{
    FLOAT x, y, z, rhw;
    DWORD color;
};
```

You can now compile and run the application. When you do, you should see the screen shown in Figure 7.6. Press Escape to exit the program.

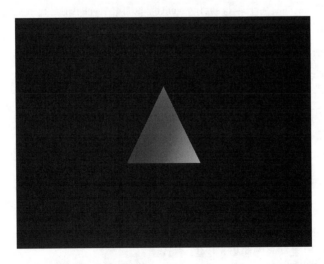

FIGURE 7.6   The TriangleApp application.

SHOP TALK

COLORS AND LIGHTING

There's not much to discuss about the TriangleApp program and its different Render() functions. Everything you need to know has already been covered in this chapter. The relationship between color and lighting in a Direct3D application, however, is worth placing under the magnifying glass. (Refer to Chapter 9 for an in-depth discussion of lighting.)

Ordinarily, in an application that specifies no lighting, Direct3D renders all objects in black. After all, with no light, nothing should be visible in your 3D world. A way around this little problem for folks who don't, for one reason or another, want to bother with lighting, is to specify colors with each 3D object's vertices, as you've done in this chapter's sample program.

The truth is that such colors are more than colors. They're actually a lighting effect. Specifically, in the case of TriangleApp, it's as if you're shining red, green, and blue lights on the triangle, one color on each point of the triangle. Direct3D uses its shading engine to determine how the three lights blend across the surface of the shape.

Ordinarily, to get lighting in your 3D world, you need to not only define a light object and the types of light it produces but also a material for each object you render in the scene. The material determines the type of light reflected by the surface of an object in a 3D world.

As you can see, specifying colors with your vertices really is a handy shortcut for drawing shapes in scenes that don't require the use of Direct3D's full-featured lighting engine.

One other thing: notice how the program calls the vertex-buffer object's Release() method when it's through with it. Most Direct3D objects require that you release them in this way.

Rendering a Point List

Now that you know the steps involved in displaying a shape with Direct3D, let's look at the other types of primitives you can draw, starting with the most basic, a point. A point is just a single dot on the screen. A Direct3D program can draw a single point or a whole set of points. No matter how many points you want to display, you define them as a point list (denoted by the D3DPT_POINTLIST constant). This process is similar to how you defined the vertices for a triangle.

The first step is to create a vertex format for the points:

```
struct CUSTOMVERTEX
{
    FLOAT x, y, z, rhw;
    DWORD color;
};
```

You can then use the vertex format to define a set of points, as shown in Listing 7.5.

LISTING 7.5   Defining a Set of Points

```
CUSTOMVERTEX points[] =
{
    {50.0, 50.0, 0.0, 1.0, D3DCOLOR_XRGB(255,0,0)},
    {100.0,  100.0, 0.0, 1.0, D3DCOLOR_XRGB(255,0,0)},
    {150.0, 150.0, 0.0, 1.0, D3DCOLOR_XRGB(255,0,0)},
    {200.0,  200.0, 0.0, 1.0, D3DCOLOR_XRGB(255,0,0)},
    {250.0, 250.0, 0.0, 1.0, D3DCOLOR_XRGB(255,0,0)},
    {300.0,  300, 0.0, 1.0, D3DCOLOR_XRGB(255,0,0)}
};
```

Here, the example defines six points, each of which will be drawn with the color red. The first three values for each point define the point's location in 3D space.

Next, create the vertex buffer:

```
IDirect3DVertexBuffer9* pVertexBuf = NULL;
HRESULT hResult = g_pDirect3DDevice->CreateVertexBuffer(
    6*sizeof(CUSTOMVERTEX), 0, D3DFVF_XYZRHW | D3DFVF_DIFFUSE,
    D3DPOOL_DEFAULT, &pVertexBuf);
```

Then you can load the buffer with the vertices:

```
VOID* pVertices;
hResult = pVertexBuf->Lock(0, 0, (void**)&pVertices, 0);
memcpy(pVertices, points, sizeof(points));
pVertexBuf->Unlock();
```

Finally, you can display the points, as shown in Listing 7.6.

LISTING 7.6   Displaying a Set of Points

```
    g_pDirect3DDevice->Clear(0, NULL, D3DCLEAR_TARGET,
        D3DCOLOR_XRGB(0,0,0), 1.0f, 0 );
    g_pDirect3DDevice->SetStreamSource(0, pVertexBuf, 0,
        sizeof(CUSTOMVERTEX));
    g_pDirect3DDevice->SetFVF(D3DFVF_XYZRHW | D3DFVF_DIFFUSE);

    g_pDirect3DDevice->BeginScene();
    g_pDirect3DDevice->DrawPrimitive(D3DPT_POINTLIST, 0, 6);
    g_pDirect3DDevice->EndScene();

    g_pDirect3DDevice->Present( NULL, NULL, NULL, NULL );
```

This process is similar to how you displayed a triangle. To see the point list in action, replace the Render() function in TriangleApp with Listing 7.7, and then rerun the program. When you do, you should see a black screen with a diagonal line of red dots. (You can find the new Render() function in the sample code's Chapter07 directory, under the name Render01.txt. For information on obtaining the sample code, see this book's introduction.)

LISTING 7.7   A Render() Function that Draws a Set of Points

```
////////////////////////////////////////////////////
// Render()
////////////////////////////////////////////////////
void Render()
{
    CUSTOMVERTEX points[] =
    {
        {50.0, 50.0, 0.0, 1.0, D3DCOLOR_XRGB(255,0,0)},
        {100.0,  100.0, 0.0, 1.0, D3DCOLOR_XRGB(255,0,0)},
        {150.0, 150.0, 0.0, 1.0, D3DCOLOR_XRGB(255,0,0)},
        {200.0,  200.0, 0.0, 1.0, D3DCOLOR_XRGB(255,0,0)},
        {250.0, 250.0, 0.0, 1.0, D3DCOLOR_XRGB(255,0,0)},
        {300.0,  300, 0.0, 1.0, D3DCOLOR_XRGB(255,0,0)}
    };

    IDirect3DVertexBuffer9* pVertexBuf = NULL;
    HRESULT hResult = g_pDirect3DDevice->CreateVertexBuffer(
        6*sizeof(CUSTOMVERTEX), 0, D3DFVF_XYZRHW | D3DFVF_DIFFUSE,
        D3DPOOL_DEFAULT, &pVertexBuf, NULL);

    VOID* pVertices;
    hResult = pVertexBuf->Lock(0, 0, (void**)&pVertices, 0);
    memcpy(pVertices, points, sizeof(points));
    pVertexBuf->Unlock();

    g_pDirect3DDevice->Clear(0, NULL, D3DCLEAR_TARGET,
        D3DCOLOR_XRGB(0,0,0), 1.0f, 0 );
    g_pDirect3DDevice->SetStreamSource(0, pVertexBuf, 0,
        sizeof(CUSTOMVERTEX));
    g_pDirect3DDevice->SetFVF(D3DFVF_XYZRHW | D3DFVF_DIFFUSE);

    g_pDirect3DDevice->BeginScene();
    g_pDirect3DDevice->DrawPrimitive(D3DPT_POINTLIST, 0, 6);
    g_pDirect3DDevice->EndScene();
```

LISTING 7.7   Continued

```
    g_pDirect3DDevice->Present( NULL, NULL, NULL, NULL );

    if (pVertexBuf)
        pVertexBuf->Release();
}
```

Rendering Line Lists

The next simplest shape Direct3D can draw is a line. Just as with points, you can draw a single line or a set of lines. No matter how many lines you want to display, you define them as a line list (denoted by the D3DPT_LINELIST constant). First, create a vertex format for the lines. (Just assume the same vertex format you've been using in this chapter.) You can then use the vertex format to define a set of lines. Because it takes a starting point and an ending point to define a line, you need to define a pair of vertices for each line you want to draw. Listing 7.8 is an example.

LISTING 7.8   Defining Vertices for Lines

```
CUSTOMVERTEX lines[] =
{
    {50.0, 50.0, 0.0, 1.0, D3DCOLOR_XRGB(255,0,0)},
    {400.0,  50.0, 0.0, 1.0, D3DCOLOR_XRGB(0,255,0)},

    {50.0, 150.0, 0.0, 1.0, D3DCOLOR_XRGB(255,0,0)},
    {400.0,  150.0, 0.0, 1.0, D3DCOLOR_XRGB(0,255,0)},

    {50.0, 250.0, 0.0, 1.0, D3DCOLOR_XRGB(255,0,0)},
    {400.0,  250, 0.0, 1.0, D3DCOLOR_XRGB(0,255,0)}
};
```

Here, the example defines three lines, each of which starts red and then blends to green at the other end.

Next, you create the vertex buffer, load the buffer with the vertices, and display the result.

To see the line list in action, replace the Render() function in TriangleApp with Listing 7.9 (you can find the code in the sample code's Chapter07 directory, under the name Render02.txt), and then rerun the program. When you do, you should see a black screen with three horizontal lines, as shown in Figure 7.7.

LISTING 7.9   A `Render()` Function that Draws a Set of Horizontal Lines

```
///////////////////////////////////////////////////
// Render()
///////////////////////////////////////////////////
void Render()
{
    CUSTOMVERTEX lines[] =
    {
        {50.0, 50.0, 0.0, 1.0, D3DCOLOR_XRGB(255,0,0)},
        {400.0,  50.0, 0.0, 1.0, D3DCOLOR_XRGB(0,255,0)},

        {50.0, 150.0, 0.0, 1.0, D3DCOLOR_XRGB(255,0,0)},
        {400.0,  150.0, 0.0, 1.0, D3DCOLOR_XRGB(0,255,0)},

        {50.0, 250.0, 0.0, 1.0, D3DCOLOR_XRGB(255,0,0)},
        {400.0,  250, 0.0, 1.0, D3DCOLOR_XRGB(0,255,0)}
    };

    IDirect3DVertexBuffer9* pVertexBuf = NULL;
    HRESULT hResult = g_pDirect3DDevice->CreateVertexBuffer(
        6*sizeof(CUSTOMVERTEX), 0, D3DFVF_XYZRHW | D3DFVF_DIFFUSE,
        D3DPOOL_DEFAULT, &pVertexBuf, NULL);

    VOID* pVertices;
    hResult = pVertexBuf->Lock(0, 0, (void**)&pVertices, 0);
    memcpy(pVertices, lines, sizeof(lines));
    pVertexBuf->Unlock();

    g_pDirect3DDevice->Clear(0, NULL, D3DCLEAR_TARGET,
        D3DCOLOR_XRGB(0,0,0), 1.0f, 0 );
    g_pDirect3DDevice->SetStreamSource(0, pVertexBuf, 0,
        sizeof(CUSTOMVERTEX));
    g_pDirect3DDevice->SetFVF(D3DFVF_XYZRHW | D3DFVF_DIFFUSE);

    g_pDirect3DDevice->BeginScene();
    g_pDirect3DDevice->DrawPrimitive(D3DPT_LINELIST, 0, 3);
    g_pDirect3DDevice->EndScene();

    g_pDirect3DDevice->Present( NULL, NULL, NULL, NULL );

    if (pVertexBuf)
        pVertexBuf->Release();
}
```

FIGURE 7.7   Drawing a line list.

Rendering Line Strips

Another type of line shape that you can draw with Direct3D is a line strip (denoted by the D3DPT_LINESTRIP constant), which is just a series of interconnected lines. When you define a line strip, the first pair of vertices defines the first line, with each vertex after that defining the next point to which Direct3D should draw. If you've had experience with drawing lines under Windows, you'll recognize a line strip as being the same as a MoveTo() command followed by a series of LineTo() commands.

The process goes like this: First, create a vertex format for the lines. (Again, just assume the same vertex format you've been using in this chapter.) You can then use the vertex format to define a set of interconnected lines. Because it takes a starting point and an ending point to define a line, you need to define a pair of vertices for the first line. The rest of the lines need only a "draw to" vertex. Listing 7.10 is an example.

LISTING 7.10   Defining a Line Strip

```
CUSTOMVERTEX lines[] =
{
    {50.0, 50.0, 0.0, 1.0, D3DCOLOR_XRGB(255,0,0)},
    {400.0,  50.0, 0.0, 1.0, D3DCOLOR_XRGB(0,255,0)},

    {50.0, 150.0, 0.0, 1.0, D3DCOLOR_XRGB(255,0,0)},
    {400.0,  150.0, 0.0, 1.0, D3DCOLOR_XRGB(0,255,0)},
    {50.0, 250.0, 0.0, 1.0, D3DCOLOR_XRGB(255,0,0)},
    {400.0,  250, 0.0, 1.0, D3DCOLOR_XRGB(0,255,0)}
};
```

Here, the example defines five connected lines, each of which starts red and then blends to green at the other end. As always, you must also create the vertex buffer, load the buffer with the vertices, and display the result.

To see the line strip in action, replace the Render() function in TriangleApp with Listing 7.11 (you can find the code in the sample code's Chapter07 directory, under the name Render03.txt) and then rerun the program. (The only thing different from the previous version of Render() is the call to DrawPrimitive().) When you do, you should see a black screen with five connected lines, as shown in Figure 7.8.

LISTING 7.11 A Render() Function that Draws a Line Strip

```
///////////////////////////////////////////////////
// Render()
///////////////////////////////////////////////////
void Render()
{
    CUSTOMVERTEX lines[] =
    {
        {50.0, 50.0, 0.0, 1.0, D3DCOLOR_XRGB(255,0,0)},
        {400.0,  50.0, 0.0, 1.0, D3DCOLOR_XRGB(0,255,0)},
        {50.0, 150.0, 0.0, 1.0, D3DCOLOR_XRGB(255,0,0)},
        {400.0,  150.0, 0.0, 1.0, D3DCOLOR_XRGB(0,255,0)},
        {50.0, 250.0, 0.0, 1.0, D3DCOLOR_XRGB(255,0,0)},
        {400.0,  250, 0.0, 1.0, D3DCOLOR_XRGB(0,255,0)}
    };

    IDirect3DVertexBuffer9* pVertexBuf = NULL;
    HRESULT hResult = g_pDirect3DDevice->CreateVertexBuffer(
        6*sizeof(CUSTOMVERTEX), 0, D3DFVF_XYZRHW | D3DFVF_DIFFUSE,
        D3DPOOL_DEFAULT, &pVertexBuf, NULL);

    VOID* pVertices;
    hResult = pVertexBuf->Lock(0, 0, (void**)&pVertices, 0);
    memcpy(pVertices, lines, sizeof(lines));
    pVertexBuf->Unlock();

    g_pDirect3DDevice->Clear(0, NULL, D3DCLEAR_TARGET,
        D3DCOLOR_XRGB(0,0,0), 1.0f, 0 );
    g_pDirect3DDevice->SetStreamSource(0, pVertexBuf, 0,
        sizeof(CUSTOMVERTEX));
    g_pDirect3DDevice->SetFVF(D3DFVF_XYZRHW | D3DFVF_DIFFUSE);
```

LISTING 7.11   Continued

```
g_pDirect3DDevice->BeginScene();
g_pDirect3DDevice->DrawPrimitive(D3DPT_LINESTRIP, 0, 5);
g_pDirect3DDevice->EndScene();

g_pDirect3DDevice->Present( NULL, NULL, NULL, NULL );

if (pVertexBuf)
    pVertexBuf->Release();
}
```

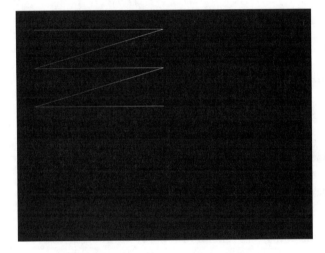

FIGURE 7.8   Drawing a line strip.

Rendering Triangle Lists

You've already had experience rendering triangle lists because that's the type of graphics primitive you used to display the triangle in the original TriangleApp program. But you can use a triangle list (denoted by the D3DPT_TRIANGLELIST constant) to render multiple triangles. Here's how: First, create a vertex format for the triangles. (Again, just assume the same vertex format you've been using in this chapter.) You can then use the vertex format to define a set of individual triangles. Because it takes three points to define a triangle, you need to define three vertices for each triangle. Listing 7.12 is an example.

LISTING 7.12   Defining a Triangle List

```
CUSTOMVERTEX triangles[] =
{
    {100.0f,  60.0f, 0.0f, 1.0f, D3DCOLOR_XRGB(255,0,0),},
    {300.0f, 300.0f, 0.0f, 1.0f, D3DCOLOR_XRGB(255,0,0),},
    {50.0f, 200.0f, 0.0f, 1.0f, D3DCOLOR_XRGB(255,0,0),},

    {400.0f,  180.0f, 0.0f, 1.0f, D3DCOLOR_XRGB(255,0,0),},
    {500.0f, 380.0f, 0.0f, 1.0f, D3DCOLOR_XRGB(0,255,0),},
    {300.0f, 380.0f, 0.0f, 1.0f, D3DCOLOR_XRGB(0,0,255),},

    {500.0f,  280.0f, 0.0f, 1.0f, D3DCOLOR_XRGB(0,0,255),},
    {700.0f, 479.0f, 0.0f, 1.0f, D3DCOLOR_XRGB(0,0,255),},
    {300.0f, 479.0f, 0.0f, 1.0f, D3DCOLOR_XRGB(0,0,255),},
};
```

Here, the example defines three triangles of different colors, locations, and sizes. As always, you must also create the vertex buffer, load the buffer with the vertices, and display the result.

To see the triangle list in action, replace the Render() function in TriangleApp with Listing 7.13 (you can find the code in the sample code's Chapter07 directory, under the name Render04.txt) and then rerun the program. When you do, you should see a black screen with three triangles, as shown in Figure 7.9.

LISTING 7.13   A Render() Function that Draws a Triangle List

```
//////////////////////////////////////////////////////
// Render()
//////////////////////////////////////////////////////
void Render()
{
    CUSTOMVERTEX triangles[] =
    {
        {100.0f,  60.0f, 0.0f, 1.0f, D3DCOLOR_XRGB(255,0,0),},
        {300.0f, 300.0f, 0.0f, 1.0f, D3DCOLOR_XRGB(255,0,0),},
        {50.0f, 200.0f, 0.0f, 1.0f, D3DCOLOR_XRGB(255,0,0),},
```

LISTING 7.13   Continued

```
        {400.0f,  180.0f, 0.0f, 1.0f, D3DCOLOR_XRGB(255,0,0),},
        {500.0f, 380.0f, 0.0f, 1.0f, D3DCOLOR_XRGB(0,255,0),},
        {300.0f, 380.0f, 0.0f, 1.0f, D3DCOLOR_XRGB(0,0,255),},

        {500.0f,  280.0f, 0.0f, 1.0f, D3DCOLOR_XRGB(0,0,255),},
        {700.0f, 479.0f, 0.0f, 1.0f, D3DCOLOR_XRGB(0,0,255),},
        {300.0f, 479.0f, 0.0f, 1.0f, D3DCOLOR_XRGB(0,0,255),},
    };

    IDirect3DVertexBuffer9* pVertexBuf = NULL;
    HRESULT hResult = g_pDirect3DDevice->CreateVertexBuffer(
        9*sizeof(CUSTOMVERTEX), 0, D3DFVF_XYZRHW | D3DFVF_DIFFUSE,
        D3DPOOL_DEFAULT, &pVertexBuf, NULL);

    VOID* pVertices;
    hResult = pVertexBuf->Lock(0, 0, (void**)&pVertices, 0);
    memcpy(pVertices, triangles, sizeof(triangles));
    pVertexBuf->Unlock();

    g_pDirect3DDevice->Clear(0, NULL, D3DCLEAR_TARGET,
        D3DCOLOR_XRGB(0,0,0), 1.0f, 0 );
    g_pDirect3DDevice->SetStreamSource(0, pVertexBuf, 0,
        sizeof(CUSTOMVERTEX));
    g_pDirect3DDevice->SetFVF(D3DFVF_XYZRHW | D3DFVF_DIFFUSE);

    g_pDirect3DDevice->BeginScene();
    g_pDirect3DDevice->DrawPrimitive(D3DPT_TRIANGLELIST, 0, 3);
    g_pDirect3DDevice->EndScene();

    g_pDirect3DDevice->Present( NULL, NULL, NULL, NULL );

    if (pVertexBuf)
        pVertexBuf->Release();
}
```

FIGURE 7.9   Drawing a triangle list.

Rendering Triangle Strips

Another triangle shape you can draw with Direct3D is a *triangle strip* (denoted by the D3DPT_TRIANGLESTRIP constant), which is a series of connected triangles. Each triangle shares an edge with the previously drawn triangle, which means that after defining the three vertices for the first triangle in the strip, you need only define one vertex for each additional triangle in the strip. (The adjoining side implicitly defines the other two vertices.)

The order in which you define the vertices of a triangle strip is important. The first triangle in the strip has its vertices defined as in Figure 7.10.

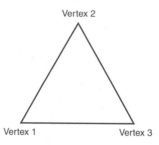

FIGURE 7.10   The vertices of the first triangle in a triangle strip.

The rules that govern triangle strips dictate that the side shared by the next triangle is defined by vertex 2 and vertex 3. Vertex 4 defines the next triangle in the strip, as shown in Figure 7.11.

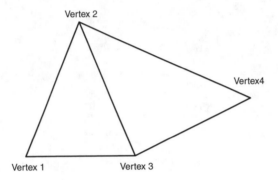

FIGURE 7.11   Adding the second triangle to the strip.

Similarly, now vertex 3 and vertex 4 define the adjoining side for the third triangle in the strip, as shown in Figure 7.12.

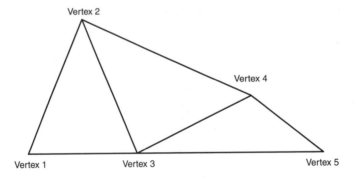

FIGURE 7.12   Adding the third triangle to the strip.

As you add triangles to the strip, the adjoining sides are determined in the same way as shown previously. For example, a fourth triangle would share the side created by vertices 4 and 5, as shown in Figure 7.13.

Following is a version of the Render() function that draws a triangle strip. Replace the Render() in TriangleApp with Listing 7.14 (you can find the code in the sample code's Chapter07 directory, under the name Render05.txt) and run the program. You'll then see the multicolor, solid object formed by the four triangles in the triangle strip, as shown in Figure 7.14. Figure 7.15 shows the same 3D object with lines that delineate the four triangles that make up the shape.

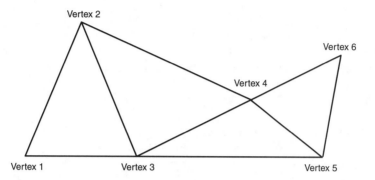

FIGURE 7.13   Adding the fourth triangle to the strip.

LISTING 7.14   A Render() Function that Draws a Triangle Strip

```
////////////////////////////////////////////////////
// Render()
////////////////////////////////////////////////////
void Render()
{
    CUSTOMVERTEX triangles[] =
    {
        {100.0f,  500.0f, 0.0f, 1.0f, D3DCOLOR_XRGB(255,0,0),},
        {300.0f, 200.0f, 0.0f, 1.0f, D3DCOLOR_XRGB(255,0,0),},
        {200.0f, 500.0f, 0.0f, 1.0f, D3DCOLOR_XRGB(255,0,0),},

        {500.0f,  180.0f, 0.0f, 1.0f, D3DCOLOR_XRGB(0,255,0),},
        {600.0f, 380.0f, 0.0f, 1.0f, D3DCOLOR_XRGB(0,0,255),},
        {750.0f, 380.0f, 0.0f, 1.0f, D3DCOLOR_XRGB(255,0,0),},
    };

    IDirect3DVertexBuffer9* pVertexBuf = NULL;
    HRESULT hResult = g_pDirect3DDevice->CreateVertexBuffer(
        6*sizeof(CUSTOMVERTEX), 0, D3DFVF_XYZRHW | D3DFVF_DIFFUSE,
        D3DPOOL_DEFAULT, &pVertexBuf, NULL);

    VOID* pVertices;
    hResult = pVertexBuf->Lock(0, 0, (void**)&pVertices, 0);      memcpy(pVertices,
triangles, sizeof(triangles));
    pVertexBuf->Unlock();
```

LISTING 7.14   Continued

```
g_pDirect3DDevice->Clear(0, NULL, D3DCLEAR_TARGET,
    D3DCOLOR_XRGB(0,0,0), 1.0f, 0 );
g_pDirect3DDevice->SetStreamSource(0, pVertexBuf, 0,
    sizeof(CUSTOMVERTEX));
g_pDirect3DDevice->SetFVF(D3DFVF_XYZRHW | D3DFVF_DIFFUSE);

g_pDirect3DDevice->BeginScene();
g_pDirect3DDevice->DrawPrimitive(D3DPT_TRIANGLESTRIP, 0, 4);
g_pDirect3DDevice->EndScene();

g_pDirect3DDevice->Present( NULL, NULL, NULL, NULL );

if (pVertexBuf)
    pVertexBuf->Release();
}
```

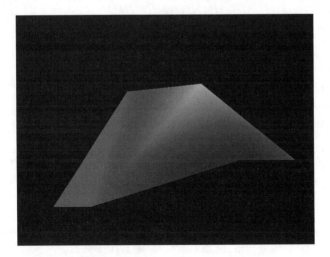

FIGURE 7.14   Rendering a triangle strip.

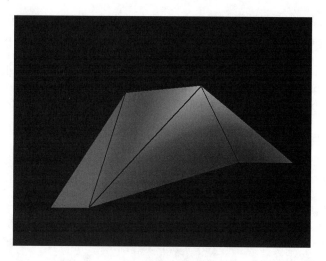

FIGURE 7.15   The four triangles in the triangle strip.

Rendering Triangle Fans

The last way you can draw triangles with Direct3D is as a *triangle fan* (denoted by the D3DPT_TRIANGLEFAN constant), which is a series of triangles that all share a single vertex defining the pivot of a fan shape. Like a triangle strip, a triangle fan is created by defining three vertices for the first triangle. Then, because each succeeding triangle shares a side with the previous triangle, you define a single vertex for each additional triangle in the fan. Figure 7.16 shows the order in which you must define the vertices of a triangle fan.

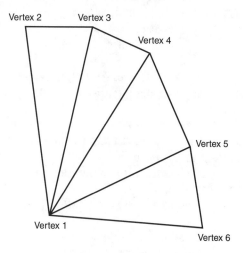

FIGURE 7.16   Defining a triangle fan.

Listing 7.15 is a version of the `Render()` function that draws a triangle fan. Replace the `Render()` in TriangleApp with this one (you can find the code in the sample code's Chapter07 directory, under the name Render06.txt)and run the program. You'll then see the multicolor, solid object formed by the four triangles in the triangle fan, as shown in Figure 7.17. Figure 7.18 shows the same 3D object with lines that delineate the four triangles that make up the shape.

LISTING 7.15   A `Render()` Function that Draws a Triangle Fan

```
///////////////////////////////////////////////////////
// Render()
///////////////////////////////////////////////////////
void Render()
{
    CUSTOMVERTEX triangles[] =
    {
        {300.0f,  500.0f, 0.0f, 1.0f, D3DCOLOR_XRGB(255,0,0),},
        {100.0f,  200.0f, 0.0f, 1.0f, D3DCOLOR_XRGB(255,0,0),},
        {200.0f,  200.0f, 0.0f, 1.0f, D3DCOLOR_XRGB(255,0,0),},

        {350.0f,   50.0f, 0.0f, 1.0f, D3DCOLOR_XRGB(0,255,0),},
        {500.0f,  280.0f, 0.0f, 1.0f, D3DCOLOR_XRGB(0,0,255),},
        {750.0f,  180.0f, 0.0f, 1.0f, D3DCOLOR_XRGB(255,0,0),},
    };

    IDirect3DVertexBuffer9* pVertexBuf = NULL;
    HRESULT hResult = g_pDirect3DDevice->CreateVertexBuffer(
        6*sizeof(CUSTOMVERTEX), 0, D3DFVF_XYZRHW | D3DFVF_DIFFUSE,
        D3DPOOL_DEFAULT, &pVertexBuf, NULL);

    VOID* pVertices;
    hResult = pVertexBuf->Lock(0, 0, (void**)&pVertices, 0);
    memcpy(pVertices, triangles, sizeof(triangles));
    pVertexBuf->Unlock();

    g_pDirect3DDevice->Clear(0, NULL, D3DCLEAR_TARGET,
        D3DCOLOR_XRGB(0,0,0), 1.0f, 0 );
    g_pDirect3DDevice->SetStreamSource(0, pVertexBuf, 0,
        sizeof(CUSTOMVERTEX));
    g_pDirect3DDevice->SetFVF(D3DFVF_XYZRHW | D3DFVF_DIFFUSE);

    g_pDirect3DDevice->BeginScene();
    g_pDirect3DDevice->DrawPrimitive(D3DPT_TRIANGLEFAN, 0, 4);
    g_pDirect3DDevice->EndScene();
```

LISTING 7.15 *LISTING 7.15* Continued

```
g_pDirect3DDevice->Present( NULL, NULL, NULL, NULL );

if (pVertexBuf)
    pVertexBuf->Release();
}
```

FIGURE 7.17 Rendering a triangle fan.

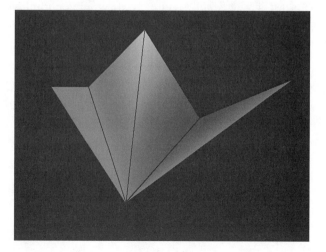

FIGURE 7.18 The four triangles in the triangle fan.

In Brief

- A vertex is a point that defines where two edges of a shape come together.

- With Direct3D, a vertex can include all kinds of information about a point, including its color, texture coordinates, blending information, and more.

- Vertex values are managed in Direct3D using what's called flexible vertex format (FVF) flags, which are constants defined by Direct3D that specify the types of information contained in a vertex.

- Transformed coordinates are simply values that tell Direct3D the exact screen coordinates at which a shape should be drawn.

- Untransformed coordinates must be processed by Direct3D's various transformations to become transformed coordinates.

- A vertex buffer is a block of memory that contains the vertices needed to draw a shape. An application's Direct3D device object defines the `CreateVertexBuffer()` method for exactly this task.

- After creating the vertex buffer, the program must load the vertex data into the buffer.

- Direct3D can draw six types of graphics primitives in sets called point lists, line lists, line strips, triangle lists, triangle strips, and triangle fans.

- To tell Direct3D where vertices are stored, your program calls the Direct3D device object's `SetStreamSource()` method.

- To tell Direct3D how to apply shading to the graphics primitive, you can call the Direct3D device object's `SetFVF()` method, which tells Direct3D the vertex format.

- To draw a shape, you call the Direct3D device object's `DrawPrimitive()` method.

- Before you start drawing a Direct3D display, you must call the Direct3D device object's `BeginScene()` method, and when you're finished drawing, you must call the `EndScene()` method, after which you call `Present()` to display the final scene on the screen.

Direct3D Transformations

8

IN THIS CHAPTER

- ▶ **Understanding Direct3D Transformations**
- ▶ **Building the MatrixTriangleApp**
- ▶ **Seeing Transformations in Action**
- ▶ **Building 3D Objects from Polygons**
- ▶ **Performing Multiple Transformations**
- ▶ **Understanding the Order of Transformations**
- ▶ **In Brief**

Understanding Direct3D Transformations

Early in this book, you learned about the basic types of transformations you can apply to graphical objects in a 3D application. These transformations are translation, rotation, and scaling. Direct3D, however, provides a set of higher level transformations you must use to render a 3D world. These are the world, view, and projection transformations. In this section, you learn what these important transformations do.

World Transformation

The *world transformation* is the one most closely related to the transformations you already learned about. This transformation determines the location and position of graphical objects in the 3D world and so is where you apply translations, rotations, and scaling.

> **DIRECT3D AND MATRICES**
>
> Just like the basic 3D application you wrote back in Chapter 4, "Programming 3D Computer Graphics," Direct3D uses matrices to perform the world transformation. However, unlike in your early 3D explorations where you had to create and manipulate matrices from scratch, Direct3D handles the matrices for you, including performing all matrix math.

The world transformation starts with your program declaring the matrix that'll be used in the transformation. To make this easy, Direct3D provides the D3DMATRIX data type. So, to declare your matrix, you'd write something like this:

```
D3DXMATRIX worldMatrix;
```

Now, all you have to do is tell Direct3D how you want the translations, rotations, and scaling performed. Direct3D's utility library features a set of functions that make this process easy, too. These functions are as follows:

- D3DXMatrixTranslation()—Applies a translation to a matrix

- D3DXMatrixRotationX()—Applies rotation around the X axis to a matrix

- D3DXMatrixRotationY()—Applies rotation around the Y axis to a matrix

- D3DXMatrixRotationZ()—Applies rotation around the Z axis to a matrix

- D3DXMatrixScaling()—Applies scaling to a matrix

After setting up the matrix for one or more of these transformations, you give Direct3D the result by calling the device's SetTransform() method, which Direct3D declares like this:

```
HRESULT SetTransform(
    D3DTRANSFORMSTATETYPE State,
    CONST D3DMATRIX* pMatrix
);
```

Here's what the two arguments mean:

- *state*—The type of transformation to apply. This can be D3DTS_WORLD, D3DTS_VIEW, or D3DTS_PROJECTION.

- *pMatrix*—A pointer to the matrix that contains the world transformation data.

Performing Translation

When you want to move an object to a new position in your 3D world, you need to perform translation on one or more of the X, Y, and Z axes. To do this, you call D3DMatrixTranslation(), which Direct3D declares like this:

```
D3DXMATRIX *D3DXMatrixTranslation(
    D3DXMATRIX* pOut,
    FLOAT x,
    FLOAT y,
    FLOAT z
);
```

Here's what the four arguments mean:

- *pOut*—A pointer to the matrix that will hold the result of the operation
- *x*—The number of units to translate on the X axis
- *y*—The number of units to translate on the Y axis
- *z*—The number of units to translate on the Z axis

Suppose that you want to translate the objects in your 3D world five units to the right on the X axis. You'd then write something like this:

```
D3DXMATRIX worldMatrix;
D3DXMatrixTranslation(&worldMatrix, 5, 0, 0);
g_pDirect3DDevice->SetTransform(D3DTS_WORLD, &worldMatrix);
```

Performing Rotation

Because a 3D world has three axes around which objects can be rotated, Direct3D defines three utility functions for rotation: D3DXMatrixRotationX(), D3DXMatrixRotationY(), and D3DXMatrixRotationZ(). When you want to rotate the objects around the X axis, for example, you call D3DMatrixRotationX(), which Direct3D declares like this:

```
D3DXMATRIX *D3DXMatrixRotationX(
    D3DXMATRIX* pOut,
    FLOAT Angle
);
```

Here's what the two arguments mean:

- *pOut*—A pointer to the matrix that will hold the result of the operation
- *angle*—The rotation angle in radians

Suppose that you want to rotate objects in your 3D world 45 degrees around the X axis. You'd then write something like this:

```
D3DXMATRIX worldMatrix;
double radians = 6.283185308 / (360.0 / 45);
D3DXMatrixRotationX(&worldMatrix, radians);
g_pDirect3DDevice->SetTransform(D3DTS_WORLD, &worldMatrix);
```

The D3DXMatrixRotationY() and D3DXMatrixRotationZ() functions work the same way, the only difference being the axis around which the rotation is performed.

Performing Scaling

When you want to scale a 3D scene, you call D3DMatrixScaling(), which Direct3D declares like this:

```
D3DXMATRIX *D3DXMatrixScaling(
    D3DXMATRIX* pOut,
    FLOAT sx,
    FLOAT sy,
    FLOAT sz
);
```

Here's what the four arguments mean:

- *pOut*—A pointer to the matrix that will hold the result of the operation

- *sx*—The scaling factor for the X axis

- *sy*—The scaling factor for the Y axis

- *sz*—The scaling factor for the Z axis

Suppose that you want to double the size of a 3D scene on all axes. You'd then write something like this:

```
D3DXMATRIX worldMatrix;
D3DXMatrixScaling(&worldMatrix, 2, 2, 2);
g_pDirect3DDevice->SetTransform(D3DTS_WORLD, &worldMatrix);
```

View Transformation

To prepare for the Direct3D view transformation, you must define three vectors of the D3DXVECTOR3 data type. These vectors are as follows:

- Eye—This is the viewpoint from which the 3D scene will be viewed. You can also think of this as being the position of the camera.

- Look At—This is the point at which the camera is pointed.

- Up—This is a vector that defines the up direction. Often, this vector points up the Y axis.

To define these vectors, you might write something like this:

```
D3DXVECTOR3 vEyePt(0.0f, 0.0f, -3.0f);
D3DXVECTOR3 vLookatPt(0.0f, 0.0f, 0.0f);
D3DXVECTOR3 vUpVec(0.0f, 1.0f, 0.0f);
```

After you have the vectors defined, you set up a matrix for the transformation by calling the Direct3D utility function D3DXMatrixLookAtLH(), which Direct3D declares like this:

```
D3DXMATRIX *D3DXMatrixLookAtLH(
    D3DXMATRIX* pOut,
    CONST D3DXVECTOR3* pEye,
    CONST D3DXVECTOR3* pAt,
    CONST D3DXVECTOR3* pUp
);
```

Here's what the arguments mean:

- *pOut*—A pointer to the matrix that will receive the data for the transformation
- *pEye*—A pointer to the D3DXVECTOR3 value that defines the scene's camera position
- *pAt*—A pointer to the D3DXVECTOR3 value that defines the scene's Look-At point
- *pUp*—A pointer to the D3DXVECTOR3 value that defines the scene's up direction

In your program, the call to D3DXMatrixLookAtLH() might look like this:

```
D3DXMATRIX viewMatrix;
D3DXMatrixLookAtLH(&viewMatrix, &vEyePt, &vLookatPt, &vUpVec);
```

Finally, just as with the world transformation, the last step is to give the transformation to Direct3D via the SetTransform() method:

```
g_pDirect3DDevice->SetTransform(D3DTS_VIEW, &viewMatrix);
```

SHOP TALK

THE VIEW TRANSFORMATION

No doubt you're familiar with an old conundrum that goes like this: If a tree fell in a forest and no one was there, would the tree make a sound? For our purposes in this book, you could also say this: If there was a 3D world but no one to see it, would the world still be visible? In Direct3D programming, the answer to that question is no. Before a 3D scene becomes visible on the screen, you must position the point from which the scene is being viewed.

Imagine, for example, a cardboard box containing a dollhouse. The cardboard box is completely sealed up so that the dollhouse is not visible from outside the box. This is analogous to a 3D scene in a Direct3D application that hasn't yet defined a viewpoint. Now imagine that you have a small camera that you can put inside the cardboard box. You can view the dollhouse through the camera. So, the

SHOP TALK

camera defines the point from which you can look at the scene in the box. If you move the camera, what you see changes based on the camera's position.

This is what Direct3D's view transformation does. It takes the position of a viewpoint and determines what the 3D scene looks like from that position. In a flight simulator program, for example, the viewpoint is usually the plane's cockpit. As the plane moves through a 3D world, the scene changes based on the plane's position. The position of the camera, then, is in the plane's virtual cockpit.

Projection Transformation

After your program has your 3D world set up and fully transformed, you need to tell Direct3D how to create a 2D display from the 3D world. This 2D display appears on the computer's monitor. To set up a matrix for the projection transformation, you call the utility function D3DXMatrixPerspectiveFovLH(), which Direct3D declares like this:

```
D3DXMATRIX *D3DXMatrixPerspectiveFovLH(
    D3DXMATRIX* pOut,
    FLOAT fovY,
    FLOAT Aspect,
    FLOAT zn,
    FLOAT zf
);
```

Here's how you use the five arguments:

- *pOut*—A pointer to the matrix that will receive the data for the transformation

- *fovY*—The field of view in radians

- *Aspect*—The scene's aspect ratio

- *zn*—The location of the near clipping plane

- *zf*—The location of the far clipping plane

A typical call to D3DXMatrixPerspectiveFovLH() might look like this:

```
D3DXMATRIX projectionMatrix;
D3DXMatrixPerspectiveFovLH(&projectionMatrix,
    D3DX_PI/4, 1.0f, 1.0f, 50.0f);
```

As usual, after performing the transformation on the matrix, you give the results to Direct3D by calling SetTransform():

```
g_pDirect3DDevice->SetTransform(D3DTS_PROJECTION, &projectionMatrix);
```

A BIT OF TERMINOLOGY

If you have little experience with 3D graphics programming, you may be a bit confused by some terms used in this discussion. The *eye* is the point from which you're currently viewing the scene. The *near clipping plane* is the beginning of the viewing volume; that is, any objects or parts of objects between the eye and the near plane do not appear in the scene. The *far clipping plane* represents the end of the viewing volume. Any objects or parts of objects beyond the far plane also do not appear in the scene.

Building the MatrixTriangleApp

Now let's apply all this stuff you've been learning to the TriangleApp application you created in Chapter 7, "Drawing Graphics Primitives." Specifically, you're going to convert TriangleApp into MaxtrixTriangleApp by adding Direct3D transformations to the program.

Creating the Basic Project

Perform the following steps to get the main Direct3D application project started:

1. Start a new empty Win32 project named MatrixTriangleApp.

2. On the Project menu, select the Add New Item command. The Add New Item dialog box appears.

3. Add a new C++ File (.cpp) named MatrixTriangleApp.cpp.

4. Copy the contents of the TriangleApp.cpp file (from Chapter 7) into the new MatrixTriangleApp code window.

5. Change the name in the comment at the top of the file to MatrixTriangleApp.cpp.

6. In the `RegisterWindowClass()` function, change `wc.lpszClassName = "TriangleApp"` to `wc.lpszClassName = "MatrixTriangleApp"`.

7. In the `CreateAppWindow()` function, change `"TriangleApp"` to `"MatrixTriangleApp"`, and then change `"Triangle Application"` to `"Matrix Triangle Application"`.

Adding the DirectX References

Next, you need to tell the program where the required DirectX header files and libraries are located. To do that, follow these steps:

1. Right-click the project's name in the Solution Explorer, and select Properties from the menu that appears. The MatrixTriangleApp Property Pages dialog box appears.

2. Click the C/C++ selection in the left-hand pane, and select General from the displayed choices.

3. In the Additional Include Directories box, enter the path to the DirectX 9 SDK's include folder. If you installed the SDK using the default settings, this path should be `c:\DXSDK\include`.

4. Click the Linker selection in the left-hand pane, and select General from the displayed choices.

5. In the Additional Library Directories box, enter the path to the DirectX 9 SDK's library folder. If you installed the SDK using the default settings, this path should be `c:\DXSDK\lib`.

6. Click the Linker's Input selection in the left-hand pane.

7. In the Additional Dependencies box in the right-hand pane, enter **d3d9.lib**, **d3dx9.lib**, and **dxerr9.lib**.

8. Compile and run the application to make sure that it works. Press Escape to exit the application.

Adding Source Code

Now all you have to do is add the Direct3D code that'll get your triangle up on the screen. Perform the following steps to get this task done:

1. Add the following lines to the function prototypes near the top of the program:

```
void InitVertices();
void InitMatrices();
BOOL CheckDevice();
```

2. Add the following lines to the global variable declarations:

```
IDirect3DVertexBuffer9* g_pVertexBuf = NULL;
IDirect3DSurface9* g_pBackBuffer = NULL;
IDirect3DSurface9* g_pBitmapSurface = NULL;
```

3. Replace the current CUSTOMVERTEX structure with the one that follows:

```
struct CUSTOMVERTEX
{
    FLOAT x, y, z;
    DWORD color;
};
```

4. In the `WinMain()` function replace the lines

```
if (SUCCEEDED(hResult))
    WPARAM result = StartMessageLoop();
```

with these lines:

```
if (SUCCEEDED(hResult))
{
    InitVertices();
    WPARAM result = StartMessageLoop();
}
```

5. Replace the current `InitD3D()` function with the one in Listing 8.1.

LISTING 8.1   The New `InitDirect3D()` Function

```
///////////////////////////////////////////////
// InitDirect3D()
///////////////////////////////////////////////
HRESULT InitDirect3D()
{
    // Create the application's Direct3D object.
    g_pDirect3D = Direct3DCreate9(D3D_SDK_VERSION);
    if (g_pDirect3D == NULL)
        return E_FAIL;

    // Verify that the hardware can handle the required display mode.
    HRESULT hResult = g_pDirect3D->CheckDeviceType(D3DADAPTER_DEFAULT,
        D3DDEVTYPE_REF, D3DFMT_X8R8G8B8, D3DFMT_X8R8G8B8, FALSE);
    if (hResult != D3D_OK)
    {
        MessageBox(g_hWnd,
            "Sorry. This program won't\nrun on your system.",
            "DirectX Error", MB_OK);
        return E_FAIL;
    }

    // Create the application's Direct3D device object.
    D3DPRESENT_PARAMETERS D3DPresentParams;
    ZeroMemory(&D3DPresentParams, sizeof(D3DPRESENT_PARAMETERS));
    D3DPresentParams.Windowed = FALSE;
    D3DPresentParams.BackBufferCount = 1;
    D3DPresentParams.BackBufferWidth = 640;
    D3DPresentParams.BackBufferHeight = 480;
```

LISTING 8.1   Continued

```
D3DPresentParams.BackBufferFormat = D3DFMT_X8R8G8B8;
D3DPresentParams.SwapEffect = D3DSWAPEFFECT_DISCARD;
D3DPresentParams.hDeviceWindow = g_hWnd;
hResult = g_pDirect3D->CreateDevice(D3DADAPTER_DEFAULT,
    D3DDEVTYPE_HAL, g_hWnd, D3DCREATE_SOFTWARE_VERTEXPROCESSING,
    &D3DPresentParams, &g_pDirect3DDevice);
if (FAILED(hResult))
    return E_FAIL;

// Get a pointer to the backbuffer.
g_pDirect3DDevice->GetBackBuffer(0, 0,
    D3DBACKBUFFER_TYPE_MONO, &g_pBackBuffer);

// Create and load a surface for the background bitmap.
g_pDirect3DDevice->CreateOffscreenPlainSurface(640, 480,
    D3DFMT_X8R8G8B8, D3DPOOL_DEFAULT, &g_pBitmapSurface, NULL);
D3DXLoadSurfaceFromFile(g_pBitmapSurface, NULL, NULL,
    "image.bmp", NULL, D3DX_DEFAULT, 0, NULL);

// Turn off Direct3D's lighting functions.
g_pDirect3DDevice->SetRenderState(D3DRS_LIGHTING, FALSE);

return D3D_OK;
}
```

6. Add Listing 8.2 to the beginning of the `CleanUpDirect3D()` function.

LISTING 8.2   New Lines for the `CleanUpDirect3D()` Function

```
if (g_pBitmapSurface)
    g_pBitmapSurface->Release();
if (g_pVertexBuf)
    g_pVertexBuf->Release();
if (g_pBackBuffer)
    g_pBackBuffer->Release();
```

7. Replace the current `Render()` function with the one in Listing 8.3.

LISTING 8.3   The New `Render()` Function

```
//////////////////////////////////////////////////////
// Render()
//////////////////////////////////////////////////////
```

LISTING 8.3   Continued

```
void Render()
{
    // Stop rendering of the app has lost its Direct3D device.
    if (!CheckDevice()) return;

    // Clear the back buffer to black.
    g_pDirect3DDevice->Clear(0, NULL, D3DCLEAR_TARGET,
        D3DCOLOR_XRGB(0,0,0), 1.0f, 0 );

    // Set up the Direct3D transformations.
    InitMatrices();

    // Copy the background bitmap to the back buffer.
    g_pDirect3DDevice->StretchRect(g_pBitmapSurface,
        NULL, g_pBackBuffer, NULL, D3DTEXF_NONE);

    // Give Direct3D the vertex buffer and vertex format.
    g_pDirect3DDevice->SetStreamSource(0, g_pVertexBuf, 0,
        sizeof(CUSTOMVERTEX));
    g_pDirect3DDevice->SetFVF(D3DFVF_XYZ | D3DFVF_DIFFUSE);

    // Render the scene.
    g_pDirect3DDevice->BeginScene();
    g_pDirect3DDevice->DrawPrimitive(D3DPT_TRIANGLESTRIP, 0, 1);
    g_pDirect3DDevice->EndScene();
    g_pDirect3DDevice->Present(NULL, NULL, NULL, NULL);
}
```

8. Add the functions in Listing 8.4 to the end of the program.

LISTING 8.4   New Functions for the Application

```
/////////////////////////////////////////////////////
// InitVertices()
/////////////////////////////////////////////////////
void InitVertices()
{
    CUSTOMVERTEX triangles[] =
    {
        { 0.5f, -0.5f, 0.0f, D3DCOLOR_XRGB(255,0,0)}, // Lower right
        {-0.5f, -0.5f, 0.0f, D3DCOLOR_XRGB(255,0,0)}, // Lower left
        { 0.0f,  0.5f, 0.0f, D3DCOLOR_XRGB(255,0,0)}  // Top
    };
```

LISTING 8.4   Continued

```
    // Create the vertex buffer.
    g_pDirect3DDevice->CreateVertexBuffer(3*sizeof(CUSTOMVERTEX),
        0, D3DFVF_XYZ | D3DFVF_DIFFUSE, D3DPOOL_DEFAULT,
        &g_pVertexBuf, NULL);

    // Copy the vertices into the buffer.
    VOID* pVertices;
    g_pVertexBuf->Lock(0, sizeof(triangles), (void**)&pVertices, 0);
    memcpy(pVertices, triangles, sizeof(triangles));
    g_pVertexBuf->Unlock();
}


//////////////////////////////////////////////////////
// InitMatrices()
//////////////////////////////////////////////////////
void InitMatrices()
{
    // Set up the world transformation.
    D3DXMATRIX worldMatrix;
    D3DXMatrixTranslation(&worldMatrix, 0, 0, 0);
    g_pDirect3DDevice->SetTransform(D3DTS_WORLD, &worldMatrix);

    // Set up the view transformation.
    D3DXVECTOR3 vEyePt(0.0f, 0.0f, -3.0f);
    D3DXVECTOR3 vLookatPt(0.0f, 0.0f, 0.0f);
    D3DXVECTOR3 vUpVec(0.0f, 1.0f, 0.0f);
    D3DXMATRIX viewMatrix;
    D3DXMatrixLookAtLH(&viewMatrix, &vEyePt, &vLookatPt, &vUpVec);
    g_pDirect3DDevice->SetTransform(D3DTS_VIEW, &viewMatrix);

    // Set up the projection transformation.
    D3DXMATRIX projectionMatrix;
    D3DXMatrixPerspectiveFovLH(&projectionMatrix,
        D3DX_PI/4, 1.0f, 1.0f, 50.0f);
    g_pDirect3DDevice->SetTransform(D3DTS_PROJECTION, &projectionMatrix);
}


//////////////////////////////////////////////////////
// CheckDevice()
//////////////////////////////////////////////////////
BOOL CheckDevice()
{
    HRESULT hResult = g_pDirect3DDevice->TestCooperativeLevel();
```

LISTING 8.4   Continued

```
    if (hResult == D3DERR_DEVICELOST)
        return FALSE;
    else if (hResult == D3DERR_DEVICENOTRESET)
    {
        CleanUpDirect3D();
        InitDirect3D();
        InitVertices();
        return TRUE;
    }
    else
        return TRUE;
}
```

9. Copy the Image.bmp file from the sample source code's
   Chapter08\MatrixTriangleApp directory to your project's folder.

When you compile and run this program, you should see the screen shown in Figure
8.1. The image in the background is just a background bitmap that the program
loads into the back-buffer surface. The triangle, however, is a 3D object that's fully
under the control of Direct3D's various transformations.

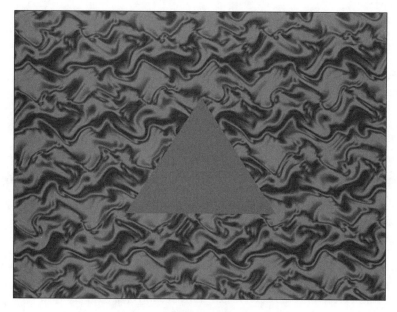

FIGURE 8.1   The running MatrixTriangleApp application.

Examining the Program

Let's examine exactly how the program renders its final image. Except for calls to a couple of helper functions, the action all happens in the Render() function, which the program calls repeatedly from the application's main message loop.

Understanding the General Rendering Process

The Render() function represents the general processes needed to create a final image on the screen. Render() first checks that the application still has access to its device, returning if not:

```
// Stop rendering of the app has lost its Direct3D device.
if (!CheckDevice()) return;
```

If the application still has its device and surfaces, Render() can continue. The first thing it does is clear the back buffer:

```
// Clear the back buffer to black.
g_pDirect3DDevice->Clear(0, NULL, D3DCLEAR_TARGET,
    D3DCOLOR_XRGB(0,0,0), 1.0f, 0 );
```

The program then sets up the matrices needed to perform the required transformations. It performs this task by calling the InitMatrices() helper function:

```
// Set up the Direct3D transformations.
InitMatrices();
```

Next, the program copies the background image to the back buffer:

```
// Copy the background bitmap to the back buffer.
g_pDirect3DDevice->StretchRect(g_pBitmapSurface,
    NULL, g_pBackBuffer, NULL, D3DTEXF_NONE);
```

Finally, the program can render the triangle just as you've seen done before, as shown in Listing 8.5.

LISTING 8.5   Rendering the Triangle

```
// Give Direct3D the vertex buffer and vertex format.
g_pDirect3DDevice->SetStreamSource(0, g_pVertexBuf, 0,
    sizeof(CUSTOMVERTEX));
g_pDirect3DDevice->SetFVF(D3DFVF_XYZ | D3DFVF_DIFFUSE);

// Render the scene.
g_pDirect3DDevice->BeginScene();
g_pDirect3DDevice->DrawPrimitive(D3DPT_TRIANGLESTRIP, 0, 1);
g_pDirect3DDevice->EndScene();
g_pDirect3DDevice->Present(NULL, NULL, NULL, NULL);
```

A DIFFERENT VERTEX FORMAT

The big difference between MatrixTriangleApp and previous programs is the vertex format, which is now D3DFVF_XYZ | D3DFVF_DIFFUSE, rather than the format D3DFVF_XYZRHW | D3DFVF_DIFFUSE that you used before. This format, without the "RHW," specifies that the vertex data contains *untransformed* X,Y,Z coordinates and a color value. The untransformed coordinates will become transformed coordinates after Direct3D performs its world, view, and projection transformations.

Exploring the Application

Although the Render() function illustrates the steps needed to render a 3D display, it's lacking many of the details, which are hidden away in helper functions or were taken care of at initialization time. The vertices, for example, are initialized at program startup in the InitVertices() function, which is called from WinMain(). You already know how to create a vertex buffer. What's important to notice about the vertices is their format and values:

```
CUSTOMVERTEX triangles[] =
{
    { 0.5f, -0.5f, 0.0f, D3DCOLOR_XRGB(255,0,0)}, // Lower right
    {-0.5f, -0.5f, 0.0f, D3DCOLOR_XRGB(255,0,0)}, // Lower left
    { 0.0f,  0.5f, 0.0f, D3DCOLOR_XRGB(255,0,0)}  // Top
};
```

The vertex format specifies untransformed X,Y,Z coordinates, along with a color value. In the triangles[] array, you can see that the program uses that format to define the three vertices of a triangle. You can also see that the vertices describe a triangle one unit wide and one unit high, as shown in Figure 8.2.

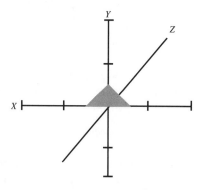

FIGURE 8.2   The triangle defined in the MatrixTriangleApp application.

Another detail to notice is in the InitDirect3D() function, which also gets called from WinMain(). In InitDirect3D(), the program creates its Direct3D objects, including the device and offscreen surface. What's new there, however, is the call to the device object's SetRenderState() method:

```
// Turn off Direct3D's lighting functions.
g_pDirect3DDevice->SetRenderState(D3DRS_LIGHTING, FALSE);
```

Because the program doesn't use Direct3D's lighting features (instead specifying colors directly for each vertex), the program must shut off the lighting, which is what this method call does.

Finally, there's the InitMatrices() function, which gets called from Render(). This is where the program sets up the transformations. First is the matrix for the world transformation:

```
// Set up the world transformation.
D3DXMATRIX worldMatrix;
D3DXMatrixTranslation(&worldMatrix, 0, 0, 0);
g_pDirect3DDevice->SetTransform(D3DTS_WORLD, &worldMatrix);
```

This transformation is being set up to perform a translation. However, this is actually a dummy transformation because all the translation values are 0. You'll experiment with these values soon to see how the translation works.

After the world transformation, the program sets up the view transformation, as shown in Listing 8.6.

LISTING 8.6   Setting Up the View Transformation

```
// Set up the view transformation.
D3DXVECTOR3 vEyePt(0.0f, 0.0f, -3.0f);
D3DXVECTOR3 vLookatPt(0.0f, 0.0f, 0.0f);
D3DXVECTOR3 vUpVec(0.0f, 1.0f, 0.0f);
D3DXMATRIX viewMatrix;
D3DXMatrixLookAtLH(&viewMatrix, &vEyePt, &vLookatPt, &vUpVec);
g_pDirect3DDevice->SetTransform(D3DTS_VIEW, &viewMatrix);
```

Here, you can see that the camera is centered on the X and Y axis origin but is pulled back three units on the Z axis. The negative Z value has the effect of pulling the camera away from the scene. The camera is pointed directly at the origin, as defined by the vertex vLookatPt, and the upward direction is straight up the Y axis, as defined by the vertex vUpVec. Figure 8.3 shows the position of the camera represented by this transformation.

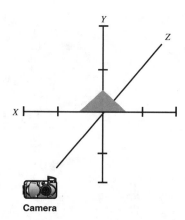

FIGURE 8.3   The camera's position in the scene.

Finally, the program sets up the matrix for the projection transformation:

```
// Set up the projection transformation.
D3DXMATRIX projectionMatrix;
D3DXMatrixPerspectiveFovLH(&projectionMatrix,
    D3DX_PI/4, 1.0f, 1.0f, 50.0f);
g_pDirect3DDevice->SetTransform(D3DTS_PROJECTION, &projectionMatrix);
```

Seeing Transformations in Action

Now that you see how the whole thing works, how about experimenting a bit to see what happens when you perform translation, rotation, and scaling with Direct3D's matrices. Right now, the program is set up to perform translations, but because the translation values given to D3DXMatrixTranslation() are zeroes, nothing really gets translated. How about moving the triangle one unit (which is also the width of the triangle) to the right on the X axis? To do this, change the D3DXMatrixTranslation() call to this:

```
D3DXMatrixTranslation(&worldMatrix, 1, 0, 0);
```

Now rerun the program, and you should see the display shown in Figure 8.4.

Want to move the triangle up one unit, too? Change the D3DXMatrixTranslation() call to this:

```
D3DXMatrixTranslation(&worldMatrix, 1, 1, 0);
```

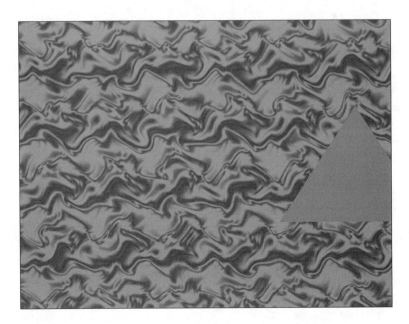

FIGURE 8.4   The triangle translated to the right.

Now rerun the program, and you should see the display shown in Figure 8.5.

FIGURE 8.5   The triangle translated to the right and up.

Currently, the triangle is so close to the camera that even a one-unit translation moves the triangle partially off the screen. One way to correct this problem is to move the triangle farther away down the Z axis. The following call to `D3DXMatrixTranslation()` accomplishes this task:

```
D3DXMatrixTranslation(&worldMatrix, 1, 1, 5);
```

Again run the program, and you should see the display shown in Figure 8.6.

FIGURE 8.6   The triangle translated to the right, up, and farther from the camera.

Another way to separate the camera and the triangle is the move the camera back. To do that, first change the Z translation back to 0, like this:

```
D3DXMatrixTranslation(&worldMatrix, 1, 1, 0);
```

Run the program to prove that the triangle is back closer to the camera. Then change the eye vector to this:

```
D3DXVECTOR3 vEyePt(0.0f, 0.0f, -8.0f);
```

This vector places the camera eight units back from the scene, which is five units more than before. Moving the camera back from the triangle by five units has exactly the same effect as translating the triangle five units away from the camera. Run the program to see that this is true.

Now let's try some scaling. Remove the call to D3DXMatrixTranslation() and replace it with this line:

```
D3DXMatrixScaling(&worldMatrix, 4, 2, 0);
```

When you run the program now, you should see the screen shown in Figure 8.7, where the triangle is four times as wide and twice as high as the original.

FIGURE 8.7   The triangle scaled at 4X width and 2X height.

Finally, you can try rotation. Just replace the call to D3DXMatrixScaling() with these lines:

```
double radians = 6.283185308 / (360.0 / 45);
D3DXMatrixRotationZ(&worldMatrix, radians);
```

When you run the program, you should see the screen shown in Figure 8.8, where the triangle is rotated 45 degrees around the Z axis.

FIGURE 8.8   The triangle rotated by 45 degrees.

Building 3D Objects from Polygons

The problem with your triangle is that, although it's being manipulated in 3D space, it's not much of a 3D object. Your triangle is more like a shape cut from a piece of paper. To get the feeling of 3D, you need to assemble a more sophisticated shape, such as a cube, from multiple triangles.

Imagine, for example, that you've got six 1-inch squares of paper, each of which was created from two triangles (see Figure 8.9). Now, you want to put those squares together to form a cube. Imagine further that you have a larger cube that's created from a 3D Cartesian grid. This second cube represents the world in which you'll assemble the paper squares into an object. You create the paper cube by placing the paper squares into the grid cube at positions such that the final cube ends up centered on the grid coordinates 0,0,0. That is, the 3D coordinates 0,0,0 are exactly centered inside both cubes, as shown in Figure 8.10.

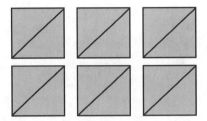

FIGURE 8.9   The 12 triangles needed to form a cube.

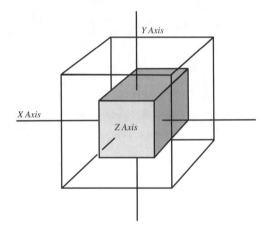

FIGURE 8.10   The assembled cube.

This is exactly the way that you create 3D objects in a Direct3D program, except, of course, you don't use paper. Instead, you tell Direct3D the coordinates of each triangle by supplying a list of vertices. This list not only tells Direct3D how to draw the triangles but also where to position them within the 3D Cartesian grid.

Using the cube in Figure 8.10 as a reference, values on the X axis increase from left to right, values on the Y axis increase from bottom to top, and values on the Z axis increase from front to back. So, to form the cube shown in Figure 8.2, you'd use Listing 8.7 to specify each triangle's vertices.

LISTING 8.7   The Vertices for a Cube

```
CUSTOMVERTEX triangles[] =
{
    // Front of cube.
    { -0.5f, 0.5f, -0.5f, D3DCOLOR_XRGB(255,0,0)},
    {0.5f, -0.5f, -0.5f, D3DCOLOR_XRGB(255,0,0)},
    {-0.5f,  -0.5f, -0.5f, D3DCOLOR_XRGB(255,0,0)},
    { -0.5f, 0.5f, -0.5f, D3DCOLOR_XRGB(0,255,0)},
```

LISTING 8.7   Continued

```
    {0.5f,  0.5f, -0.5f, D3DCOLOR_XRGB(0,255,0)},
    {0.5f, -0.5f, -0.5f, D3DCOLOR_XRGB(0,255,0)},

    // Right side of cube.
    {0.5f, 0.5f, -0.5f, D3DCOLOR_XRGB(0,0,255)},
    {0.5f, -0.5f, 0.5f, D3DCOLOR_XRGB(0,0,255)},
    {0.5f,  -0.5f, -0.5f, D3DCOLOR_XRGB(0,0,255)},
    {0.5f, 0.5f, -0.5f, D3DCOLOR_XRGB(255,255,0)},
    {0.5f,  0.5f, 0.5f, D3DCOLOR_XRGB(255,255,0)},
    {0.5f, -0.5f, 0.5f, D3DCOLOR_XRGB(255,255,0)},

    // Back of cube.
    {0.5f,  0.5f, 0.5f, D3DCOLOR_XRGB(255,0,255)},
    {-0.5f, -0.5f, 0.5f, D3DCOLOR_XRGB(255,0,255)},
    {0.5f,  -0.5f, 0.5f, D3DCOLOR_XRGB(255,0,255)},
    {0.5f, 0.5f, 0.5f, D3DCOLOR_XRGB(0,255,255)},
    {-0.5f,  0.5f, 0.5f, D3DCOLOR_XRGB(0,255,255)},
    {-0.5f, -0.5f, 0.5f, D3DCOLOR_XRGB(0,255,255)},

    // Left side of cube.
    {-0.5f,  0.5f, 0.5f, D3DCOLOR_XRGB(64,192,64)},
    {-0.5f, -0.5f, -0.5f, D3DCOLOR_XRGB(64,192,64)},
    {-0.5f,  -0.5f, 0.5f, D3DCOLOR_XRGB(64,192,64)},
    {-0.5f, 0.5f, 0.5f, D3DCOLOR_XRGB(64,255,255)},
    {-0.5f,  0.5f, -0.5f, D3DCOLOR_XRGB(64,255,255)},
    {-0.5f, -0.5f, -0.5f, D3DCOLOR_XRGB(64,255,255)},

    // Top of cube.
    {-0.5f,  0.5f, -0.5f, D3DCOLOR_XRGB(3,187,116)},
    {-0.5f, 0.5f, 0.5f, D3DCOLOR_XRGB(3,187,116)},
    {0.5f,  0.5f, -0.5f, D3DCOLOR_XRGB(3,187,116)},
    {-0.5f, 0.5f, 0.5f, D3DCOLOR_XRGB(203,253,42)},
    {0.5f,  0.5f, 0.5f, D3DCOLOR_XRGB(203,253,42)},
    {0.5f, 0.5f, -0.5f, D3DCOLOR_XRGB(203,253,42)},

    // Bottom of cube.
    {-0.5f,  -0.5f, -0.5f, D3DCOLOR_XRGB(255,120,120)},
    {0.5f, -0.5f, -0.5f, D3DCOLOR_XRGB(255,120,120)},
    {-0.5f,  -0.5f, 0.5f, D3DCOLOR_XRGB(255,120,120)},
    {0.5f, -0.5f, -0.5f, D3DCOLOR_XRGB(169,167,245)},
    {0.5f,  -0.5f, 0.5f, D3DCOLOR_XRGB(169,167,245)},
    {-0.5f, -0.5f, 0.5f, D3DCOLOR_XRGB(169,167,245)}
};
```

A cube has six sides, and it takes two triangles to form a side. That's 12 triangles times 3 vertices each for a total of 36 vertices.

To see how these vertices form a 3D cube, how about some more Direct3D experimentation? First, you need to start a new programming project. Perform the following steps to get the application project started:

1. Start a new empty (don't forget to select the Empty option) Win32 project named MatrixCubeApp.

2. On the Project menu, select the Add New Item command. The Add New Item dialog box appears.

3. Add a new C++ File (.cpp) named MatrixCubeApp.cpp.

4. Copy the contents of the MatrixTriangleApp file into the new MatrixCubeApp code window.

5. Change the name in the comment at the top of the file to MatrixCubeApp.cpp.

6. In the `RegisterWindowClass()` function, change `wc.lpszClassName = "MatrixTriangleApp"` to `wc.lpszClassName = "MatrixCubeApp"`.

7. In the `CreateAppWindow()` function, change `"MatrixTriangleApp"` to `"MatrixCubeApp"`, and then change `"Matrix Triangle Application"` to `"Matrix Cube Application"`.

8. Right-click the project's name in the Solution Explorer, and select Properties from the menu that appears. The MatrixCubeApp Property Pages dialog box appears.

9. Click the C/C++ selection in the left-hand pane, and select General from the displayed choices.

10. In the Additional Include Directories box, enter the path to the DirectX 9 SDK's include folder. If you installed the SDK using the default settings, this path should be `c:\DXSDK\include`.

11. Click the Linker selection in the left-hand pane, and select General from the displayed choices.

12. In the Additional Library Directories box, enter the path to the DirectX 9 SDK's library folder. If you installed the SDK using the default settings, this path should be `c:\DXSDK\lib`.

13. Click the Linker's Input selection in the left-hand pane.

14. In the Additional Dependencies box in the right-hand pane, enter `d3d9.lib`, `d3dx9.lib`, `dxerr9.lib`, and `winmm.lib`.

15. Copy the Image.bmp file from the MatrixTriangleApp directory to your new MatrixCubeApp directory.

16. Compile and run the application to make sure that it works. Press Escape to exit the application.

When you run the application, you should see exactly the same display you saw with MatrixTriangleApp. Now, however, you're going to start making changes to the program until you end up with an animated 3D cube. You'll be changing the program a little and then running it to see the result. In this way, you'll see exactly how every piece of the program works.

The first thing to do is to define the vertices for the cube. To do that, replace the current `triangles[]` array definition in `InitVertices()` with the new `triangles[]` array shown previously. (The one that defines the cube's vertices.)

Now, change the 3 in the call to `CreateVertexBuffer()` to 36 because that's how many vertices need to be copied to the vertex buffer.

Finally, go to the `Render()` function, and in the call to `DrawPrimitive()`, change the `D3DPT_TRIANGLESTRIP` to `D3DPT_TRIANGLELIST`. Notice that the `DrawPrimitive()` method still has a 1 as its last argument, which means it's only going to draw one triangle. For now, that's all you want to draw. Go ahead and run the program. You should see the screen shown in Figure 8.11.

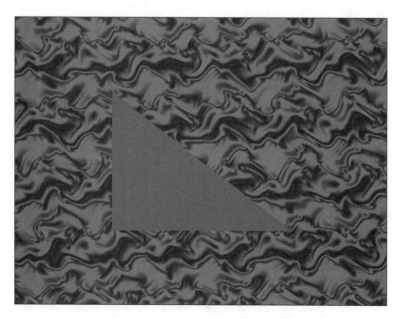

FIGURE 8.11   The first of many triangles in the cube.

You can now see the first triangle of the two that make up the cube's front side. To give you a little more perspective, take a look at Figure 8.12, which shows how the triangle is positioned in its local 3D space.

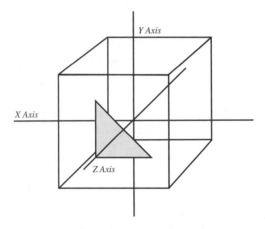

FIGURE 8.12   The first triangle as it relates to its local 3D space.

Now, go ahead and change the 1 in the DrawPrimitive() call to a 2 so that you can draw the remaining triangle in the cube's front side. When you do, rerun the program, and you should see the screen shown in Figure 8.13. Figure 8.14 shows both triangles as they are oriented in their local 3D space.

FIGURE 8.13   The cube's completed front side.

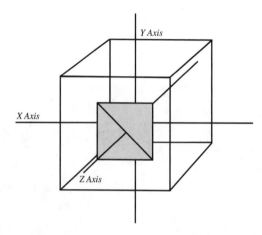

FIGURE 8.14   The first two triangles in their local 3D space.

Let's draw the first triangle on the cube's right side. To do this, change the 2 in the DrawPrimitive() call to a 3. Run the program, and it draws three triangles, in the orientation shown in Figure 8.15. However, the display still shows only two triangles. What's up? The third triangle is hidden behind the front side. To see it, the program must rotate the cube.

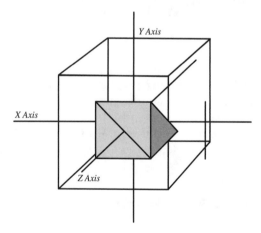

FIGURE 8.15   The first three triangles in their local 3D space.

Because you're going to want to see all triangles in the cube, the best way to do the rotation is as a continuous animation. To set this up, go to the InitMatrices() function and replace the D3DXMatrixTranslation() call with these lines:

```
double radians = timeGetTime() / 1000.0f;
D3DXMatrixRotationY(&worldMatrix, radians);
```

These lines cause your partial cube to continually rotate around the Y axis. When you run the program, you'll see your triangles rotating around the origin, as shown in Figure 8.16.

FIGURE 8.16   The rotated triangles.

But why, you ask, do the triangles continually appear and disappear as they turn? This phenomenon is due to something called *back-face culling*. This means that Direct3D shows only the front of each triangle and not the back. When the triangles rotate so that only their backs are facing you, Direct3D draws nothing. As you'll soon see, culling is much more useful than it might seem to you at the moment. For now, though, let's turn it off. To do this, go to the InitDirect3D() function and add these lines after the line that turns off the lighting:

```
// Turn off Direct3D's culling.
g_pDirect3DDevice->SetRenderState(D3DRS_CULLMODE, D3DCULL_NONE);
```

Rerun the program, and the triangles get drawn no matter which way they're facing. But because culling is off, the blue triangle gets drawn even when it should be hiding behind the others. This causes a kind of weird effect, as shown in Figure 8.17, as the shape rotates.

FIGURE 8.17   A side effect of no culling.

FRONT OR BACK?

You may wonder now how Direct3D knows which side of a triangle is the front. You specify this when you define each triangle's vertices. By default, Direct3D considers the side of the triangle with the vertices defined in clockwise order as the front. You must keep this in mind when you define your vertices.

Just ignore this no-culling side effect for now, and change the 3 in the DrawPrimitive() call to a 4. When you run the program now, two sides of the cube are complete, as shown in Figure 8.18. Figure 8.19 shows how the triangles are organized in their 3D space.

FIGURE 8.18   Two sides of the cube complete.

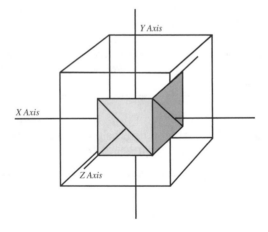

FIGURE 8.19   The first four triangles in their local 3D space.

You should now understand how these triangles fit together to draw a cube. Go ahead and change the 4 in the DrawPrimitive() call to 12 so that the program draws the entire cube. Run the program and watch the cube spin. Figure 8.20 gives you an idea of what you should see; the lack of culling is really messing things up now. Comment out the line that shuts off the culling and rerun the program. The cube looks much better when Direct3D stops drawing the backs of the triangles.

FIGURE 8.20   The full cube without culling.

Performing Multiple Transformations

Right now, your MatrixCubeApp performs only a rotation around the Y axis, but what if you want to rotate around more than one axis, or even want to perform translation or scaling? Just as with the traditional 3D matrix operations you learned about in Chapter 4, you can use Direct3D to multiply matrices into a single matrix that contains all the translation, scaling, and rotation operations you want to perform on your 3D world. To multiply two matrices, you call the utility function `D3DXMatrixMultiply()`, which Direct3D declares like this:

```
D3DXMATRIX *D3DXMatrixMultiply(
    D3DXMATRIX* pOut,
    CONST D3DXMATRIX* pM1,
    CONST D3DXMATRIX* pM2
);
```

Here's what the arguments are

- *pOut*—A pointer to the matrix that will receive the results of the operation

- *pM1*—A pointer to the first matrix that should be used in the operation

- *pM2*—A pointer to the second matrix that should be used in the operation

You also need to know about a Direct3D utility function that initializes a matrix to an identity matrix, which, if you recall from Chapters 3 and 4, is the matrix equivalent of the number 1. That is, the result of any matrix M multiplied by an identity matrix is M. The function that initializes an identity matrix is D3DXMatrixIdentity(), which Direct3D declares like this:

```
D3DXMATRIX *D3DXMatrixIdentity(
    D3DXMATRIX* pOut
);
```

The single argument here is a pointer to the matrix that will receive the result of the operation. In other words, after the call to D3DXMatrixIdentity(), the matrix pointed to by pOut will be an identity matrix.

So, here's how the whole process should go. First, you need to define two matrices, your world matrix and a temporary matrix:

```
D3DXMATRIX worldMatrix;
D3DXMATRIX tempMatrix;
```

Then, initialize your world matrix to its identity state:

```
D3DXMatrixIdentity(&worldMatrix);
```

Now, suppose that you want to rotate your 3D world around all three axes. Start by setting up the temporary matrix for the first rotation:

```
double radians = 6.283185308 / (360.0 / 45);
D3DXMatrixRotationX(&tempMatrix, radians);
```

The matrix tempMatrix now contains the values needed to rotate the 3D world around the X axis by 45 degrees. Now, you need to get this result into the world matrix, which you do with the D3DXMatrixMultiply() function:

```
D3DXMatrixMultiply(&worldMatrix, &worldMatrix, &tempMatrix);
```

This function call multiples worldMatrix times tempMatrix with the result being stored back in worldMatrix. Because worldMatrix starts off as an identity matrix, after the multiplication, worldMatrix will contain a copy of tempMatrix.

The next step is to load up tempMatrix with the values for the next rotation:

```
D3DXMatrixRotationY(&tempMatrix, radians);
```

The matrix tempMatrix now contains the values needed to rotate the 3D world around the Y axis by 45 degrees. You need to combine this result with the rotation already in the world matrix, which you do with another call to the D3DXMatrixMultiply() function:

```
D3DXMatrixMultiply(&worldMatrix, &worldMatrix, &tempMatrix);
```

Now worldMatrix contains the values needed for both rotations. Adding a third rotation is a simple matter of repeating the process:

```
D3DXMatrixRotationZ(&tempMatrix, radians);
D3DXMatrixMultiply(&worldMatrix, &worldMatrix, &tempMatrix);
```

A single call to SetTransform() now sends all three rotations to Direct3D for processing:

```
g_pDirect3DDevice->SetTransform(D3DTS_WORLD, &worldMatrix);
```

To see these rotations in your MatrixCubeApp program, simply find the InitMatrices() function and replace the lines

```
D3DXMATRIX worldMatrix;
double radians = timeGetTime() / 1000.0f;
D3DXMatrixRotationY(&worldMatrix, radians);
g_pDirect3DDevice->SetTransform(D3DTS_WORLD, &worldMatrix);
```

with Listing 8.8.

LISTING 8.8   New Lines for the InitMatrices() Function

```
D3DXMATRIX worldMatrix;
D3DXMATRIX tempMatrix;
D3DXMatrixIdentity(&worldMatrix);
double radians = timeGetTime() / 1000.0f;
D3DXMatrixRotationX(&tempMatrix, radians);
D3DXMatrixMultiply(&worldMatrix, &worldMatrix, &tempMatrix);
D3DXMatrixRotationY(&tempMatrix, radians);
D3DXMatrixMultiply(&worldMatrix, &worldMatrix, &tempMatrix);
D3DXMatrixRotationZ(&tempMatrix, radians);
D3DXMatrixMultiply(&worldMatrix, &worldMatrix, &tempMatrix);
g_pDirect3DDevice->SetTransform(D3DTS_WORLD, &worldMatrix);
```

Compile and run the program, and you'll see the screen shown in Figure 8.21, except that your cube will be in constant motion.

FIGURE 8.21   The final version of the MatrixCubeApp program.

Understanding the Order of Transformations

You know that you can translate, scale, and rotate objects in a 3D world, but what you may not know is that the order in which you perform these operations can make a big difference in the end result. For example, rotating a shape followed by a translation gives you a totally different result than translating the shape first and then doing the rotation.

To illustrate the difference, you'll now perform a few more Direct3D experiments. First, make a copy of your MatrixCubeApp project (just copy the entire folder). You'll use this copy as the starting point for your new Direct3D explorations.

Suppose that you want to have the cube rotated 45 degrees around each of its axes, but you also want the cube translated up the Z axis so that it appears to be farther away. To perform these transformations, find the `InitMatrices()` function and replace the line

```
double radians = timeGetTime() / 1000.0f;
```

with this:

```
double radians = 6.283185308 / (360.0 / 45);
```

and add the following lines right before the call to SetTransform():

```
D3DXMatrixTranslation(&tempMatrix, 0, 0, 5);
D3DXMatrixMultiply(&worldMatrix, &worldMatrix, &tempMatrix);
```

Run the program, and you should see the screen shown in Figure 8.22. You can see that the result is what you expect, with the cube rotated and farther away from the camera as compared to the original version of the program.

FIGURE 8.22   Rotating and translating the cube.

Now place the lines that perform the translation before the ones that do the rotation. You should end up with Listing 8.9.

LISTING 8.9   Changing the Transformation Order

```
// Set up the world transformation.
D3DXMATRIX worldMatrix;
D3DXMATRIX tempMatrix;
D3DXMatrixIdentity(&worldMatrix);
D3DXMatrixTranslation(&tempMatrix, 0, 0, 5);
D3DXMatrixMultiply(&worldMatrix, &worldMatrix, &tempMatrix);
double radians = 6.283185308 / (360.0 / 45);
D3DXMatrixRotationX(&tempMatrix, radians);
```

LISTING 8.9   Continued

```
D3DXMatrixMultiply(&worldMatrix, &worldMatrix, &tempMatrix);
D3DXMatrixRotationY(&tempMatrix, radians);
D3DXMatrixMultiply(&worldMatrix, &worldMatrix, &tempMatrix);
D3DXMatrixRotationZ(&tempMatrix, radians);
D3DXMatrixMultiply(&worldMatrix, &worldMatrix, &tempMatrix);
g_pDirect3DDevice->SetTransform(D3DTS_WORLD, &worldMatrix);
```

Run the program. When you do, the cube is nowhere to be seen. It has been rotated out of view of the camera.

Remember that, when you perform a rotation, you're actually rotating the entire 3D world, not just a single object. When you performed the rotation followed by the translation, everything worked fine because the cube was still located at the 3D world's origin. In this case, when you rotated the 3D world, it gave the effect of just rotating the cube. Then the translation pushed the cube farther away from the camera.

When you performed the translation first, however, you started by pushing the cube up the Z axis. Then, the cube was no longer at the origin, and when you performed the rotations, the 3D world rotated the cube out of view.

To see that this is true, let's add some animation to the rotation so that you can actually see the cube rotating around the 3D world. To do this, all you have to do is change the line:

```
double radians = 6.283185308 / (360.0 / 45);
```

back to this:

```
double radians = timeGetTime() / 1000.0f;
```

Now the angle used for the rotations changes constantly based on the system time. When you run the program, the screen starts off without the cube, but keep watching. Soon you'll see the cube rotate into (see Figure 8.23) and then out of view.

Want to get even a better view of the action? Just move the camera back from the scene, so that it's far enough back to keep the cube in view. Just change the line:

```
D3DXVECTOR3 vEyePt(0.0f, 0.0f, -3.0f);
```

to this:

```
D3DXVECTOR3 vEyePt(0.0f, 0.0f, -15.0f);
```

FIGURE 8.23   The cube rotated into view.

Here, you're changing the -3.0 in the call to -15.0, which has the effect of moving the camera back farther from the area in the 3D world where the cube is rotating. When you run the program, you can watch the cube floating around the screen without going off the edges of the screen.

You can keep moving the camera back by making the Z coordinate for the vEyePt vector smaller and smaller. Something weird happens, though, when the Z coordinate gets to be about -46. The cube vanishes now and then as it rotates. Can you guess why?

Remember in the projection transformation where you specify the near and far clipping planes? Here's what the code looks like:

```
// Set up the projection transformation.
D3DXMATRIX projectionMatrix;
D3DXMatrixPerspectiveFovLH(&projectionMatrix,
    D3DX_PI/4, 1.0f, 1.0f, 50.0f);
g_pDirect3DDevice->SetTransform(D3DTS_PROJECTION, &projectionMatrix);
```

You can see in the call to D3DXMatrixPerspectiveFovLH() that the far clipping plane is set to 50. This means that anything in the 3D world that's farther than 50 units away from the camera will be clipped out of the scene. By changing the Z coordinate for the camera to -46, you've caused the cube's rotation to move both in front of and behind the far clipping plane. In other words, when the cube vanishes, it's behind the clipping plane. To bring the entire cube's rotation back into view, just increase the far clipping plane's distance from the camera, like this:

```
D3DXMatrixPerspectiveFovLH(&projectionMatrix,
    D3DX_PI/4, 1.0f, 1.0f, 100.0f);
```

Now you can get the camera *way* back from the scene, as shown in Figure 8.24.

FIGURE 8.24   The cube way back in the distance.

In Brief

- The world transformation determines the location and position of graphical objects in the 3D world and so is where you apply translations, rotations, and scaling.

- Direct3D's utility library features a set of functions that set up matrices for the various transformations, including D3DXMatrixTranslation(), D3DXMatrixRotationX(), D3DXMatrixRotationY(), D3DXMatrixRotationZ(), and D3DXMatrixScaling().

- After setting up a matrix for one or more transformations, you give Direct3D the result by calling the device's SetTransform() method.

- Direct3D's view transformation takes the position of a viewpoint and determines what the 3D scene looks like from that position.

- To prepare for the Direct3D view transformation, you must define three vectors of the D3DXVECTOR3 data type for the location of the camera, the position at which the camera is pointed, and the up direction in the 3D world.

- After you define the vectors, you set up a matrix for the transformation by calling the Direct3D utility function D3DXMatrixLookAtLH().

- Direct3D's projection transformation specifies how to create a 2D display from the 3D world. To set up a matrix for the projection transformation, you call the utility function D3DXMatrixPerspectiveFovLH().

- The near clipping plane is the beginning of the viewing volume; that is, any objects or parts of objects between the camera and the near plane do not appear in the scene.

- The far clipping plane represents the end of the viewing volume. Any objects or parts of objects beyond the far plane also do not appear in the scene.

- Back-face culling is the process of drawing only the front sides of a 3D object and removing all back faces from the scene.

- To multiply two matrices, you call the utility function D3DXMatrixMultiply().

Lighting 3D Objects

9

Understanding Types of Source Light

Whether you're talking about the real world or a virtual Direct3D world, light comes in several forms and can be created by many types of objects. The sun, for example, gives off a type of light considerably different in its characteristics than light given off by a spotlight on a stage. The Direct3D engine can render four types of source light:

- Point light—A *point light* has color and position but not direction. That is, point light emits in every direction from the source. An example of a point light is a bulb in a lamp.

- Directional light—*Directional light* has color and direction but no discernable position. It's a parallel light that travels through a scene from a far away light source such as the sun.

- Spotlight—A *spotlight* has color, direction, and position, emitting a cone of light that is more intense toward the center of the cone and dimmer toward the edges of the cone.

- Ambient light—*Ambient light* is everywhere in a scene and has no discernable source. The brighter the ambient light, the brighter every object in the scene becomes (assuming the objects' materials are set to reflect ambient light), regardless of where the object is located. You can think of ambient light as coming from so many sources, directions, and reflections that it is simply everywhere.

Types of Reflective Light

The source light types produce light in a 3D scene, but what happens to the light depends on a number of things, not the least of which is the objects in the scene and how they're defined. Think about light in the real world. When you turn on a lamp, you've created a source of light that Direct3D programmers would call a point light. The light has a color and a position but no direction, except in the sense that it radiates everywhere from the bulb.

However, different things happen to the light as it travels from the light bulb and into the room. For example, it may reflect off the edge of a shiny object, causing a bright spot. The light may also reflect off the surface of a flat object, with the color of the light and the color of the flat object's surface combining to determine the color of light reflected from the object.

Direct3D can handle these types of what I like to call reflective light:

- *Diffuse*—This light results from the color of an object's material and the color of the light that strikes the object. Diffuse light greatly affects the final color of an object in a 3D scene.

- *Specular*—This light results from bright reflections off shiny surfaces. For example, a shiny red ball may have a bright spot of white light, which is an example of specular light.

- *Ambient*—Ambient light affects the color of an object by combining with the other types of light reflected or emitted from the object's surface.

- *Emissive*—Emissive light comes directly from an object in a scene. In other words, the object gives off the light. For this reason, one might be tempted to list emissive light with the source light types. However, emissive light has no reflective effects on other objects in a scene and so doesn't qualify as a light source. Emissive light is used simply to provide color, or "glow," to an object without the use of a formally defined light object.

SHOP TALK

THE VISIBILITY OF LIGHTS

If you're not used to using light objects in 3D programs, all this talk comparing lights to the sun, a lamp, and other types of real-world objects may get a little confusing. When you add a light object to a 3D scene, you can't actually see the source of the light, except as it affects the objects in the scene.

For example, if you place a spotlight in a 3D world and then position your viewpoint in the scene to look right at the light, you won't see a light bulb! This may seem obvious, but you may expect to see *something*. The truth is that, unless other objects are in the scene, you'll see nothing at all, not even light. In short, if there's nothing to reflect light in a 3D scene, no light is visible.

How do you add real-world lights to your 3D scenes? You need to create your own images and position them at the same location as the Direct3D light object you want to represent. Good examples of this are the Lighting and LightVS demos that come with the DirectX 9 SDK. Be sure to check them out.

Exploring Other Attributes of Lights

You've learned about several types of source light, as well as different ways that light reflects from the surface of an object. There are, however, still other factors that determine the lighting for the final image of a scene. These factors are as follows:

- *Position*—This is the X,Y,Z position of the light in world coordinates. This attribute is specified using the D3DVECTOR structure. All lights except directional and ambient have position.

- *Direction*—This is the direction the source light travels through the scene. This attribute is also specified using the D3DVECTOR structure. All lights except point and ambient have position.

- *Range*—This is the distance in world coordinates the light travels. Objects beyond this distance, which is specified with a float value, get no lighting.

- *Attenuation*—Determines how light diminishes as it travels from its source to the limit of its range. This attribute is also specified using floating-point values.

Defining a Direct3D Light

Obviously, it takes a lot of data to define a Direct3D light. To better organize all this information, Direct3D declares the D3DLIGHT9 structure. Direct3D defines the D3DLIGHT9 structure like this:

```
typedef struct _D3DLIGHT9 {
    D3DLIGHTTYPE Type;
    D3DCOLORVALUE Diffuse;
    D3DCOLORVALUE Specular;
    D3DCOLORVALUE Ambient;
    D3DVECTOR Position;
    D3DVECTOR Direction;
    float Range;
    float Falloff;
    float Attenuation0;
    float Attenuation1;
    float Attenuation2;
    float Theta;
    float Phi;
} D3DLIGHT9;
```

To define and prepare a light for use in your Direct3D program, you must perform the following steps:

1. Declare a variable of the D3DLIGHT9 structure.

2. Initialize the D3DLIGHT9 structure to all zeroes.

3. Set the light type, using one of the predefined constants D3DLIGHT_POINT, D3DLIGHT_SPOT, or D3DLIGHT_DIRECTIONAL. (As you'll soon see, ambient light is a special case and so does not have a light-type constant.)

4. Specify the amount and color of reflective light (ambient, diffuse, and specular) produced by the light source.

5. If appropriate for the type of light being used, specify the light source's position.

6. If appropriate for the type of light being used, specify the light source's direction.

7. If necessary, set the light source's attenuation and range.

8. Create the light.

9. Enable the light.

As you can see, setting up a light can be a lot of work, but it's more meticulous than it is hard. Suppose, for example, that you want to create a directional light source that introduces white, diffuse light into a scene, without regard for attenuation. First declare the light structure and initialize it to all zeroes:

```
D3DLIGHT9 light;
ZeroMemory(&light, sizeof(light));
```

Next, set the light type to D3DLIGHT_DIRECTIONAL:

```
light.Type = D3DLIGHT_DIRECTIONAL;
```

The next step is to set the diffuse color to white:

```
light.Diffuse.r  = 1.0f;
light.Diffuse.g  = 1.0f;
light.Diffuse.b  = 1.0f;
```

RGB VALUES OF A DIFFERENT TYPE

Unlike many RGB values you may have used to define colors, the values you use in the D3DLIGHT9 structure for RGB values typically go from 0.0 to 1.0, rather than from 0 to 255. Also, for special effects, these color values can be greater than 1.0 or even negative numbers.

The next step is to define the light's direction in the 3D scene. To do this, define a variable of the D3DVECTOR structure and then use it to set the value of the D3DLIGHT9 structure's Direction member:

```
D3DVECTOR dir = {1.0f, -1.0f, 1.0f};
light.Direction = dir;
```

The dir vector defined here points the light into the scene slightly downward and to the right. If you wanted a vector that aimed the light directly down the Z axis, you'd define the D3DVECTOR structure like this:

```
D3DVECTOR dir = {0.0f, 0.0f, 1.0f};
```

All these vectors are defined in relation to a virtual origin. That is, to figure out the light direction, you first plot the point defined by the X,Y,Z coordinates given by the vector. Then, you draw a line from the virtual origin (0,0,0) to the point. The direction traveled by the vector away from the origin is the direction traveled by the light.

After setting the light's direction, you specify the light's range, which is how far into the scene the light will travel:

```
light.Range = 100.0f;
```

The actual value you use for the range depends on your scene.

Next to last, you give the light to Direct3D by calling the device object's SetLight() method:

```
g_pDirect3DDevice->SetLight(0, &light);
```

Finally, you call the device's LightEnable() method to turn on the light:

```
g_pDirect3DDevice->LightEnable(0, TRUE);
```

You can turn off the light by calling LightEnable() with FALSE.

THE LIMIT ON LIGHTS

The MaxActiveLights member of the D3DCAPS9 structure specifies the maximum number of active lights that the device can handle.

Defining an Object's Material

Defining lights is only half the battle. Now you have to define materials for the objects in your scene. Just as a silver vase and a black bookshelf reflect light differently, so too do objects in a Direct3D scene produce different results, depending on their material and the light that strikes that material. Simply, a material determines what type, how much, and what color of light an object reflects.

Just as with a light, it takes a lot of data to define a Direct3D material. To better organize all this information, Direct3D declares the D3DMATERIAL9 structure. Direct3D defines the D3DMATERIAL9 structure like this:

```
typedef struct _D3DMATERIAL9 {
    D3DCOLORVALUE Diffuse, Ambient, Specular, Emissive;
    float Power;
} D3DMATERIAL9;
```

The first thing to notice here is that the structure has four D3DCOLORVALUE members, one for each of the types of light that a material can reflect. That is, for a material to reflect a particular type of light, that light type's member in the D3DMATERIAL9 structure must have a nonzero value. The Power member of the structure specifies the intensity of specular light.

Listing 9.1 sets a material to reflect ambient light and to give off emissive light.

LISTING 9.1   Setting a Material

```
D3DMATERIAL9 material;
ZeroMemory(&material, sizeof(material));
material.Ambient.r = 1.0f;
material.Ambient.g = 0.0f;
material.Ambient.b = 0.0f;
material.Ambient.a = 0.0f;
material.Emissive.r = 0.5f;
material.Emissive.g = 0.75f;
material.Emissive.b = 0.75f;
material.Emissive.a = 0.0f;
```

After initializing the material's D3DMATERIAL9 structure, you give the material to Direct3D by calling the device's SetMaterial() method:

```
g_pDirect3DDevice->SetMaterial(&material);
```

Defining Normals

There's one more complication to Direct3D's lighting: normals. To properly light a scene, Direct3D needs to know which way each triangle in the scene faces. However, although all triangles used to render a scene are planar (that is, their surfaces are flat), such triangles are often used to represent curved surfaces.

As an example, consider a globe. If the Direct3D lighting engine provided shading based only on the facing direction of each triangle, the result would look more like a mirror ball than a smoothly rounded globe. That is, it would be obvious that the globe comprised hundreds or thousands of small, flat surfaces. Direct3D names this effect *flat shading*.

For more realistic lighting effects, most Direct3D programs use *Gourand shading*, which hides each individual triangle by making planar surfaces look curved. To provide this type of lighting, it's not enough for Direct3D to know which way a triangle faces. Instead, the lighting engine needs to know the facing direction of each vertex in the triangle. So, for most Direct3D lighting effects, normals called *vertex normals* are associated with each vertex in a triangle.

But what exactly is a normal? A normal is nothing more than a vector of length 1. That is, a normal is a *normalized vector*. In the case of Direct3D's shading effects, normals tell Direct3D the facing direction of each vertex in a triangle. In return for this information, Direct3D can offer more realistic shading effects.

Whereas the concept of a normal is pretty simple, defining one often is not. This is because it takes some fancy math to determine the direction in which a normal points. Specifically, you need to know how to calculate vectors, find the cross products of vectors, and normalize the results. Luckily, Direct3D provides the math functions you need to calculate normals.

Calculating Face Normals

Face normals, which specify the facing direction of a triangle, are the easiest to understand and calculate. In three steps, you can calculate a face normal for a triangle whose vertices are defined in clockwise order:

1. Calculate two vectors, the first of which goes from vertex 1 to vertex 2, and the second of which goes from vertex 1 to vertex 3.

2. Find the cross product of the two vectors calculated in step 1.

3. Normalize the result of step 2.

In Direct3D code, the previous calculations would look something like Listing 9.2.

LISTING 9.2   Calculating Face Normals

```
// A forward-facing triangle's vertices expressed as vectors.
D3DXVECTOR3 vec1(-0.5f,  0.5f, -0.5f);
D3DXVECTOR3 vec2(0.5f, -0.5f, -0.5f);
D3DXVECTOR3 vec3(-0.5f, -0.5f, -0.5f);

// Step 1 of calculations.
D3DXVECTOR3 result1;
D3DXVec3Subtract(&result1, &vec1, &vec2);
D3DXVECTOR3 result2;
D3DXVec3Subtract(&result2, &vec1, &vec3);

// Step 2 of calculations.
D3DXVECTOR3 result3;
D3DXVec3Cross(&result3, &result1, &result2);

// Step 3 of calculations.
D3DXVECTOR3 faceNormal;
D3DXVec3Normalize(&faceNormal, &result3);
```

After the preceding calculations, the vector `faceNormal` contains X,Y,Z values of 0,0,-1, which specifies that the triangle front face is aimed directly down the negative Z axis.

That's all there is to calculating a face normal. However, what Direct3D usually wants is vertex normals.

Calculating Vertex Normals

Vertex normals are easy to calculate after you know how to calculate face normals. Here are the steps:

1. Determine which triangles share the vertex for which you need the normal.

2. For each triangle from step 1, generate an un-normalized face normal.

3. Sum the normals from step 2.

4. Normalize the result from step 3.

Building the LightApp Application

All the information presented so far in this chapter may have your head spinning. The best way to slow that spinning is to create a program and experiment with the code to understand how lighting works. In this section, you create a program that uses the simplest form of light, emissive, to provide color for a rotating cube. Remember that you can find the complete source code online, and so can copy and paste code rather than type everything. (See this book's introduction for instructions on downloading the source code.)

Creating the Basic Project

Perform the following steps to get the main Direct3D application project started:

1. Start a new empty Win32 project named LightApp.

2. On the Project menu, select the Add New Item command. The Add New Item dialog box appears.

3. Add a new C++ File (.cpp) named LightApp.cpp.

4. Copy the contents of the BasicDirect3DApp.cpp file (from Chapter 5, "Getting Direct3D Up and Running") into the new LightApp code window.

5. Change the name in the comment at the top of the file to LightApp.cpp.

6. In the `RegisterWindowClass()` function, change `wc.lpszClassName = "Direct3D"` to `wc.lpszClassName = "LightApp"`.

7. In the `CreateAppWindow()` function, change `"Direct3D"` to `"LightApp"`, and then change `"Basic Direct3D Application"` to `"Direct3D Lighting Application"`.

Adding the DirectX References

Next, you need to tell the program where the required DirectX header files and libraries are located. To do that, follow these steps:

1. Right-click the project's name in the Solution Explorer, and select Properties from the menu that appears. The LightApp Property Pages dialog box appears.

2. Click the C/C++ selection in the left-hand pane, and select General from the displayed choices.

3. In the Additional Include Directories box, enter the path to the DirectX 9 SDK's include folder. If you installed the SDK using the default settings, this path should be `C:\DXSDK\include`.

4. Click the Linker selection in the left-hand pane, and select General from the displayed choices.

5. In the Additional Library Directories box, enter the path to the DirectX 9 SDK's library folder. If you installed the SDK using the default settings, this path should be `C:\DXSDK\lib`.

6. Click the Linker's Input selection in the left-hand pane.

7. In the Additional Dependencies box in the right-hand pane, enter **d3d9.lib**, **d3dx9.lib**, and **dxerr9.lib**.

8. Compile and run the application to make sure that it works. Press Escape to exit the application.

Adding Source Code

Now all you have to do is add the Direct3D code that'll get your lighted cube up on the screen. Perform the following steps to get this task done:

1. Add the following line to the #include statements near the top of the program:

```
#include <d3dx9.h>
```

2. Add the following lines to the function prototypes near the top of the program:

```
HRESULT InitVertices();
void InitMatrices();
void InitLights();
```

3. Add the following lines to the global variable declarations:

```
IDirect3DVertexBuffer9* g_pVertexBuf = NULL;
int g_iNumTriangles;
```

4. Add the following vertex structure right after the global variables:

```
struct CUSTOMVERTEXSTRUCT
{
    float fX,
          fY,
          fZ;
    D3DVECTOR normal;
};
```

5. Replace the current WinMain() function with Listing 9.3.

LISTING 9.3   The New WinMain() Function

```
/////////////////////////////////////////////////////
// WinMain()
/////////////////////////////////////////////////////
```

LISTING 9.6   Continued

```
{
    if (g_pVertexBuf)
    {
        g_pVertexBuf->Release();
        g_pVertexBuf = NULL;
    }
    if (g_pDirect3DDevice)
    {
        g_pDirect3DDevice->Release();
        g_pDirect3DDevice = NULL;
    }
    if (g_pDirect3D)
    {
        g_pDirect3D->Release();
        g_pDirect3D = NULL;
    }
}
```

9. Add the InitVertices() function shown in Listing 9.7 to the program.

LISTING 9.7   The New InitVertices() Function

```
/////////////////////////////////////////////////////
// InitVertices()
/////////////////////////////////////////////////////
HRESULT InitVertices()
{
    CUSTOMVERTEXSTRUCT cube[] =
    {
        // Front of cube.
        {-0.5f,  0.5f, -0.5f, 0.0f, 0.0f, -1.0f}, // Top left.
        { 0.5f, -0.5f, -0.5f, 0.0f, 0.0f, -1.0f}, // Bottom right.
        {-0.5f, -0.5f, -0.5f, 0.0f, 0.0f, -1.0f}, // Bottom left.
        {-0.5f,  0.5f, -0.5f, 0.0f, 0.0f, -1.0f}, // Top left.
        { 0.5f,  0.5f, -0.5f, 0.0f, 0.0f, -1.0f}, // Top right.
        { 0.5f, -0.5f, -0.5f, 0.0f, 0.0f, -1.0f},  // Bottom right.

        // Right side of cube.
        {0.5f,  0.5f, -0.5f, 1.0f, 0.0f, 0.0f},
        {0.5f, -0.5f,  0.5f, 1.0f, 0.0f, 0.0f},
        {0.5f, -0.5f, -0.5f, 1.0f, 0.0f, 0.0f},
        {0.5f,  0.5f, -0.5f, 1.0f, 0.0f, 0.0f},
```

LISTING 9.7   Continued

```
            {0.5f,  0.5f,  0.5f, 1.0f, 0.0f, 0.0f},
            {0.5f, -0.5f,  0.5f, 1.0f, 0.0f, 0.0f},

            // Back of cube.
            { 0.5f,  0.5f, 0.5f, 0.0f, 0.0f, 1.0f},
            {-0.5f, -0.5f, 0.5f, 0.0f, 0.0f, 1.0f},
            { 0.5f, -0.5f, 0.5f, 0.0f, 0.0f, 1.0f},
            { 0.5f,  0.5f, 0.5f, 0.0f, 0.0f, 1.0f},
            {-0.5f,  0.5f, 0.5f, 0.0f, 0.0f, 1.0f},
            {-0.5f, -0.5f, 0.5f, 0.0f, 0.0f, 1.0f},

            // Left side of cube.
            {-0.5f,  0.5f,  0.5f, -1.0f, 0.0f, 0.0f},
            {-0.5f, -0.5f, -0.5f, -1.0f, 0.0f, 0.0f},
            {-0.5f, -0.5f,  0.5f, -1.0f, 0.0f, 0.0f},
            {-0.5f,  0.5f,  0.5f, -1.0f, 0.0f, 0.0f},
            {-0.5f,  0.5f, -0.5f, -1.0f, 0.0f, 0.0f},
            {-0.5f, -0.5f, -0.5f, -1.0f, 0.0f, 0.0f},

            // Top of cube.
            {-0.5f, 0.5f, -0.5f, 0.0f, 1.0f, 0.0f},
            {-0.5f, 0.5f,  0.5f, 0.0f, 1.0f, 0.0f},
            { 0.5f, 0.5f, -0.5f, 0.0f, 1.0f, 0.0f},
            {-0.5f, 0.5f,  0.5f, 0.0f, 1.0f, 0.0f},
            { 0.5f, 0.5f,  0.5f, 0.0f, 1.0f, 0.0f},
            { 0.5f, 0.5f, -0.5f, 0.0f, 1.0f, 0.0f},

            // Bottom of cube.
            {-0.5f, -0.5f, -0.5f, 0.0f, -1.0f, 0.0f},
            { 0.5f, -0.5f, -0.5f, 0.0f, -1.0f, 0.0f},
            {-0.5f, -0.5f,  0.5f, 0.0f, -1.0f, 0.0f},
            { 0.5f, -0.5f, -0.5f, 0.0f, -1.0f, 0.0f},
            { 0.5f, -0.5f,  0.5f, 0.0f, -1.0f, 0.0f},
            {-0.5f, -0.5f,  0.5f, 0.0f, -1.0f, 0.0f}
    };

    // Create the vertex buffer.
    if(FAILED(g_pDirect3DDevice ->CreateVertexBuffer(sizeof(cube),
            0, D3DFVF_XYZ|D3DFVF_NORMAL, D3DPOOL_DEFAULT,
            &g_pVertexBuf, NULL)))
        return E_FAIL;
```

```
CUSTOMVERTEXSTRUCT* pVertices;
if(FAILED(g_pVertexBuf->Lock( 0, 0, (void**)&pVertices, 0)))
    return E_FAIL;
memcpy(pVertices, cube, sizeof(cube));
g_pVertexBuf->Unlock();

g_iNumTriangles = (sizeof(cube) / sizeof(float)) / 18;

return S_OK;
}
```

10. Add the InitMatrices() function shown in Listing 9.8 to the program.

LISTING 9.8   The New InitMatrices() Function

```
//////////////////////////////////////////////////////
// InitMatrices()
//////////////////////////////////////////////////////
VOID InitMatrices()
{
    D3DXMATRIXA16 matWorld;
    D3DXMatrixIdentity(&matWorld);
    static float angle = 0.0f;
    D3DXMatrixRotationY(&matWorld, angle);
    angle += 0.01f;
    g_pDirect3DDevice->SetTransform(D3DTS_WORLD, &matWorld);

    D3DXVECTOR3 vEyePt(0.0f, 1.0f, -3.0f);
    D3DXVECTOR3 vLookatPt(0.0f, 0.0f, 0.0f);
    D3DXVECTOR3 vUpVec(0.0f, 1.0f, 0.0f);
    D3DXMATRIXA16 matView;
    D3DXMatrixLookAtLH(&matView, &vEyePt, &vLookatPt, &vUpVec);
    g_pDirect3DDevice->SetTransform(D3DTS_VIEW, &matView);

    D3DXMATRIXA16 matProj;
    D3DXMatrixPerspectiveFovLH(&matProj, D3DX_PI/4, 1.0f, 1.0f, 100.0f);
    g_pDirect3DDevice->SetTransform(D3DTS_PROJECTION, &matProj);
}
```

11. Add the `InitLights()` function shown in Listing 9.9 to the end of the program.

LISTING 9.9   The New `InitLights()` Function

```
/////////////////////////////////////////////////
// InitLights()
/////////////////////////////////////////////////
VOID InitLights()
{
    D3DMATERIAL9 material;
    ZeroMemory(&material, sizeof(material));
    material.Emissive.r = 0.5f;
    material.Emissive.g = 0.75f;
    material.Emissive.b = 0.75f;
    material.Emissive.a = 0.0f;
    g_pDirect3DDevice->SetMaterial(&material);
}
```

Experimenting with Lights

When you compile and run the program, you should see the window shown in Figure 9.1. However, throughout this section, you'll modify the program to create different types of lighting effects. All changes to the program will be limited to the `InitLights()` function.

SHOP TALK

MANAGING LIGHT ATTRIBUTES

I can tell you firsthand that the many attributes and settings you can apply to Direct3D lights can drive you crazy. That is, unless everything is set just right, you may think that your lights aren't working, when in fact, they may only be pointing in the wrong direction, placed in the wrong location, or giving off the wrong kind of light.

When you create your light objects and set their attributes, look over your code carefully to make sure that you've followed all the steps and set their attributes appropriately. Also, don't forget that lights must be enabled, which is the Direct3D version of turning them on.

To make sure that you understand how lights work, you should experiment with working examples, such as the programs included with this chapter or with the DirectX SDK. When you start off with a working program and make changes one by one, running the program after each change, you can quickly identify the places where you don't understand a setting.

This is exactly the method I used to try out Direct3D lights for myself. If I hadn't learned the ins and outs of Direct3D lighting and materials this way, there's a good chance you wouldn't be reading this chapter right now! At the very least, it would have taken me much longer to figure out Direct3D lights and materials. Many variables are involved in setting up lights and materials, and there are dozens of ways you can go wrong.

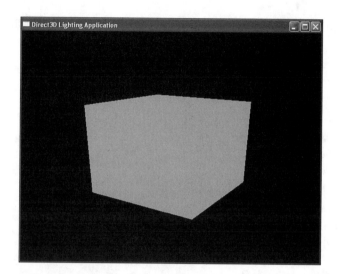

FIGURE 9.1   A cube giving off emissive light.

Using Emitted Light

You're seeing on the screen a 3D cube comprised of 12 triangles. The cube itself emits blue light, which is what gives the cube its color. However, notice how the cube lacks detail. That is, the cube looks more like a blue shadow than a 3D object. The only way you can tell that this is a 3D object is by its rotation, which gives you clues to the object's full shape. The lack of detail is a product of the emissive light, which provides no shading, giving off equal light from every surface.

The thing to notice about the program at this point is that you have defined no lights at all, yet the spinning cube is lit. Emissive light is one of the simplest lights to use because it requires only a material.

The program sets up the material by first declaring a variable of the D3DMATERIAL9 structure and initializing all its members to 0:

```
D3DMATERIAL9 material;
ZeroMemory(&material, sizeof(material));
```

Then the program sets the material's Emissive member to specify a light blue emitted light:

```
material.Emissive.r = 0.5f;
material.Emissive.g = 0.75f;
material.Emissive.b = 0.75f;
material.Emissive.a = 0.0f;
```

Finally, the program calls `SetMaterial()` to give the material to Direct3D:

```
g_pDirect3DDevice->SetMaterial(&material);
```

Direct3D now uses this as the material for every primitive it draws and continues to do so until the program sets a new material.

To prove that the cube really is emitting blue light, comment out the call to `SetMaterial()` and rerun the program. When you do, the cube vanishes from the scene. More accurately, Direct3D renders the cube as solid black. Because the background is also black, the cube vanishes.

Using Ambient Light

Ambient light is the next easiest type of light to use in your Direct3D programs. Just as with emissive light, ambient light is easy to use because you need not formally define light objects. To see how this works, replace the current version of `InitLights()` with Listing 9.10.

LISTING 9.10   Another `InitLights()` Function

```
/////////////////////////////////////////////////////
// InitLights()
/////////////////////////////////////////////////////
VOID InitLights()
{
    D3DMATERIAL9 material;
    ZeroMemory(&material, sizeof(material));
    material.Ambient.r = 0.5f;
    material.Ambient.g = 0.75f;
    material.Ambient.b = 0.75f;
    material.Ambient.a = 0.0f;
    g_pDirect3DDevice->SetMaterial(&material);
    g_pDirect3DDevice-> SetRenderState(D3DRS_AMBIENT,
        D3DCOLOR_ARGB(0, 255, 255, 255));
}
```

When you run the program now, you see exactly the same display you did with the previous version, except now the blue color reflected by the cube is produced by ambient light rather than emissive light. Like emissive light, ambient light causes an object to give off light equally from all surfaces, so again the cube lacks detail. The difference is that, with emissive light, the light comes from the cube itself, whereas with ambient light, you add light to the scene, and that light is then reflected back by the cube. The end result, however, looks exactly the same.

Notice in the new InitLights() function that you're no longer defining the material to generate emissive light. Instead, you've defined the material to reflect ambient light:

```
material.Ambient.r = 0.5f;
material.Ambient.g = 0.75f;
material.Ambient.b = 0.75f;
material.Ambient.a = 0.0f;
```

Specifically, the material will reflect 50 percent of any red ambient light, 75 percent of any green ambient light, and 75 percent of any blue ambient light.

Where does this ambient light come from? To turn it on, you don't need to define a light object. All you have to do is call the device's SetRenderState() method with the D3DRS_AMBIENT flag and the color of the ambient light you want to use:

```
g_pDirect3DDevice-> SetRenderState(D3DRS_AMBIENT,
    D3DCOLOR_ARGB(0, 255, 255, 255));
```

An easy way to define the light color is to employ the D3DCOLOR_ARGB macro, which produces the required D3DCOLOR value from the alpha, red, green, and blue color elements. In this particular case, the call to SetRenderState() creates pure white ambient light, which contains equal amounts of red, green, and blue light.

LIGHT COLOR AND REFLECTION

The light source and the material enjoy a close connection when it comes to how light is reflected. For example, if the ambient light added to a scene contains a red color element of 0, the object material could not reflect red light, even if it is defined to do so. Suppose that the ambient light's color is defined as D3DCOLOR_ARGB(0, 0, 255, 255), and the material's red ambient setting is material.Ambient.r = 0.5f. No red ambient light would reflect from the material because 50% of 0 is still 0.

With another modification to the InitLights() function, you can prove that emissive and ambient light really are different and independent of each other. To do so, replace the current InitLights() with Listing 9.11.

LISTING 9.11   Yet Another InitLights() Function

```
/////////////////////////////////////////////////////
// InitLights()
/////////////////////////////////////////////////////
VOID InitLights()
{
    D3DMATERIAL9 material;
    ZeroMemory(&material, sizeof(material));
```

LISTING 9.11 Continued

```
    material.Ambient.r = 1.0f;
    material.Ambient.g = 0.0f;
    material.Ambient.b = 0.0f;
    material.Ambient.a = 0.0f;
    material.Emissive.r = 0.5f;
    material.Emissive.g = 0.75f;
    material.Emissive.b = 0.75f;
    material.Emissive.a = 0.0f;
    g_pDirect3DDevice->SetMaterial(&material);
    g_pDirect3DDevice->SetRenderState(D3DRS_AMBIENT,
        D3DCOLOR_ARGB(0, 255, 255, 255));
}
```

Now, you've defined a material that reflects 100 percent of any red ambient light that strikes its surface but none of the green or blue ambient light. Moreover, the material emits its own blue light. The ambient light introduced to the scene is still pure white. The cube's final color, then, will be a combination of the two, which will look pinkish. If you change the red ambient value of 255 to 0, the cube will go back to blue, because there will no longer be any red ambient light to reflect.

Using Point Light

As you've seen, using emissive and ambient light requires no actual Direct3D light objects. That's not true with other forms of light. The first of which you'll look at is point light. As you've already learned, point light has position but no direction (except in the sense that it radiates in every direction simultaneously). An example of a real-world point light is a light bulb. To see a point light in action, replace your current InitLights() function with Listing 9.12.

LISTING 9.12 The Latest Version of the InitLights() Function

```
//////////////////////////////////////////////////////
// InitLights()
//////////////////////////////////////////////////////
VOID InitLights()
{
    D3DLIGHT9 light0;
    ZeroMemory(&light0, sizeof(light0));

    light0.Type = D3DLIGHT_POINT;
    light0.Diffuse.r  = 1.0f;
    light0.Diffuse.g  = 1.0f;
```

LISTING 9.12 Continued

```
    light0.Diffuse.b  = 1.0f;
    light0.Position.x = 0.0f;
    light0.Position.y = 10.0f;
    light0.Position.z = -10.0f;
    light0.Range = 15.0f;
    light0.Attenuation0 = 1.0f;

    g_pDirect3DDevice->SetLight(0, &light0);
    g_pDirect3DDevice->LightEnable(0, TRUE);

    D3DMATERIAL9 material;
    ZeroMemory(&material, sizeof(material));
    material.Diffuse.r = 1.0f;
    material.Diffuse.g = 0.3f;
    material.Diffuse.b = 1.0f;
    material.Diffuse.a = 0.0f;
    g_pDirect3DDevice->SetMaterial(&material);
}
```

When you run the program now, you see the window shown in Figure 9.2. Notice that the cube now has plenty of detail, thanks to shading. Unlike with emissive or ambient light, Direct3D uses the reflective properties of a point light and diffuse light to create the shading that makes the cube look like an actual 3D object rather than just a blob of color.

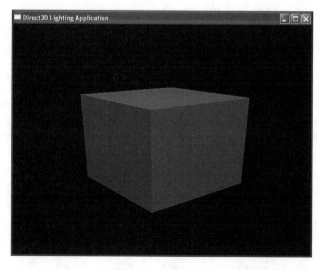

FIGURE 9.2 A cube reflecting diffuse light from a source point light.

This is the first version of the `InitLights()` function that creates a light object, in addition to material for the cube. The function first creates a variable of the `D3DLIGHT9` structure and initializes it to all zeroes:

```
D3DLIGHT9 light0;
ZeroMemory(&light0, sizeof(light0));
```

Then the function sets the type of light to use:

```
light0.Type = D3DLIGHT_POINT;
```

Because this version of the program deals only with diffuse light, the function sets the color for only the `Diffuse` member of the light structure:

```
light0.Diffuse.r  = 1.0f;
light0.Diffuse.g  = 1.0f;
light0.Diffuse.b  = 1.0f;
```

By setting each value to 1.0, the light provides pure white diffuse light.

The next step is to place the light somewhere in the 3D scene:

```
light0.Position.x = 0.0f;
light0.Position.y = 10.0f;
light0.Position.z = -10.0f;
```

Using world coordinates, the preceding values position the light a bit above and in front of the cube.

Now the program must specify how far into the scene the light will travel. The light is already 10 units back on the Z axis, so it'll take a value of 10 just to get the light to the beginning of the scene. Turns out that a value of 15 works fine to light the entire cube:

```
light0.Range = 15.0f;
```

As mentioned previously, attenuation is how fast the light fades out as it travels into the scene. Three members of the light structure control this effect. To prevent attenuation from occurring, the program sets `Attenuation0` to 1. `Attenuation1` and `Attenuation2` are already 0:

```
light0.Attenuation0 = 1.0f;
```

LIGHT ATTENUATION

Dealing with light attenuation can be confusing. For most purposes, if you want to use attenuation, setting `Attenuation0` to 0, `Attenuation1` to 1, and `Attenuation2` to 0 works well to provide light that fades realistically and evenly.

Finally, the program sets and turns on the light:

```
g_pDirect3DDevice->SetLight(0, &light0);
g_pDirect3DDevice->LightEnable(0, TRUE);
```

So now the program has a light that's giving off a white diffuse element. Next, the program needs to create a material that reflects this light:

```
D3DMATERIAL9 material;
ZeroMemory(&material, sizeof(material));
material.Diffuse.r = 1.0f;
material.Diffuse.g = 0.3f;
material.Diffuse.b = 1.0f;
material.Diffuse.a = 0.0f;
g_pDirect3DDevice->SetMaterial(&material);
```

The material the function defines reflects 100 percent of red and blue diffuse light in the scene, but only 30 percent of the green. This results in a purple cube.

Spend some time experimenting with the different values used in the InitLights() function, changing the colors of the light and material, as well as positioning the light in different places. As an example, look at the version of InitLights() in Listing 9.13.

LISTING 9.13   Changing the Light's Position

```
///////////////////////////////////////////////////////
// InitLights()
///////////////////////////////////////////////////////
VOID InitLights()
{
    D3DLIGHT9 light0;
    ZeroMemory(&light0, sizeof(light0));

    light0.Type = D3DLIGHT_POINT;
    light0.Diffuse.r  = 1.0f;
    light0.Diffuse.g  = 1.0f;
    light0.Diffuse.b  = 1.0f;
    light0.Position.x = -5.0f;
    light0.Position.y = -1.0f;
    light0.Position.z = -10.0f;
    light0.Range = 50.0f;
    light0.Attenuation0 = 1.0f;
```

LISTING 9.13   Continued

```
        g_pDirect3DDevice->SetLight(0, &light0);
        g_pDirect3DDevice->LightEnable(0, TRUE);

        D3DMATERIAL9 material;
        ZeroMemory(&material, sizeof(material));
        material.Diffuse.r = 0.5f;
        material.Diffuse.g = 0.5f;
        material.Diffuse.b = 0.5f;
        material.Diffuse.a = 0.0f;
        g_pDirect3DDevice->SetMaterial(&material);
}
```

If you use this version of the InitLights() function in your program, you'll get the window shown in Figure 9.3. Now the light is positioned down and to the left, which means that the top of the cube receives no light. Moreover, the changes in the material result in a gray, rather than purple cube.

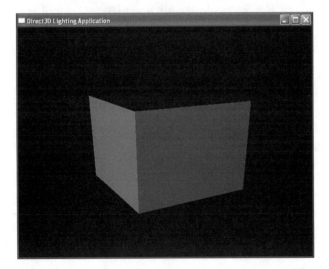

FIGURE 9.3   After repositioning the light and changing the material color.

The light in this program currently provides only diffuse light to the scene. A normal white light, however, would also provide ambient and specular light, and the material would reflect these types of light. However, flat surfaces don't reflect much specular light, so there's not much point in creating a material for a cube that sets the Specular member of the structure. Listing 9.14 is the resulting InitLights() function.

LISTING 9.14 A Final Point Light Example

```
///////////////////////////////////////////////////
// InitLights()
///////////////////////////////////////////////////
VOID InitLights()
{
    D3DLIGHT9 light0;
    ZeroMemory(&light0, sizeof(light0));

    light0.Type = D3DLIGHT_POINT;
    light0.Diffuse.r  = 1.0f;
    light0.Diffuse.g  = 1.0f;
    light0.Diffuse.b  = 1.0f;
    light0.Ambient.r  = 1.0f;
    light0.Ambient.g  = 1.0f;
    light0.Ambient.b  = 1.0f;
    light0.Specular.r  = 1.0f;
    light0.Specular.g  = 1.0f;
    light0.Specular.b  = 1.0f;
    light0.Position.x = -5.0f;
    light0.Position.y = -1.0f;
    light0.Position.z = -10.0f;
    light0.Range = 50.0f;
    light0.Attenuation0 = 1.0f;

    g_pDirect3DDevice->SetLight(0, &light0);
    g_pDirect3DDevice->LightEnable(0, TRUE);

    D3DMATERIAL9 material;
    ZeroMemory(&material, sizeof(material));
    material.Diffuse.r = 0.5f;
    material.Diffuse.g = 0.5f;
    material.Diffuse.b = 0.5f;
    material.Diffuse.a = 0.0f;
    material.Ambient.r = 0.3f;
    material.Ambient.g = 0.3f;
    material.Ambient.b = 0.3f;
    material.Ambient.a = 0.0f;
    g_pDirect3DDevice->SetMaterial(&material);
}
```

When you use this version of the function in the program, you see the window shown in Figure 9.4. The addition of ambient light to the scene has lightened all surfaces of the cube so that the top is again visible. Also, even though the cube remains gray, it's a brighter gray.

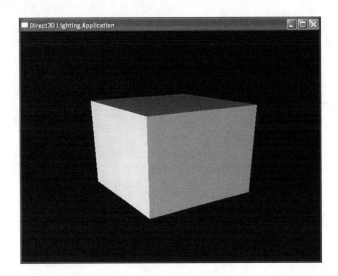

FIGURE 9.4   After adding ambient light to the scene.

Using Directional Light

Much of what you've learned with point lights applies to directional lights. The difference is that a directional light has no position, only a direction in which it moves through the scene. To see the difference, replace the current InitLights() function with Listing 9.15.

LISTING 9.15   Using Directional Light

```
///////////////////////////////////////////////////
// InitLights()
///////////////////////////////////////////////////
VOID InitLights()
{
    D3DLIGHT9 light0;
    ZeroMemory(&light0, sizeof(light0));

    light0.Type = D3DLIGHT_DIRECTIONAL;
    light0.Diffuse.r  = 1.0f;
```

LISTING 9.15 Continued

```
    light0.Diffuse.g  = 1.0f;
    light0.Diffuse.b  = 1.0f;
    light0.Ambient.r  = 1.0f;
    light0.Ambient.g  = 1.0f;
    light0.Ambient.b  = 1.0f;
    light0.Specular.r = 1.0f;
    light0.Specular.g = 1.0f;
    light0.Specular.b = 1.0f;
    light0.Direction.x = -1.0f;
    light0.Direction.y = 0.0f;
    light0.Direction.z = 0.0f;

    g_pDirect3DDevice->SetLight(0, &light0);
    g_pDirect3DDevice->LightEnable(0, TRUE);

    D3DMATERIAL9 material;
    ZeroMemory(&material, sizeof(material));
    material.Diffuse.r = 1.0f;
    material.Diffuse.g = 0.0f;
    material.Diffuse.b = 0.0f;
    material.Diffuse.a = 0.0f;
    g_pDirect3DDevice->SetMaterial(&material);
}
```

When you run the program now, you see the window shown in Figure 9.5. The directional light in the scene is coming directly from the right, and moving left through the scene, so that only the right side of the cube ever receives light. As the cube revolves, that side gets darker until it vanishes and the next side starts getting light.

Only a couple of things are different with the directional light as compared with the previous point light examples. The first difference is the light type setting:

```
light0.Type = D3DLIGHT_DIRECTIONAL;
```

The color and content of the light can all remain the same. However, rather than setting a position for the light, the program must set a direction:

```
light0.Direction.x = -1.0f;
light0.Direction.y = 0.0f;
light0.Direction.z = 0.0f;
```

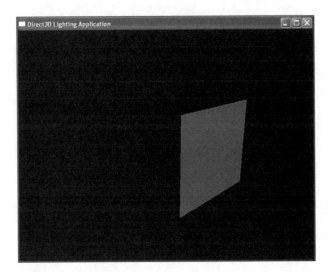

FIGURE 9.5   A cube lit with directional light coming from the direct right.

These values place the light directly to the right because the X coordinate points in the negative X direction. If you wanted the light to come from the left, you would change the X value to positive 1, resulting in the window shown in Figure 9.6.

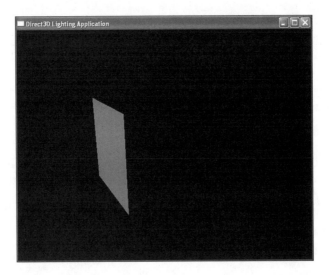

FIGURE 9.6   A cube lit with directional light coming from the direct left.

As another example, if you wanted the light to come from in front of the scene, as shown in Figure 9.7, you would use these values:

```
light0.Direction.x = 0.0f;
light0.Direction.y = 0.0f;
light0.Direction.z = 1.0f;
```

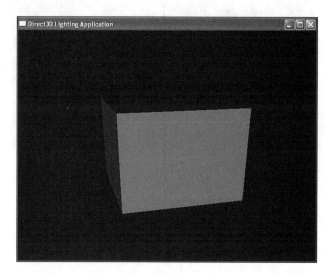

FIGURE 9.7   A cube lit with directional light coming from the front.

You can angle the light by setting more than one of the X, Y, or Z coordinates. For example, the following values place the directional light source above and to the right of the cube, resulting in Figure 9.8:

```
light0.Direction.x = -1.0f;
light0.Direction.y = -1.0f;
light0.Direction.z = 0.0f;
```

Getting back to the program, another difference is that, because directional light isn't affected by range or attenuation, the program sets none of the structure members related to those characteristics. Finally, the last change is to the material, setting it to reflect only red diffuse light.

The lack of ambient light gives the directional light a more dramatic effect. For example, consider the first version of the directional-light example, where the light comes directly from the right. By adding ambient light-reflecting properties to the material, you can see the other surfaces of the cube even when they receive no light for the directional light source (see Figure 9.9). Listing 9.16 shows the new InitLights() function.

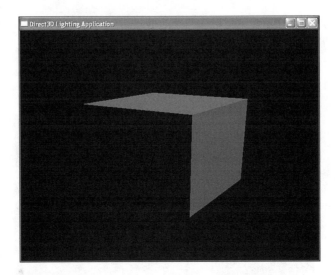

FIGURE 9.8   A cube lit with directional light coming from above and to the right.

LISTING 9.16   Another Example of Directional Light

```
/////////////////////////////////////////////////
// InitLights()
/////////////////////////////////////////////////
VOID InitLights()
{
    D3DLIGHT9 light0;
    ZeroMemory(&light0, sizeof(light0));

    light0.Type = D3DLIGHT_DIRECTIONAL;
    light0.Diffuse.r  = 1.0f;
    light0.Diffuse.g  = 1.0f;
    light0.Diffuse.b  = 1.0f;
    light0.Ambient.r  = 1.0f;
    light0.Ambient.g  = 1.0f;
    light0.Ambient.b  = 1.0f;
    light0.Specular.r  = 1.0f;
    light0.Specular.g  = 1.0f;
    light0.Specular.b  = 1.0f;
    light0.Direction.x = -1.0f;
    light0.Direction.y = 0.0f;
    light0.Direction.z = 0.0f;
```

LISTING 9.16 Continued

```
g_pDirect3DDevice->SetLight(0, &light0);
g_pDirect3DDevice->LightEnable(0, TRUE);

D3DMATERIAL9 material;
ZeroMemory(&material, sizeof(material));
material.Diffuse.r = 1.0f;
material.Diffuse.g = 0.0f;
material.Diffuse.b = 0.0f;
material.Diffuse.a = 0.0f;
material.Ambient.r = 0.4f;
material.Ambient.g = 0.0f;
material.Ambient.b = 0.0f;
material.Ambient.a = 0.0f;
g_pDirect3DDevice->SetMaterial(&material);
}
```

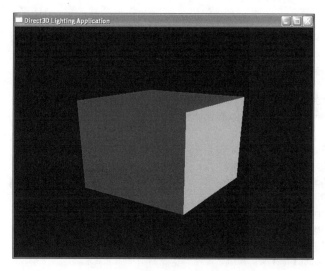

FIGURE 9.9 Adding ambient light to the original directional light.

Using a Spotlight

Spotlights are the toughest to use for a couple of reasons. From a programmer's point of view, they require a lot of settings to create. From the application's point of view, they require more processing power than any of the other light types. Of course, you get what you pay for: spotlights provide realistic lighting effects.

To review, spotlights have—besides the usual color settings—direction and position. Moreover, they are affected by range and attenuation. To complicate matters even further, they require that you set the Phi, Theta, and Falloff members of the light structure.

These last three values define the cone of light produced by the spotlight. Phi is an angle in radians that specifies the full width of the cone of light, whereas Theta is the width of a smaller cone of light inside the full cone. Theta is also an angle in radians and must be smaller than Phi.

The smaller cone of light represents the way a spotlight produces light that's brighter in the center than it is at the extremes of the cone. The Falloff value specifies how the light attenuates between the two cones. Most programmers set Falloff to 1.0 and forget about it.

To see a spotlight in action, replace the current InitLights() function with Listing 9.17. When you run the program, you'll see the window shown in Figure 9.10.

LISTING 9.17   Setting Up a Spotlight

```
/////////////////////////////////////////////////////
// InitLights()
/////////////////////////////////////////////////////
VOID InitLights()
{
    D3DLIGHT9 light0;
    ZeroMemory(&light0, sizeof(light0));

    light0.Type = D3DLIGHT_SPOT;
    light0.Diffuse.r  = 1.0f;
    light0.Diffuse.g  = 1.0f;
    light0.Diffuse.b  = 1.0f;
    light0.Ambient.r  = 1.0f;
    light0.Ambient.g  = 1.0f;
    light0.Ambient.b  = 1.0f;
    light0.Specular.r  = 1.0f;
    light0.Specular.g  = 1.0f;
    light0.Specular.b  = 1.0f;
    light0.Position.x = 1.0f;
    light0.Position.y = 1.0f;
    light0.Position.z = 0.0f;
    light0.Direction.x = -1.0f;
    light0.Direction.y = -1.0f;
    light0.Direction.z = 0.0f;
    light0.Attenuation0 = 1.0f;
```

LISTING 9.17 Continued

```
    light0.Range = 50.0f;
    light0.Phi = 2.0f;
    light0.Theta = 1.0f;
    light0.Falloff = 1.0f;

    g_pDirect3DDevice->SetLight(0, &light0);
    g_pDirect3DDevice->LightEnable(0, TRUE);

    D3DMATERIAL9 material;
    ZeroMemory(&material, sizeof(material));
    material.Diffuse.r = 1.0f;
    material.Diffuse.g = 0.0f;
    material.Diffuse.b = 0.0f;
    material.Diffuse.a = 0.0f;
    material.Ambient.r = 0.4f;
    material.Ambient.g = 0.0f;
    material.Ambient.b = 0.0f;
    material.Ambient.a = 0.0f;
    g_pDirect3DDevice->SetMaterial(&material);
}
```

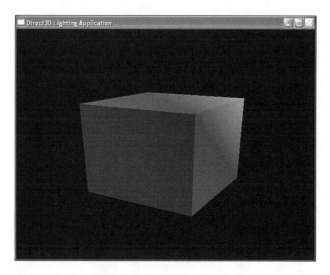

FIGURE 9.10 Lighting the cube with a spotlight.

The program defines the light object similarly to the other types, except that the type is now D3DLIGHT_SPOT:

```
D3DLIGHT9 light0;
ZeroMemory(&light0, sizeof(light0));
light0.Type = D3DLIGHT_SPOT;
```

The program specifies the light's color exactly as it did with the other types, as shown in Listing 9.18:

LISTING 9.18   Specifying the Light's Colors

```
light0.Diffuse.r  = 1.0f;
light0.Diffuse.g  = 1.0f;
light0.Diffuse.b  = 1.0f;
light0.Ambient.r  = 1.0f;
light0.Ambient.g  = 1.0f;
light0.Ambient.b  = 1.0f;
light0.Specular.r  = 1.0f;
light0.Specular.g  = 1.0f;
light0.Specular.b  = 1.0f;
```

In this version of the program, the light is positioned slightly up and to the right:

```
light0.Position.x = 1.0f;
light0.Position.y = 1.0f;
light0.Position.z = 0.0f;
```

In addition, the spotlight points down and to the left:

```
light0.Direction.x = -1.0f;
light0.Direction.y = -1.0f;
light0.Direction.z = 0.0f;
```

The program sets the attenuation and range similarly to the other light examples:

```
light0.Attenuation0 = 1.0f;
light0.Range = 50.0f;
```

The last settings define the two cones that make up the light beam produced by the spotlight:

```
light0.Phi = 2.0f;
light0.Theta = 1.0f;
light0.Falloff = 1.0f;
```

Then the light is handed off to Direct3D and turned on:

```
g_pDirect3DDevice->SetLight(0, &light0);
g_pDirect3DDevice->LightEnable(0, TRUE);
```

Last but not least, the program creates a material that reflects red diffuse and ambient light, as shown in Listing 9.19.

LISTING 9.19   Specifying a Material that Reflects Red Light

```
D3DMATERIAL9 material;
ZeroMemory(&material, sizeof(material));
material.Diffuse.r = 1.0f;
material.Diffuse.g = 0.0f;
material.Diffuse.b = 0.0f;
material.Diffuse.a = 0.0f;
material.Ambient.r = 0.4f;
material.Ambient.g = 0.0f;
material.Ambient.b = 0.0f;
material.Ambient.a = 0.0f;
g_pDirect3DDevice->SetMaterial(&material);
```

In Brief

- A point light has color and position, but not direction.

- Directional light has color and direction, but no discernable position.

- A spotlight has color, direction, and position, emitting a cone of light that is more intense toward the center of the cone and dimmer toward the edges of the cone.

- Ambient light is everywhere in a scene and has no discernable source.

- Diffuse light results from the color of an object's material and the color of the light that strikes the object.

- Specular light results from bright reflections off shiny surfaces.

- Ambient light affects the color of an object by combining with the other types of light reflected or emitted from the object's surface.

- Emissive light comes directly from an object in a scene.

- Direct3D lights have four possible attributes: position, direction, range, and attenuation.

- To define and prepare a light for use in your Direct3D program, you must declare a variable of the D3DLIGHT9 structure and use it to initialize the light data. Then you must call the device's SetLight() and LightEnable() methods.

- Usually, you will also define a material using the D3DMATERIAL9 structure. To set a material, you call the device's SetMaterial() method.

- For more realistic lighting effects, most Direct3D programs use Gourand shading, which hides each individual triangle by making planar surfaces look curved.

- To provide realistic lighting, Direct3D needs to know the facing direction of each vertex in the triangle. So, for most Direct3D lighting effects, normals called vertex normals are associated with each vertex in a triangle.

Using Direct3D Textures

10

Applying Texture Mapping to a Polygon

As you know, a filled polygon lacks the graphical details that make that polygon look like the object you're trying to create. For example, you might want to build a child's alphabet block from six polygons formed into a cube. Unfortunately, a simple cube doesn't look much like the block you want in your final image. You need some way to paint the details of a child's block onto the polygons that make up the cube. You do this with texture mapping, which "pastes" an image onto the surface of a polygon.

Although texture mapping is a complicated process requiring extensive computation, Direct3D handles all the math for you. To texture-map a polygon, you need only set a few parameters and tell Direct3D where to find the image you want mapped onto the polygon.

Creating a Texture Surface

Before you can display a texture on a polygon, you must load it into memory. Usually, the image you want to use for a texture will be stored on disk as a bitmap file, although Direct3D can handle other types of resources, as well. Thanks to Direct3D's utility function library, loading a bitmap into memory is easy.

Just as with most types of graphics, Direct3D stores textures in a surface—in the case of textures, the type of surface is an object of the IDirect3DTexture9 interface, as shown here:

```
IDirect3DTexture9* g_pTexture;
```

After you've declared a pointer to the texture surface, you can use the Direct3D `D3DXCreateTextureFromFile()` function to load the texture image into the surface and initialize the texture surface's pointer:

```
HRESULT hResult = D3DXCreateTextureFromFile(g_pDirect3DDevice,
    "texture.bmp", &g_pTexture);
```

Here's how Direct3D declares the `D3DXCreateTextureFromFile()` utility function:

```
HRESULT D3DXCreateTextureFromFile(
    LPDIRECT3DDEVICE9 pDevice,
    LPCTSTR pSrcFile,
    LPDIRECT3DTEXTURE9 *ppTexture
);
```

Here's what the function's three arguments mean:

- *pDevice*—A pointer to the Direct3D device

- *pSrcFile*—The texture image's filename

- *ppTexture*—The address where the function should store the pointer to the new texture-surface object

TEXTURES AND THE POWER OF 2

The width and height of a texture image must be a power of 2 and usually cannot be larger than 256×256. Common sizes for texture images are 64×64, 128×128, and 256×256.

Understanding Texture Coordinates

The texture image is now in memory, where Direct3D can access it to apply it to the graphics primitives you draw. However, before you can get Direct3D to use your texture, you have to understand texture coordinates.

You already know how to define vertices for the objects you want to draw in a 3D scene. You've discovered that a Direct3D vertex can contain many types of information, including not only the vertex's X,Y,Z coordinates but also color information and normals.

A vertex can also hold information about textures. This information is in the form of *texture coordinates*. The texture coordinates tell Direct3D what part of the texture should be applied to a shape. Here's an example of a vertex that holds coordinates, a normal, and texture coordinates:

```
struct CUSTOMVERTEXSTRUCT
{
```

```
    D3DVECTOR coords;
    D3DVECTOR normal;
    float tu, tv;
};
```

Here, the floating-point values `tu` and `tv` are the texture coordinates. These values must be between 0.0 and 1.0, inclusive, where the coordinates 0.0,0.0 specify the texture image's upper-left corner, and the coordinates 1.0,1.0 specify the texture image's lower-right corner. Figure 10.1 illustrates the concept of texture coordinates.

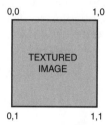

FIGURE 10.1   A texture image and its texture coordinates.

Because textures can be many different sizes, yet may need to be applied to surfaces that don't match those sizes, Direct3D needs a way to map a texture image onto a graphics primitive. That's what texture coordinates are for. No matter the size in pixels of a texture, it always uses texture coordinates between 0.0 and 1.0, as shown in Figure 10.2.

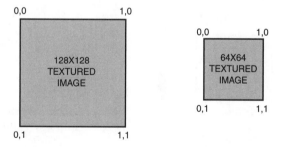

FIGURE 10.2   The mapping of texture coordinates onto texture images of different sizes.

Using Texture Coordinates

Texture coordinates, then, relieve you of having to worry about the actual physical size of a texture. Direct3D handles all the mapping for you. All you have to do is specify texture coordinates when you define your vertices.

Suppose that you have a rectangle composed from two triangles. Suppose further that you want to texture the rectangle. When you create the vertices for your two triangles, you specify the texture coordinates that match the area of the texture that you want Direct3D to apply. The first triangle's vertices might look like this:

```
{-0.5f,  0.5f, -0.5f, 0.0f, 0.0f, -1.0f, 0.0f, 0.0f},
{ 0.5f, -0.5f, -0.5f, 0.0f, 0.0f, -1.0f, 1.0f, 1.0f},
{-0.5f, -0.5f, -0.5f, 0.0f, 0.0f, -1.0f, 0.0f, 1.0f},
```

Each line here defines one vertex for the triangle. The first three values of each vertex are the vertex's X,Y,Z coordinates, the second three values are the vertex's normal, and the last two values are the texture coordinates. Figure 10.3 shows the triangle created by these vertices, with the texture coordinates shown at each vertex. Figure 10.4, on the other hand, shows the texture image and how it ends up being applied to the triangle.

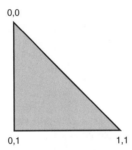

FIGURE 10.3   A triangle and its texture coordinates.

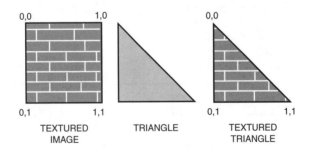

FIGURE 10.4   Applying the texture to the triangle.

One triangle, however, is only half the rectangle you want to end up with. You must define the second triangle something like this:

```
{-0.5f,  0.5f, -0.5f, 0.0f, 0.0f, -1.0f, 0.0f, 0.0f},
{ 0.5f,  0.5f, -0.5f, 0.0f, 0.0f, -1.0f, 1.0f, 0.0f},
{ 0.5f, -0.5f, -0.5f, 0.0f, 0.0f, -1.0f, 1.0f, 1.0f},
```

Thanks to the way each vertex specifies a texture coordinate, the result of rendering the two triangles will be that shown in Figure 10.5.

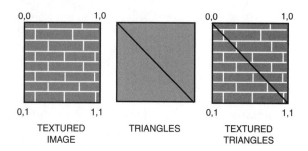

FIGURE 10.5 The final textured rectangle.

You can easily see how Direct3D uses the texture coordinates to texture a polygon. It may also have occurred to you that the size of the polygon is mostly irrelevant. That is, Direct3D stretches or shrinks the texture as required to fit it into the area specified by the texture coordinates.

Also, you don't need to use the entire texture. Suppose, for example, that you only wanted to use the left half of an image to texture a rectangle. You would then define the triangles and their texture coordinates something like Listing 10.1.

LISTING 10.1 Defining Texture Coordinates

```
{-0.5f,  0.5f, -0.5f, 0.0f, 0.0f, -1.0f, 0.0f, 0.0f},
{ 0.5f, -0.5f, -0.5f, 0.0f, 0.0f, -1.0f, 0.5f, 1.0f},
{-0.5f, -0.5f, -0.5f, 0.0f, 0.0f, -1.0f, 0.0f, 1.0f},

{-0.5f,  0.5f, -0.5f, 0.0f, 0.0f, -1.0f, 0.0f, 0.0f},
{ 0.5f,  0.5f, -0.5f, 0.0f, 0.0f, -1.0f, 0.5f, 0.0f},
{ 0.5f, -0.5f, -0.5f, 0.0f, 0.0f, -1.0f, 0.5f, 1.0f},
```

Notice that some of the texture coordinates are now specified as 0.5. The rectangle created by these vertices would end up looking like Figure 10.6. Now, the left half of the texture has been applied to the rectangle and stretched to fit. You can see that the bricks have been stretched horizontally across the rectangle.

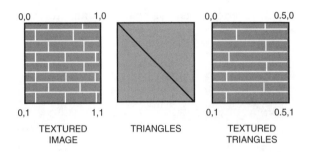

FIGURE 10.6   The rectangle textured with the left half of a texture image.

Rendering Textures

Loading your texture and specifying texture coordinates with your vertices is just the first battle. Now you must set a number of Direct3D states related to textures. To go over all these states in this book would take forever, so you'll just learn the most common. Refer to your Direct3D documentation for more information on Direct3D states. For many texturing tasks, though, Listing 10.2 should work pretty well.

LISTING 10.2   Setting Texture Stage States

```
g_pDirect3DDevice->SetTextureStageState(0,
    D3DTSS_COLOROP, D3DTOP_MODULATE);
g_pDirect3DDevice->SetTextureStageState(0,
    D3DTSS_COLORARG1, D3DTA_TEXTURE);
g_pDirect3DDevice->SetTextureStageState(0,
    D3DTSS_COLORARG2, D3DTA_DIFFUSE);
g_pDirect3DDevice->SetTextureStageState(0,
    D3DTSS_ALPHAOP, D3DTOP_DISABLE);
```

Notice that what you have here are four calls to the Direct3D device object's `SetTextureStageState()` method. Direct3D declares this method as follows:

```
HRESULT SetTextureStageState(
    DWORD Stage,
    D3DTEXTURESTAGESTATETYPE Type,
    DWORD Value
);
```

Here's what the function's three arguments mean:

- *Stage*—The texture stage ID, which can be from 0 to 7.

- *Type*—The texture state to be set. There are more than 20 of these, which Direct3D defines in the D3DTEXTURESTAGESTATETYPE enumeration.

- *Value*—The value to which to set the state.

To give you at least a little idea of what these states do, look at the first line from the previous example:

```
g_pDirect3DDevice->SetTextureStageState(0,
    D3DTSS_COLOROP, D3DTOP_MODULATE);
```

The zero as the first argument means that the call will set a state for the texture stage 0. You can have up to eight texture stages, which means that you can have Direct3D apply and blend up to eight textures on each polygon you draw.

The second argument tells Direct3D which state of texture stage 0 you want to set. In this case, D3DTSS_COLOROP specifies that you want to set the type of color blending Direct3D will use when applying the texture.

The third argument, D3DTOP_MODULATE, is the value to which the color operation will be set and means that Direct3D should multiply the values involved. (Don't worry about the details.) There are nearly 30 of these color-blending values, so you can see why you won't be exploring all the possibilities in this book!

The rest of the lines set other state values. You can use them exactly as they are shown here for most common texture tasks. However, you'll definitely want to spend some time learning the different texture states when you're ready to try more advanced texturing techniques.

SHOP TALK

TEXTURE STAGE STATES

Because the texture stage states are states, they are always set to something regardless of whether your program explicitly sets them. Direct3D sets all states to default values, and, as it turns out, the default values for the texture stage states work just fine for many texturing tasks. That is, you may find that your program doesn't need to set the states at all.

Of course, explicitly setting states in your program, even when you're only using the default states, is a good way to make your program self-documenting. You can then tell at a glance how the states are set, without having to remember what the default states are.

Setting the Texture

Finally, the last step before rendering is to give Direct3D the texture you want to use. You do this with the Direct3D device object's `SetTexture()` method, which Direct3D declares like this:

```
HRESULT SetTexture(
  DWORD Stage,
  IDirect3DBaseTexture8* pTexture
);
```

Here's what the arguments mean:

- *Stage*—The texture stage for which you're setting the texture

- *pTexture*—A pointer to the IDirect3DTexture8 object associated with your texture image

An actual call to the method in your program would look something like this:

```
g_pDirect3DDevice->SetTexture(0, g_pTexture);
```

Creating the TextureApp Application

Enough of the theoretical stuff for now. It's time to bring all this theory into the real world and build a program that does everything you've just learned about. The following sections lead you through the building of the TextureApp application. Remember that you don't have to type the code if you don't want to. You can just copy it from the completed projects included with this book's sample projects. See the introduction to learn how to download these projects.

Creating the Basic Project

Perform the following steps to get the main Direct3D application project started:

1. Start a new empty Win32 project named TextureApp.

2. On the Project menu, select the Add New Item command. The Add New Item dialog box appears.

3. Add a new C++ File (.cpp) named TextureApp.cpp.

4. Copy the contents of the LightApp.cpp file, from Chapter 9's LightApp, Spotlight Version folder, into the new TextureApp code window.

5. Change the name in the comment at the top of the file to TextureApp.cpp.

6. In the `RegisterWindowClass()` function, change `wc.lpszClassName = "LightApp"` to `wc.lpszClassName = "TextureApp"`.

7. In the `CreateAppWindow()` function, change `"LightApp"` to `"TextureApp"`, and then change `"Direct3D Lighting Application"` to `"Direct3D Texture Application"`.

Adding the DirectX References

Next, you need to tell the program where the required DirectX header files and libraries are located. To do that, follow these steps:

1. Right-click the project's name in the Solution Explorer, and select Properties from the menu that appears. The TextureApp Property Pages dialog box appears.

2. Click the C/C++ selection in the left-hand pane, and select General from the displayed choices.

3. In the Additional Include Directories box, enter the path to the DirectX 9 SDK's include folder. If you installed the SDK using the default settings, this path should be `c:\DXSDK\include`.

4. Click the Linker selection in the left-hand pane, and select General from the displayed choices.

5. In the Additional Library Directories box, enter the path to the DirectX 9 SDK's library folder. If you installed the SDK using the default settings, this path should be `c:\DXSDK\lib`.

6. Click the Linker's Input selection in the left-hand pane.

7. In the Additional Dependencies box in the right-hand pane, enter **d3d9.lib**, **d3dx9.lib**, and **dxerr9.lib**.

8. Compile and run the application to make sure that it works. Press Escape to exit the application.

Adding Source Code

Now all you have to do is add the Direct3D code that'll get a textured cube up on the screen. Perform the following steps:

1. Add the following line to the program's global variable declarations:

```
IDirect3DTexture9* g_pTexture;
```

This line declares a pointer for the texture object.

2. Replace the existing CUSTOMVERTEXSTRUCT declaration with the following one:

```
struct CUSTOMVERTEXSTRUCT
{
    D3DVECTOR coords;
    D3DVECTOR normal;
        float tu, tv;
};
```

This structure adds the texture coordinates, tu and tv, to the vertex information.

3. Place the code shown in Listing 10.3 at the end of the InitDirect3D() function, right before the function's return statement,

LISTING 10.3   New Code for the InitDirect3D() Function

```
HRESULT hResult = D3DXCreateTextureFromFile(g_pDirect3DDevice,
    "texture.bmp", &g_pTexture);
g_pDirect3DDevice->SetTextureStageState(0,
    D3DTSS_COLOROP, D3DTOP_MODULATE);
g_pDirect3DDevice->SetTextureStageState(0,
    D3DTSS_COLORARG1, D3DTA_TEXTURE);
g_pDirect3DDevice->SetTextureStageState(0,
    D3DTSS_COLORARG2, D3DTA_DIFFUSE);
g_pDirect3DDevice->SetTextureStageState(0,
    D3DTSS_ALPHAOP, D3DTOP_DISABLE);
```

These lines load the texture from disk and set the various stage states for texture stage 0.

4. Replace the current CleanUpDirect3D() function with the one in Listing 10.4. (The only change to the function is the code that releases the g_pTexture pointer.)

LISTING 10.4   The New CleanUpDirect3D() Function

```
/////////////////////////////////////////////////////
// CleanUpDirect3D()
/////////////////////////////////////////////////////
void CleanUpDirect3D()
{
    if (g_pVertexBuf)
    {
```

LISTING 10.4 Continued

```
            g_pVertexBuf->Release();
            g_pVertexBuf = NULL;
        }
        if (g_pTexture)
        {
            g_pTexture->Release();
            g_pTexture = NULL;
        }
        if (g_pDirect3DDevice)
        {
            g_pDirect3DDevice->Release();
            g_pDirect3DDevice = NULL;
        }
        if (g_pDirect3D)
        {
            g_pDirect3D->Release();
            g_pDirect3D = NULL;
        }
    }
}
```

5. In the `Render()` function, add the following line right after the call to
`SetStreamSource()`:

```
g_pDirect3DDevice->SetTexture(0, g_pTexture);
```

This line tells Direct3D which texture to use when rendering the polygons.

6. Also in the `Render()` function, change the call to `SetFVF()` so that it looks like this:

```
g_pDirect3DDevice->SetFVF(D3DFVF_XYZ|D3DFVF_NORMAL|D3DFVF_TEX1);
```

This line tells Direct3D that the vertex information contains the vertex's X,Y,Z
coordinates, its normal, and its texture coordinates.

7. In the `InitVertices()` function, replace the `cube[]` array with Listing 10.5.

LISTING 10.5 The New `cube[]` Array

```
CUSTOMVERTEXSTRUCT cube[] =
{
    // Front of cube.
```

LISTING 10.5 Continued

```
{-0.5f,  0.5f, -0.5f, 0.0f, 0.0f, -1.0f, 0.0f, 0.0f},
{ 0.5f, -0.5f, -0.5f, 0.0f, 0.0f, -1.0f, 1.0f, 1.0f},
{-0.5f, -0.5f, -0.5f, 0.0f, 0.0f, -1.0f, 0.0f, 1.0f},
{-0.5f,  0.5f, -0.5f, 0.0f, 0.0f, -1.0f, 0.0f, 0.0f},
{ 0.5f,  0.5f, -0.5f, 0.0f, 0.0f, -1.0f, 1.0f, 0.0f},
{ 0.5f, -0.5f, -0.5f, 0.0f, 0.0f, -1.0f, 1.0f, 1.0f},

// Right side of cube.
{0.5f,  0.5f, -0.5f, 1.0f, 0.0f, 0.0f, 0.0f, 0.0f},
{0.5f, -0.5f,  0.5f, 1.0f, 0.0f, 0.0f, 1.0f, 1.0f},
{0.5f, -0.5f, -0.5f, 1.0f, 0.0f, 0.0f, 0.0f, 1.0f},
{0.5f,  0.5f, -0.5f, 1.0f, 0.0f, 0.0f, 0.0f, 0.0f},
{0.5f,  0.5f,  0.5f, 1.0f, 0.0f, 0.0f, 1.0f, 0.0f},
{0.5f, -0.5f,  0.5f, 1.0f, 0.0f, 0.0f, 1.0f, 1.0f},

// Back of cube.
{ 0.5f,  0.5f, 0.5f, 0.0f, 0.0f, 1.0f, 0.0f, 0.0f},
{-0.5f, -0.5f, 0.5f, 0.0f, 0.0f, 1.0f, 1.0f, 1.0f},
{ 0.5f, -0.5f, 0.5f, 0.0f, 0.0f, 1.0f, 0.0f, 1.0f},
{ 0.5f,  0.5f, 0.5f, 0.0f, 0.0f, 1.0f, 0.0f, 0.0f},
{-0.5f,  0.5f, 0.5f, 0.0f, 0.0f, 1.0f, 1.0f, 0.0f},
{-0.5f, -0.5f, 0.5f, 0.0f, 0.0f, 1.0f, 1.0f, 1.0f},

// Left side of cube.
{-0.5f,  0.5f,  0.5f, -1.0f, 0.0f, 0.0f, 0.0f, 0.0f},
{-0.5f, -0.5f, -0.5f, -1.0f, 0.0f, 0.0f, 1.0f, 1.0f},
{-0.5f, -0.5f,  0.5f, -1.0f, 0.0f, 0.0f, 0.0f, 1.0f},
{-0.5f,  0.5f,  0.5f, -1.0f, 0.0f, 0.0f, 0.0f, 0.0f},
{-0.5f,  0.5f, -0.5f, -1.0f, 0.0f, 0.0f, 1.0f, 0.0f},
{-0.5f, -0.5f, -0.5f, -1.0f, 0.0f, 0.0f, 1.0f, 1.0f},

// Top of cube.
{-0.5f, 0.5f, -0.5f, 0.0f, 1.0f, 0.0f, 0.0f, 0.0f},
{-0.5f, 0.5f,  0.5f, 0.0f, 1.0f, 0.0f, 1.0f, 0.0f},
{ 0.5f, 0.5f, -0.5f, 0.0f, 1.0f, 0.0f, 0.0f, 1.0f},
{-0.5f, 0.5f,  0.5f, 0.0f, 1.0f, 0.0f, 1.0f, 0.0f},
{ 0.5f, 0.5f,  0.5f, 0.0f, 1.0f, 0.0f, 1.0f, 1.0f},
{ 0.5f, 0.5f, -0.5f, 0.0f, 1.0f, 0.0f, 0.0f, 1.0f},

// Bottom of cube.
{-0.5f, -0.5f, -0.5f, 0.0f, -1.0f, 0.0f, 0.0f, 0.0f},
```

LISTING 10.5   Continued

```
      { 0.5f, -0.5f, -0.5f, 0.0f, -1.0f, 0.0f, 0.0f, 0.0f},
      {-0.5f, -0.5f,  0.5f, 0.0f, -1.0f, 0.0f, 0.0f, 0.0f},
      { 0.5f, -0.5f, -0.5f, 0.0f, -1.0f, 0.0f, 0.0f, 0.0f},
      { 0.5f, -0.5f,  0.5f, 0.0f, -1.0f, 0.0f, 0.0f, 0.0f},
      {-0.5f, -0.5f,  0.5f, 0.0f, -1.0f, 0.0f, 0.0f, 0.0f}
};
```

This new array adds texture coordinates to each vertex.

8. Add the following line to the InitVertices() function, right after the new cube[] array:

```
int i_numCoordsPerVertex = 24;
```

This change has nothing to do with textures and has been added only to make the code more readable.

9. Change the call to CreateVertexBuffer() in InitVertices() so that it looks like this (you're just adding the D3DFVF_TEX1 flag):

```
if(FAILED(g_pDirect3DDevice ->CreateVertexBuffer(sizeof(cube),
        0, D3DFVF_XYZ|D3DFVF_NORMAL|D3DFVF_TEX1, D3DPOOL_DEFAULT,
        &g_pVertexBuf, NULL)))
```

10. Change the line that sets the g_iNumTriangles variable to the following:

```
g_iNumTriangles = (sizeof(cube) / sizeof(float)) / i_numCoordsPerVertex;
```

Replacing the hard-coded value at the end of the original line with the local variable i_numCoordsPerVertex makes the code more readable.

11. In the InitLights() function, change the code that defines and sets the material to that shown in Listing 10.6.

LISTING 10.6   Defining the New Material

```
D3DMATERIAL9 material;
ZeroMemory(&material, sizeof(material));
material.Diffuse.r = 1.0f;
material.Diffuse.g = 1.0f;
material.Diffuse.b = 1.0f;
material.Diffuse.a = 1.0f;
```

LISTING 10.6   Continued

```
material.Ambient.r = 1.0f;
material.Ambient.g = 1.0f;
material.Ambient.b = 1.0f;
material.Ambient.a = 1.0f;
g_pDirect3DDevice->SetMaterial(&material);
```

These lines set the material so that it reflects white diffuse and ambient light.

12. Place a 128×128 bitmap named Texture.bmp into your project's TextureApp folder, or copy the one from the Chapter10\TextureApp folder of this book's sample code.

Compile and run the program. When you do, you should see a window like that shown in Figure 10.7. As you can see, the program produces a textured cube.

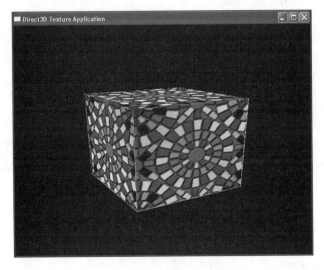

FIGURE 10.7   The running TextureApp application.

Implementing Transparency

Often in your programs, you'll want to implement a graphics technique known as *transparency*. Transparency is important because it enables a graphics application to display bitmaps that appear to be nonrectangular or that have areas that allow the background to show through. That is, the transparent areas of the bitmap don't appear on the screen. The process goes something like this:

1. You create a rectangular bitmap, using a specific color (pure black, with an RGB value of 0,0,0 is typical) to indicate the areas of the bitmap that you want to be transparent.

2. You tell Direct3D the transparent color you've chosen.

3. You tell Direct3D to draw the bitmap using transparency.

4. Direct3D draws the bitmap on the screen, ignoring every pixel in the bitmap that matches the transparent color.

With Direct3D and textures, though, the process is actually a little more complicated. This is because transparency is implemented through the use of *alpha values*. An alpha value tells Direct3D exactly how transparent a color is. Here are the rules:

- An alpha value of 255 specifies that the color is opaque and any pixel drawn in that color will completely obliterate the pixel over which it's drawn.

- An alpha value of 0 specifies that the color is completely transparent and any pixel of that color won't be drawn at all.

- Alpha values between 0 and 255 specify varying degrees of transparency and determine how the colors of the source color (the color that you're drawing) and destination color (the color over which you're drawing the source color) are mixed together.

Alpha values make transparency an even more powerful feature, enabling you to do very cool things. For example, you could have a rectangle that represents a window in your game world, and to give the effect of looking through glass, you could use alpha values to specify that you want most of the source colors (in this case, the scene outside the window) to show through the window, but with a slight blue tint. In this book, though, you'll be concerned with only two types of transparency: fully opaque or fully transparent.

The first step in using a texture is, of course, to create in a paint program the bitmap you'll use for the texture. After you do that, however, you must load the texture into your memory. You've already learned how to create texture surfaces and how to load bitmaps into those surfaces. You follow a similar procedure to get a texture with transparent colors into memory, except that you call the DirectX utility function `D3DXCreateTextureFromFileEx()`, which Direct3D declares like this:

```
HRESULT D3DXCreateTextureFromFileEx(
    LPDIRECT3DDEVICE8 pDevice,
    LPCTSTR pSrcFile,
    UINT Width,
    UINT Height,
    UINT MipLevels,
    DWORD Usage,
```

```
    D3DFORMAT Format,
    D3DPOOL Pool,
    DWORD Filter,
    DWORD MipFilter,
    D3DCOLOR ColorKey,
    D3DXIMAGE_INFO* pSrcInfo,
    PALETTEENTRY* pPalette,
    LPDIRECT3DTEXTURE8* ppTexture
);
```

Here's what all of the arguments mean:

- *pDevice*—A pointer to the Direct3D device that's associated with the texture.

- *pSrcFile*—The path to the texture.

- *Width*—The width of the texture. Use D3DX_DEFAULT to use width specified in the file.

- *Height*—The height of the texture. Use D3DX_DEFAULT to use height specified in the file.

- *MipLevels*—The number of mip levels, something you won't need to worry about in this book. Just use the value 1 here.

- *Usage*—For your purposes in this book, always 0.

- *Format*—The texture's pixel format.

- *Pool*—The texture's memory class. For this book, you'll always use D3DPOOL_MANAGED.

- *Filter*—The type of filtering to use. You'll be using D3DX_DEFAULT.

- *MipFilter*—Another filtering setting for which you'll use D3DX_DEFAULT.

- *ColorKey*—The 32-bit color value that specifies the transparent color. This is in the format ARGB, so for solid black, you'd use the value 0xFF000000. (The FF is the alpha value, which is required here.)

- *pSrcInfo*—In this book, you'll always use NULL here.

- *pPalette*—Again, in this book, you'll always use NULL here.

- *ppTexture*—The address of a pointer to the texture object.

Here's what a real call to D3DXCreateTextureFromFileEx() might look like in your program:

```
IDirect3DTexture8* g_pTexture;
g_hResult = D3DXCreateTextureFromFileEx(g_pDirect3DDevice,
    "Texture.bmp", D3DX_DEFAULT, D3DX_DEFAULT, 1, 0, D3DFMT_A8R8G8B8,
    D3DPOOL_MANAGED, D3DX_DEFAULT, D3DX_DEFAULT, 0xFF000000,
    NULL, NULL, &g_pTexture);
```

If the call goes okay, the last argument will hold a pointer to a texture object, which, as you can see from the example, is an object of the IDirect3DTexture8 interface.

Next, you need to set the Direct3D's rendering state to enable alpha blending. The following settings should work fine for many applications. For more information about rendering states, consult your Direct3D documentation:

```
g_pDirect3DDevice->SetRenderState(D3DRS_ALPHATESTENABLE, TRUE);
g_pDirect3DDevice->SetRenderState(D3DRS_ALPHAREF, 0x01);
g_pDirect3DDevice->SetRenderState(D3DRS_ALPHAFUNC, D3DCMP_GREATEREQUAL);
```

Creating the TransparencyApp Application

Now it's time to add transparency to the TextureApp application you completed previously in this chapter. The following sections guide you through the process of creating TransparencyApp, which, as you'll see, is similar to TextureApp.

Creating the Basic TransparencyApp Project

Perform the following steps to get the main Direct3D application project started:

1. Start a new empty Win32 project named TransparencyApp.

2. On the Project menu, select the Add New Item command. The Add New Item dialog box appears.

3. Add a new C++ File (.cpp) named TransparencyApp.cpp.

4. Copy the contents of the TextureApp.cpp file, from Chapter 10's TextureApp folder, into the new TransparencyApp code window.

5. Change the name in the comment at the top of the file to TransparencyApp.cpp.

6. In the RegisterWindowClass() function, change wc.lpszClassName = "TextureApp" to wc.lpszClassName = "TransparencyApp".

7. In the CreateAppWindow() function, change "TextureApp" to "TransparencyApp", and then change "Direct3D Texture Application" to "Direct3D Transparency Application".

Adding the DirectX References

Next, you need to tell the program where the required DirectX header files and libraries are located. To do that, follow these steps:

1. Right-click the project's name in the Solution Explorer, and select Properties from the menu that appears. The TransparencyApp Property Pages dialog box appears.

2. Click the C/C++ selection in the left-hand pane, and select General from the displayed choices.

3. In the Additional Include Directories box, enter the path to the DirectX 9 SDK's include folder. If you installed the SDK using the default settings, this path should be `c:\DXSDK\include`.

4. Click the Linker selection in the left-hand pane, and select General from the displayed choices.

5. In the Additional Library Directories box, enter the path to the DirectX 9 SDK's library folder. If you installed the SDK using the default settings, this path should be `c:\DXSDK\lib`.

6. Click the Linker's Input selection in the left-hand pane.

7. In the Additional Dependencies box in the right-hand pane, enter **d3d9.lib**, **d3dx9.lib**, and **dxerr9.lib**.

8. Copy the texture.bmp file from the TransparencyApp folder of this book's sample code into your TransparencyApp folder. (You must use this bitmap, rather than one of your own.)

9. Compile and run the application to make sure that it works. You should see the window shown in Figure 10.8.

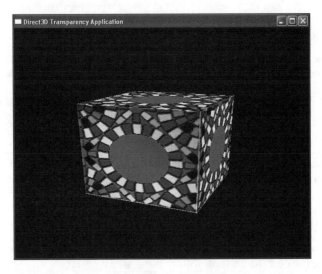

FIGURE 10.8   The running basic TransparencyApp application.

When you run the application, notice that the texture image now has a large red circle in the center. This is the area of the bitmap that will be transparent.

Adding Source Code

Now all you have to do is add the Direct3D code that'll get a textured cube, with its transparent areas, up on the screen. Perform the following steps:

1. Place the following lines in the `InitDirect3D()` function, right after the line `g_pDirect3DDevice->SetRenderState(D3DRS_ZENABLE, TRUE)` that's already there:

   ```
   g_pDirect3DDevice->SetRenderState(D3DRS_ALPHATESTENABLE, TRUE);
   g_pDirect3DDevice->SetRenderState(D3DRS_ALPHAREF, 0x01);
   g_pDirect3DDevice->SetRenderState(D3DRS_ALPHAFUNC, D3DCMP_GREATEREQUAL);
   ```

   These lines set the Direct3D rendering state to allow transparency through alpha blending.

2. Replace the call to `D3DXCreateTextureFromFile()` with the following:

   ```
   HRESULT hResult = D3DXCreateTextureFromFileEx(g_pDirect3DDevice,
       "texture.bmp", D3DX_DEFAULT, D3DX_DEFAULT, D3DX_DEFAULT, 0,
       D3DFMT_A8R8G8B8, D3DPOOL_MANAGED, D3DX_FILTER_TRIANGLE,
       D3DX_FILTER_TRIANGLE, D3DCOLOR_RGBA(255,0,0,255), NULL, NULL, &g_pTexture);
   ```

   Take a close look at the eleventh argument here, `D3DCOLOR_RGBA(255,0,0,255)`. This is the value that tells Direct3D that solid red will be the texture's transparent color.

Now you can compile and run the application. When you do, you should see the window shown in Figure 10.9. The red areas of the texture don't get drawn because the program has told Direct3D that pure red is transparent, which means that Direct3D will not draw any pure red pixel.

Direct3D can do even better things with transparency. But to do so, it needs to have alpha blending turned on. Right now in your program, it's off, so in the `InitDirect3D()` function, change the line

```
g_pDirect3DDevice->SetTextureStageState(0,
    D3DTSS_ALPHAOP, D3DTOP_DISABLE);
```

to

```
g_pDirect3DDevice->SetTextureStageState(0,
    D3DTSS_ALPHAOP, D3DTOP_SELECTARG1);
```

Now recompile and run the program. When the application's window appears, you'll see one of the cool things you can do with transparency, as shown in Figure 10.10.

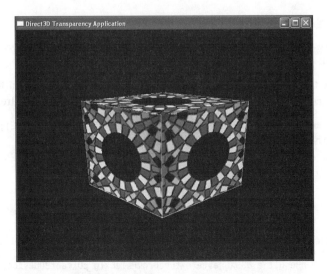

FIGURE 10.9   The running TransparencyApp application.

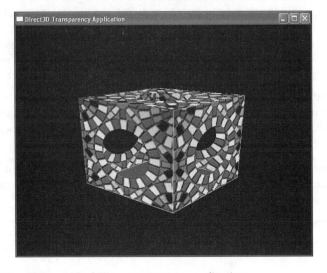

FIGURE 10.10   The modified TransparencyApp application.

In Brief

- Texture mapping "pastes" an image onto the surface of a polygon, providing an easy way to add detail to your 3D worlds.

- Just as with most types of graphics, Direct3D stores textures in a surface—in the case of textures, the type of surface is an object of the `IDirect3DTexture9` interface.

- After you've declared a pointer to the texture surface, you can use the Direct3D `D3DXCreateTextureFromFile()` function to load the texture image into the surface and initialize the texture surface's pointer.

- A vertex can also hold information about textures. This information is in the form of *texture coordinates*, which tell Direct3D what part of the texture should be applied to a shape.

- To set Direct3D texture states, you call the Direct3D device object's `SetTextureStageState()` method.

- You give a texture to Direct3D's rendering engine by calling the Direct3D device object's `SetTexture()` method.

- In Direct3D, transparency is implemented through the use of alpha values.

- To load a texture with transparent areas, you must call the `D3DXCreateTextureFromFileEx()` function.

Programming Alpha Blending and Fog

11

Introducing Transparency with Alpha Blending

In the previous chapter, you discovered how to use textures to display bitmaps with transparent areas. That technique works great for many applications. Sometimes, however, what you really want is something between the extremes of invisible and opaque.

For example, suppose that you're programming a 3D scene in which the user should be able to look through a window. For the most realistic effect, you want the window's glass to be a semitransparent rectangle whose color affects the colors of the scene outside the window. That is, if the window's glass has a slight blue tint, you want the scene visible through the window to have a slight blue tint, too. This gives the illusion of looking through a plate of glass rather than just a hole in the wall.

Imagine an even more complex situation: What if the window is a design formed from stained-glass? The ability to affect the colors of the scene visible through the window becomes critical in this situation. In the following sections, you learn to use transparency to implement such scenes in your 3D applications. You also learn to use a similar technique called fog, which causes 3D objects to seem to fade into the distance.

Understanding Alpha Blending

Simply, *alpha blending* enables a 3D scene to have semitransparent objects. You might, for example, want to have a semitransparent red rectangle in front of a solid white rectangle. In this case, when the scene's camera is in front of the semitransparent object, the white object behind should be tinted pink, which is a combination of red and white. Figure 11.1 illustrates this example.

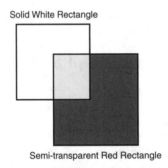

Solid White Rectangle

Semi-transparent Red Rectangle

FIGURE 11.1   The result of using alpha blending.

In Chapter 10, "Using Direct3D Textures," you learned about alpha values, which control the amount of transparency used to render an object in a 3D scene. Alpha blending is the 3D programming technique that uses alpha values to create this transparency—any type of transparency, from fully opaque to fully transparent, with 254 levels of transparency between the extremes.

Implementing such a sophisticated graphics technique might seem as if it would be difficult, but the truth is that Direct3D makes it pretty easy, although you do have to choose between five different types of alpha blending. These different types are as follows:

- Vertex alpha

- Material alpha

- Texture alpha

- Frame buffer alpha

- Render target alpha

The different types of alpha blending differ mainly in where Direct3D looks for the alpha values. For example, with vertex alpha blending, the vertex data holds the alpha values, whereas with texture alpha blending, the texture bitmap holds the alpha values. In this chapter, you'll examine vertex alpha blending.

To set up vertex alpha blending, you first need vertex data that can hold alpha values, which means adding diffuse color data to the vertex structure, as shown here:

```
struct CUSTOMVERTEXSTRUCT
{
    D3DVECTOR coords;
    D3DVECTOR normal;
    DWORD dwColor;
    float tu, tv;
};
```

This structure provides local coordinates, a normal, a diffuse color value, and texture coordinates for a vertex.

Next, you need to define the vertex data, as shown in Listing 11.1.

LISTING 11.1   Defining the Vertex Data

```
CUSTOMVERTEXSTRUCT square[] =
{
    {-1.0f,  1.0f, 1.0f, 0.0f, 0.0f, -1.0f,
        D3DCOLOR_ARGB(128,255,255,255), 0.0f, 0.0f},
    { 1.0f, -1.0f, 1.0f, 0.0f, 0.0f, -1.0f,
        D3DCOLOR_ARGB(128,255,255,255), 1.0f, 1.0f},
    {-1.0f, -1.0f, 1.0f, 0.0f, 0.0f, -1.0f,
        D3DCOLOR_ARGB(128,255,255,255), 0.0f, 1.0f},
    {-1.0f,  1.0f, 1.0f, 0.0f, 0.0f, -1.0f,
        D3DCOLOR_ARGB(128,255,255,255), 0.0f, 0.0f},
    { 1.0f,  1.0f, 1.0f, 0.0f, 0.0f, -1.0f,
        D3DCOLOR_ARGB(128,255,255,255), 1.0f, 0.0f},
    { 1.0f, -1.0f, 1.0f, 0.0f, 0.0f, -1.0f,
        D3DCOLOR_ARGB(128,255,255,255), 1.0f, 1.0f}
};
```

This vertex data defines the diffuse color data using the D3DCOLOR_ARGB macro, which means that the macro's arguments are the alpha, red, green, and blue color elements, in that order.

Looking at the data, you can see that the alpha value for each vertex is 128, which makes that vertex half transparent. The value of the red, green, and blue elements depends on your application. If you're not using vertex color, Direct3D ignores the RGB values.

The final step is to set up the application's rendering state for alpha blending. You can do this a number of ways, but the following lines are typical:

```
g_pDirect3DDevice->SetRenderState(D3DRS_ALPHABLENDENABLE, true);
g_pDirect3DDevice->SetRenderState(D3DRS_SRCBLEND, D3DBLEND_SRCALPHA);
g_pDirect3DDevice->SetRenderState(D3DRS_DESTBLEND, D3DBLEND_INVSRCALPHA);
```

The first line turns on alpha blending. If you don't do this, Direct3D will not render with alpha blending. The next two lines tell Direct3D how to use the alpha values to blend the source and destination colors. The *source color* is the color of the pixel about to be rendered, whereas the *destination color* is the color of the currently existing pixel in the scene—that is, the pixel that is about to be blended with the source pixel.

The call to SetRenderState() with the arguments D3DRS_SRCBLEND and D3DBLEND_SRCALPHA tells Direct3D to use the alpha value from the source pixel to draw the source pixel. In the case of vertex alpha blending, the source is the alpha value defined in the vertices. Direct3D takes this value and creates alpha values for every pixel of the object you're rendering, much in the same way it determines the color of each pixel when rendering with vertex color information.

The call to SetRenderState() with the arguments D3DRS_DESTBLEND and D3DBLEND_INVSRCALPHA tells Direct3D to use the alpha value from the source pixel for the destination pixel, too, but the actual value will be 1 - SRCALPHA. In other words, if the source alpha value is 200, Direct3D calculates a destination alpha value of 155, which is 255 - 200.

THE VALUES OF ALPHA

You may be wondering how 1 - SRCALPHA can possibly end up as a value between 0 and 255. It doesn't! Internally, Direct3D uses values between 0.0 and 1.0 for the alpha, converting the alpha values you supply to fit into that range.

After setting up the rendering state for alpha blending, you need to call SetTextureStageState() with the arguments D3DTSS_ALPHAARG1 and D3DTA_DIFFUSE to tell Direct3D to look for the texture's alpha values in the diffuse color:

```
g_pDirect3DDevice->SetTextureStageState(0, D3DTSS_ALPHAARG1, D3DTA_DIFFUSE);
```

Creating the VertexAlphaApp Application

Ready to see alpha blending in action? The following sections lead you through the building of the VertexAlphaApp application, which puts together everything you just discovered about vertex alpha blending. Remember that you don't have to type the code if you don't want to. You can just copy it from the completed projects included with this book's sample code. Refer to this book's introduction for information on how to obtain the sample code.

Creating the Basic Project

Perform the following steps to get the main Direct3D application project started:

1. Start a new empty Win32 project named VertexAlphaApp.

2. On the Project menu, select the Add New Item command. The Add New Item dialog box appears.

3. Add a new C++ File (.cpp) named VertexAlphaApp.cpp.

4. Copy the contents of the TextureApp.cpp file, from the sample code's Chapter11\TextureApp folder, into the new VertexAlphaApp code window.

5. Change the name in the comment at the top of the file to VertexAlphaApp.cpp.

6. In the `RegisterWindowClass()` function, change `wc.lpszClassName = "TextureApp"` to `wc.lpszClassName = "VertexAlphaApp"`.

7. In the `CreateAppWindow()` function, change `"TextureApp"` to `"VertexAlphaApp"`, and then change `"Direct3D Lighting Application"` to `"Direct3D Vertex Alpha Application"`.

Adding the DirectX References

Next, you need to tell the program where the required DirectX header files and libraries are located. To do that, follow these steps:

1. Display the VertexAlphaApp project's Property Pages dialog box.

2. In the C/C++ General options, enter the path to the DirectX 9 SDK's include folder into the Additional Include Directories box.

3. In the Linker General options, enter the path to the DirectX 9 SDK's library into the Additional Library Directories box.

4. In the Linker Input options, enter **d3d9.lib**, **d3dx9.lib**, and **dxerr9.lib** into the Additional Dependencies box.

5. Place a 128×128 texture image named texture.bmp in your VertexAlphaApp project folder. If you want, you can copy the texture.bmp file from the sample code's Chapter11\VetexAlphaApp folder.

6. Compile and run the application to make sure that it works.

Adding Source Code

Now you need to add the Direct3D code that'll get your transparent rectangle up on the screen. Perform the following steps:

1. In the global variable declarations near the top of the program, delete the following lines:

```
IDirect3DVertexBuffer9* g_pVertexBuf = NULL;
int g_iNumTriangles;
IDirect3DTexture9* g_pTexture;
```

   The new version of the program will still use vertex buffers and textures, but the vertex and texture objects will have different names.

2. Add the following lines to the program's global variable declarations:

```
IDirect3DVertexBuffer9* g_pSolidSquareVertexBuf = NULL;
IDirect3DVertexBuffer9* g_pTransparentSquareVertexBuf = NULL;
IDirect3DTexture9* g_pSolidSquareTexture;
IDirect3DTexture9* g_pTransparentSquareTexture;
```

   These lines declare pointers for the new vertex-buffer and texture objects the program will use.

3. Replace the existing CUSTOMVERTEXSTRUCT declaration with the following lines:

```
struct CUSTOMVERTEXSTRUCT
{
    D3DVECTOR coords;
    D3DVECTOR normal;
    DWORD dwColor;
    float tu, tv;
};
```

   This structure adds diffuse color information (dwColor) to the vertex data. This color data will hold the alpha values that Direct3D will use to calculate the amount of transparency associated with each vertex.

4. Replace the current InitDirect3D() function with Listing 11.2.

LISTING 11.2   The New InitDirect3D() Function

```
//////////////////////////////////////////////////////////
// InitDirect3D()
//////////////////////////////////////////////////////////
```

LISTING 11.2   Continued

```
HRESULT InitDirect3D()
{
    if((g_pDirect3D = Direct3DCreate9(D3D_SDK_VERSION)) == NULL)
        return E_FAIL;

    D3DPRESENT_PARAMETERS D3DPresentParams;
    ZeroMemory(&D3DPresentParams, sizeof(D3DPRESENT_PARAMETERS));
    D3DPresentParams.Windowed = TRUE;
    D3DPresentParams.BackBufferFormat = D3DFMT_UNKNOWN;
    D3DPresentParams.SwapEffect = D3DSWAPEFFECT_DISCARD;
    D3DPresentParams.hDeviceWindow = g_hWnd;
    D3DPresentParams.EnableAutoDepthStencil = TRUE;
    D3DPresentParams.AutoDepthStencilFormat = D3DFMT_D16;

    if (FAILED(g_pDirect3D->CreateDevice(D3DADAPTER_DEFAULT,
            D3DDEVTYPE_HAL, g_hWnd, D3DCREATE_SOFTWARE_VERTEXPROCESSING,
            &D3DPresentParams, &g_pDirect3DDevice)))
        return E_FAIL;

    g_pDirect3DDevice->SetRenderState(D3DRS_CULLMODE, D3DCULL_NONE);
    g_pDirect3DDevice->SetRenderState(D3DRS_ZENABLE, TRUE);
    g_pDirect3DDevice->SetRenderState(D3DRS_ALPHABLENDENABLE, true);
    g_pDirect3DDevice->SetRenderState(D3DRS_SRCBLEND, D3DBLEND_SRCALPHA);
    g_pDirect3DDevice->SetRenderState(D3DRS_DESTBLEND, D3DBLEND_INVSRCALPHA);

    HRESULT hResult = D3DXCreateTextureFromFile(g_pDirect3DDevice,
        "texture03.bmp", &g_pTransparentSquareTexture);
    hResult = D3DXCreateTextureFromFile(g_pDirect3DDevice,
        "texture02.bmp", &g_pSolidSquareTexture);
    g_pDirect3DDevice->SetTextureStageState(0,
        D3DTSS_ALPHAARG1, D3DTA_DIFFUSE);

    return D3D_OK;
}
```

Besides the typical Direct3D startup, this new function sets the render state to enable alpha blending and loads the two textures from disk. The texture stage state is set to use the diffuse color component of a vertex as the alpha channel.

5. Replace the current `CleanUpDirect3D()` function with Listing 11.3.

LISTING 11.3   The New `CleanUpDirect3D()` Function

```
/////////////////////////////////////////////////////
// CleanUpDirect3D()
/////////////////////////////////////////////////////
void CleanUpDirect3D()
{
    if (g_pSolidSquareVertexBuf)
    {
        g_pSolidSquareVertexBuf->Release();
        g_pSolidSquareVertexBuf = NULL;
    }
    if (g_pTransparentSquareVertexBuf)
    {
        g_pTransparentSquareVertexBuf->Release();
        g_pTransparentSquareVertexBuf = NULL;
    }
    if (g_pSolidSquareTexture)
    {
        g_pSolidSquareTexture->Release();
        g_pSolidSquareTexture = NULL;
    }
    if (g_pTransparentSquareTexture)
    {
        g_pTransparentSquareTexture->Release();
        g_pTransparentSquareTexture = NULL;
    }
    if (g_pDirect3DDevice)
    {
        g_pDirect3DDevice->Release();
        g_pDirect3DDevice = NULL;
    }
    if (g_pDirect3D)
    {
        g_pDirect3D->Release();
        g_pDirect3D = NULL;
    }
}
```

This function releases from memory the many Direct3D objects created by the program.

6. Replace the current Render() function with Listing 11.4.

LISTING 11.4   The New Render() Function

```
/////////////////////////////////////////////////////
// Render()
/////////////////////////////////////////////////////
VOID Render()
{
    g_pDirect3DDevice->Clear(0, NULL, D3DCLEAR_TARGET|D3DCLEAR_ZBUFFER,
        D3DCOLOR_XRGB(0,0,0), 1.0f, 0);

    if( SUCCEEDED(g_pDirect3DDevice->BeginScene()))
    {
        InitLights();
        InitMatrices();
        g_pDirect3DDevice->SetFVF(D3DFVF_XYZ|D3DFVF_NORMAL |
            D3DFVF_DIFFUSE | D3DFVF_TEX1);
        g_pDirect3DDevice->SetTexture(0, g_pSolidSquareTexture);
        g_pDirect3DDevice->SetStreamSource(0, g_pSolidSquareVertexBuf, 0,
            sizeof(CUSTOMVERTEXSTRUCT));
        g_pDirect3DDevice->DrawPrimitive(D3DPT_TRIANGLELIST,
            0, 2);
        g_pDirect3DDevice->SetTexture(0, g_pTransparentSquareTexture);
        g_pDirect3DDevice->SetStreamSource(0, g_pTransparentSquareVertexBuf,
0,
            sizeof(CUSTOMVERTEXSTRUCT));
        g_pDirect3DDevice->DrawPrimitive(D3DPT_TRIANGLELIST,
            0, 2);
        g_pDirect3DDevice->EndScene();
    }

    g_pDirect3DDevice->Present( NULL, NULL, NULL, NULL );
}
```

This new version of the function renders two different rectangles with their own textures.

7. Replace the current `InitVertices()` function with Listing 11.5.

LISTING 11.5   The New `InitVertices()` Function

```
///////////////////////////////////////////////////
// InitVertices()
///////////////////////////////////////////////////
HRESULT InitVertices()
{
    CUSTOMVERTEXSTRUCT solidSquare[] =
    {
        {-1.0f,  1.0f, 1.0f, 0.0f, 0.0f, -1.0f,
            D3DCOLOR_ARGB(255,255,255,255), 0.0f, 0.0f},
        { 1.0f, -1.0f, 1.0f, 0.0f, 0.0f, -1.0f,
            D3DCOLOR_ARGB(255,255,255,255), 1.0f, 1.0f},
        {-1.0f, -1.0f, 1.0f, 0.0f, 0.0f, -1.0f,
            D3DCOLOR_ARGB(255,255,255,255), 0.0f, 1.0f},
        {-1.0f,  1.0f, 1.0f, 0.0f, 0.0f, -1.0f,
            D3DCOLOR_ARGB(255,255,255,255), 0.0f, 0.0f},
        { 1.0f,  1.0f, 1.0f, 0.0f, 0.0f, -1.0f,
            D3DCOLOR_ARGB(255,255,255,255), 1.0f, 0.0f},
        { 1.0f, -1.0f, 1.0f, 0.0f, 0.0f, -1.0f,
            D3DCOLOR_ARGB(255,255,255,255), 1.0f, 1.0f}
    };

    CUSTOMVERTEXSTRUCT transparentSquare[] =
    {
        { 0.75f,  0.75f, 0.2f, 0.0f, 0.0f, 1.0f,
            D3DCOLOR_ARGB(170,255,255,255), 0.0f, 0.0f},
        {-0.75f, -0.75f, 0.2f, 0.0f, 0.0f, 1.0f,
            D3DCOLOR_ARGB(170,255,255,255), 1.0f, 1.0f},
        { 0.75f, -0.75f, 0.2f, 0.0f, 0.0f, 1.0f,
            D3DCOLOR_ARGB(170,255,255,255), 0.0f, 1.0f},
        { 0.75f,  0.75f, 0.2f, 0.0f, 0.0f, 1.0f,
            D3DCOLOR_ARGB(170,255,255,255), 0.0f, 0.0f},
        {-0.75f,  0.75f, 0.2f, 0.0f, 0.0f, 1.0f,
            D3DCOLOR_ARGB(170,255,255,255), 1.0f, 0.0f},
        {-0.75f, -0.75f, 0.2f, 0.0f, 0.0f, 1.0f,
            D3DCOLOR_ARGB(170,255,255,255), 1.0f, 1.0f}
    };

    if(FAILED(g_pDirect3DDevice ->CreateVertexBuffer(sizeof(solidSquare),
            0, D3DFVF_XYZ|D3DFVF_NORMAL | D3DFVF_DIFFUSE | D3DFVF_TEX1,
        D3DPOOL_DEFAULT, &g_pSolidSquareVertexBuf, NULL)))
        return E_FAIL;
```

LISTING 11.5   Continued

```
    if(FAILED(g_pDirect3DDevice ->
            CreateVertexBuffer(sizeof(transparentSquare),
            0, D3DFVF_XYZ|D3DFVF_NORMAL | D3DFVF_DIFFUSE | D3DFVF_TEX1,
            D3DPOOL_DEFAULT, &g_pTransparentSquareVertexBuf, NULL)))
        return E_FAIL;

    CUSTOMVERTEXSTRUCT* pVertices;
    if(FAILED(g_pSolidSquareVertexBuf->Lock(0, 0, (void**)&pVertices, 0)))
        return E_FAIL;
    memcpy(pVertices, solidSquare, sizeof(solidSquare));
    g_pSolidSquareVertexBuf->Unlock();
    if(FAILED(g_pTransparentSquareVertexBuf->
            Lock(0, 0, (void**)&pVertices, 0)))
        return E_FAIL;
    memcpy(pVertices, transparentSquare, sizeof(transparentSquare));
    g_pTransparentSquareVertexBuf->Unlock();

    return S_OK;
}
```

This new version of the function creates vertex buffers for two rectangles, each with its own level of transparency.

8. In the InitMatrices() function, replace the line D3DXVECTOR3 vEyePt(0.0f, 1.0f, -3.0f) with the following (just change the -3.0f to -4.0f):

```
D3DXVECTOR3 vEyePt(0.0f, 1.0f, -4.0f);
```

This change moves the scene's camera back a little.

9. In the InitLights() function, change the lines

```
light0.Position.x = 1.0f;
light0.Position.y = 1.0f;
```

to

```
light0.Position.x = 2.0f;
light0.Position.y = 2.0f;
```

This change moves the spotlight back a little from the scene, providing a slightly wider beam of light.

10. Copy the texture02.bmp and texture03.bmp files from the sample code's Chapter11\VertexAlphaApp directory to your own VertexAlphaApp directory, or provide your own 128×128 textures.

Compile and run the program. When you do, you'll see the window shown in Figure 11.2. In the window, two rectangles rotate around the Y axis. One rectangle is semitransparent, whereas the second is opaque. Figure 11.3 shows the application when the opaque rectangle is facing the camera.

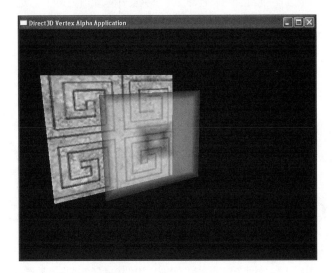

FIGURE 11.2   The running VertexAlphaApp application.

To make both rectangles opaque, all you have to do is comment out the line

```
g_pDirect3DDevice->SetRenderState(D3DRS_ALPHABLENDENABLE, true);
```

in the InitDirect3D() function. This turns off alpha blending, because off is the default setting for the D3DRS_ALPHABLENDENABLE render state. When you run the program now, you'll see a window similar to Figure 11.4. Notice that both rectangles are now opaque. That is, Direct3D renders the scene without alpha blending.

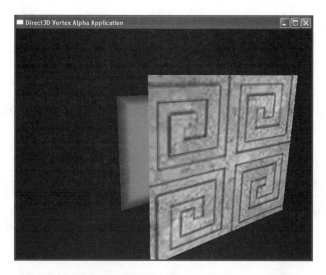

FIGURE 11.3   The running VertexAlphaApp application showing the opaque rectangle in front.

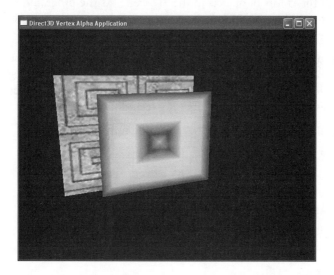

FIGURE 11.4   The VertexAlphaApp application with alpha blending turned off.

Using Fog

In the real world, air is not fully transparent, which is why objects appear more obscured the farther they are from us. This lack of transparency is the result of tiny particles that fill the air. The density of these particles (that is, the number of particles in the air) determines visibility. The denser the particles in the air, the worse the visibility. Extreme density, such as inside a black smoke cloud or in dense fog, can completely obscure objects that are nearly in front of us.

THE PRACTICALITY OF FOG

3D-application programmers use fog not only to create more realistic scenes but also to limit the number of 3D objects an application must render to display a scene. That is, 3D objects obscured by fog need not be processed and rendered. Limiting the number of objects that must be rendered speeds up the entire rendering process, especially when a scene must be rendered many times a second.

Direct3D can simulate the effect of airborne particles by adding fog to a scene. In fact, fogging is similar to alpha blending because Direct3D must blend the color of the fog with the colors of objects in the 3D scene. As the programmer, you have full control over the amount of fog in a scene, as well as over the type of calculations Direct3D uses to produce the fog effect.

Direct3D provides a couple of ways to produce fog in a scene, but you'll study only one of them in this chapter. The method you'll study, called *vertex fog*, works well for many situations in which you want to add fog to a scene. Your Direct3D documentation provides information about other fog techniques.

Fog is actually easy to add to a scene, requiring only four steps:

1. Enable fog blending.

2. Set the fog mode.

3. Set the fog color.

4. Set fog parameters, such as density and depth.

Enabling Fog Blending

To turn on fog blending, you call SetRenderState() with the arguments D3DRS_FOGEN-ABLE and true, as shown here:

```
g_pDirect3DDevice->SetRenderState(D3DRS_FOGENABLE, true);
```

The default value for the D3DRS_FOGENABLE render state is false, so there's no getting around calling SetRenderState() to enable fog.

Setting the Fog Mode

The fog mode determines the type of calculations Direct3D performs to display the fog. Direct3D supports three modes of fog: linear fog and two types of exponential fog. You specify these modes using the D3DFOG_LINEAR, D3DFOG_EXP, and D3DFOG_EXP2 constants, which Direct3D defines for you. SetRenderState() sets the fog mode, as shown here:

```
g_pDirect3DDevice->SetRenderState(D3DRS_FOGVERTEXMODE, D3DFOG_EXP2);
```

This call sets Direct3D to supply vertex fog in the second exponential mode.

Setting the Fog Color

Fog can be any color. The color you use depends on the effect you're trying to create. For example, to simulate the effect of a cloud of smoke, you might use a fog color of dark gray or black, whereas to create the kind of fog you get on a damp, warm night, you'd probably use white for the fog color.

To set the fog color, call SetRenderState() again, this time with D3DRS_FOGCOLOR and a color as the two arguments. Such a call looks something like this, depending on the color you choose:

```
g_pDirect3DDevice->SetRenderState(D3DRS_FOGCOLOR,
    D3DXCOLOR(255,255,255,255));
```

This call to SetRenderState() sets the fog color to white.

Setting Fog Parameters

The fog parameters you need to set depend on the fog mode you choose. If you set up Direct3D for linear fog, you need to set the starting and ending points for the fog in the scene. As usual, SetRenderState() does the job, as shown here:

```
float fFogStart = 2.0f;
float fFogEnd = 15.0f;
g_pDirect3DDevice->SetRenderState(D3DRS_FOGSTART, *(DWORD*) (&fFogStart));
g_pDirect3DDevice->SetRenderState(D3DRS_FOGEND, *(DWORD*) (&fFogEnd));
```

Here, fFogStart is the world coordinate at which the fog effect begins, whereas fFogEnd is the world coordinate at which the fog stops. The second argument's strange-looking casting presents to Direct3D a floating-point value as a DWORD, which is the data type required by SetRenderState().

If you're using exponential fog, which tends to look the most realistic, you need to call `SetRenderState()` to specify the fog density, like this:

```
float fDensity = 0.1f;
g_pDirect3DDevice->SetRenderState(D3DRS_FOGDENSITY, *(DWORD*)(&fDensity));
```

Creating the VertexFogApp Application

It's time to build this chapter's fog demonstration program. The following sections lead you through the building of the VertexFogApp application. Remember that you don't have to type the code if you don't want to. You can just copy it from the completed projects included with this book's sample code. Refer to this book's introduction for information on how to obtain the sample code.

Creating the Basic Project

Perform the following steps to get the main Direct3D application project started:

1. Start a new empty Win32 project named VertexFogApp.

2. On the Project menu, select the Add New Item command. The Add New Item dialog box appears.

3. Add a new C++ File (.cpp) named VertexFogApp.cpp.

4. Copy the contents of the TextureApp.cpp file from the sample code's Chapter10\TextureApp folder into the new VertexFogApp code window.

5. Change the name in the comment at the top of the file to VertexFogApp.cpp.

6. In the `RegisterWindowClass()` function, change `wc.lpszClassName = "TextureApp"` to `wc.lpszClassName = "VertexFogApp"`.

7. In the `CreateAppWindow()` function, change `"TextureApp"` to `"VertexFogApp"`, and then change `"Direct3D Lighting Application"` to `"Direct3D Vertex Fog Application"`.

Adding the DirectX References

Next, you need to tell the program where the required DirectX header files and libraries are located. To do that, follow these steps:

1. Right-click the project's name in the Solution Explorer, and select Properties from the menu that appears. The VertexFogApp Property Pages dialog box appears.

2. Click the C/C++ selection in the left-hand pane, and select General from the displayed choices.

3. In the Additional Include Directories box, enter the path to the DirectX 9 SDK's include folder. If you installed the SDK using the default settings, this path should be `c:\DXSDK\include`.

4. Click the Linker selection in the left-hand pane, and select General from the displayed choices.

5. In the Additional Library Directories box, enter the path to the DirectX 9 SDK's library folder. If you installed the SDK using the default settings, this path should be `c:\DXSDK\lib`.

6. Click the Linker's Input selection in the left-hand pane.

7. In the Additional Dependencies box in the right-hand pane, enter **d3d9.lib**, **d3dx9.lib**, and **dxerr9.lib**.

8. Place a 128×128 texture image named texture.bmp in your VertexFogApp project folder. (You can copy the one from the sample code's Chapter10\TextureApp folder, if you want.)

9. Compile and run the application to make sure that it works.

Adding Source Code

Now you'll add the Direct3D code that will complete the VertexFogApp application. Perform the following steps:

1. Add the following line to the program's global variable declarations:

```
float zDistance = -1.5f;
```

This line declares a variable that will be used to animate the application's rendering.

2. Delete the following line from the program's global variable declarations:

```
int g_iNumTriangles;
```

3. In the `WndProc()` function, add Listing 11.6 to `WM_KEYDOWN` case section.

LISTING 11.6   New Code for the `WndProc()` Function

```
case VK_DOWN:
    zDistance -= 0.1f;
    if (zDistance < -18.0f)
        zDistance = -18.0f;
    break;
case VK_UP:
```

LISTING 11.6   Continued

```
zDistance += 0.1f;
if (zDistance > -1.5f)
    zDistance = -1.5f;
break;
```

These lines change the position of the camera whenever the user presses the up or down arrows on his keyboard.

4. Replace the current `InitDirect3D()` function with Listing 11.7.

LISTING 11.7   The New `InitDirect3D()` Function

```
//////////////////////////////////////////////////
// InitDirect3D()
//////////////////////////////////////////////////
HRESULT InitDirect3D()
{
    if((g_pDirect3D = Direct3DCreate9(D3D_SDK_VERSION)) == NULL)
        return E_FAIL;

    D3DPRESENT_PARAMETERS D3DPresentParams;
    ZeroMemory(&D3DPresentParams, sizeof(D3DPRESENT_PARAMETERS));
    D3DPresentParams.Windowed = TRUE;
    D3DPresentParams.BackBufferFormat = D3DFMT_UNKNOWN;
    D3DPresentParams.SwapEffect = D3DSWAPEFFECT_DISCARD;
    D3DPresentParams.hDeviceWindow = g_hWnd;
    D3DPresentParams.EnableAutoDepthStencil = TRUE;
    D3DPresentParams.AutoDepthStencilFormat = D3DFMT_D16;

    if (FAILED(g_pDirect3D->CreateDevice(D3DADAPTER_DEFAULT,
            D3DDEVTYPE_HAL, g_hWnd, D3DCREATE_SOFTWARE_VERTEXPROCESSING,
            &D3DPresentParams, &g_pDirect3DDevice)))
        return E_FAIL;

    g_pDirect3DDevice->SetRenderState(D3DRS_FOGENABLE, TRUE);
    g_pDirect3DDevice->SetRenderState(D3DRS_FOGCOLOR, D3DXCOLOR(0,0,0,0));
    g_pDirect3DDevice->SetRenderState(D3DRS_FOGVERTEXMODE, D3DFOG_EXP2);
    float density = 0.1f;
    g_pDirect3DDevice->SetRenderState(D3DRS_FOGDENSITY, *(DWORD
*)(&density));
```

LISTING 11.7   Continued

```
HRESULT hResult = D3DXCreateTextureFromFile(g_pDirect3DDevice,
    "texture04.bmp", &g_pTexture);
if (FAILED(hResult))
    MessageBox(g_hWnd, "Couldn't load texture file.",
    "Error", MB_OK | MB_ICONEXCLAMATION);

return D3D_OK;
}
```

Besides the typical Direct3D startup, this new function sets the render state to enable fog and loads the texture from disk. This application uses the default states for textures and so doesn't call SetTextureStageState().

5. Replace the current Render() function with Listing 11.8.

LISTING 11.8   The New Render() Function

```
/////////////////////////////////////////////////////
// Render()
/////////////////////////////////////////////////////
VOID Render()
{
    g_pDirect3DDevice->Clear(0, NULL, D3DCLEAR_TARGET|D3DCLEAR_ZBUFFER,
        D3DCOLOR_XRGB(0,0,0), 1.0f, 0);

    if(SUCCEEDED(g_pDirect3DDevice->BeginScene()))
    {
        InitLights();
        InitMatrices();
        g_pDirect3DDevice->SetFVF(D3DFVF_XYZ|D3DFVF_NORMAL|D3DFVF_TEX1);
        g_pDirect3DDevice->SetTexture(0, g_pTexture);
        g_pDirect3DDevice->SetStreamSource(0, g_pVertexBuf, 0,
            sizeof(CUSTOMVERTEXSTRUCT));
        g_pDirect3DDevice->DrawPrimitive(D3DPT_TRIANGLELIST, 0, 2);
        g_pDirect3DDevice->EndScene();
    }
    else
    {
        MessageBox(g_hWnd, "Rendering Error", "Error",
            MB_OK | MB_ICONEXCLAMATION);
```

LISTING 11.8   Continued

```
        PostQuitMessage(WM_QUIT);
    }

    g_pDirect3DDevice->Present( NULL, NULL, NULL, NULL );
}
```

6. Replace the current InitVertices() function with Listing 11.9.

LISTING 11.9   The New InitVertices() Function

```
////////////////////////////////////////////////////
// InitVertices()
////////////////////////////////////////////////////
HRESULT InitVertices()
{
    CUSTOMVERTEXSTRUCT square[] =
    {
        {-1.0f,  1.0f, 1.0f, 0.0f, 0.0f, -1.0f, 0.0f, 0.0f},
        { 1.0f, -1.0f, 1.0f, 0.0f, 0.0f, -1.0f, 1.0f, 1.0f},
        {-1.0f, -1.0f, 1.0f, 0.0f, 0.0f, -1.0f, 0.0f, 1.0f},
        {-1.0f,  1.0f, 1.0f, 0.0f, 0.0f, -1.0f, 0.0f, 0.0f},
        { 1.0f,  1.0f, 1.0f, 0.0f, 0.0f, -1.0f, 1.0f, 0.0f},
        { 1.0f, -1.0f, 1.0f, 0.0f, 0.0f, -1.0f, 1.0f, 1.0f}
    };

    if(FAILED(g_pDirect3DDevice ->CreateVertexBuffer(sizeof(square),
            0, D3DFVF_XYZ|D3DFVF_NORMAL|D3DFVF_TEX1,
            D3DPOOL_DEFAULT, &g_pVertexBuf, NULL)))
        return E_FAIL;

    CUSTOMVERTEXSTRUCT* pVertices;
    if(FAILED(g_pVertexBuf->Lock(0, 0, (void**)&pVertices, 0)))
        return E_FAIL;
    memcpy(pVertices, square, sizeof(square));
    g_pVertexBuf->Unlock();

    return S_OK;
}
```

This new version of the function creates vertex buffers for one rectangle.

7. Replace the InitMatrices() function with Listing 11.10.

LISTING 11.10   The New InitMatrices() Function

```
//////////////////////////////////////////////////////
// InitMatrices()
//////////////////////////////////////////////////////
VOID InitMatrices()
{
    D3DXVECTOR3 vEyePt(0.0f, 0.0f, zDistance);
    D3DXVECTOR3 vLookatPt(0.0f, 0.0f, 0.0f);
    D3DXVECTOR3 vUpVec(0.0f, 1.0f, 0.0f);
    D3DXMATRIXA16 matView;
    D3DXMatrixLookAtLH(&matView, &vEyePt, &vLookatPt, &vUpVec);
    g_pDirect3DDevice->SetTransform(D3DTS_VIEW, &matView);

    D3DXMATRIXA16 matProj;
    D3DXMatrixPerspectiveFovLH(&matProj, D3DX_PI/4, 1.0f, 1.0f, 100.0f);
    g_pDirect3DDevice->SetTransform(D3DTS_PROJECTION, &matProj);
}
```

This function now enables the application to change the camera position based on the current value of the zDistance variable. Notice that the function performs no world transformations, such as rotation or translation. The camera position creates all changes in the scene.

8. Replace the current InitLights() function with Listing 11.11.

LISTING 11.11   The New InitLight() Function

```
//////////////////////////////////////////////////////
// InitLights()
//////////////////////////////////////////////////////
VOID InitLights()
{
    D3DLIGHT9 light0;
    ZeroMemory(&light0, sizeof(light0));

    light0.Type = D3DLIGHT_SPOT;
    light0.Diffuse.r  = 1.0f;
    light0.Diffuse.g  = 1.0f;
    light0.Diffuse.b  = 1.0f;
    light0.Ambient.r  = 1.0f;
```

LISTING 11.11   Continued

```
light0.Ambient.g  = 1.0f;
light0.Ambient.b  = 1.0f;
light0.Position.x = 2.0f;
light0.Position.y = 2.0f;
light0.Position.z = 0.0f;
light0.Direction.x = -1.0f;
light0.Direction.y = -1.0f;
light0.Direction.z = 0.0f;
light0.Attenuation0 = 1.0f;
light0.Range = 50.0f;
light0.Phi = 2.0f;
light0.Theta = 1.0f;
light0.Falloff = 1.0f;

g_pDirect3DDevice->SetLight(0, &light0);
g_pDirect3DDevice->LightEnable(0, TRUE);

D3DMATERIAL9 material;
ZeroMemory(&material, sizeof(material));
material.Diffuse.r = 1.0f;
material.Diffuse.g = 1.0f;
material.Diffuse.b = 1.0f;
material.Diffuse.a = 1.0f;
material.Ambient.r = 1.0f;
material.Ambient.g = 1.0f;
material.Ambient.b = 1.0f;
material.Ambient.a = 1.0f;
g_pDirect3DDevice->SetMaterial(&material);
}
```

This new version of the function removes specular light from the scene and slightly repositions the light in the scene.

9. Copy the texture04.bmp file from the sample code's Chapter11\VertexFogApp directory to your own VertexFogApp directory, or provide your own 128×128 texture.

Compile and run the program. When you do, you should see a window like that shown in Figure 11.5. As you can see, the program displays a textured rectangle. Press the down arrow on your keyboard to move the camera away from the rectangle. The farther you move away, the dimmer the rectangle becomes, as if it's fading in the distance (see Figure 11.6). Press the up arrow to move closer to the rectangle.

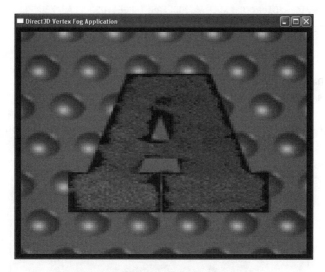

FIGURE 11.5   The running VertexFogApp application.

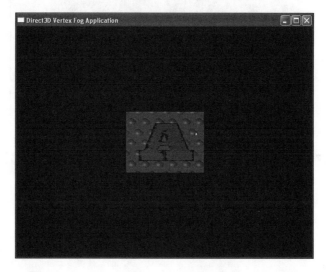

FIGURE 11.6   Moving the camera away from the fogged 3D object.

To create the effect of the rectangle fading in the distance, the application uses black fog to obscure the rectangle as it gets farther from the camera. Black works well here because the window's background color is black. To see what's really going on, change the line

```
g_pDirect3DDevice->Clear(0, NULL, D3DCLEAR_TARGET|D3DCLEAR_ZBUFFER,
    D3DCOLOR_XRGB(0,0,0), 1.0f, 0);
```

in the InitDirect3D() function to

```
g_pDirect3DDevice->Clear(0, NULL, D3DCLEAR_TARGET|D3DCLEAR_ZBUFFER,
    D3DCOLOR_XRGB(255,255,255), 1.0f, 0);
```

and rerun the application. Now the background color is white, so you can see how Direct3D uses the black fog to blend the rectangle with a black background, as shown in Figures 11.7 through 11.9.

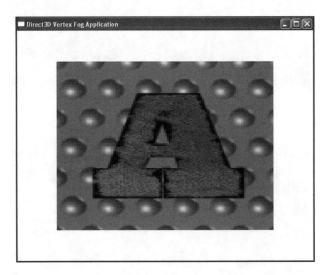

FIGURE 11.7   Changing to a white background with black fog.

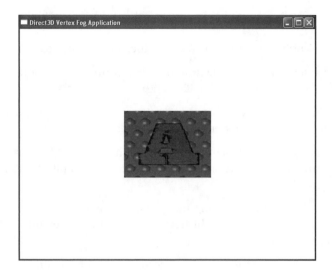

FIGURE 11.8   Fading...fading....

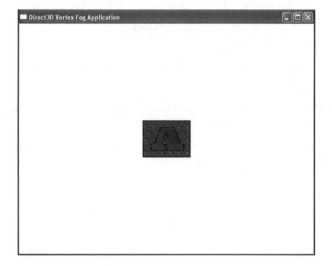

FIGURE 11.9   Faded to black.

In Brief

- Alpha blending enables a 3D scene to include semitransparent objects.

- Alpha values, which can be from 0 to 255, control the amount of transparency used to render an object in a 3D scene.

- Direct3D supports five types of alpha blending: vertex alpha, material alpha, texture alpha, frame buffer alpha, and render target alpha.

- To set up vertex alpha blending, you must have vertex data that can hold alpha values and must call `SetRenderState()` to set up the application's rendering state for alpha blending.

- After setting up the rendering state for alpha blending, you need to call `SetTextureStageState()` to tell Direct3D to look for the texture's alpha values in the diffuse color.

- Direct3D simulates the effect of airborne particles by adding fog to a scene.

- Vertex fog is easy to add to a scene, requiring only four steps: enable fog blending, set the fog mode, set the fog color, set the appropriate fog parameters.

- To turn on fog blending, you call `SetRenderState()` with the arguments `D3DRS_FOGENABLE` and `true`.

- Direct3D supports three modes of fog: linear fog and two types of exponential fog.

- To set the fog color, call `SetRenderState()` with `D3DRS_FOGCOLOR` and a color as the two arguments.

- Each type of fog is associated with a number of parameters that you must set in the program.

Creating a 3D World

12

IN THIS CHAPTER

▶ Introducing
  Direct3DDemoApp

▶ Exploring the Program

▶ Exploring the Full Program

▶ In Brief

Introducing Direct3DDemoApp

Throughout this book, you've learned the basic techniques you need to create 3D worlds. However, most of the discussions were demonstrated using a single 3D object. Not much of a "world." Most 3D applications must render many 3D objects simultaneously to create an immersive 3D environment for the user. This is one topic that we've avoided—up until now.

Even more important, though, this chapter represents a review of most of the Direct3D programming techniques you learned in previous chapters. Here, you'll explore a complete 3D application that does everything from performing standard 3D transformations such as rotation and scaling, to managing textures, using transparency, and generating fog.

You won't spend any time in this chapter building an application. First, you've already built many applications as you've worked through this book, so you should know how to do it by now. Second, this chapter's example program, Direct3DDemoApp, is too big to present as a step-by-step project. Instead of building the program, you'll examine the source code piece by piece to make sure that you understand the core concepts you learned in this book.

A PRACTICAL STUDY GUIDE

For your convenience, in place of the usual step-by-step project, this chapter features the entire printed source code for Direct3DDemoApp. You can find this listing at the end of the chapter. After you go through the piece-by-piece explanation of the program, study the listing to make sure that you understand how all the pieces fit together in the context of a full application. The listing is heavily commented to help with your understanding.

Your first job in this chapter is to run the program and see what it can do. You can find the application in the sample code's Chapter12\Direct3DDemoApp folder. You can copy this folder to your hard drive and compile the project, or you can just run the program's executable file, also included in the folder. (Refer to this book's introduction to find out how to get the sample code.)

When you run the application (make sure that your system is set to the 32-bit color mode with a resolution of at least 800×600), you'll see the window shown in Figure 12.1. The sign is comprised of three rectangles, each with an assigned texture. Actually, in the case of the sign board, two textures alternate, providing a flashing effect.

FIGURE 12.1   The running Direct3DDemoApp application.

Use your keyboard's Up arrow key to move through the sign and into the 3D world beyond. Figure 12.2 shows what you'll see. The various shapes use different world transformations to create the animation. You can also see two types of transparency in effect: full transparency using a color key and partial transparency using alpha blending.

Use your Up and Down arrow keys to move forward or backward through the scene. You can even step inside a couple of the cubes. Figure 12.3, for example, shows the viewpoint from inside the cube with the circular openings.

FIGURE 12.2   Direct3DDemoApp's 3D world beyond the sign.

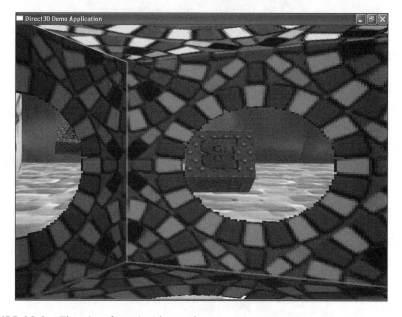

FIGURE 12.3   The view from inside a cube.

If you hold down the Up arrow key, you'll move through the entire scene. When you get beyond the last 3D object, the viewpoint automatically reverses so that you're looking at the scene from the back while you continue to move farther and farther from the 3D objects (see Figure 12.4). The farther away you move, the more you can see fog having an effect (see Figure 12.5).

FIGURE 12.4   The reversed view.

FIGURE 12.5   The effects of fog.

SHOP TALK

MOVING THROUGH A 3D WORLD

You may wonder why you can move only forward and backward through Direct3DDemoApp's 3D world. The easy answer—and the most honest—is that I was lazy. Moving a viewpoint through a 3D world is easy when you need to update the camera location on only one axis. In the case of this program, only the camera's Z coordinate changes.

Moving at an angle, though, requires a bit of math that I didn't want to get into here. Not that I couldn't do it; I just didn't want to obscure the basic Direct3D principles presented in the code. To this end, I've kept the code as simple as possible. You've got enough to study without having to deal with trigonometry, too.

That being said, I urge you to spend a lot of time experimenting with the Direct3DDemoApp application (make sure that you keep a backup of the original). See whether you can enable the user to move in any direction in the 3D world. You'll soon see that the process isn't as easy as you might at first think.

The program also enables you to manipulate many of the Direct3D effects. For example, press the L key to turn lighting on and off. When you turn off lighting, you'll then see a scene something like Figure 12.6. (The background image remains unaffected by Direct3D because it's not a rendered 3D object. It's just a background bitmap.)

FIGURE 12.6   The scene with lighting off.

If you press the T key, you turn off the texturing process, giving you the scene shown in Figure 12.7. Without the textures, you can see that the scene loses its transparency effects, too. Pressing T a second time, replaces the textures in the scene.

FIGURE 12.7   The scene with texturing off.

Use the M key to control the amount of ambient light added to the scene. As you hold down the M key, ambient light gets brighter and brighter until it reaches its maximum and cycles back to its minimum setting. Notice that the less ambient light in the scene, the stronger the shadow effects, which are generated by each object's reflection of diffuse light.

Hold down the P key to change the position of the single spotlight, sweeping it through the scene. The F key toggles the fog effect, whereas the E key changes fog density. You can turn the background on and off with the K key. When the background is off, the fog color changes from white to black, so you can see the effect of 3D objects vanishing in the distance as you move away from them (see Figure 12.8).

The R, G, and B keys change the red, green, and blue color content of the material used in the scene, enabling you to tint the 3D objects. This effect is especially apparent when you have texturing turned off. Press the A key to toggle alpha blending on and off.

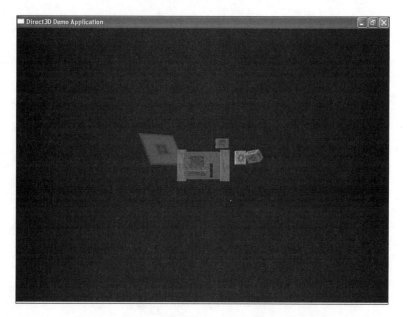

FIGURE 12.8   The scene with the background off.

The C key cycles through the different culling modes. The default setting for the program is culling off. By pressing the C key, you can see the culling of vertices defined in counterclockwise order. Press C again to see the culling of vertices defined in clockwise order. In the case of this program—in which all vertices are actually defined in clockwise order—the change in culling mode changes whether Direct3D culls rear surfaces or front surfaces. Press C a third time to turn off culling again.

Three more controls to go. Press the spacebar to reverse your viewpoint in the scene, and use the Z key to toggle Z-buffering (see Figure 12.9). Use the W and Q keys to reposition the sign in the scene (see Figure 12.10), and finally, press the D key to reset all Direct3D effects to their application-defined default values.

NEAR AND FAR

When Z-buffering is off, Direct3D has no idea which objects are closer to the camera, causing it to render all objects, even those that should be hidden behind others.

FIGURE 12.9 The scene with Z-buffering off.

FIGURE 12.10 The scene with the sign in a new position.

Exploring the Program

Now that you know what the program does, it's time to learn how the program works. For the rest of this chapter, you'll explore the source code piece by piece. In case you need to review a certain topic, each discussion refers you to the chapter in the book that covers the topic being discussed.

Reviewing the Windows Code

I'm not going to spend a lot of time on this topic because it doesn't have a lot to do with Direct3D. But it is important to understand how a Windows application interfaces with Direct3D.

The program's entry point is, of course, the WinMain() function, which in this application, breaks the application run into three phases: initialization, running, and cleanup (see Listing 12.1).

LISTING 12.1   The WinMain() Function

```
INT WINAPI WinMain(HINSTANCE hInstance, HINSTANCE, LPSTR, INT)
{
    InitApp(hInstance);
    RunApp();
    CleanUpApp();
    return 0;
}
```

The InitApp() function gets the window on the screen, as well as starts a Windows timer, as shown in Listing 12.2.

LISTING 12.2   The InitApp() Function

```
void InitApp(HINSTANCE hInstance)
{
    RegisterWindowClass(hInstance);
    CreateAppWindow(hInstance);
    ShowWindow(g_hWnd, SW_SHOWDEFAULT);
    UpdateWindow(g_hWnd);
    SetTimer(g_hWnd, 1, 500, NULL);
}
```

REVIEWING WINDOWS PROGRAMMING TECHNIQUES

You should be familiar with the functions InitApp() calls (except maybe SetTimer())
because you've used them in every program in this book. If you need to review the details,
refer to Chapter 2, "Writing a Windows Program."

The RunApp() function simply initializes Direct3D and starts the application's message
loop, as shown in Listing 12.3.

LISTING 12.3   The InitApp() Function

```
void RunApp()
{
    if (SUCCEEDED(InitDirect3D()))
    {
        InitVertices();
        WPARAM result = StartMessageLoop();
    }
}
```

We'll cover the Direct3D initialization soon, including the InitDirect3D() and
InitVertices() functions called from RunApp(). If you need to review how message
loops work, refer to Chapter 2.

Finally, the CleanUpApp() function destroys the Windows timer and calls the function
that performs the Direct3D cleanup:

```
void CleanUpApp()
{
    KillTimer(g_hWnd, 1);
    CleanUpDirect3D();
}
```

When the application's message loop starts pumping, it delivers the application's
messages to the WndProc() function, which handles the usual WM_CREATE, WM_DESTROY,
and WM_PAINT messages, as well as the timer and keypresses (see Listing 12.4).

LISTING 12.4   The WndProc() Function

```
LRESULT WINAPI WndProc(HWND hWnd, UINT msg, WPARAM wParam, LPARAM lParam)
{
    switch(msg)
    {
    case WM_CREATE:
        return 0;
```

LISTING 12.4   Continued

```
    case WM_DESTROY:
        PostQuitMessage( 0 );
        return 0;

    case WM_PAINT:
        ValidateRect(g_hWnd, NULL);
        return 0;

    case WM_TIMER:
        UpdateAnimation();
        return 0;

    case WM_KEYDOWN:
        HandleKeys(wParam);
        return 0;
    }
    return DefWindowProc(hWnd, msg, wParam, lParam);
}
```

Each time the timer reaches its set value (in this case, one second), it sends a WM_TIMER message to the program. Similarly, every time the user presses a key on his keyboard, the application gets a WM_KEYDOWN message. And that's the Windows stuff in a nutshell. For more information, refer to Chapter 2.

Initializing Direct3D

As you should already know, before you can use Direct3D to render your 3D worlds, you must initialize Direct3D. You do this by creating a Direct3D object and a Direct3D device. This is the first thing that happens in the application-defined InitDirect3D() function. Here's the code that creates the Direct3D object:

```
// Create the main Direct3D object.
if((g_pDirect3D = Direct3DCreate9(D3D_SDK_VERSION)) == NULL)
{
    MessageBox(g_hWnd, "Couldn't create main Direct3D object.",
        "FinalApp - Error", MB_OK | MB_ICONEXCLAMATION);
    return E_FAIL;
}
```

If the program creates the Direct3D object successfully, it checks the current screen mode to make sure that the program runs okay (see Listing 12.5).

LISTING 12.5   Checking the Screen Mode

```
// Get the current display mode.
D3DDISPLAYMODE d3ddisplaymode;
if (FAILED(g_pDirect3D->GetAdapterDisplayMode(
        D3DADAPTER_DEFAULT, &d3ddisplaymode)))
{
    MessageBox(g_hWnd, "Couldn't determine display mode.",
        "FinalApp - Error", MB_OK | MB_ICONEXCLAMATION);
    return E_FAIL;
}

// Determine whether the display mode is compatible with this app.
if (d3ddisplaymode.Format != D3DFMT_X8R8G8B8)
{
    MessageBox(g_hWnd, "This application requires the 32-bit display mode.",
        "FinalApp - Error", MB_OK | MB_ICONEXCLAMATION);
    return E_FAIL;
}
```

Finally, assuming that the display mode is acceptable, the program creates its Direct3D device:

```
// Create the Direct3D device.
if (FAILED(CreateDevice()))
{
    MessageBox(g_hWnd, "Couldn't create main Direct3D device.",
        "FinalApp - Error", MB_OK | MB_ICONEXCLAMATION);
    return E_FAIL;
}
```

CreateDevice() is an application-defined function, not a Direct3D function. The program defines CreateDevice() as shown in Listing 12.6.

LISTING 12.6   The CreateDevice() Function

```
HRESULT CreateDevice()
{
    D3DPRESENT_PARAMETERS D3DPresentParams;
    ZeroMemory(&D3DPresentParams, sizeof(D3DPRESENT_PARAMETERS));
    D3DPresentParams.Windowed = TRUE;
    D3DPresentParams.BackBufferFormat = D3DFMT_UNKNOWN;
    D3DPresentParams.SwapEffect = D3DSWAPEFFECT_DISCARD;
    D3DPresentParams.hDeviceWindow = g_hWnd;
```

LISTING 12.6   Continued

```
    D3DPresentParams.EnableAutoDepthStencil = TRUE;
    D3DPresentParams.AutoDepthStencilFormat = D3DFMT_D16;

    HRESULT hResult = g_pDirect3D->CreateDevice(D3DADAPTER_DEFAULT,
            D3DDEVTYPE_HAL, g_hWnd, D3DCREATE_SOFTWARE_VERTEXPROCESSING,
            &D3DPresentParams, &g_pDirect3DDevice);
    return hResult;
}
```

The created device uses (as it must because this is a windowed application) the currently set display mode and pixel format. The device uses hardware acceleration (D3DDEVTYPE_HAL) and software vertex processing (D3DCREATE_SOFTWARE_VERTEXPROCESSING).

If you need to review Direct3D initialization, refer to Chapter 5, "Getting Direct3D Up and Running."

Setting Global Rendering States

The program sets some rendering states only once, and these states remain in effect for the entire program run. I refer to these values as *global rendering states*, because all rendering done in the program will use them. The InitDirect3D() function calls the application-defined SetRenderingStates() function to handle this task:

```
// Set global rendering states.
if (FAILED(SetRenderingStates()))
{
    MessageBox(g_hWnd, "Couldn't set rendering states.",
        "FinalApp - Error", MB_OK | MB_ICONEXCLAMATION);
    PostQuitMessage(WM_QUIT);
}
```

The SetRenderingStates() function first sets the rendering states that control alpha blending:

```
if (FAILED(g_pDirect3DDevice->SetRenderState(D3DRS_SRCBLEND,
        D3DBLEND_SRCALPHA)))
    return E_FAIL;
if (FAILED(g_pDirect3DDevice->SetRenderState(D3DRS_DESTBLEND,
        D3DBLEND_INVSRCALPHA)))
    return E_FAIL;
```

SetRenderingStates() tells Direct3D to use vertex alpha blending with this call:

```
if (FAILED(g_pDirect3DDevice->SetRenderState(
        D3DRS_DIFFUSEMATERIALSOURCE, D3DMCS_COLOR1)))
    return E_FAIL;
```

For more information about alpha blending, review Chapter 11, "Programming Alpha Blending and Fog."

The program also sets rendering states for alpha testing, which helps accelerate alpha testing used to render the scene:

```
if (FAILED(g_pDirect3DDevice->SetRenderState(D3DRS_ALPHAREF, 96)))
    return E_FAIL;
if (FAILED(g_pDirect3DDevice->SetRenderState(D3DRS_ALPHAFUNC,
        D3DCMP_GREATEREQUAL)))
    return E_FAIL;
```

These lines tell Direct3D to process only pixels that have a value equal to or greater than 96.

Finally, SetRenderingStates() sets the type of fog to use in the scene:

```
if (FAILED(g_pDirect3DDevice->
        SetRenderState(D3DRS_FOGVERTEXMODE, D3DFOG_EXP2)))
    return E_FAIL;
```

FOG COLOR

Because the fog color and density can be controlled from the user's keyboard, the application sets those states elsewhere in the program.

For a review of fog techniques, refer to Chapter 11.

Loading Textures

Direct3DDemoApp uses nine different textures to render its 3D world. All those textures have to be loaded into texture surfaces, and one of them—the texture with the transparent circles—requires special handling. InitDirect3D() calls the application-defined function LoadTextures() to handle these tasks:

```
if (FAILED(LoadTextures()))
{
    MessageBox(g_hWnd, "Couldn't load textures.",
        "FinalApp - Error", MB_OK | MB_ICONEXCLAMATION);
    PostQuitMessage(WM_QUIT);
}
```

The LoadTextures() function first loads the texture that requires special handling:

```
if (FAILED(D3DXCreateTextureFromFileEx(g_pDirect3DDevice,
        "texture.bmp", D3DX_DEFAULT, D3DX_DEFAULT, D3DX_DEFAULT, 0,
        D3DFMT_A8R8G8B8, D3DPOOL_MANAGED, D3DX_FILTER_TRIANGLE,
        D3DX_FILTER_TRIANGLE, D3DCOLOR_RGBA(255,0,0,255),
        NULL, NULL, &g_pTransparentTexture)))
    return E_FAIL;
```

This is the texture that uses a color key to produce the transparent holes in the cube on which the texture is displayed. If you don't understand how this works, refer to Chapter 10, "Using Direct3D Textures."

The program loads the remaining textures using the simpler D3DXCreateTextureFromFile() function (rather than D3DXCreateTextureFromFileEx()), as shown in Listing 12.7.

LISTING 12.7   Loading Textures

```
if (FAILED(D3DXCreateTextureFromFile(g_pDirect3DDevice,
        "Texture_A.bmp", &g_pTextureA)))
    return E_FAIL;
if (FAILED(D3DXCreateTextureFromFile(g_pDirect3DDevice,
        "Texture_B.bmp", &g_pTextureB)))
    return E_FAIL;
if (FAILED(D3DXCreateTextureFromFile(g_pDirect3DDevice,
        "Texture_C.bmp", &g_pTextureC)))
    return E_FAIL;
if (FAILED(D3DXCreateTextureFromFile(g_pDirect3DDevice,
        "Texture_Star.bmp", &g_pTextureStar)))
    return E_FAIL;
if (FAILED(D3DXCreateTextureFromFile(g_pDirect3DDevice,
        "texture03.bmp", &g_pTransparentSquareTexture)))
    return E_FAIL;
```

LISTING 12.7   Continued

```
if (FAILED(D3DXCreateTextureFromFile(g_pDirect3DDevice,
        "Texture_Pillar.bmp", &g_pTexturePillar)))
    return E_FAIL;
if (FAILED(D3DXCreateTextureFromFile(g_pDirect3DDevice,
        "Texture_Welcome1.bmp", &g_pTextureWelcome1)))
    return E_FAIL;
if (FAILED(D3DXCreateTextureFromFile(g_pDirect3DDevice,
        "Texture_Welcome2.bmp", &g_pTextureWelcome2)))
    return E_FAIL;
```

Again, for more information, consult Chapter 10.

After loading the textures, program execution returns to InitDirect3D(), where the program sets the g_pTextureWelcome pointer to the first of two textures that will animate the flashing sign:

```
g_pTextureWelcome = g_pTextureWelcome1;
```

Loading the Background Bitmap

The application-defined LoadBackgroundBitmap() function, which InitDirect3D() calls next, takes care of loading the image displayed behind the 3D objects. InitDirect3D() calls that function like this:

```
if (FAILED(LoadBackgroundBitmap()))
{
    MessageBox(g_hWnd, "Couldn't load background bitmap.",
        "FinalApp - Error", MB_OK | MB_ICONEXCLAMATION);
    PostQuitMessage(WM_QUIT);
}
```

The LoadBackgroundBitmap() function looks like Listing 12.8.

LISTING 12.8   The LoadBackgroundBitmap() Function

```
HRESULT LoadBackgroundBitmap()
{
    // Create a surface for the background bitmap.
    if (FAILED(g_pDirect3DDevice->CreateOffscreenPlainSurface(800, 600,
            D3DFMT_X8R8G8B8, D3DPOOL_DEFAULT, &g_pBackgroundSurface, NULL)))
        return E_FAIL;
```

LISTING 12.8   Continued

```
// Load the background bitmap into the surface.
if (FAILED(D3DXLoadSurfaceFromFile(g_pBackgroundSurface, NULL, NULL,
        "Background.bmp", NULL, D3DX_DEFAULT, 0, NULL)))
    return E_FAIL;

return D3D_OK;
}
```

Here, the program first creates an offscreen surface in which to store the bitmap. Then a call to the D3DXLoadSurfaceFromFile() loads the bitmap into the surface, where it is accessible through the g_pBackgroundSurface pointer.

The program also needs to access the application's back buffer, which is where the background bitmap must be copied during scene rendering. The InitDirect3D() function gets the back buffer pointer by calling the Direct3D device function, GetBackBuffer():

```
if (FAILED(g_pDirect3DDevice->GetBackBuffer(0, 0,
    D3DBACKBUFFER_TYPE_MONO, &g_pBackBuffer)))
{
    MessageBox(g_hWnd, "Couldn't acquire back buffer.",
        "FinalApp - Error", MB_OK | MB_ICONEXCLAMATION);
    PostQuitMessage(WM_QUIT);
}
```

All this material was covered in Chapter 6, "Understanding Direct3D Surfaces."

Initializing Vertices

The last thing the program must do to initialize its Direct3D objects is to load two sets of vertices into the appropriate vertex buffers. The RunApp() function calls the application-defined InitVertices() function to take care of this task. That function first creates a vertex buffer for the cube shape, as shown in Listing 12.9.

LISTING 12.9   Creating the Vertex Buffer

```
int i_numCoordsPerVertex = 24;

// Create the vertex buffer.
if(FAILED(g_pDirect3DDevice ->CreateVertexBuffer(sizeof(cube),
        0, D3DFVF_XYZ|D3DFVF_NORMAL|D3DFVF_TEX1, D3DPOOL_DEFAULT,
        &g_pVertexBuf, NULL)))
    return E_FAIL;
```

LISTING 12.9   Continued

```
CUSTOMVERTEXSTRUCT* pVertices;
if(FAILED(g_pVertexBuf->Lock( 0, 0, (void**)&pVertices, 0)))
    return E_FAIL;
memcpy(pVertices, cube, sizeof(cube));
g_pVertexBuf->Unlock();

g_iNumTriangles = (sizeof(cube) / sizeof(float)) / i_numCoordsPerVertex;
```

THE VERTEX DATA IN QUESTION

Due to its length, the actual vertex data isn't shown here—you can see it in the complete listing at the end of this chapter—but the code that creates the first buffer is all here. If you need a review of the functions used, refer to Chapter 7, "Drawing Graphics Primitives."

The vertices in question are of the CUSTOMVERTEXSTRUCT type, which is a structure declared near the top of the listing like this:

```
struct CUSTOMVERTEXSTRUCT
{
    D3DVECTOR coords;
    D3DVECTOR normal;
    float tu, tv;
};
```

This structure declares model coordinates, a normal, and texture coordinates.

The program actually renders two types of custom vertices. After defining the first vertex buffer, InitVertices() defines the second, as shown in Listing 12.10.

LISTING 12.10   Creating the Second Vertex Buffer

```
TRANSCUSTOMVERTEXSTRUCT transparentSquare[] =
{
    { 0.75f,  0.75f, 0.2f, 0.0f, 0.0f, 1.0f,
        D3DCOLOR_ARGB(96,255,255,255), 0.0f, 0.0f},
    {-0.75f, -0.75f, 0.2f, 0.0f, 0.0f, 1.0f,
        D3DCOLOR_ARGB(96,255,255,255), 1.0f, 1.0f},
    { 0.75f, -0.75f, 0.2f, 0.0f, 0.0f, 1.0f,
        D3DCOLOR_ARGB(96,255,255,255), 0.0f, 1.0f},
    { 0.75f,  0.75f, 0.2f, 0.0f, 0.0f, 1.0f,
        D3DCOLOR_ARGB(96,255,255,255), 0.0f, 0.0f},
    {-0.75f,  0.75f, 0.2f, 0.0f, 0.0f, 1.0f,
```

LISTING 12.10   Continued

```
        D3DCOLOR_ARGB(96,255,255,255), 1.0f, 0.0f},
    {-0.75f, -0.75f, 0.2f, 0.0f, 0.0f, 1.0f,
        D3DCOLOR_ARGB(96,255,255,255), 1.0f, 1.0f}
};

if(FAILED(g_pDirect3DDevice ->CreateVertexBuffer(sizeof(transparentSquare),
        0, D3DFVF_XYZ | D3DFVF_NORMAL | D3DFVF_DIFFUSE | D3DFVF_TEX1,
        D3DPOOL_DEFAULT, &g_pTransparentSquareVertexBuf, NULL)))
    return E_FAIL;
if(FAILED(g_pTransparentSquareVertexBuf->Lock(0, 0, (void**)&pVertices, 0)))
    return E_FAIL;
memcpy(pVertices, transparentSquare, sizeof(transparentSquare));
g_pTransparentSquareVertexBuf->Unlock();
```

This set of vertices is used for the semitransparent square in the scene and is of the TRANSCUSTOMVERTEXSTRUCT structure, which the program defines like this:

```
struct TRANSCUSTOMVERTEXSTRUCT
{
    D3DVECTOR coords;
    D3DVECTOR normal;
    DWORD dwColor;
    float tu, tv;
};
```

This structure defines model coordinates, a normal, a diffuse color, and texture coordinates. Because the program displays the square using vertex alpha blending, Direct3D gets the alpha values from each vertex's diffuse color, represented by the dwColor member of the structure. For a review of alpha blending, refer to Chapter 11.

Preparing to Render

At this point, all the general initialization is complete, and the program enters its message loop. The first time that there's no message to process, the loop calls the application-defined Render() function to draw the display.

Render() is a fairly concise function, considering how much work it has to do. This is because most of the work gets done in helper functions called from inside Render(). As is typical, Render() must first clear the display:

```
g_pDirect3DDevice->Clear(0, NULL, D3DCLEAR_TARGET|D3DCLEAR_ZBUFFER,
    D3DCOLOR_XRGB(0,0,0), 1.0f, 0);
```

If you don't understand this Direct3D function call, refer to Chapter 5.

Next, `Render()` calls the application-defined `DisplayBackgroundImage()` helper function to transfer the background image to the device's back buffer, which it does as shown in Listing 12.11.

LISTING 12.11   Transferring the Background Image

```
RECT SrcRect;
RECT DstRect;
SrcRect.left = 0;     SrcRect.right = 799;
SrcRect.top = 0;      SrcRect.bottom = 599;
DstRect.left = 0;     DstRect.top = 0;
DstRect.right = 792;  DstRect.bottom = 566;

// Blit the background image to the target surface.
if (g_bShowBackground)
    g_pDirect3DDevice->StretchRect(g_pBackgroundSurface,
        &SrcRect, g_pBackBuffer, &DstRect, D3DTEXF_NONE);
```

You learned about `StretchRect()` in Chapter 5.

Next up for `Render()` is a call to the application-defined function `SetVariableRenderStates()` function, which sets variable states based on the values of the render-state variables that the user can control with the various keystrokes outlined earlier in this chapter. The program sets the fog color based on whether the background image is being displayed:

```
// Set fog color based on whether background is displayed.
if (g_bShowBackground)
    g_pDirect3DDevice->SetRenderState(D3DRS_FOGCOLOR,
        D3DXCOLOR(255,255,255,255));
else
    g_pDirect3DDevice->SetRenderState(D3DRS_FOGCOLOR,
        D3DXCOLOR(0,0,0,0));
```

The `g_bZBufferingOn` Boolean variable controls whether the program renders using Z-buffering:

```
// Turn Z-buffering on and off.
g_pDirect3DDevice->SetRenderState(D3DRS_ZENABLE, g_bZBufferingOn);
```

Backface culling, which determines whether Direct3D draws rear-facing primitives, is also controlled by a variable. This time, the variable is g_iCullingMode, which can be one of three values, as seen here:

```
// Turn back-face culling on or off.
if (g_iCullingMode == CULLCOUNTERCLOCKWISE)
    g_pDirect3DDevice->SetRenderState(D3DRS_CULLMODE, D3DCULL_CCW);
else if (g_iCullingMode == CULLCLOCKWISE)
    g_pDirect3DDevice->SetRenderState(D3DRS_CULLMODE, D3DCULL_CW);
else if (g_iCullingMode == CULLNONE)
    g_pDirect3DDevice->SetRenderState(D3DRS_CULLMODE, D3DCULL_NONE);
```

Finally, the g_bFogOn and g_fFogDensity variables control fog enabling and fog density:

```
// Turn fog on or off.
g_pDirect3DDevice->SetRenderState(D3DRS_FOGENABLE, g_bFogOn);

// Set fog density.
g_pDirect3DDevice->SetRenderState(D3DRS_FOGDENSITY,
        *(DWORD *)(&g_fFogDensity));
```

If you need a review of SetRenderState() with respect to culling, refer to Chapter 8, "Direct3D Transformations." If you need a review of SetRenderState() with respect to fog, refer to Chapter 11.

Beginning the Rendering Process

With the background cleared and redrawn, and the variable render states set to their current values, Render() is ready to start drawing 3D objects. As always, to start the rendering process, the program must call the device object's BeginScene() function:

```
if(SUCCEEDED(g_pDirect3DDevice->BeginScene()))
```

Setting Up Lights

The next step is to set up all the things that are universal to the scene. This includes (in this case) lighting, the view transformation, and the projection transformation. Render() calls the application-defined InitLights() to get the scene's lighting set up. That function first defines a Direct3D light object:

```
D3DLIGHT9 light0;
ZeroMemory(&light0, sizeof(light0));
```

With the light object ready to go, InitLights() uses the object to define and position a spotlight that provides ambient and diffuse light to the scene (see Listing 12.12).

LISTING 12.12   Setting Up the Light Object

```
light0.Type = D3DLIGHT_SPOT;
light0.Ambient.r  = g_fAmbientLight;
light0.Ambient.g  = g_fAmbientLight;
light0.Ambient.b  = g_fAmbientLight;
light0.Diffuse.r  = 1.0f;
light0.Diffuse.g  = 1.0;
light0.Diffuse.b  = 1.0;
light0.Position.x = g_fLightPosition;
light0.Position.y = g_fLightPosition;
light0.Position.z = 0.0f;
light0.Direction.x = -1.0f;
light0.Direction.y = -1.0f;
light0.Direction.z = 0.0f;
light0.Attenuation0 = 1.0f;
light0.Range = 50.0f;
light0.Phi = 2.0f;
light0.Theta = 1.0f;
light0.Falloff = 1.0f;
```

As you can see here, the `g_fAmbientLight` and `g_fLightPosition` variables control the intensity of the ambient light, as well as the light's position. The values of these variables are under the user's control through the application's keyboard commands.

With the light object fully defined, the Direct3D device method `SetLight()` tells Direct3D to use the light when rendering the scene. The `LightEnable()` method, which is under the control of the `g_bLightingOn` Boolean variable, turns on lighting in the scene:

```
g_pDirect3DDevice->SetLight(0, &light0);
g_pDirect3DDevice->LightEnable(0, g_bLightingOn);
```

For more information about setting up Direct3D lighting, refer to Chapter 9, "Lighting 3D Objects."

Setting Up Materials

Lights don't do much good if the 3D objects in the scene reflect no light. To create this reflection, the objects must be rendered using a material. Because lights and materials are so closely related, the `InitLights()` function also takes care of creating materials, first defining a Direct3D material object:

```
D3DMATERIAL9 material;
ZeroMemory(&material, sizeof(material));
```

`InitLights()` then sets the material to reflect ambient and diffuse light:

```
material.Ambient.r = g_fMaterialRed;
material.Ambient.g = g_fMaterialGreen;
material.Ambient.b = g_fMaterialBlue;
material.Ambient.a = 1.0f;
material.Diffuse.r = 1.0;
material.Diffuse.g = 1.0;
material.Diffuse.b = 1.0;
material.Diffuse.a = 1.0f;
```

The material's diffuse component is set to white, but three variables—`g_fMaterialRed`, `g_fMaterialGreen`, and `g_fMaterialBlue`—control the color of ambient light reflected by the object. The user can adjust the values of these variables from the keyboard.

To make the material active when rendering 3D objects, the program calls the device object's `SetMaterial()` function:

```
g_pDirect3DDevice->SetMaterial(&material);
```

Until `SetMaterial()` gets called again (which it doesn't until the next frame), Direct3D uses this material for each 3D object rendered in the scene. For more information about materials, refer to Chapter 9.

Setting Up the View and Projection Transformations

In this application, the view and projection transformations are the same for each rendering frame, so they get set once before rendering all of the individual 3D object. The application-defined `SetViewTransformation()` function, called from `Render()`, takes care of this task (see Listing 12.13).

LISTING 12.13   The `SetViewTransformation()` Function

```
void SetViewTransformation()
{
    D3DXVECTOR3 vEyePt(0.0f, 0.0f, g_fZDistance);
    D3DXVECTOR3 vLookatPt(0.0f, 0.0f, g_fZLookAt);
    D3DXVECTOR3 vUpVec(0.0f, 1.0f, 0.0f);
    D3DXMATRIXA16 matView;
    D3DXMatrixLookAtLH(&matView, &vEyePt, &vLookatPt, &vUpVec);
    g_pDirect3DDevice->SetTransform(D3DTS_VIEW, &matView);
}
```

Essentially, this function defines the camera's position and the point at which the camera is pointed. Notice the use of the `g_fZDistance` and `g_fZLookAt` variables to control these camera values. The g_fZDistance variable enables the user to move the camera through the scene, and the g_fZLookAt variable enables the user to reverse the direction in which she's looking. Both of these variables get new values whenever the user presses the Up arrow, Down arrow, or spacebar keys on her keyboard.

For more information about Direct3D and the view transformation, refer to Chapter 8.

Basically, the projection transformation determines how objects are scaled based on their distance from the camera, as well as how much of the scene gets rendered in the first place (that is, this projection determines the clipping planes for the scene). Render() calls the application-defined function SetProjectionTransformation() to set up this critical transformation:

```
void SetProjectionTransformation()
{
    D3DXMATRIXA16 matProj;
    D3DXMatrixPerspectiveFovLH(&matProj, D3DX_PI/4, 1.0f, 1.0f, 100.0f);
    g_pDirect3DDevice->SetTransform(D3DTS_PROJECTION, &matProj);
}
```

For more information about Direct3D and the projection transformation, refer to Chapter 8.

Rendering the 3D Objects

At last it's time to start drawing the 3D objects that make up the 3D world. The first object the program draws is the cube with the fully transparent ports. Render() calls the application-defined function RenderTransparentCube() to get this object up on the screen. Because the cube's animation is actually a number of rotations, the program needs to keep track of the cube's current rotation angle, which it does in the static angle variable:

```
static float angle = 0.0f;
angle += 0.01f;
```

With the angle updated, you get to a part of the program that does things a little differently than you've been used to. In previous programs, the world, view, and projection transformations were all done once per frame, using the same transformations for any object in the 3D scene. Now, however, only the view and projection transformation are performed once per frame. The world projection is performed once before each object that's rendered. After setting the angle variable, RenderTransparentCube() calls the application-defined helper function SetWorldTransformation(), like this:

```
SetWorldTransformation(
    0.0f, angle, 0.0f, /* Rotations    */
    0.0f, 0.0f, 1.0f,  /* Translations */
    1.0f, 1.0f, 1.0f); /* Scaling      */
```

Here's how the program declares SetWorldTransformation():

```
VOID SetWorldTransformation(float fXRot, float fYRot, float fZRot,
        float fXTrans, float fYTrans, float fZTrans,
        float fXScale, float fYScale, float fZScale);
```

Here's what each argument means:

- *fXRot*—The angle in radians of the rotation around the X axis

- *fYRot*—The angle in radians of the rotation around the Y axis

- *fZRot*—The angle in radians of the rotation around the Z axis

- *fXTrans*—The amount of translation on the X axis

- *fYTrans*—The amount of translation on the Y axis

- *fZTrans*—The amount of translation on the Z axis

- *fXScale*—The amount of scaling to perform on the X axis

- *fYScale*—The amount of scaling to perform on the Y axis

- *fZScale*—The amount of scaling to perform on the Z axis

Just call SetWorldTransformation() with the appropriate values, and the world transformation is taken care of. When you're creating a 3D world with many 3D objects, you need to call SetWorldTransformation() before each object is rendered—unless a set of objects uses the same world transformation. Listing 12.14 shows what SetWorldTransformation() looks like.

LISTING 12.14   The SetWorldTransformation() Function

```
VOID SetWorldTransformation(float fXRot, float fYRot, float fZRot,
        float fXTrans, float fYTrans, float fZTrans,
        float fXScale, float fYScale, float fZScale)
{
    D3DXMATRIX worldMatrix;
    D3DXMATRIX tempMatrix;
    D3DXMatrixIdentity(&worldMatrix);
    D3DXMatrixScaling(&tempMatrix, fXScale, fYScale, fZScale);
    D3DXMatrixMultiply(&worldMatrix, &worldMatrix, &tempMatrix);
```

LISTING 12.14   Continued

```
    D3DXMatrixRotationX(&tempMatrix, fXRot);
    D3DXMatrixMultiply(&worldMatrix, &worldMatrix, &tempMatrix);
    D3DXMatrixRotationY(&tempMatrix, fYRot);
    D3DXMatrixMultiply(&worldMatrix, &worldMatrix, &tempMatrix);
    D3DXMatrixRotationZ(&tempMatrix, fZRot);
    D3DXMatrixMultiply(&worldMatrix, &worldMatrix, &tempMatrix);
    D3DXMatrixTranslation(&tempMatrix, fXTrans, fYTrans, fZTrans);
    D3DXMatrixMultiply(&worldMatrix, &worldMatrix, &tempMatrix);
    g_pDirect3DDevice->SetTransform(D3DTS_WORLD, &worldMatrix);
}
```

There's nothing new here, except for the way the various Direct3D functions use the arguments passed into the function. If you need to refresh your memory about these functions and the world transformation, refer to Chapter 8. You'll also find a lot of information in Chapter 3, "Programming 2D Computer Graphics," and Chapter 4, "Programming 3D Computer Graphics."

After taking care of the world transformation, RenderTransparentCube() calls SetStreamSource() to tell Direct3D where the vertices to be rendered are stored:

```
g_pDirect3DDevice->SetStreamSource(0, g_pVertexBuf, 0,
    sizeof(CUSTOMVERTEXSTRUCT));
```

Next, Direct3D needs to know how to handle the textures, which means a few calls to the Direct3D device method SetTextureStageState():

```
g_pDirect3DDevice->SetTextureStageState(0, D3DTSS_COLORARG1, D3DTA_TEXTURE);
g_pDirect3DDevice->SetTextureStageState(0, D3DTSS_COLORARG2, D3DTA_CURRENT);
g_pDirect3DDevice->SetTextureStageState(0, D3DTSS_COLOROP, D3DTOP_MODULATE);
g_pDirect3DDevice->SetTextureStageState(0, D3DTSS_ALPHAARG1, D3DTA_TEXTURE);
g_pDirect3DDevice->SetTextureStageState(0, D3DTSS_ALPHAOP, D3DTOP_SELECTARG1);
```

These lines are shown without the comments you'll find in the full listing. In order of occurrence, here's what these SetTextureStageState() calls do:

1. Tells Direct3D that the first color argument comes from the texture color.

2. Tells Direct3D that the second color argument comes from the previous stage. Because there is no previous stage, this setting is the same as setting the state to D3DTA_DIFFUSE.

3. Tells Direct3D to multiply the color arguments.

4. Tells Direct3D to get the alpha value from the texture.

5. Tells Direct3D to use the unmodified first color argument as the color for the alpha operation. Transparent black, which replaced the color-key color in the texture, goes undrawn, leaving areas transparent.

For more information about textures, review Chapter 10. For more information about transparency and alpha blending, refer to Chapters 10 and 11.

For alpha blending to work, it must be enabled. `RenderTransparentCube()` calls `SetRenderState()` to accomplish this task:

```
g_pDirect3DDevice->SetRenderState(D3DRS_ALPHABLENDENABLE, g_bAlphaBlendingOn);
```

If the `g_bAlphaBlendingOn` variable is FALSE, alpha blending does not get turned on, and the transparent areas of the cube will be rendered as black.

This 3D object also uses alpha testing during rendering, to help cut down the number of pixels that need to be involved in alpha operations:

```
g_pDirect3DDevice->SetRenderState(D3DRS_ALPHATESTENABLE, TRUE);
```

Because the user can turn off texturing from the keyboard, the object may or may not be drawn with a texture. `RenderTransparentCube()` takes care of this complication as follows:

```
if (g_bUseTextures)
    g_pDirect3DDevice->SetTexture(0, g_pTransparentTexture);
else
    g_pDirect3DDevice->SetTexture(0, NULL);
```

Finally, the function sets the proper vertex type and draws the cube:

```
g_pDirect3DDevice->SetFVF(D3DFVF_XYZ|D3DFVF_NORMAL|D3DFVF_TEX1);
g_pDirect3DDevice->DrawPrimitive(D3DPT_TRIANGLELIST,
    0, g_iNumTriangles);
```

The program draws the remaining 3D objects similarly, so there's no need to go through each of them. Each of the functions that draw objects are well commented.

After the scene has been rendered, the `Render()` function calls the Direct3D device method `EndScene()`:

```
g_pDirect3DDevice->EndScene();
```

Finally, a call to `Present()` gets the scene up on the screen:

```
g_pDirect3DDevice->Present( NULL, NULL, NULL, NULL );
```

Rendering Several Objects as One

One of the 3D objects in Direct3DDemoApp's world is actually several objects combined into one. I'm talking about the signpost you first see when you run the program. This sign is made up of two stretched cubes, which are the sign posts, and a simple rectangle, which represents the sign board between the posts. The RenderSign() function draws the objects in question. This function first sets the appropriate texture states:

```
g_pDirect3DDevice->SetTextureStageState(0, D3DTSS_COLORARG1, D3DTA_TEXTURE);
g_pDirect3DDevice->SetTextureStageState(0, D3DTSS_COLORARG2, D3DTA_CURRENT);
g_pDirect3DDevice->SetTextureStageState(0, D3DTSS_COLOROP, D3DTOP_MODULATE);
```

Because the sign requires no transparency, alpha blending and alpha testing get turned off:

```
g_pDirect3DDevice->SetRenderState(D3DRS_ALPHABLENDENABLE, FALSE);
g_pDirect3DDevice->SetRenderState(D3DRS_ALPHATESTENABLE, FALSE);
```

Next, RenderSign() sets up the world transformation for the first sign post:

```
SetWorldTransformation(
    0.0f, 0.0f, 0.0f,                /* Rotations    */
    -2.5f, 0.0f, g_fSignTranslation, /* Translations */
    1.0f, 5.0f, 1.0f);               /* Scaling      */
```

Take a close look at the values used for the three transformations. The first three arguments, all zeroes, mean that no rotation will be applied to the primitive. Because the user can move the sign from the keyboard, the sign post's Z translation is the value stored in the g_fSignTranslation variable. Finally, because the sign post shouldn't look like a cube, the second scaling argument of 5.0 stretches the primitive to five times its normal height.

Before drawing the primitive, the program must give Direct3D the vertex buffer to use:

```
g_pDirect3DDevice->SetStreamSource(0, g_pVertexBuf, 0,
    sizeof(CUSTOMVERTEXSTRUCT));
```

And, because the user can turn textures on or off from the keyboard, the program must check the state of the g_bUseTextures variable before assigning a texture to the primitive about to be drawn:

```
if (g_bUseTextures)
    g_pDirect3DDevice->SetTexture(0, g_pTexturePillar);
else
    g_pDirect3DDevice->SetTexture(0, NULL);
```

A call to DrawPrimitive() gets the 3D object up on the screen:

```
g_pDirect3DDevice->DrawPrimitive(D3DPT_TRIANGLELIST,
    0, g_iNumTriangles);
```

The second sign post gets rendered in much the same way, the main difference being that it's translated farther to the right:

```
SetWorldTransformation(
    0.0f, 0.0f, 0.0f,                 /* Rotations    */
    2.5f, 0.0f, g_fSignTranslation,  /* Translations */.
    1.0f, 5.0f, 1.0f);               /* Scaling      */
g_pDirect3DDevice->DrawPrimitive(D3DPT_TRIANGLELIST,
    0, g_iNumTriangles);
```

The sign board gets a transformation that includes rotations, translations, and scaling, placing it between the two sign posts:

```
SetWorldTransformation(
    0.0f, 3.14f, 0.0f,                /* Rotations    */
    0.0f, 0.0f, g_fSignTranslation,  /* Translations */
    3.0, 3.0, 1.0);                  /* Scaling      */
```

Because the sign board uses a different vertex buffer and texture, all settings related to these values must be reset appropriately, as shown in Listing 12.15.

LISTING 12.15   Resetting Texture Values

```
g_pDirect3DDevice->SetStreamSource(0, g_pTransparentSquareVertexBuf, 0,
    sizeof(TRANSCUSTOMVERTEXSTRUCT));

if (g_bUseTextures)
    g_pDirect3DDevice->SetTexture(0, g_pTextureWelcome);
else
    g_pDirect3DDevice->SetTexture(0, NULL);

g_pDirect3DDevice->SetFVF(D3DFVF_XYZ|D3DFVF_NORMAL|D3DFVF_DIFFUSE|D3DFVF_TEX1);
```

Finally, the program draws the sign board, completing the entire sign:

```
g_pDirect3DDevice->DrawPrimitive(D3DPT_TRIANGLELIST, 0, 2);
```

And that's pretty much the whole ball of wax. The program draws the other objects in the scene in a similar manner. If you don't understand any of the program, make sure to check back with the chapters recommended in each discussion.

Exploring the Full Program

You didn't learn much new in this chapter; you just applied the techniques you already learned to create a full-featured 3D world. Listing 12.16 is the complete listing for the Direct3DDemoApp program. It's here to make it easy for you to study it from your favorite armchair, so take the time to explore every line of code until you're comfortable with the program. As for me, I'll be watching for your first 3D opus on the software shelves.

LISTING 12.16   The Full Program Listing

```cpp
//////////////////////////////////////////////////////
// Direct3DDemoApp.cpp
//////////////////////////////////////////////////////

#include <windows.h>
#include <d3d9.h>
#include <d3dx9.h>

// Constants
const CULLCOUNTERCLOCKWISE = 0;
const CULLCLOCKWISE = 1;
const CULLNONE = 2;

// Function prototypes.
LRESULT WINAPI WndProc(HWND hWnd, UINT msg,
     WPARAM wParam, LPARAM lParam);
void InitApp(HINSTANCE hInstance);
void RunApp();
void CleanUpApp();
void RegisterWindowClass(HINSTANCE hInstance);
void CreateAppWindow(HINSTANCE hInstance);
WPARAM StartMessageLoop();
void HandleKeys(WPARAM wParam);
HRESULT InitDirect3D();
HRESULT CreateDevice();
HRESULT SetRenderingStates();
HRESULT LoadTextures();
HRESULT LoadBackgroundBitmap();
void CleanUpDirect3D();
void Render();
HRESULT InitVertices();
VOID SetWorldTransformation(float fXRot, float fYRot, float fZRot,
        float fXTrans, float fYTrans, float fZTrans,
```

LISTING 12.16   Continued

```
        float fXScale, float fYScale, float fZScale);
void SetViewTransformation();
void SetProjectionTransformation();
void InitLights();
void RenderTransparentCube();
void RenderSign();
void RenderCubeA();
void RenderCubeB();
void RenderCubeC();
void RenderStarCube();
void RenderTransparentRectangles();
void UpdateAnimation();
void RestoreDefaultSettings();
void SetVariableRenderStates();
void DisplayBackgroundImage();

// Global variables.
HWND g_hWnd;
IDirect3D9* g_pDirect3D = NULL;
IDirect3DDevice9* g_pDirect3DDevice = NULL;
IDirect3DVertexBuffer9* g_pVertexBuf = NULL;
IDirect3DVertexBuffer9* g_pTransparentSquareVertexBuf = NULL;
IDirect3DTexture9* g_pTransparentTexture = NULL;
IDirect3DTexture9* g_pTextureA = NULL;
IDirect3DTexture9* g_pTextureB = NULL;
IDirect3DTexture9* g_pTextureC = NULL;
IDirect3DTexture9* g_pTextureStar = NULL;
IDirect3DTexture9* g_pTexturePillar = NULL;
IDirect3DTexture9* g_pTextureWelcome = NULL;
IDirect3DTexture9* g_pTextureWelcome1 = NULL;
IDirect3DTexture9* g_pTextureWelcome2 = NULL;
IDirect3DTexture9* g_pTransparentSquareTexture = NULL;
IDirect3DSurface9* g_pBackgroundSurface = NULL;
IDirect3DSurface9* g_pBackBuffer = NULL;
FLOAT g_fZDistance = -12.0f;
FLOAT g_fZLookAt = 100.0f;
BOOL g_bFogOn = TRUE;
BOOL g_bAlphaBlendingOn = TRUE;
BOOL g_bZBufferingOn = TRUE;
INT g_iCullingMode = CULLNONE;
BOOL g_bLightingOn = TRUE;
INT g_iNumTriangles;
```

LISTING 12.16   Continued

```
FLOAT g_fLightPosition = 15.0f;
FLOAT g_fAmbientLight = 0.4f;
FLOAT g_fMaterialRed = 1.0f;
FLOAT g_fMaterialGreen = 1.0f;
FLOAT g_fMaterialBlue = 1.0f;
BOOL g_bShowBackground = TRUE;
FLOAT g_fFogDensity = 0.02f;
BOOL g_bUseTextures = TRUE;
FLOAT g_fSignTranslation = -3.0;

// Custom vertices for primitives using vertex alpha.
struct TRANSCUSTOMVERTEXSTRUCT
{
    D3DVECTOR coords;
    D3DVECTOR normal;
    DWORD dwColor;
    float tu, tv;
};

// Custom vertices for primitives NOT using vertex alpha blending.
struct CUSTOMVERTEXSTRUCT
{
    D3DVECTOR coords;
    D3DVECTOR normal;
    float tu, tv;
};

//////////////////////////////////////////////////////
// WinMain()
//////////////////////////////////////////////////////
INT WINAPI WinMain(HINSTANCE hInstance, HINSTANCE, LPSTR, INT)
{
    InitApp(hInstance);
    RunApp();
    CleanUpApp();
    return 0;
}

//////////////////////////////////////////////////////
// InitApp()
//////////////////////////////////////////////////////
```

LISTING 12.16 Continued

```c
void InitApp(HINSTANCE hInstance)
{
    RegisterWindowClass(hInstance);
    CreateAppWindow(hInstance);
    ShowWindow(g_hWnd, SW_SHOWDEFAULT);
    UpdateWindow(g_hWnd);
    SetTimer(g_hWnd, 1, 500, NULL);
}


/////////////////////////////////////////////////////
// RunApp()
/////////////////////////////////////////////////////
void RunApp()
{
    if (SUCCEEDED(InitDirect3D()))
    {
        InitVertices();
        WPARAM result = StartMessageLoop();
    }
}


/////////////////////////////////////////////////////
// CleanUpApp()
/////////////////////////////////////////////////////
void CleanUpApp()
{
    KillTimer(g_hWnd, 1);
    CleanUpDirect3D();
}


/////////////////////////////////////////////////////
// RegisterWindowClass()
/////////////////////////////////////////////////////
void RegisterWindowClass(HINSTANCE hInstance)
{
    WNDCLASSEX wc;
    wc.cbSize = sizeof(WNDCLASSEX);
    wc.style = CS_HREDRAW | CS_VREDRAW | CS_OWNDC;
    wc.lpfnWndProc = WndProc;
    wc.cbClsExtra = 0;
    wc.cbWndExtra = 0;
```

LISTING 12.16   Continued

```
    wc.hInstance = hInstance;
    wc.hIcon = LoadIcon(NULL, IDI_APPLICATION);
    wc.hCursor = (HCURSOR)LoadCursor(NULL, IDC_ARROW);
    wc.hbrBackground = (HBRUSH)GetStockObject(WHITE_BRUSH);
    wc.lpszMenuName = NULL;
    wc.lpszClassName = "D3DDemoApp";
    wc.hIconSm = NULL;

    RegisterClassEx(&wc);
}

/////////////////////////////////////////////////////
// CreateAppWindow()
/////////////////////////////////////////////////////
void CreateAppWindow(HINSTANCE hInstance)
{
    g_hWnd = CreateWindowEx(
        NULL,
        "D3DDemoApp",
        "Direct3D Demo Application",
        WS_OVERLAPPEDWINDOW,
        100,
        100,
        800,
        600,
        GetDesktopWindow(),
        NULL,
        hInstance,
        NULL);
}

/////////////////////////////////////////////////////
// StartMessageLoop()
/////////////////////////////////////////////////////
WPARAM StartMessageLoop()
{
    MSG msg;
    while(1)
    {
        if (PeekMessage(&msg, NULL, 0, 0, PM_REMOVE))
        {
            if (msg.message == WM_QUIT)
```

LISTING 12.16   Continued

```
                break;
            TranslateMessage(&msg);
            DispatchMessage(&msg);
        }
        else
        {
            // Use idle time here.
            Render();
        }
    }
    return msg.wParam;
}


//////////////////////////////////////////////////////
// WndProc()
//////////////////////////////////////////////////////
LRESULT WINAPI WndProc(HWND hWnd, UINT msg, WPARAM wParam, LPARAM lParam)
{
    switch(msg)
    {
    case WM_CREATE:
        return 0;

    case WM_DESTROY:
        PostQuitMessage( 0 );
        return 0;

    case WM_PAINT:
        ValidateRect(g_hWnd, NULL);
        return 0;

    case WM_TIMER:
        UpdateAnimation();
        return 0;

    case WM_KEYDOWN:
        HandleKeys(wParam);
        return 0;
    }
    return DefWindowProc(hWnd, msg, wParam, lParam);
}
```

LISTING 12.16   Continued

```
/////////////////////////////////////////////////
// HandleKeys()
/////////////////////////////////////////////////
void HandleKeys(WPARAM wParam)
{
    switch(wParam)
    {
    case VK_ESCAPE:
        PostQuitMessage(WM_QUIT);
        break;
    case VK_DOWN:
        g_fZDistance -= 0.2f;
        if (g_fZDistance < -6.0f)
            g_fZLookAt = 100.0;
        break;
    case VK_UP:
        g_fZDistance += 0.2f;
        if (g_fZDistance > 15)
            g_fZLookAt = -100.0f;
        break;
    case VK_SPACE:
        g_fZLookAt = -g_fZLookAt;
        break;
    case 65: // A
        g_bAlphaBlendingOn = !g_bAlphaBlendingOn;
        break;
    case 66: // B
        if ((g_fMaterialBlue += 0.01f) > 1.0f)
            g_fMaterialBlue = 0.0f;
        break;
    case 67: // C
        ++g_iCullingMode;
        if (g_iCullingMode > CULLNONE)
            g_iCullingMode = CULLCOUNTERCLOCKWISE;
        break;
    case 68: // D
        RestoreDefaultSettings();
        break;
    case 69: // E
        if ((g_fFogDensity += 0.01f) > 1.0f)
            g_fFogDensity = 0.02f;
```

LISTING 12.16   Continued

```
        break;
    case 70: // F
        g_bFogOn = !g_bFogOn;
        break;
    case 71: // G
        if ((g_fMaterialGreen += 0.01f) > 1.0f)
            g_fMaterialGreen = 0.0f;
        break;
    case 75: // K
        g_bShowBackground = !g_bShowBackground;
        break;
    case 76: // L
        g_bLightingOn = !g_bLightingOn;
        break;
    case 77: // M
        if ((g_fAmbientLight += 0.01f) > 1.0f)
            g_fAmbientLight = 0.0f;
        break;
    case 80: // P
        if ((g_fLightPosition += 0.2f) > 15)
            g_fLightPosition = 0.0f;
        break;
    case 81: // Q
        g_fSignTranslation += 0.2f;
        break;
    case 82: // R
        if ((g_fMaterialRed += 0.01f) > 1.0f)
            g_fMaterialRed = 0.0f;
        break;
    case 84: // T
        g_bUseTextures = !g_bUseTextures;
        break;
    case 87: // W
        g_fSignTranslation -= 0.2f;
        break;
    case 90: // Z
        g_bZBufferingOn = !g_bZBufferingOn;
        break;
    }
}
```

LISTING 12.16   Continued

```
///////////////////////////////////////////////////
// RestoreDefaultSettings()
///////////////////////////////////////////////////
void RestoreDefaultSettings()
{
    g_bFogOn = TRUE;
    g_bAlphaBlendingOn = TRUE;
    g_bZBufferingOn = TRUE;
    g_iCullingMode = CULLNONE;
    g_bLightingOn = TRUE;
    g_iNumTriangles;
    g_fLightPosition = 15.0f;
    g_fAmbientLight = 0.4f;
    g_fMaterialRed = 1.0f;
    g_fMaterialGreen = 1.0f;
    g_fMaterialBlue = 1.0f;
    g_bShowBackground = TRUE;
    g_fFogDensity = 0.02f;
    g_bUseTextures = TRUE;
    g_fSignTranslation = -3.0f;
}


///////////////////////////////////////////////////
// InitDirect3D()
///////////////////////////////////////////////////
HRESULT InitDirect3D()
{
    // Create the main Direct3D object.
    if((g_pDirect3D = Direct3DCreate9(D3D_SDK_VERSION)) == NULL)
    {
        MessageBox(g_hWnd, "Couldn't create main Direct3D object.",
            "FinalApp - Error", MB_OK | MB_ICONEXCLAMATION);
        return E_FAIL;
    }

    // Get the current display mode.
    D3DDISPLAYMODE d3ddisplaymode;
    if (FAILED(g_pDirect3D->GetAdapterDisplayMode(
            D3DADAPTER_DEFAULT, &d3ddisplaymode)))
    {
        MessageBox(g_hWnd, "Couldn't determine display mode.",
```

LISTING 12.16   Continued

```
            "FinalApp - Error", MB_OK | MB_ICONEXCLAMATION);
        return E_FAIL;
    }

    // Determine whether the display mode is compatible with this app.
    if (d3ddisplaymode.Format != D3DFMT_X8R8G8B8)
    {
        MessageBox(g_hWnd,
            "This application requires the 32-bit display mode.",
            "FinalApp - Error", MB_OK | MB_ICONEXCLAMATION);
        return E_FAIL;
    }

    // Create the Direct3D device.
    if (FAILED(CreateDevice()))
    {
        MessageBox(g_hWnd, "Couldn't create main Direct3D device.",
            "FinalApp - Error", MB_OK | MB_ICONEXCLAMATION);
        return E_FAIL;
    }

    // Set global rendering states.
    if (FAILED(SetRenderingStates()))
    {
        MessageBox(g_hWnd, "Couldn't set rendering states.",
            "FinalApp - Error", MB_OK | MB_ICONEXCLAMATION);
        PostQuitMessage(WM_QUIT);
    }

    // Load the textures.
    if (FAILED(LoadTextures()))
    {
        MessageBox(g_hWnd, "Couldn't load textures.",
            "FinalApp - Error", MB_OK | MB_ICONEXCLAMATION);
        PostQuitMessage(WM_QUIT);
    }

    // Set first texture for animated sign.
    g_pTextureWelcome = g_pTextureWelcome1;
```

LISTING 12.16   Continued

```
    // Load background bitmap.
    if (FAILED(LoadBackgroundBitmap()))
    {
        MessageBox(g_hWnd, "Couldn't load background bitmap.",
            "FinalApp - Error", MB_OK | MB_ICONEXCLAMATION);
        PostQuitMessage(WM_QUIT);
    }

    // Get a pointer to the back buffer.
    if (FAILED(g_pDirect3DDevice->GetBackBuffer(0, 0,
        D3DBACKBUFFER_TYPE_MONO, &g_pBackBuffer)))
    {
        MessageBox(g_hWnd, "Couldn't acquire back buffer.",
            "FinalApp - Error", MB_OK | MB_ICONEXCLAMATION);
        PostQuitMessage(WM_QUIT);
    }

    return D3D_OK;
}

/////////////////////////////////////////////////////
// CreateDevice()
/////////////////////////////////////////////////////
HRESULT CreateDevice()
{
    D3DPRESENT_PARAMETERS D3DPresentParams;
    ZeroMemory(&D3DPresentParams, sizeof(D3DPRESENT_PARAMETERS));
    D3DPresentParams.Windowed = TRUE;
    D3DPresentParams.BackBufferFormat = D3DFMT_UNKNOWN;
    D3DPresentParams.SwapEffect = D3DSWAPEFFECT_DISCARD;
    D3DPresentParams.hDeviceWindow = g_hWnd;
    D3DPresentParams.EnableAutoDepthStencil = TRUE;
    D3DPresentParams.AutoDepthStencilFormat = D3DFMT_D16;

    HRESULT hResult = g_pDirect3D->CreateDevice(D3DADAPTER_DEFAULT,
            D3DDEVTYPE_HAL, g_hWnd, D3DCREATE_SOFTWARE_VERTEXPROCESSING,
            &D3DPresentParams, &g_pDirect3DDevice);
    return hResult;
}
```

LISTING 12.16   Continued

```
///////////////////////////////////////////////////////
// SetRenderingStates()
///////////////////////////////////////////////////////
HRESULT SetRenderingStates()
{
    // Set up Alpha blending. NOTE: Enabling alpha blending,
    // is controlled by the A-key switch and the
    // g_bAlphaBlendingOn variable. See Render().
    if (FAILED(g_pDirect3DDevice->SetRenderState(D3DRS_SRCBLEND,
            D3DBLEND_SRCALPHA)))
        return E_FAIL;
    if (FAILED(g_pDirect3DDevice->SetRenderState(D3DRS_DESTBLEND,
            D3DBLEND_INVSRCALPHA)))
        return E_FAIL;

    // Setup the application for vertex alpha blending.
    if (FAILED(g_pDirect3DDevice->SetRenderState(
            D3DRS_DIFFUSEMATERIALSOURCE, D3DMCS_COLOR1)))
        return E_FAIL;

    // Set up alpha testing.
    if (FAILED(g_pDirect3DDevice->SetRenderState(D3DRS_ALPHAREF, 96)))
        return E_FAIL;
    if (FAILED(g_pDirect3DDevice->SetRenderState(D3DRS_ALPHAFUNC,
            D3DCMP_GREATEREQUAL)))
        return E_FAIL;

    // Set up fog, except for enabling fog, which is controlled
    // by the F-key switch and the g_bFogOn variable, and fog
    // color, which is controlled by the K-key switch and
    // the g_bShowBackground variable. See Render().
    if (FAILED(g_pDirect3DDevice->
            SetRenderState(D3DRS_FOGVERTEXMODE, D3DFOG_EXP2)))
        return E_FAIL;

    return D3D_OK;
}


///////////////////////////////////////////////////////
// LoadTextures()
///////////////////////////////////////////////////////
```

LISTING 12.16   Continued

```
HRESULT LoadTextures()
{
    // Load texture with fully transparent areas (color key).
    if (FAILED(D3DXCreateTextureFromFileEx(g_pDirect3DDevice,
            "texture.bmp", D3DX_DEFAULT, D3DX_DEFAULT, D3DX_DEFAULT, 0,
            D3DFMT_A8R8G8B8, D3DPOOL_MANAGED, D3DX_FILTER_TRIANGLE,
            D3DX_FILTER_TRIANGLE, D3DCOLOR_RGBA(255,0,0,255),
            NULL, NULL, &g_pTransparentTexture)))
        return E_FAIL;

    // Load remaining textures.
    if (FAILED(D3DXCreateTextureFromFile(g_pDirect3DDevice,
            "Texture_A.bmp", &g_pTextureA)))
        return E_FAIL;
    if (FAILED(D3DXCreateTextureFromFile(g_pDirect3DDevice,
            "Texture_B.bmp", &g_pTextureB)))
        return E_FAIL;
    if (FAILED(D3DXCreateTextureFromFile(g_pDirect3DDevice,
            "Texture_C.bmp", &g_pTextureC)))
        return E_FAIL;
    if (FAILED(D3DXCreateTextureFromFile(g_pDirect3DDevice,
            "Texture_Star.bmp", &g_pTextureStar)))
        return E_FAIL;
    if (FAILED(D3DXCreateTextureFromFile(g_pDirect3DDevice,
            "texture03.bmp", &g_pTransparentSquareTexture)))
        return E_FAIL;
    if (FAILED(D3DXCreateTextureFromFile(g_pDirect3DDevice,
            "Texture_Pillar.bmp", &g_pTexturePillar)))
        return E_FAIL;
    if (FAILED(D3DXCreateTextureFromFile(g_pDirect3DDevice,
            "Texture_Welcome1.bmp", &g_pTextureWelcome1)))
        return E_FAIL;
    if (FAILED(D3DXCreateTextureFromFile(g_pDirect3DDevice,
            "Texture_Welcome2.bmp", &g_pTextureWelcome2)))
        return E_FAIL;

    return D3D_OK;
}


//////////////////////////////////////////////////////
// LoadBackgroundBitmap()
//////////////////////////////////////////////////////
```

LISTING 12.16   Continued

```
HRESULT LoadBackgroundBitmap()
{
    // Create a surface for the background bitmap.
    if (FAILED(g_pDirect3DDevice->CreateOffscreenPlainSurface(800, 600,
            D3DFMT_X8R8G8B8, D3DPOOL_DEFAULT, &g_pBackgroundSurface, NULL)))
        return E_FAIL;

    // Load the background bitmap into the surface.
    if (FAILED(D3DXLoadSurfaceFromFile(g_pBackgroundSurface, NULL, NULL,
            "Background.bmp", NULL, D3DX_DEFAULT, 0, NULL)))
        return E_FAIL;

    return D3D_OK;
}


//////////////////////////////////////////////////////
// CleanUpDirect3D()
//////////////////////////////////////////////////////
void CleanUpDirect3D()
{
    if (g_pBackgroundSurface)
    {
        g_pBackgroundSurface->Release();
        g_pBackgroundSurface = NULL;
    }
    if (g_pVertexBuf)
    {
        g_pVertexBuf->Release();
        g_pVertexBuf = NULL;
    }
    if (g_pTransparentSquareVertexBuf)
    {
        g_pTransparentSquareVertexBuf->Release();
        g_pTransparentSquareVertexBuf = NULL;
    }
    if (g_pTransparentSquareTexture)
    {
        g_pTransparentSquareTexture->Release();
        g_pTransparentSquareTexture = NULL;
    }
    if (g_pTextureWelcome2)
```

LISTING 12.16   Continued

```
{
    g_pTextureWelcome2->Release();
    g_pTextureWelcome2 = NULL;
}
if (g_pTextureWelcome1)
{
    g_pTextureWelcome1->Release();
    g_pTextureWelcome1 = NULL;
}
if (g_pTexturePillar)
{
    g_pTexturePillar->Release();
    g_pTexturePillar = NULL;
}
if (g_pTextureStar)
{
    g_pTextureStar->Release();
    g_pTextureStar = NULL;
}
if (g_pTextureC)
{
    g_pTextureC->Release();
    g_pTextureC = NULL;
}
if (g_pTextureB)
{
    g_pTextureB->Release();
    g_pTextureB = NULL;
}
if (g_pTextureA)
{
    g_pTextureA->Release();
    g_pTextureA = NULL;
}
if (g_pTransparentTexture)
{
    g_pTransparentTexture->Release();
    g_pTransparentTexture = NULL;
}
if (g_pBackBuffer)
{
```

LISTING 12.16   Continued

```
        g_pBackBuffer->Release();
        g_pBackBuffer = NULL;
    }
    if (g_pDirect3DDevice)
    {
        g_pDirect3DDevice->Release();
        g_pDirect3DDevice = NULL;
    }
    if (g_pDirect3D)
    {
        g_pDirect3D->Release();
        g_pDirect3D = NULL;
    }
}


////////////////////////////////////////////////////
// UpdateAnimation()
////////////////////////////////////////////////////
VOID UpdateAnimation()
{
    static bool bFirstFrame = TRUE;
    if (bFirstFrame)
        g_pTextureWelcome = g_pTextureWelcome1;
    else
        g_pTextureWelcome = g_pTextureWelcome2;
    bFirstFrame = !bFirstFrame;
}


////////////////////////////////////////////////////
// Render()
////////////////////////////////////////////////////
VOID Render()
{
    // Clear the target surface.
    g_pDirect3DDevice->Clear(0, NULL, D3DCLEAR_TARGET|D3DCLEAR_ZBUFFER,
        D3DCOLOR_XRGB(0,0,0), 1.0f, 0);

    DisplayBackgroundImage();
    SetVariableRenderStates();
```

LISTING 12.16   Continued

```
    // Render the 3D scene.
    if(SUCCEEDED(g_pDirect3DDevice->BeginScene()))
    {
        InitLights();
        SetViewTransformation();
        SetProjectionTransformation();
        RenderTransparentCube();
        RenderSign();
        RenderCubeA();
        RenderCubeB();
        RenderCubeC();
        RenderStarCube();
        RenderTransparentRectangles();
        g_pDirect3DDevice->EndScene();
    }

    // Display the newly rendered scene.
    g_pDirect3DDevice->Present( NULL, NULL, NULL, NULL );
}


//////////////////////////////////////////////////////
// DisplayBackgroundImage()
//////////////////////////////////////////////////////
void DisplayBackgroundImage()
{
    // Set up source and destination rectangles for the background blit.
    RECT SrcRect;
    RECT DstRect;
    SrcRect.left = 0;     SrcRect.right = 799;
    SrcRect.top = 0;      SrcRect.bottom = 599;
    DstRect.left = 0;     DstRect.top = 0;
    DstRect.right = 792;  DstRect.bottom = 566;

    // Blit the background image to the target surface.
    if (g_bShowBackground)
        g_pDirect3DDevice->StretchRect(g_pBackgroundSurface,
            &SrcRect, g_pBackBuffer, &DstRect, D3DTEXF_NONE);
}


//////////////////////////////////////////////////////
// SetVariableRenderingStates()
//////////////////////////////////////////////////////
```

LISTING 12.16   Continued

```
void SetVariableRenderStates()
{
    // Set fog color based on whether background is displayed.
    if (g_bShowBackground)
        g_pDirect3DDevice->SetRenderState(D3DRS_FOGCOLOR,
            D3DXCOLOR(255,255,255,255));
    else
        g_pDirect3DDevice->SetRenderState(D3DRS_FOGCOLOR,
            D3DXCOLOR(0,0,0,0));

    // Turn Z-buffering on and off.
    g_pDirect3DDevice->SetRenderState(D3DRS_ZENABLE, g_bZBufferingOn);

    // Turn back-face culling on or off.
    if (g_iCullingMode == CULLCOUNTERCLOCKWISE)
        g_pDirect3DDevice->SetRenderState(D3DRS_CULLMODE, D3DCULL_CCW);
    else if (g_iCullingMode == CULLCLOCKWISE)
        g_pDirect3DDevice->SetRenderState(D3DRS_CULLMODE, D3DCULL_CW);
    else if (g_iCullingMode == CULLNONE)
        g_pDirect3DDevice->SetRenderState(D3DRS_CULLMODE, D3DCULL_NONE);

    // Turn fog on or off.
    g_pDirect3DDevice->SetRenderState(D3DRS_FOGENABLE, g_bFogOn);

    // Set fog density.
    g_pDirect3DDevice->SetRenderState(D3DRS_FOGDENSITY,
            *(DWORD *)(&g_fFogDensity));
}


////////////////////////////////////////////////////
// RenderTransparentCube()
////////////////////////////////////////////////////
void RenderTransparentCube()
{
    static float angle = 0.0f;
    angle += 0.01f;
    SetWorldTransformation(
        0.0f, angle, 0.0f, /* Rotations    */
        0.0f, 0.0f, 1.0f,  /* Translations */
        1.0f, 1.0f, 1.0f); /* Scaling      */
    g_pDirect3DDevice->SetStreamSource(0, g_pVertexBuf, 0,
        sizeof(CUSTOMVERTEXSTRUCT));
```

LISTING 12.16   Continued

```
// Set the first color argument to the texture color.
g_pDirect3DDevice->SetTextureStageState(0,
    D3DTSS_COLORARG1, D3DTA_TEXTURE);

// Set the second color argument to be the output of the previous stage.
// Because there is no previous stage, this argument results in
// the same value as the D3DTA_DIFFUSE setting, which is the vertex
// diffuse color or, lacking that, the default color of 0xFFFFFFFF.
g_pDirect3DDevice->SetTextureStageState(0,
    D3DTSS_COLORARG2, D3DTA_CURRENT);

// Set the color operation to multiply the colors (which is the default).
g_pDirect3DDevice->SetTextureStageState(0,
    D3DTSS_COLOROP, D3DTOP_MODULATE);

// Set the alpha argument to the texture, because that's where the
// D3DXCreateTextureFromFileEx() function placed the alpha data.
g_pDirect3DDevice->SetTextureStageState(0,
    D3DTSS_ALPHAARG1, D3DTA_TEXTURE);

// Set the operation to use for alpha blending.
// In this case, use the stage's
// first argument (the texture color) as the output. Thanks to the
// D3DXCreateTextureFromFileEx() function, transparent areas will
// have the transparent-black color and so won't appear. Other colors pass
// through exactly as they are.
g_pDirect3DDevice->SetTextureStageState(0,
    D3DTSS_ALPHAOP, D3DTOP_SELECTARG1);

// Turn alpha blending on or off, based on the g_bAlphaBlendingOn variable.
g_pDirect3DDevice->SetRenderState(D3DRS_ALPHABLENDENABLE,
    g_bAlphaBlendingOn);

// Turn on alpha testing.
g_pDirect3DDevice->SetRenderState(D3DRS_ALPHATESTENABLE, TRUE);

// Set the texture to use.
if (g_bUseTextures)
    g_pDirect3DDevice->SetTexture(0, g_pTransparentTexture);
else
    g_pDirect3DDevice->SetTexture(0, NULL);
```

LISTING 12.16   Continued

```
    // Set the vertex format, and draw the cube.
    g_pDirect3DDevice->SetFVF(D3DFVF_XYZ|D3DFVF_NORMAL|D3DFVF_TEX1);
    g_pDirect3DDevice->DrawPrimitive(D3DPT_TRIANGLELIST,
        0, g_iNumTriangles);
}


//////////////////////////////////////////////////////
// RenderSign()
//////////////////////////////////////////////////////
void RenderSign()
{
    // Set the first color argument to the texture color.
    g_pDirect3DDevice->SetTextureStageState(0,
        D3DTSS_COLORARG1, D3DTA_TEXTURE);

    // Set the second color argument to be the output of the previous stage.
    // Because there is no previous stage, this argument results in
    // the same value as the D3DTA_DIFFUSE setting, which is the vertex
    // diffuse color or, lacking that, the default color of 0xFFFFFFFF.
    g_pDirect3DDevice->SetTextureStageState(0,
        D3DTSS_COLORARG2, D3DTA_CURRENT);

    // Set the color operation to multiply the colors (which is the default).
    g_pDirect3DDevice->SetTextureStageState(0,
        D3DTSS_COLOROP, D3DTOP_MODULATE);

    // No alpha blending or testing.
    g_pDirect3DDevice->SetRenderState(D3DRS_ALPHABLENDENABLE, FALSE);
    g_pDirect3DDevice->SetRenderState(D3DRS_ALPHATESTENABLE, FALSE);

    // Render the first pillar.
    SetWorldTransformation(
        0.0f, 0.0f, 0.0f,                 /* Rotations    */
        -2.5f, 0.0f, g_fSignTranslation, /* Translations */
        1.0f, 5.0f, 1.0f);                /* Scaling      */
    g_pDirect3DDevice->SetStreamSource(0, g_pVertexBuf, 0,
        sizeof(CUSTOMVERTEXSTRUCT));

    if (g_bUseTextures)
        g_pDirect3DDevice->SetTexture(0, g_pTexturePillar);
    else
```

LISTING 12.16   Continued

```
        g_pDirect3DDevice->SetTexture(0, NULL);
    g_pDirect3DDevice->DrawPrimitive(D3DPT_TRIANGLELIST,
        0, g_iNumTriangles);

    // Render the second pillar.
    SetWorldTransformation(
        0.0f, 0.0f, 0.0f,                    /* Rotations    */
        2.5f, 0.0f, g_fSignTranslation, /* Translations */
        1.0f, 5.0f, 1.0f);                   /* Scaling      */
    g_pDirect3DDevice->DrawPrimitive(D3DPT_TRIANGLELIST,
        0, g_iNumTriangles);

    // Render the sign board.
    SetWorldTransformation(
        0.0f, 3.14f, 0.0f,                   /* Rotations    */
        0.0f, 0.0f, g_fSignTranslation, /* Translations */
        3.0, 3.0, 1.0);                      /* Scaling      */
    g_pDirect3DDevice->SetStreamSource(0, g_pTransparentSquareVertexBuf, 0,
        sizeof(TRANSCUSTOMVERTEXSTRUCT));
    if (g_bUseTextures)
        g_pDirect3DDevice->SetTexture(0, g_pTextureWelcome);
    else
        g_pDirect3DDevice->SetTexture(0, NULL);

    // Set the vertex format, and draw the sign board.
    g_pDirect3DDevice->
        SetFVF(D3DFVF_XYZ|D3DFVF_NORMAL|D3DFVF_DIFFUSE|D3DFVF_TEX1);
    g_pDirect3DDevice->DrawPrimitive(D3DPT_TRIANGLELIST, 0, 2);
}


//////////////////////////////////////////////////
// RenderCubeA()
//////////////////////////////////////////////////
void RenderCubeA()
{
    double radians = timeGetTime() / 1000.0f;
    SetWorldTransformation(
        (float)radians, (float)radians, (float)radians, /* Rotations    */
        -4.0f, 1.0f, 14.0f,                             /* Translations */
        1.0f, 1.0f, 1.0f);                              /* Scaling      */
    g_pDirect3DDevice->SetStreamSource(0, g_pVertexBuf, 0,
        sizeof(CUSTOMVERTEXSTRUCT));
```

LISTING 12.16   Continued

```
    // See RenderSign() for an explanation of the texture stage settings.
    g_pDirect3DDevice->SetTextureStageState(0,
        D3DTSS_COLORARG1, D3DTA_TEXTURE);
    g_pDirect3DDevice->SetTextureStageState(0,
        D3DTSS_COLORARG2, D3DTA_CURRENT);
    g_pDirect3DDevice->SetRenderState(D3DRS_ALPHABLENDENABLE, FALSE);
    g_pDirect3DDevice->SetRenderState(D3DRS_ALPHATESTENABLE, FALSE);

    if (g_bUseTextures)
        g_pDirect3DDevice->SetTexture(0, g_pTextureA);
    else
        g_pDirect3DDevice->SetTexture(0, NULL);
    g_pDirect3DDevice->SetFVF(D3DFVF_XYZ|D3DFVF_NORMAL|D3DFVF_TEX1);
    g_pDirect3DDevice->DrawPrimitive(D3DPT_TRIANGLELIST,
        0, g_iNumTriangles);
}


//////////////////////////////////////////////////////
// RenderCubeB()
//////////////////////////////////////////////////////
void RenderCubeB()
{
    static float angle = 0.0f;
    angle += 0.01f;
    SetWorldTransformation(
        angle, 0.0f, 0.0f, /* Rotations    */
        0.5f, 0.0f, 14.0f, /* Translations */
        2.0f, 2.0f, 2.0f); /* Scaling      */
    g_pDirect3DDevice->SetStreamSource(0, g_pVertexBuf, 0,
        sizeof(CUSTOMVERTEXSTRUCT));

    // See RenderSign() for an explanation of these texture stage settings.
    g_pDirect3DDevice->SetTextureStageState(0,
        D3DTSS_COLORARG1, D3DTA_TEXTURE);
    g_pDirect3DDevice->SetTextureStageState(0,
        D3DTSS_COLORARG2, D3DTA_CURRENT);
    g_pDirect3DDevice->SetRenderState(D3DRS_ALPHABLENDENABLE, FALSE);
    g_pDirect3DDevice->SetRenderState(D3DRS_ALPHATESTENABLE, FALSE);

    if (g_bUseTextures)
        g_pDirect3DDevice->SetTexture(0, g_pTextureB);
    else
```

LISTING 12.16   Continued

```
        g_pDirect3DDevice->SetTexture(0, NULL);
    g_pDirect3DDevice->DrawPrimitive(D3DPT_TRIANGLELIST,
        0, g_iNumTriangles);
}


//////////////////////////////////////////////////////
// RenderCubeC()
//////////////////////////////////////////////////////
void RenderCubeC()
{
    static float height = 0.0f;
    static int multiplier = 1;
    height += 0.02f * multiplier;
    if (height > 3.0f)
        multiplier = -1;
    else if (height < -1.0f)
        multiplier = 1;
    SetWorldTransformation(
        0.0f, 0.0f, 0.0f,     /* Rotations    */
        -1.5f, height, 13.0f, /* Translations */
        1.0f, 1.0f, 1.0f);    /* Scaling      */
    g_pDirect3DDevice->SetStreamSource(0, g_pVertexBuf, 0,
        sizeof(CUSTOMVERTEXSTRUCT));

    // See RenderSign() for an explanation of these texture stage settings.
    g_pDirect3DDevice->SetTextureStageState(0,
        D3DTSS_COLORARG1, D3DTA_TEXTURE);
    g_pDirect3DDevice->SetTextureStageState(0,
        D3DTSS_COLORARG2, D3DTA_CURRENT);
    g_pDirect3DDevice->SetRenderState(D3DRS_ALPHABLENDENABLE, FALSE);
    g_pDirect3DDevice->SetRenderState(D3DRS_ALPHATESTENABLE, FALSE);

    if (g_bUseTextures)
        g_pDirect3DDevice->SetTexture(0, g_pTextureC);
    else
        g_pDirect3DDevice->SetTexture(0, NULL);
    g_pDirect3DDevice->DrawPrimitive(D3DPT_TRIANGLELIST,
        0, g_iNumTriangles);
}
```

LISTING 12.16   Continued

```
/////////////////////////////////////////////////////
// RenderStarCube()
/////////////////////////////////////////////////////
void RenderStarCube()
{
    static float scale = 1.0f;
    scale += 0.02f;
    if (scale > 5.0f)
        scale = 1.0f;
    SetWorldTransformation(
        0.0f, 0.0f, 0.0f, /* Rotations    */
        -3.5f, 1.0, 7.0f, /* Translations */
        1.0, scale, 1.0); /* Scaling      */
    g_pDirect3DDevice->SetStreamSource(0, g_pVertexBuf, 0,
        sizeof(CUSTOMVERTEXSTRUCT));

    // See RenderSign() for an explanation of these texture stage settings.
    g_pDirect3DDevice->SetTextureStageState(0,
        D3DTSS_COLORARG1, D3DTA_TEXTURE);
    g_pDirect3DDevice->SetTextureStageState(0,
        D3DTSS_COLORARG2, D3DTA_CURRENT);
    g_pDirect3DDevice->SetRenderState(D3DRS_ALPHABLENDENABLE, FALSE);
    g_pDirect3DDevice->SetRenderState(D3DRS_ALPHATESTENABLE, FALSE);

    if (g_bUseTextures)
        g_pDirect3DDevice->SetTexture(0, g_pTextureStar);
    else
        g_pDirect3DDevice->SetTexture(0, NULL);
    g_pDirect3DDevice->DrawPrimitive(D3DPT_TRIANGLELIST,
        0, g_iNumTriangles);
}


/////////////////////////////////////////////////////
// RenderTransparentRectangles()
/////////////////////////////////////////////////////
void RenderTransparentRectangles()
{
    static float angle = 0.0f;
    angle += 0.01f;
```

LISTING 12.16   Continued

```
// Set the first color argument to the texture color.
g_pDirect3DDevice->SetTextureStageState(0,
    D3DTSS_COLORARG1, D3DTA_TEXTURE);

// Set the second color argument to be the output of the previous stage.
// Because there is no previous stage, this argument results in
// the same value as the D3DTA_DIFFUSE setting, which is the vertex
// diffuse color or, lacking that, the default color of 0xFFFFFFFF.
g_pDirect3DDevice->SetTextureStageState(0,
    D3DTSS_COLORARG2, D3DTA_CURRENT);

// Set the color operation to multiply the colors (which is the default).
g_pDirect3DDevice->SetTextureStageState(0,
    D3DTSS_COLOROP, D3DTOP_MODULATE);

// Use the alpha value stored in the vertex's diffuse color.
g_pDirect3DDevice->SetTextureStageState(0,
    D3DTSS_ALPHAARG1, D3DTA_DIFFUSE);
g_pDirect3DDevice->SetTextureStageState(0,
    D3DTSS_ALPHAARG2, D3DTA_CURRENT);
g_pDirect3DDevice->SetTextureStageState(0,
    D3DTSS_ALPHAOP, D3DTOP_SELECTARG1);

// Turn alpha blending on or off, based on the g_bAlphaBlendingOn variable.
g_pDirect3DDevice->SetRenderState(D3DRS_ALPHABLENDENABLE,
    g_bAlphaBlendingOn);

// Turn on alpha testing.
g_pDirect3DDevice->SetRenderState(D3DRS_ALPHATESTENABLE, TRUE);

SetWorldTransformation(
    angle, angle*2, 0.0f,  /* Rotations    */
    4.0f, 2.0f, 7.0f,      /* Translations */
    3.0, 3.0, 1.0);        /* Scaling      */
g_pDirect3DDevice->SetStreamSource(0, g_pTransparentSquareVertexBuf, 0,
    sizeof(TRANSCUSTOMVERTEXSTRUCT));
if (g_bUseTextures)
    g_pDirect3DDevice->SetTexture(0, g_pTransparentSquareTexture);
else
    g_pDirect3DDevice->SetTexture(0, NULL);
```

LISTING 12.16   Continued

```
    // Set vertex type, and draw the rectangle.
    g_pDirect3DDevice->
        SetFVF(D3DFVF_XYZ|D3DFVF_NORMAL|D3DFVF_DIFFUSE|D3DFVF_TEX1);
    g_pDirect3DDevice->DrawPrimitive(D3DPT_TRIANGLELIST, 0, 2);
}


/////////////////////////////////////////////////////
// InitVertices()
/////////////////////////////////////////////////////
HRESULT InitVertices()
{
    CUSTOMVERTEXSTRUCT cube[] =
    {
        // Front of cube.
        {-0.5f,  0.5f, -0.5f, 0.0f, 0.0f, -1.0f, 0.0f, 0.0f},
        { 0.5f, -0.5f, -0.5f, 0.0f, 0.0f, -1.0f, 1.0f, 1.0f},
        {-0.5f, -0.5f, -0.5f, 0.0f, 0.0f, -1.0f, 0.0f, 1.0f},
        {-0.5f,  0.5f, -0.5f, 0.0f, 0.0f, -1.0f, 0.0f, 0.0f},
        { 0.5f,  0.5f, -0.5f, 0.0f, 0.0f, -1.0f, 1.0f, 0.0f},
        { 0.5f, -0.5f, -0.5f, 0.0f, 0.0f, -1.0f, 1.0f, 1.0f},

        // Right side of cube.
        {0.5f,  0.5f, -0.5f, 1.0f, 0.0f, 0.0f, 0.0f, 0.0f},
        {0.5f, -0.5f,  0.5f, 1.0f, 0.0f, 0.0f, 1.0f, 1.0f},
        {0.5f, -0.5f, -0.5f, 1.0f, 0.0f, 0.0f, 0.0f, 1.0f},
        {0.5f,  0.5f, -0.5f, 1.0f, 0.0f, 0.0f, 0.0f, 0.0f},
        {0.5f,  0.5f,  0.5f, 1.0f, 0.0f, 0.0f, 1.0f, 0.0f},
        {0.5f, -0.5f,  0.5f, 1.0f, 0.0f, 0.0f, 1.0f, 1.0f},

        // Back of cube.
        { 0.5f,  0.5f, 0.5f, 0.0f, 0.0f, 1.0f, 0.0f, 0.0f},
        {-0.5f, -0.5f, 0.5f, 0.0f, 0.0f, 1.0f, 1.0f, 1.0f},
        { 0.5f, -0.5f, 0.5f, 0.0f, 0.0f, 1.0f, 0.0f, 1.0f},
        { 0.5f,  0.5f, 0.5f, 0.0f, 0.0f, 1.0f, 0.0f, 0.0f},
        {-0.5f,  0.5f, 0.5f, 0.0f, 0.0f, 1.0f, 1.0f, 0.0f},
        {-0.5f, -0.5f, 0.5f, 0.0f, 0.0f, 1.0f, 1.0f, 1.0f},

        // Left side of cube.
        {-0.5f,  0.5f,  0.5f, -1.0f, 0.0f, 0.0f, 0.0f, 0.0f},
        {-0.5f, -0.5f, -0.5f, -1.0f, 0.0f, 0.0f, 1.0f, 1.0f},
        {-0.5f, -0.5f,  0.5f, -1.0f, 0.0f, 0.0f, 0.0f, 1.0f},
```

LISTING 12.16   Continued

```
        {-0.5f,  0.5f,  0.5f, -1.0f, 0.0f, 0.0f, 0.0f, 0.0f},
        {-0.5f,  0.5f, -0.5f, -1.0f, 0.0f, 0.0f, 1.0f, 0.0f},
        {-0.5f, -0.5f, -0.5f, -1.0f, 0.0f, 0.0f, 1.0f, 1.0f},

        // Top of cube.
        {-0.5f, 0.5f, -0.5f, 0.0f, 1.0f, 0.0f, 0.0f, 0.0f},
        {-0.5f, 0.5f,  0.5f, 0.0f, 1.0f, 0.0f, 1.0f, 0.0f},
        { 0.5f, 0.5f, -0.5f, 0.0f, 1.0f, 0.0f, 0.0f, 1.0f},
        {-0.5f, 0.5f,  0.5f, 0.0f, 1.0f, 0.0f, 1.0f, 0.0f},
        { 0.5f, 0.5f,  0.5f, 0.0f, 1.0f, 0.0f, 1.0f, 1.0f},
        { 0.5f, 0.5f, -0.5f, 0.0f, 1.0f, 0.0f, 0.0f, 1.0f},

        // Bottom of cube.
        {-0.5f, -0.5f, -0.5f, 0.0f, -1.0f, 0.0f, 0.0f, 0.0f},
        { 0.5f, -0.5f, -0.5f, 0.0f, -1.0f, 0.0f, 0.0f, 1.0f},
        {-0.5f, -0.5f,  0.5f, 0.0f, -1.0f, 0.0f, 1.0f, 0.0f},
        { 0.5f, -0.5f, -0.5f, 0.0f, -1.0f, 0.0f, 0.0f, 1.0f},
        { 0.5f, -0.5f,  0.5f, 0.0f, -1.0f, 0.0f, 1.0f, 1.0f},
        {-0.5f, -0.5f,  0.5f, 0.0f, -1.0f, 0.0f, 1.0f, 0.0f}
};

int i_numCoordsPerVertex = 24;

// Create the vertex buffer.
if(FAILED(g_pDirect3DDevice ->CreateVertexBuffer(sizeof(cube),
        0, D3DFVF_XYZ|D3DFVF_NORMAL|D3DFVF_TEX1, D3DPOOL_DEFAULT,
        &g_pVertexBuf, NULL)))
    return E_FAIL;

CUSTOMVERTEXSTRUCT* pVertices;
if(FAILED(g_pVertexBuf->Lock( 0, 0, (void**)&pVertices, 0)))
    return E_FAIL;
memcpy(pVertices, cube, sizeof(cube));
g_pVertexBuf->Unlock();

g_iNumTriangles = (sizeof(cube) / sizeof(float)) / i_numCoordsPerVertex;

TRANSCUSTOMVERTEXSTRUCT transparentSquare[] =
{
    { 0.75f,  0.75f, 0.2f, 0.0f, 0.0f, 1.0f,
        D3DCOLOR_ARGB(96,255,255,255), 0.0f, 0.0f},
```

LISTING 12.16   Continued

```
        {-0.75f, -0.75f, 0.2f, 0.0f, 0.0f, 1.0f,
            D3DCOLOR_ARGB(96,255,255,255), 1.0f, 1.0f},
        { 0.75f, -0.75f, 0.2f, 0.0f, 0.0f, 1.0f,
            D3DCOLOR_ARGB(96,255,255,255), 0.0f, 1.0f},
        { 0.75f,  0.75f, 0.2f, 0.0f, 0.0f, 1.0f,
            D3DCOLOR_ARGB(96,255,255,255), 0.0f, 0.0f},
        {-0.75f,  0.75f, 0.2f, 0.0f, 0.0f, 1.0f,
            D3DCOLOR_ARGB(96,255,255,255), 1.0f, 0.0f},
        {-0.75f, -0.75f, 0.2f, 0.0f, 0.0f, 1.0f,
            D3DCOLOR_ARGB(96,255,255,255), 1.0f, 1.0f}
    };

    if(FAILED(g_pDirect3DDevice ->CreateVertexBuffer(sizeof(transparentSquare),
            0, D3DFVF_XYZ | D3DFVF_NORMAL | D3DFVF_DIFFUSE | D3DFVF_TEX1,
            D3DPOOL_DEFAULT, &g_pTransparentSquareVertexBuf, NULL)))
        return E_FAIL;
    if(FAILED(g_pTransparentSquareVertexBuf->
            Lock(0, 0, (void**)&pVertices, 0)))
        return E_FAIL;
    memcpy(pVertices, transparentSquare, sizeof(transparentSquare));
    g_pTransparentSquareVertexBuf->Unlock();

    return S_OK;
}


///////////////////////////////////////////////////////
// SetWorldTransformation()
///////////////////////////////////////////////////////
VOID SetWorldTransformation(float fXRot, float fYRot, float fZRot,
        float fXTrans, float fYTrans, float fZTrans,
        float fXScale, float fYScale, float fZScale)
{
    D3DXMATRIX worldMatrix;
    D3DXMATRIX tempMatrix;
    D3DXMatrixIdentity(&worldMatrix);
    D3DXMatrixScaling(&tempMatrix, fXScale, fYScale, fZScale);
    D3DXMatrixMultiply(&worldMatrix, &worldMatrix, &tempMatrix);
    D3DXMatrixRotationX(&tempMatrix, fXRot);
    D3DXMatrixMultiply(&worldMatrix, &worldMatrix, &tempMatrix);
    D3DXMatrixRotationY(&tempMatrix, fYRot);
    D3DXMatrixMultiply(&worldMatrix, &worldMatrix, &tempMatrix);
```

LISTING 12.16   Continued

```
    D3DXMatrixRotationZ(&tempMatrix, fZRot);
    D3DXMatrixMultiply(&worldMatrix, &worldMatrix, &tempMatrix);
    D3DXMatrixTranslation(&tempMatrix, fXTrans, fYTrans, fZTrans);
    D3DXMatrixMultiply(&worldMatrix, &worldMatrix, &tempMatrix);
    g_pDirect3DDevice->SetTransform(D3DTS_WORLD, &worldMatrix);
}


/////////////////////////////////////////////////////
// SetViewTransformation()
/////////////////////////////////////////////////////
void SetViewTransformation()
{
    D3DXVECTOR3 vEyePt(0.0f, 0.0f, g_fZDistance);
    D3DXVECTOR3 vLookatPt(0.0f, 0.0f, g_fZLookAt);
    D3DXVECTOR3 vUpVec(0.0f, 1.0f, 0.0f);
    D3DXMATRIXA16 matView;
    D3DXMatrixLookAtLH(&matView, &vEyePt, &vLookatPt, &vUpVec);
    g_pDirect3DDevice->SetTransform(D3DTS_VIEW, &matView);
}


/////////////////////////////////////////////////////
// SetProjectionTransformation()
/////////////////////////////////////////////////////
void SetProjectionTransformation()
{
    D3DXMATRIXA16 matProj;
    D3DXMatrixPerspectiveFovLH(&matProj, D3DX_PI/4, 1.0f, 1.0f, 100.0f);
    g_pDirect3DDevice->SetTransform(D3DTS_PROJECTION, &matProj);
}


/////////////////////////////////////////////////////
// InitLights()
/////////////////////////////////////////////////////
VOID InitLights()
{
    D3DLIGHT9 light0;
    ZeroMemory(&light0, sizeof(light0));

    light0.Type = D3DLIGHT_SPOT;
    light0.Ambient.r  = g_fAmbientLight;
    light0.Ambient.g  = g_fAmbientLight;
```

LISTING 12.16   Continued

```
light0.Ambient.b  = g_fAmbientLight;
light0.Diffuse.r  = 1.0f;
light0.Diffuse.g  = 1.0;
light0.Diffuse.b  = 1.0;
light0.Position.x = g_fLightPosition;
light0.Position.y = g_fLightPosition;
light0.Position.z = 0.0f;
light0.Direction.x = -1.0f;
light0.Direction.y = -1.0f;
light0.Direction.z = 0.0f;
light0.Attenuation0 = 1.0f;
light0.Range = 50.0f;
light0.Phi = 2.0f;
light0.Theta = 1.0f;
light0.Falloff = 1.0f;

g_pDirect3DDevice->SetLight(0, &light0);
g_pDirect3DDevice->LightEnable(0, g_bLightingOn);

D3DMATERIAL9 material;
ZeroMemory(&material, sizeof(material));
material.Ambient.r = g_fMaterialRed;
material.Ambient.g = g_fMaterialGreen;
material.Ambient.b = g_fMaterialBlue;
material.Ambient.a = 1.0f;
material.Diffuse.r = 1.0;
material.Diffuse.g = 1.0;
material.Diffuse.b = 1.0;
material.Diffuse.a = 1.0f;
g_pDirect3DDevice->SetMaterial(&material);
}
```

In Brief

- Use your Up and Down arrow keys to move forward or backward through Direct3DDemoApp's 3D world.

- Press the L key to turn lighting on and off.

- Press the T key to turn off the texturing process. Pressing T a second time replaces the textures in the scene.

- Use the M key to control the amount of ambient light added to the scene.

- Hold down the P key to change the position of the single spotlight, sweeping it through the scene.

- The F key toggles the fog effect, whereas the E key changes fog density.

- Turn the background on and off with the K key.

- The R, G, and B keys change the red, green, and blue color content of the material used in the scene.

- Press the A key to toggle alpha blending on and off.

- The C key cycles through the different culling modes.

- Press the spacebar to reverse your viewpoint in the scene.

- Use the Z key to toggle Z-buffering.

- Use the W and Q keys to reposition the sign in the scene.

- Press the D key to reset all Direct3D effects to their application-defined default values.

Index

Numerics

M

N

O

Your Guide to Computer Technology

www.informit.com

Sams has partnered with **InformIT.com** to bring technical information to your desktop. Drawing on Sams authors and reviewers to provide additional information on topics you're interested in, **InformIT.com** has free, in-depth information you won't find anywhere else.

ARTICLES

Keep your edge with thousands of free articles, in-depth features, interviews, and information technology reference recommendations—all written by experts you know and trust.

POWERED BY
Safari

ONLINE BOOKS

Answers in an instant from **InformIT Online Books'** 600+ fully searchable online books. Sign up now and get your first 14 days **free**.

CATALOG

Review online sample chapters and author biographies to choose exactly the right book from a selection of more than 5,000 titles.

SAMS   www.samspublishing.com

KICK START

< QUICK >
< CONCISE >
< PRACTICAL >

JSTL: JSP Standard Tag Library Kick Start
By Jeff Heaton
0-672-321450-4
$34.99 US/$54.99 CAN

EJB 2.1 Kick Start
By Peter Thaggard
0-672-32178-5
$34.99 US/$54.99 CAN

JAX: Java APIs for XML Kick Start
By Aoyon Chowdhury and Parag Chaudhary
0-672-32434-2
$34.99 US/$54.99 CAN

Tomcat Kick Start
By Martin Bond and Debbie Law
0-672-32439-3
$34.99 US/$54.99 CAN

PHP 5 Kick Start
By Luke Welling and Laura Thomson
0-672-32292-7
$34.99 US/$54.99 CAN

Struts Kick Start
By James Turner and Kevin Bedell
0-672-32472-5
$34.99 US/$54.99 CAN

ASP.NET Kick Start
By Stephen Walther
0-672-32476-8
$34.99 US/$54.99 CAN

ASP.NET Data Web Controls Kick Start
By Scott Mitchell
0-672-32501-2
$34.99 US/$54.99 CAN